THE MODERNIST CITY

THE MODERNIST CITY
AN ANTHROPOLOGICAL CRITIQUE
OF BRASÍLIA

JAMES HOLSTON

THE UNIVERSITY OF CHICAGO PRESS
CHICAGO AND LONDON

The University of Chicago Press, Chicago 60637
The University of Chicago Press, Ltd., London

09 08 07 06 05 04 03 02 01 00   3 4 5 6 7

Library of Congress Cataloging-in-Publication Data

Holston, James.
    The modernist city : an anthropological critique of Brasília /
James Holston.
        p.   cm.
    Rev. ed. of thesis (doctoral)—Yale University.
    Bibliography: p.
    Includes index.
    ISBN: 0-226-34979-9 (pbk.)
    1. New towns—Brazil-Brasília. 2. City planning-Brazil-
Brasília. 3. Brasília (Brazil)—Social conditions. 4. Urban
anthropology—Case studies. 5. Architecture—Human factors.
6. Architecture, Modern—20th century. 7. Social aspects—Brazil—
Brasília.   I. Title.
HT169.57.B62B634   1989   89–33482
307.76′8′098174—dc20   CIP

Contents

Contents

Illustrations

Tables

Acknowledgments

Several institutions generously supported my study of Brasília. I conducted the fieldwork in Brazil on which it is based between 1980 and 1982 with research grants from the Organization of American States, the Tinker Foundation, and Yale University under the auspices of the Concilium on International and Area Studies and the Williams Fund for Anthropological Research. From 1983 to 1985, I was fortunate to join the staff of the Helen Kellogg Institute for International Studies as a junior faculty fellow. This fellowship allowed me to concentrate on writing the first version of the study, which I presented as my doctoral dissertation to the Department of Anthropology at Yale University. To these organizations and their members I gratefully give my thanks.

Through all stages of the doctorate, I had the great privilege of receiving criticism and encouragement from Professor M. G. Smith, who was my dissertation director, and Professor Guillermo O'Donnell. Whatever merits the dissertation may have had are due in no small measure to the intellectual standards they set and to the opportunities they provided for me to attempt to reach them. I am also indebted to the other members of my dissertation committee, Professors Alan Colquhoun and Harold Scheffler, for their suggestions on early drafts of the manuscript. In addition, I would like to acknowledge the contributions of Professors David Apter, Albert Fishlow, Fredric Jameson, and Emília Viotti da Costa. I am particularly grateful to Professor Paul Rabinow for his suggestions on the first version and to Professor Terence Turner for his comments on the revised manuscript.

One voice especially has been my guide not only in writing this book but also in surviving it, that of fellow anthropologist Teresa Pires do Rio Caldeira. To recount the times her judgment improved mine, to tell of her labors in producing the first draft, to talk of her patience and skill in considering my doubts would all be to say that her companionship has been essential.

In this work, as in my other efforts, I have been fortunate indeed to have had the sustaining support of my parents Ruth and Marc Holston and my brother Rand.

Acknowledgments

My debts are great to the many in Brazil who have given me hospitality and assistance. In particular, I want to thank Professor Roberto Cardoso de Oliveira, who kindly accepted me as a research fellow in the Department of Social Sciences of the Universidade de Brasília; Professor Hélio Jaguaribe and the directors of IUPERJ (Instituto Universitário de Pesquisas do Rio de Janeiro), who provided me with a vital foothold in Brazil when I first arrived; Dr. Mariza G. S. Peirano, whose friendship was invaluable; Dr. Jayme de Assis Almeida, who generously allowed me to use material from his personal archive on the early history of Brasília; and Rodrigo Bhering Andrade, Milton Feferman, Gustavo Lins Ribeiro, and Antonio Augusto G. S. Silva.

I owe a special debt to the people of Brasília, to the many who befriended me, who graciously accepted me and my incessant questioning, and who responded passionately about their city. If they had not insisted that I understand their experiences in Brasília, my research would have amounted to nothing. I want especially to express my deep respect for the pioneers of the new capital. I should like them to know that although I have made a critical assessment of their city, they have my admiration for the courage and dedication with which they built it. Similarly, I would like to record that although I criticize their work in Brasília, architects Lúcio Costa and Oscar Niemeyer also have my respect. With great skill and commitment, they have taken the risks of making public their vision of a new Brazil.

PART ONE

THE MYTH OF THE CONCRETE

ONE

Premises and Paradoxes

The journey to Brasília across the Central Plateau of Brazil is one of separation. It confronts the traveler with the separation of modernist Brasília from the familiar Brazil: from densely packed settlements along the coast to the emptiness of the interior; from layers of congestion and clutter in the big cities to the silent horizons of the plateau; from small town squares with their markets and conversations to the empty spaces of Brasília without squares or markets; from civilization to the frontier; from underdevelopment to the incongruously modern. Migrants make this journey mainly for economic gain. They seek jobs, higher wages, rapid advancement, and speculative opportunity in Brazil's new capital. Yet, however diverse their motives, they all share a sense of the city's separation from the rest of the country that this journey represents. For the migrant, it is this passage that establishes the identity of Brasília as frontier city, development project, utopian experiment in modern urbanism, detached center of political power, Eldorado of opportunity.

It is also this passage that contrasts the old Brazil with a plan to develop the new. As one travels across the desolate plateau toward the city, the landscape abruptly changes about 40 kilometers from the capital. The highway widens. Billboards announce lots for sale in future residential havens with names like New Brazil, New World, and New America. A gigantic, modern sculpture appears out of nowhere to suggest that something is about to happen. Still without visible signs of settlement, one is suddenly swept into a cloverleaf intersection of superspeedway proportions. At one carefully choreographed moment, Brasília begins: a 14-lane speedway roars into view and catapults the traveler into what is hailed as "the New Age of Brazil."

Brasília was built to be more than merely the symbol of this new age. Rather, its design and construction were intended as means to *create* it by transforming Brazilian society. This study analyzes the paired premises of this inversion in development—an inversion in which urban form and organization are considered instruments of social change. The first premise is that the plan for a new city can create a social order in its image; that is, one based on the values that motivate its design. The second premise projects the first as a blueprint for change in the context of national development. It proposes that the new city should be a model of radically different social practices. It argues that if this model could serve as an exemplar of progress for the rest of the nation, then it would be possible not only to generalize its innovations, but also to propel the country as a whole into the planned future it embodies. In this way, planners could stimulate leaps in the development process itself, causing the nation to skip undesired stages in its evolution. Subsequent chapters demonstrate that both premises motivated the building of Brasília in 1957 as the modernist capital of a newly industrializing Brazil. However, they also show that as Brazilian society inhabited the built city, these premises engendered a set of social processes which paradoxically yet unequivocally destroyed the planners' utopian intentions.

I have two sets of objectives in this demonstration. One concerns the case study of a modernist capital built for Brazil. The other addresses the question of how an anthropologist should study modernism and, more generally, the modern world. The objectives of the case study are several: first, to provide an ethnographic account—a description based on my field research—of the consequences of Brasília's founding premises for the development of its social orders and disorders, and second, to analyze the motivations and entailments of these planning precepts. Thus, when I refer to an analysis of premises, I mean to include what they intend, their internal coherence, the instruments and conditions they entail in the world, and the interpretations and social processes they engage.

This study requires that we differentiate between the various components of the planned city: between the architects' intentions for social change, embodied in its design, and the government's intentions to build and occupy it. In evaluating the former, I present Brasília as an exemplar of the tenets of modernist architecture and city planning. Proposed by avant-garde groups in Western Europe and the Soviet Union and adopted in Brazil, these tenets constitute a radical reconceptualization of city life. Brasília is probably their most complete realization. Nevertheless, what is found as a totality in Brasília is found as fragments large and small in cities throughout the world because in this century of phenomenal urban growth architectural theory, debate, education, and practice have been set in modernist terms. It is therefore not too great a generalization to say that the modernist vision of a new way of life has fundamentally altered the urban environment in which nearly half the world's people live. Postmodern critics tell us today that this modernism is now finished, its creativity exhausted. Yet, I would suggest another aspect of the problem: if modernism is dying, it nevertheless remains dominant, at the very least in the third world. A study of Brasília therefore offers an opportunity to evaluate its dominant assumptions in a context in which they are expressed with particular clarity.

In analyzing the second set of intentions—the government's plan to build Brasília—I suggest a number of different but related points about development. On the one hand, I analyze the role of modernist architecture and city planning in development projects which require massive state intervention and centralized coordination. This issue is especially important in third-world countries, where the modernist aesthetic appeals to governments across the political spectrum. To explain this unusual appeal, I suggest a number of affinities between modernism as an aesthetic of erasure and reinscription and modernization as an ideology of development in which governments, regardless of persuasion, seek to rewrite national histories.

On the other hand, I examine Brasília as an example of a common type of development project founded on a paradox. In portraying an imagined and desired future, Brasília represented a negation of existing conditions in Brazil. This utopian difference between the two is precisely the project's premise. Yet, at the same time, the government intended it as a means to achieve this future—as an instrument of change which would, of necessity, have to use the existing conditions it denied. My point in analyzing this apparent paradox is not to dispute the need for utopia in imagining a better world. Indeed, in the course of the book I shall oppose the postmodern abandonment of alternative futures. My aim is rather to determine the ways in which, in the construction of the city and the making of its society, the paradoxes of utopia subverted its initial premises. On this subversion—on the way in which the people of Brasília engaged these premises at their points of contradiction to reassert the social processes and cultural values utopia intended to deny—I focus my ethnographic account.

1.1 Anthropology and Modernism

When I began fieldwork in Brasília in 1980, one of my objectives was to link ethnographic activity with the set of critical attitudes known as modernism. By the latter, I refer to the disenchantments of the avant-gardes—dadaism, surrealism, constructivism, and futurism, among others—which arose in the context of European capitalism and which stood against it and its bourgeois society. What drew me, as an anthropologist, to these movements was their subversive intent: differences notwithstanding, their aim was to disrupt the imagery of what bourgeois society understood as the real and the natural, to challenge the taken-for-granted, to defamiliarize, disorient, decode, deconstruct, and de-authenticate the normative, moral, aesthetic, and familiar categories of social life. The avant-gardes developed techniques of shock—such as fragmentation, absurd juxtaposition, and montage—not so much to end in nihilistic relativism, but rather to stimulate a critical attitude toward the means-end rationalities of cultural order. By withdrawing the narcotic of official or assumed meaning, they hoped to turn peoples' attention to the principles on which such meaning is constructed, and thereby to the possibilities of changing it.

In an ethnographic study of Brasília's modernism, I thought I might find ways of investing anthropology with the critical energies of these avant-gardes. My intention was to take modernism out of its usual domain in art and literature, and its generally internal readings in related fields of criticism, by showing how it becomes linked to social practices and thereby becomes a force in the social world. Moreover, I thought that this demonstration would not only focus my attention on the anthropology of the modern world, but also emphasize the critical potential of ethnography. That it has such potential I think most anthropologists would agree, and recently Marcus and Fischer (1986: especially 111–64) and Clifford (1981) have again drawn our attention to them. If anthropology has traditionally been concerned to familiarize the alien, the exotic, and the marginal by rendering them comprehensible through description, classification, and interpretation, this very process presupposes a complement: that the familiarization of the strange will defamiliarize the familiar by breaking it open to new and unexpected possibilities. This subversive idea is implicit in a wide variety of issues central to the discipline: that what passes for the natural order of people and things is not natural or given, but culturally constructed and relative; that to juxtapose the familiar and the strange in a systematic description of the world's cultural diversity is to erode the prejudices of the former while increasing respect for the latter; that different institutional arrangements may fulfill similar functions; that culture-history-truth-making are contested domains of power; ideas, in a word, that relativize the foundations of the natural and the real wherever these are claimed.

Nonetheless, if modernism and anthropology share certain critical intentions to shake the values of Western civilization, what makes their linking problematic is that both types of subversion are largely failures—or at least unfulfilled promises. That modernist architecture and city planning not only failed in their subversive aims, but often strengthened what they challenged will be demonstrated in the case study of Brasília. That anthropology has not studied the West and modern society with the seriousness of its nonwestern, peasant, and tribal studies is obvious from any one of the number of perspectives that Marcus and Fischer (1986) outline in their useful discussion of "the repatriation of anthropology as cultural critique." Moreover, if, in Clifford's (1981: 543) apt phrase, "surrealism is ethnography's secret sharer," this alter relation has been largely unacknowledged and undeveloped in ethnographic writing.[1]

The problem is not merely that we do not have ethnographies of the West to interact with those of the non-West, to make specific and dynamic and reciprocal whatever critical potentials they may have.[2] Nor is it only, as Foucault (1973) and Fabian (1983) argue in different ways, that the sciences of society use techniques of seeing to control and distance their objects in the moment of appropriating them as scientific—especially that which is conceived as or made to become radically other, as the mad or the primitive. It is also that beyond the important Marxist critiques of capitalism (and anthropology) in the third world, the very project of what an anthropology of modern Western society could mean, and of how to develop an ethnographically critical perspective of it, have only recently emerged as significant, though not yet central, concerns.[3] Moreover, many of the ethnographies in this emergent project invoke precapitalist, precontact, precolonial, premodern, or nonwestern baselines to structure their analyses of present circumstances. Thus, they frame their studies in contrastive terms which, though important in their areas, have less relevance for many aspects of modern city life both in developed and in developing countries.

Yet, precisely because of their parallel failures, I have found it useful in thinking about my field encounter with modernism to explore its common ground with ethnography. For reasons I shall discuss shortly, I am not suggesting an exploration of the kinds of experiments in writing that Marcus and Fischer (1986: 67–73) call "modernist ethnography," or that Clifford (1981: 563–64) calls "surrealist ethnography." Nor am I suggesting a history of their common ground, which others mentioned here are pursuing. Rather, *I am proposing a critical ethnography of modernism* and suggesting that it is useful to think about the problems of the one in relation to those of the other. For if I had to deal empirically with the social forces that modernism engaged in Brasília, I found that as an anthropologist I was ill-equipped to do so. I found rather that my encounter with the field material forced me to reconsider the adequacy of my research framework. This framework had a number of blind spots in relation to the data which I realized occurred around issues key to both modernism and anthropology, such as the nature of criticism, the constitution of context, the notion of historical agency, and the politics of daily life. I therefore developed a set of reciprocal questions to let the one provoke the other: what unsolved or hidden problems in ethnography do the claims and consequences of modernist architecture and planning in Brasília suggest? And what does it mean to study this modernism anthropologically?

One such reciprocal provocation involves the issue of criticism itself. If one of my objectives was to gain a critical understanding of modernism, I could not just evaluate its claims in the same terms in which they had been proposed. Such wholly internal readings I found all too common in the field of architectural criticism, very often done by architects and planners in praise or defense of their own practices. Yet, for various reasons—due to the anthropologist's almost built-in respect for indigenous commentary, for example—I was also susceptible to conflating the history and criticism of architecture with the various discourses of architecture, that is, with the claims and manifestos of the architects themselves. Moreover, traditional anthropology gave me little guidance concerning the objectives of criticism. If there can be no neutral positions in the study of systems of power and social inequality of which the anthropologist is also part, what should critique aim to do? For example, one of the social effects of modernist master planning is the depoliticization of those who are not planners, since their political organization becomes irrelevant if not obstructive in decisions about urban development. A noninternal critical analysis of this planning would have to do more than merely rescue the voices of those left out. Although this affirmation is crucial, and although its redemptive value is one of anthropology's most cherished legitimations, a critical analysis would have to go beyond demonstrating that those marginalized have intelligent interests and important roles with respect to the social system and asking planners to respect them. Such affirmations of the nonhegemonic would not counter the planners' discourse of power. Rather, as I intend to show in the analysis of Brasília, a counter-discourse would have to demonstrate that the delirium of power in master planning itself creates conditions over which the planners stumble and consequently conditions for its own subversion. Indeed, my objective is to produce such a counter-discourse, one precisely grounded in the tension that an anthropologically critical study of modernism creates between the normative ethnographic task of recording the natives' intentions in their own terms and the aim of evaluating those intentions in terms of their results.[4]

Another problem central both to modernism and to anthropology that the study of Brasília confronts is that of history. Modernism in architecture and planning begins by distancing itself from the norms and forms of bourgeois urban life, which it tries to subvert by proposing both a radically different future and a means to get there. As it works backward from this imagined end to preconditions, its view of history is teleological. There are several significant consequences of this teleology. First, it generates one of the fundaments of modernist architecture and planning: total decontextualization, in which an imagined future is posited as the critical ground in terms of which to evaluate the present. As it therefore lacks a notion of historical context, the modernist view of history is paradoxically dehistoricizing. A noninternal critique would therefore have to work in the opposite direction: it would have to historicize the present. Yet, this type of contextualization is not usually emphasized in the foundations of anthropology, whose synchronic concerns set the ethnographic account in a timeless present. It is now well-known that in fact this bias tends to dehistoricize, and, in compensation, many ethnographers over the last few decades have set their descriptions within a historical context. Yet, the problem of history in anthropology is more complex. For it is one thing to give a historical baseline to description and quite another to consider the present as a product of historical *processes* of transformation. An ethnographic study of modernism exacerbates this problem, for while modernism establishes the former in its critique of capitalist cities, it deliberately denies the latter in proposing the possibility of transcendence. Therefore, if I were to stay in a dehistoricized present, or if I were to neglect historical process even while establishing historical context, I would inadvertently accept the modernist criteria of change.

Second, the teleological view of history dispenses with a consideration of intervening actors and intentions, of their diverse sources and conflicts. Rather, the only kind of agency modernism considers in the making of history is the intervention of the prince (state head) and the genius (architect-planner) within the structural constraints of existing technology. Moreover, this intervention is really an overcoming of history, for it attributes to the prince and the genius the power of negating the past by reference to a new future. Thus, modernism's relation to history is strangely disembodied. To avoid the assumption of what it intends to evaluate, therefore, an analysis of the worldly effects of Brasília's modernist design would have not only to historicize the present; it would also have to consider historical agency as an interplay between the transformative actions of diverse social actors (including but not limited to government officials, architects, and planners) and the force of structural constraints (including but not limited to plans and technology). Such an account also defends a place for anthropology itself in the study of the modern world. For in its claim that social context is not crucial in making history, that only impositions of genius count, modernism negates the value of any critique anthropology might offer. Therefore, to study modernist Brasília ethnographically is not only to take anthropology in new directions, but also to subvert such a decontextualized view of history with classic anthropological concerns.

Modernist architecture claims to be an international move-ment that advances national development by building new kinds of cities which in turn transform daily life. The scope of this claim raises for the anthropologist studying it the difficult problem of identifying the appropriate units of analysis. This problem is compounded by the conventional framing of ethno-graphic studies in terms of units that are spatially and tempo-rally isolated. Such framing is obviously inadequate to the task of understanding social practices, historical processes, and cultural interpretations that are engendered in a complex web of relations not only between local and national socioeconomic systems, but also between different social groups whose differ-ences are themselves historically interactive. Inadequate as well are synchronic studies of daily life which presuppose the reproduction of existing differences.

Rather, it makes more sense to say that the units of analysis and their methods cannot be determined in advance and that they will have to be negotiated at each step among the multitude of relevant factors. This complexity means that the methodolog-ical challenge of my case study is to grasp the formation of Brasília's social order, and the structure of events motivating its development, as relational processes in time and space, that is, as processes in which the structures and values of each analytic unit (whether the working classes or the modernist capital as a whole or a single street) are defined in active engagement with those of cognate units (such as the bureaucratic elites or a Brazilian baroque capital or the traffic system). Thus, it is not enough to give the point of view of just the government, or the planners, or the workers, any more than it is of one neighborhood. Rather, the complexity of the case demands cross-class and intergroup juxtapositions in analyzing the material. The challenge, therefore, is to create an interactive framework of research that generates a detailed understanding of the processes of social and cultural change without reducing them to an isolated example and thus failing to account for the complexity of conditions which create them.

To this end, I have first posed the problem of research as one of understanding how the claims of Brasília's modernism are linked to social practices and hence become forces in the social world. Second, I have organized this project in terms of five interactive and cross-class perspectives: those of context, intention, instrumentality, contradiction, and historical process. At this point, only the first four require additional comment. The study of context concerns identifying the conditions (social, cultural, economic, and political) under which Brasília was proposed, produced, and received in Brazilian society. It also identifies the constellation of issues that motivate its makers and inhabitants. The contexts that I found most relevant to the problems of research were (a) those in which the idea of Brasília attained legitimacy as a national endeavor, establishing the terms of its validation and a community of experts to elaborate them; (b) those in which modernism became the dominant model of the modern city and of development through urbanization; (c) those in which Brazilian ambitions found realization in a modernist project, linking first-, second-, and third-world concepts of development; and (d) those in which systems of political, institutional, and economic power engaged these ambitions to establish some of the structural constraints of the project.[5]

An adequate conception of what drives Brasília's development from modernist principles has to include the ways in which the main players interpret these contexts. One important way to do this is to consider that the project generated discourses, statements, texts, plans, models, drawings, and the like, which defined the intentions of those involved. These intentions are fundamental to our study because they make possible and legitimate the tactical interventions that people use to give Brasília's development its particular configuration of forms and forces. Architecture is itself a domain of intentions—for changing society, repatterning daily life, displaying status, regulating real estate, and so forth—which engages other intentions, all of which have consequence in the world. Intentionality constitutes a part of social action that can be neglected only at the cost of having a reductive and determinist view of historical development. In this case study, I shall focus on intentions as they are manifested in the production of texts of various kinds, and I shall always link these to specific people or groups, their social practices, and their historical circumstances.[6]

Moreover, intentions generate instruments for their realization, and we may study them as such. They may be of many sorts: a plan for a building (expressing an intention and also containing a set of instructions to carry it out), a certain type of rationality, a real estate contract. One way of looking at Brasília's modernism is as a discourse on the good government of society which proposes architecture and city planning as instruments of social change and management. Such proposals have a long history in the West. Since Renaissance treatises on the nature of architecture and the city and the Laws of the Indies of 1573 regulating the discovery and settlement of the New World, architecture and city planning have been prominent among those modern techniques of government that address what the order of society should be and how it should be maintained. Their instrumentality concerns not only such practical matters as how to avoid epidemics, traffic jams, and street riots, but equally how to stimulate family and civic virtue. What characterizes Brasília's instruments of social change and organization, and how they realize their intentions in social processes, will be an important part of this study.

As such intentions and instruments constitute the self-understanding of Brasília's modernism, they remain essential to its analysis. However, a critical analysis cannot simply use for its own categories those that the theoreticians of modernism developed for themselves. Rather, it must distance itself from such an internal view, and I have already suggested some of the dimensions of this distancing. Nevertheless, it seems to me that there are two great dangers in a critical interpretation that distances itself too much: reductivism and dogmatism. Discussing problems in what he calls allegorical interpretation, Jameson (1981: 22) observes that the first occurs when "the data of one narrative line are radically impoverished by their rewriting according to the paradigm of another narrative [his example is everyday experience and individual fantasy reduced to Freudian psychodynamics], which is taken as the former's master code or Ur-narrative and proposed as the ultimate hidden or unconscious *meaning* of the first one." In one form or another, the recent poststructuralist critiques of psychoanalytic, Marxist, and structuralist interpretation have all emphasized this point. Dogmatic criticism seems less a matter of such rewriting than of truth claims. It advances an alternative position against the one it criticizes and asserts that a demonstration of its truth is sufficient proof that its opponent's position is false: "I am right, therefore you must be wrong." To refute another, it only requires the proof, or even the claim, that it is true. Although it remains external to its object, this type of criticism is usually charged with imposing irrelevant criteria of evaluation, ignoring existing conditions, and being arrogant. Modernism in architecture is itself very often such a dogmatic critique of the cities and societies of bourgeois capitalism.

To avoid these charges, a critique of modernism can neither dismiss it out of hand nor reduce it to something else. What is needed instead is a method of assessment similar to what Frankfurt school theorists call immanent or dialectical criticism.[7] This procedure begins with the substance of what is to be criticized and establishes its self-understanding (its premises, intentions, categories, instruments, and the like). It then unfolds their entailments, implications, and consequences which it uses to reexamine the object of investigation. This reassessment reveals its gaps and paradoxes. As Bürger (1984: liv) remarks, one of the important insights of this method is that "for dialectical criticism, the contradictions in the criticized theory are not indications of insufficient intellectual rigor . . . but an indication of an unsolved problem or one that has remained hidden." It is in this sense that the critique proceeds from within, deriving its stimuli from the paradoxes of the theory criticized. By pursuing such paradoxes and the problems they reveal, it suggests not only a new understanding but also new possibilities for analyzing its object. This is its productive advantage, and it is in this sense that I shall focus my critical analysis of Brasília's development on its structure of premise and paradox. Ultimately, my interest in this structure is to show how its unsolved problems, gaps, and contradictions trip up the master plans, creating the conditions for their own transformation.

It is this immanent critique that distinguishes my project of critical ethnography from the experiments in writing that I mentioned earlier and that have become identified with postmodernism in anthropology. These experiments concentrate their critical attention on the various textual strategies that must organize any work of cultural representation. Their broadest critical objective is to debunk the notion that this representation may be transparent, that is, without artifice. They therefore focus on its literary production, on the way in which it is constructed in the encounter between ethnographer and native out of many voices, partial truths, disjointed observations, shifting biases, and other fragmentations in fieldwork. Thus, they conceive of ethnography as an experiment in writing precisely to reveal the devices and fractures of this construction on the one hand, and on the other to demonstrate the way most of them tend to get written out of the normative scientific account of other cultures when these are presented as an objective description by the all-seeing, intrepid, and authoritative ethnographer.

I have found their critique of such accounts very useful in helping me to understand the practice of ethnography. Nevertheless, I agree with Rabinow (1985: 12) when he says that "if in the last five years we have seen important work showing us specific ways beyond the transparency of language, I think it is now time to take those advances and move back to the world." It is in this sense of a return to the world that I intend to let the critical dimension of my study of Brasília emerge from a substantive analysis of the case itself. For if ethnography may be conceived of as a counter-discourse in the study of Brasília's modernism, then its critique must be worked out in terms of evaluating the claims at issue in light of their consequences. The critical self-consciousness of this enterprise lies not so much in the writing of a text, or in the erosion of positivist epistemologies, as in the recognition and indeed the emphasis of a tension between the goal of presenting the native's point of view and that of pursuing its paradoxes in social practice. Its self-reflection consists less in questioning the project of ethnography as an authoritative presentation of facts, than in moving beyond that question to develop ethnography as a critical register—a kind of subversive practice—with which to analyze particular cases.

The following discussion introduces the parameters of this objective in two ways. It provides an overview of the entire study in terms of the research framework just outlined, and it presents the plan of analysis.

1.2 The Idea of Brasília

To understand the intentions of building Brasília, it is first necessary to see the city as the acropolis of an enormous expanse of emptiness. The Federal District in which the capital lies is an area of 5,771 square kilometers plotted at the approximate center of the Central Plateau (map 1.1). Around it is nearly 2 million square kilometers of stunted scrub vegetation called *cerrado*, lying without significant modulation between 1000 and 1300 meters above sea level. This vast tableland includes areas within three of Brazil's five great regions—the Central West, the Northeast, and the Southeast—and comprises almost all of the

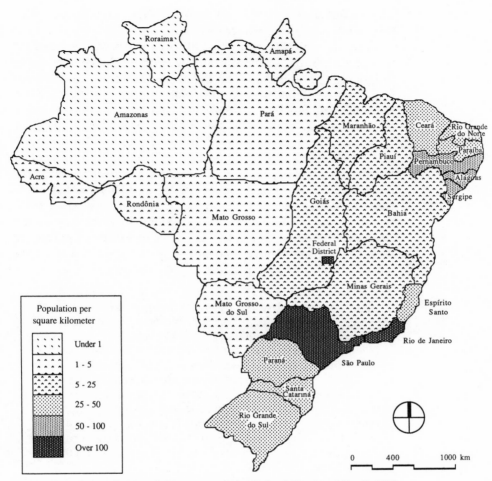

Map 1.1 Population density of the states and the Federal District of Brazil, 1980

states of Mato Grosso, Mato Grosso do Sul, and Goiás in the West and parts of Bahia and Minas Gerais in the East. Although it represents 23% of Brazil's surface area, in 1980 it contained only 6% of its population, mostly found in the isolated boom towns and agricultural stations of pioneer zones. The rest survive as pastoralists and subsistence cultivators sparsely distributed across the land. At the time of Brasília's construction, its average population density was less than one person per square kilometer. Today, it is only four.[8] As one journeys across this desolate flatness, any interruption in the landscape—a twisted palm or a chain of voluminous clouds—becomes a welcome figure of life. It is in this tradition of desert sculpture that the steel and glass oasis of Brasília arises, almost 1000 kilometers from the coastline to which, in the metaphor of Frei

15

Vicente do Salvador (1931: 19), Brazilian civilization has for over four centuries "clung like crabs."[9]

Since the middle of the eighteenth century, the idea of transferring Brazil's capital from the coast to the center of this uninhabited interior has been the dream of numerous visionaries. Their combined legacy to Brasília is that of a New World mythology in which the construction of a capital city at the heart of the Central Plateau is the means of launching a great civilization to flourish in a paradise of plenty. One of these visionaries, the Italian João Bosco, became the patron saint of Brasília for such a prophecy. According to interpretors of his revelation, he envisaged the site of the city 75 years before its construction as that of the Promised Land. On 30 August 1883, the saint dreamed that he was traveling by train across the Andes to Rio de Janeiro in the company of a celestial guide. As they crossed the Central Plateau, they surveyed not only the land's surface but also its subterranean features:

> I saw the bowels of the mountains and the depths of the plains. I had before my eyes the incomparable riches . . . which would one day be discovered. I saw numerous mines of precious metals and fossil coals, and deposits of oil of such abundance as had never before been seen in other places. But that was not all. Between the fifteenth and the twentieth degrees of latitude, there was a long and wide stretch of land which arose at a point where a lake was forming. Then a voice said repeatedly: when people come to excavate the mines hidden in the middle of these mountains, there will appear in this place the Promised Land, flowing with milk and honey. It will be of inconceivable richness. (Cited in Silva 1971: 34)

Official interpretation holds that the topography of this vision corresponds precisely to the site of Brasília, constructed between the fifteenth and the sixteenth latitudes, and that its "lake in the process of forming" refers to the city's man-made Lake Paranoá. Moreover, as one of Brasília's founding fathers and local historians writes: "To confirm once again that Saint João Bosco was referring to our capital, to the Great Civilization that is now arising on the Central Plateau of Brazil, the Saint affirmed that these dreams . . . would be lived in the third generation" after his own (Silva 1971: 35). Brasilienses—as the people of Brasília are called—consider this prognostication to indicate a period of 75 years. This establishes the late 1950s as the date of the prophecy's realization, exactly the years of Brasília's construction. João Bosco's prophecy is one of several foundation myths officially recognized in the city's history books and monuments. These myths are various versions of the same theme: they present Brasília as the civilizing agent of the Central Plateau, as the harbinger of an inverted development in which the capital creates the civilization over which it exercises a radiant sovereignty.

This New World mythology complements Brasília's foundation as an instrument of economic and political development. Since the third quarter of the eighteenth century, a multitude of reformers, revolutionaries, and empire-builders has proposed the transfer of the capital to the backlands as a means of populating, developing, and securing Brazil's vast interior. It was a proposal advocated by men of such different political objectives as the autocratic marquis of Pombal, the revolutionary Tiradentes, the patriarch of independence José Bonifácio de Andrade e Silva, and the diplomat Varnhagen. Since its inception, therefore, the "idea of Brasília" (as it is called) has had the peculiar characteristic of appealing to radically different, even violently opposed, political perspectives both as an image of a new Brazil and as a strategy of development. This idea finally attained legal form in the first Republican Constitution of 1891. Its third article set aside an area of 14,400 square kilometers in the Central Plateau for the installation of a future federal capital. In congressional debate on this article, legislators argued that the move to the interior would enable the government to establish sovereignty over the entire territory of Brazil away from the colonial coast and safe from naval attacks on the maritime capital in Rio de Janeiro. At the same time, they maintained that it would produce national integration by stimulating development of the interior's resources and thus generating axes of economic growth from the center to the farthest corners of the country.

Over the next sixty years, this constitutional directive received only intermittent attention: commissions in 1892, 1946, and 1953 were convened to chart the site of the future capital; their legal mandate was reiterated in the constitutions of 1934 and 1937 and in the Constitutional Assembly of 1946; and two presidents issued decrees to initiate construction, Presidents Epitácio Pessoa and Café Filho in 1920 and 1955, respectively. A ceremonial foundation stone was even laid in 1922 in what is today one of Brasília's satellite cities. This record of compliance with the constitution indicates the uncertainty with which political officials approached the mandated transfer of the capital. They were dissuaded not only by the economic risks involved, but perhaps even more by the political risks of undertaking a project with little likelihood of being completed within a single administration. For it is a well-known fact of Brazilian politics that public work projects left unfinished at the end of one adminis-

tration are more likely to be ridiculed and dropped than completed by the next.

However, in 1955, the idea of Brasília found full voice in the
presidential campaign of Juscelino Kubitschek. He initiated his
candidacy with a pledge to build the new capital. After his
election, the realization of this pledge became the central project
of his administration (1956–61), the target-synthesis, as he
called it, of his Target Program for national development. This
program embodied a theory of development known as developmentalism, which was promoted throughout Latin America
during the 1950s by ECLA (the United Nation's Economic
Commission for Latin America) and in Brazil by ISEB (the
Superior Institute of Brazilian Studies). It stressed state-directed
industrialization as the means by which underdeveloped countries could achieve rapid economic growth and a more favorable
position in world trade. Kubitschek's version emphasized Brazilian nationalism in establishing development targets designed
to propel Brazil over the hurdle of underdevelopment. He gave
Brasília top priority in this program for several reasons. First, he
argued that the construction of the capital in the Central Plateau
would cause both national integration ("integration through
interiorization" was his slogan) and regional development by
bringing national markets to regions of subsistence economies.
Second, he believed that the united effort required to build the
city would stimulate research, development, and innovation in
the other target projects—for example, in highway construction,
hydroelectric generation, communications, and steel production. Thus, he maintained that Brasília would produce both a
new national space and a new national epoch, the first by
incorporating the interior into the national economy and the
second by being the decisive mark on the time-line of Brazil's
emergence as a modern nation.

In Kubitschek's master plan, these innovations were supposed to create a development inversion: not only would they
propel the Central West up to the level of development in the
Southeast (i.e., of Rio de Janeiro and São Paulo), but more
important, they would cause the rest of Brazil to catch up with
the innovations of Brasília. Thus, Brasília would become "a pole
of development" for the nation, "a stone cast to create waves of
progress" as the rhetoric of developmentalism put it.[10] One of
the most succinct and popularized images of this intended
inversion is given in map 1.2. Since 1956, it has appeared in
various versions in publications as diverse as elementary school
textbooks and government reports on regional development. In
suggesting the existence of extensive linkages between Brasília
and Brazil's state capitals, the map portrays Brasília as a means

Map 1.2 Distances between Brasília and state capitals. This map frequently illustrates discussions of "Brasília and national development." For example, in a social studies textbook for elementary school children, it accompanies the following passage: "The transfer of the capital brought progress to the central west region and contributed to the settlement and development of a great part of Brazil's territory. The new capital is linked by great highways to all the regions of Brazil" (Perugine et al. 1980: 15).

to create not only the polity of a centralized state but also the civilization it will rule. Yet, like the colonizing project it represents, the map's linkages are mostly imaginary. They are merely graphic representations of linear distance, not yet built in any form. As such, they constitute a map of intentions concerning the axes of economic development, the vectors of political consolidation, and the means of progress—in short, a map of the imaginary nation Brasília was designed to generate.

Nevertheless, when the Kubitschek government announced its decision in 1956 to transfer the capital to Brasília, and audaciously set the inaugural date for 21 April 1960, it encountered opposition from all quarters. The national press, congressional leaders, local politicians of every hue, and even the popular press lampooned the project as pure folly. This opposition fell into four camps. First, there were those simply skeptical of the government's ability to build a capital "in the middle of nowhere." Second, many were doubtful that even if construction were begun, it could be completed within Kubitschek's mandate. They reasoned that the city's construction would never be continued by the succeeding administration and that it would remain an incomplete and fabulously expensive ruin. A third group argued that the entire project was economic madness, for it would fuel inflation beyond control. It suggested that if the government were really intent on committing Brazil's resources to huge development projects, then there were many other regions of the country, those at least inhabited, that needed attention first.[11] Even popular sentiment against the city depicted the Central Plateau as an unreal place populated, if inhabited at all, by Indians—which is to say barely Brazilian and hardly suitable for the center of national government.[12]

Kubitschek and his supporters countered with a skillful and successful campaign to legitimate the city's construction. Their legitimation combined New World mythology and development theory in linking the foundation of a capital city with the foundation of a new Brazil. Throughout Brazilian history, this link has had numerous names, including Nova Lisboa, Petrópole, Pedrália, Imperatória, Tiradentes, Vera Cruz, and finally Brasília—each name symbolizing the intentions of its proponents. Kubitschek and his architects amalgamated these intentions into a unified rhetorical proposition, expressed both in the modernist design of the city and in the government's plan to occupy it.

1.3 The Instruments of Change

The apartment blocks of a *superquadra* [the city's basic residential unit] are all equal: same façade, same height, same facilities, all constructed on *pilotis* [columns], all provided with garages and constructed of the same material—which prevents the hateful differentiation of social classes; that is, all the families share the same life together, the upper-echelon public functionary, the middle, and the lower.

As for the apartments themselves, some are larger and some are smaller in number of rooms. [They] are distributed, respectively, to families on the basis of the number of dependents they have. And because of this distribution and the inexistence of social class discrimination, the residents of a *superquadra* are forced to live as if in the sphere of one big family, in perfect social coexistence, which results in benefits for the children who live, grow up, play, and study in the same environment of sincere camaraderie, friendship, and wholesome upbringing. . . . And thus is raised, on the plateau, the children who will construct the Brazil of tomorrow, since Brasília is the glorious cradle of a new civilization. (*Brasília* 1963 [65–81]: 15)

This description of "perfect social coexistence" comes neither from the pages of a utopian novel, nor from the New World annals of Fourierite socialism. Rather, it is taken from the periodical of the state corporation that planned, built, and administered Brasília—from a "report" on living conditions in the new capital. Nevertheless, it presents a fundamentally utopian premise: that the design and organization of Brasília were meant to transform Brazilian society. Moreover, it does so according to the conventions of utopian discourse: by an implicit comparison with and negation of existing social conditions. In this case, the subtext is the rest of Brazil, where society is stratified into pernicious social classes, where access to city services and facilities is differentially distributed by class, and where residential organization and architecture are primary markers of social standing. Brasília is put forth not merely as the antithesis of this stratification, but also as its antidote, as the "cradle" of a new society. Thus, when the city's planners presuppose that lower-level government employees live "the same life together" with higher officials, it is not because they assume that such egalitarianism already exists as a basic value in Brazilian society. They know that it does not. Rather, they are presupposing the value they *want* to create among the residents, especially the children, of Brasília. To complete the deliberate *petitio principii*—the assumption of what one wishes to prove— which seems fundamental to this sort of discourse, they state their intention as fact, as a transformation in the present tense: they claim that the unequal distribution of advantage due to differences in class, race, employment, wealth, and family that structures urban life elsewhere in Brazil is in Brasília already negated.

The mechanism of this negation is its embodiment in the residential organization of the city. It lies not only in the distribution of apartments according to need but moreover in their design. Thus, the planners claim that the "equality" or standardization of architectural elements "prevents" social discrimination. In this embodiment of intention, they propose an instrumental relation between architecture and society: the people who inhabit their buildings will be "forced" to adopt the new forms of social experience, collective association, and personal habit their architecture represents. This forced conduction to radical changes in social values and relations is the essential means by which Brasília's planners hoped to institute their egalitarian prescriptions for a new Brazilian society. It is in this sense that they considered architecture an instrument of social change. Moreover, in designing an entire city, a total environment, they viewed this conduction as an inescapable inversion of social evolution in which architects and city planners would design fundamental features of society.

Parts 1 and 2 of this study examine the embodiment of these intentions in Brasília's architecture and planning. Chapter 2 establishes Brasília's pedigree as a modernist city, setting out its basic features in its European and Russian context by focusing on its explicitly political objective: to transform the city of industrial capitalism and, by extension, capitalist society. Chapter 3 relates these features to the intentions of Brasília's planners to change Brazilian society. It shows how the city's foundation charter, its Master Plan, paradoxically disguises these intentions by dehistoricizing their relations to the rest of Brazil and mythologizing the agenda for social change that motivates its specific proposals.

These proposals are evaluated in part 2. There are five of them, and together they claim to redefine the "key functions" of urban life: (1) to organize the city into exclusive and homogeneous zones of activity based on a predetermined typology of urban functions and building forms; (2) to concentrate the function of work in relation to dispersed dormitory settlements; (3) to institute a new type of residential architecture and organization; (4) to create a green city, a city in the park; and (5) to impose a new system of traffic circulation. Analyzed separately in chapter 4, this last proposal not only eliminates the street system of public spaces and the urban crowd that streets traditionally support in Brazilian cities; it also destroys the basic architectural structure of the type of city modernism attacks. To understand the significance of this transformation, I consider the street in the preindustrial Brazilian cities of eighteenth-century Ouro Preto and nineteenth-century Rio de Janeiro. In these cities, the street defines a context for social life in terms of a contrast between public space and private building. It is this context, and contrast, that Brasília subverts.

I evaluate these proposals in terms of the claims of Brasília's founding premises. This assessment occurs at several levels of analysis. On the one hand, my objective is to provide an account of how the planners' proposals structure the built city. On the other, it is to evaluate the consequences of this structure for the development of Brasiliense society. In the first case, I analyze the entailments of these proposals, focusing on their internal coherence and contradiction. By entailments, I refer to those conditions that derive both from the definition and from the mode of expression of the planners' intentions, in other words, from the proposals and from the values they supposedly embody. This analysis is important in order to counter a simplistic assumption often made by planners themselves: that their intentions are more or less perfectly realized in their plans. This assumption enables them to blame external forces beyond their control if plans go awry. However, the analysis of entailments reveals two sets of issues that undercut this assumption in the case of Brasília. First, we must consider the values that the planners thought they were concretizing in their proposals. For example, we shall want to know whether a social program characterized as egalitarian, socialist, or collectivist may be internally contradicted if it attempts to restructure residential relations but neglects those of work. Second, we must consider whether the planners were mistaken about the real nature of the social program to which their proposals refer. We must determine whether their proposals are the right instruments to bring about the desired ends, or whether they contradict the intentions they presumably concretize and therefore represent, once built, very different values from the ones imagined.

1.4 The Negation of the Negation

The second type of evaluation made in part 2, and carried on in part 3, focuses on the consequences of planning for the development of Brasiliense society. Although Brasília was conceived to create one kind of society, it was necessarily built and inhabited by another—by the rest of Brazil the former denied. Brasília's social development is driven by the tensions and contradictions between these two societies. I look at this development in terms of the reaction of Brasilienses to the defamiliarizations of the architectural and planning proposals—both to the unintended consequences of their internal contradictions and to their intended realizations. I analyze two facets of this response: how Brasilienses have interpreted Brasília's negation of the life of other Brazilian cities, and what kind of social and cultural processes this interpretation has generated. These processes reveal that the paradox of Brasília's development is not that its radical premises failed to produce something new, but rather, that what they did produce contradicted what was intended.

The first generation of migrants in postinaugural Brasília expressed their reactions in a way that suggests the scope of this paradox. They coined the expression *brasilite*, meaning 'Brasíl(ia)-itis,' to describe the impact of Brasília as a trauma. *Brasilite* is an ambiguous description because it includes both negative and positive reactions to the planned city (interviews, Brasília, 1980–82). Nevertheless, in terms of the city's utopian premises, this ambiguity merely reveals a double paradox. The negative aspects of *brasilite* are linked to a rejection of the defamiliarizing intentions of Brasília's design. What they reject is the negation of the familiar urban Brazil in the city's organization and architecture. Thus, not only did these migrants view the "same façades" as monotonous but they considered that their standardization produced anonymity among residents, not equality. Moreover, they rejected the mixing of social classes in the same *superquadra* as explosive, as igniting conflicts among neighbors of irreconcilably different life styles and values. In addition, while they appreciated the absence of traffic jams, they complained that the elimination of streets and street corners also eliminated the crowds that they enjoyed in cities. Without the bustle of street life, they found Brasília "cold." Although separating the functions of work, residence, recreation, and traffic produced organizational clarity in the city's plan, it also reduced their *use* of urban space to a commuter shuttle between work and residence. In this regard, they used the term *brasilite* to refer to their feelings about a daily life without the pleasures—the distractions, conversations, flirtations, and little rituals—of the outdoor public life of other Brazilian cities.

This rejection of the utopian city led them to reassert familiar conceptual schemes about urban life—to familiarize a defamiliarized city. For example, they repudiated the antistreet intentions of the Master Plan by putting their shops back on the street, in contact with curbs and traffic. Although limited to a few commercial sectors, this conversion reproduced the life of the market street where it had been architecturally denied. Although they could not change the façades of the apartment blocks, many upper-echelon bureaucrats moved out of them, preferring to build individual houses on the other side of the lake. Often with considerable ostentation and in a variety of historical styles, these houses display their residents' wealth, status, and personality in elaborate façades that negate the modernist aesthetic. Moreover, finding the "same life together" intolerable, the elite abandoned the idea of constructing egalitarian social clubs in the *superquadras* as had been planned. Instead, many joined private clubs organized according to exclusive criteria antithetical to the utopian aims of Brasília's residential organization. As a result, an important aspect of its planned collective structure collapsed. Thus, in rejecting the negation of established patterns of urban life, Brasilienses reasserted social processes and cultural values that the architectural design intended to deny. What resulted was not of course the old Brazil, but neither was it the imagined city.

When we look at the positive aspects of *brasilite*, we see that the response was no less paradoxical. The idea of Brasília denied the old Brazil twice: it negated its underdevelopment as well as its urban life. Although Brasilienses rejected the defamiliarization of the latter, not surprisingly they accepted Brasília's negation of the former. Thus, their accounts of *brasilite* have this positive aspect: they consistently appreciate the economic opportunity and higher standards of living in the city. They may reject its forced social life, but they praise its conditions of prosperity. That these conditions should be considered part of its trauma is a measure of just how incongruously modern the city is in Brazil. Foremost among these positive evaluations are those concerning economic opportunity. Their emphasis on work brings into focus the role of the state not only as the builder and developer of the city but also, as we shall discuss in chapter 5, as the overwhelmingly predominant provider of jobs and urban services. In what follows, I shall briefly illustrate the benefits of this provision. I do so at this point not only because they reveal what residents like about Brasília, but moreover because they suggest a paradoxical conclusion: that in achieving economic development, the government reiterated some of the basic social conditions of underdevelopment that it had initially sought to preclude.

In a number of ways, the 1980 census confirms Brasília's preeminent position in Brazil as a place to work. For example, it reports that of Brazil's states and territories the Federal District has the highest proportion of people in the labor force.[13] The census also reports that proportionately more women are economically active and proportionately less children and adolescents than anywhere else.[14] Moreover, as table 1.1 indicates, the rewards of working in Brasília are likely to be greater: nearly double the national proportion earns over 5 minimum salaries per month, while the percentage at the bottom is significantly lower. Thus, a much greater percentage of Brasília's labor force is in the middle-income brackets.

In a nation where over three quarters of the population are poor, the relative conditions of urban poverty are a crucial consideration. If one compares these conditions in Brasília with those in other Brazilian cities, even the relative prosperity of its

TABLE 1.1
Employed Population by Monthly Income (Minimum Salaries):
Brazil, São Paulo, Federal District (1980); Sobradinho, DF (1980);
São Miguel Paulista, SP (1977)

Monthly Income (Minimum Salaries)	Percentage of Employed Population				
	Brazil	São Paulo	Federal District	Sobradinho	São Miguel Paulista
<1–3	77.2	64.6	63.4	71.9	80.2
>5	11.9	17.1	22.3	12.8	6.7
5–10	7.2	11.0	10.8	9.4	[3.4][a]
>10	4.7	6.1	11.5	3.4	[3.3][b]

Sources: For Brazil, São Paulo, and Federal District, IBGE 1981a; for Sobradinho, IBGE 1980 census (unpublished data); for São Miguel Paulista, Caldeira 1984: 73 (table 10).

Note: Minimum salary for 1977 (May) was Cr$1,106 (U.S.$78.20) and for 1980 (May), Cr$4,150 (U.S.$78.73).

[a]From 5 to 7 minimum salaries.

[b]Greater than 7 minimum salaries.

poor becomes apparent. As most of Brazil's impoverished citizens live on the periphery of its big cities, table 1.1 contrasts one of the typical poor neighborhoods of São Paulo's periphery, São Miguel Paulista, with one of Brasília's satellite cities, Sobradinho. Although the numbers of poor people in each are overwhelming, they are noticeably lower in Sobradinho as a percentage of the total population. More significant, the proportion of those earning over 5 minimum salaries monthly is double. In addition to low income, the most important condition of poverty on the periphery of Brazil's cities is the lack of basic urban services. Here again, due to government investments, services in Brasília's peripheral neighborhoods are remarkably better than São Paulo's. Let us compare a number of services in the poorest of São Paulo's peripheries, Area VIII (in which São Miguel Paulista is located), with those in the poorest of Brasília's satellite cities, Ceilândia. In the late 1970s and early 1980s, only 19% of the residences in Area VIII had sanitary sewage; 5% had telephones; 80% had trash removal; and 25% of the mostly unpaved streets had public lighting. By contrast, in Ceilândia 60% had sewage, 11% telephones, 100% trash removal, and 74% of the streets were illuminated.[15] In terms of educational services, São Miguel Paulista had one elementary school for every 1,429 students, while in Ceilândia there was one school for 1,080 students, and in Sobradinho, one for 499.[16] Together, these conditions substantiate a well-known saying in the capital: if one has to be poor in Brazil, it is better to be poor in Brasília.

When we consider the urban conditions and job opportunities provided in the modernist city itself—called the Plano Piloto ('Pilot Plan') to distinguish it from the periphery of satellite cities (map 1.3)—it is evident that measured in these terms its quality of life is exceptional. Not only are its infrastructural services excellent, but what makes this characterization extraordinary in Brazil is that it may be applied to the *entire* city. In interview after interview, residents register this basic difference: the Plano Piloto is free from problems afflicting other Brazilian cities— from congestion, high crime rate, omnipresent misery, lack of urban services, and pollution. The Plano Piloto is free from "all that disorder." Rather, in the capital, "things function"; the work day is "convenient"; daily life is "tranquil." When one adds to these conveniences the opportunity, security, salary, and perquisites of government employment, the "good life" of Brasília is quite seductive; that is, in people's evaluation, its practical advantages come to outweigh its defamiliarizations. Especially as urban conditions elsewhere have progressively deteriorated in the last two decades, the appeal of order in Brasília eventually—and sometimes rapidly—succeeds the sense of loss that Plano Piloto residents commonly feel for the urban life of hometown Brazil.

These opinions are, of course, difficult to gauge as opinion. However, just as the negative evaluations of Brasília are manifested in social processes, actions, and statuses, so too are the

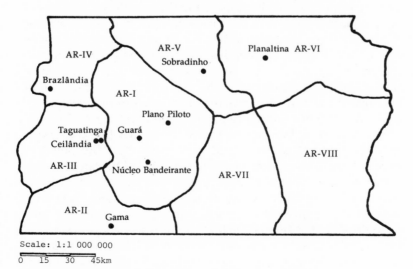

Scale: 1:1 000 000

0   15   30   45km

Map 1.3 Plano Piloto, satellite cities, and administrative regions of the Federal District, 1980

positive ones. One such indication is the long-term residence in the city of people who have great opportunity to leave: those who occupy the highest positions in the federal bureaucracy, especially in the ministries. These people usually hold jobs that are untenured and commonly called *cargos de confiança*, 'positions of confidence'; that is, they are appointees whose jobs depend on the fortunes of their superiors. As a result, not only do they have greater opportunity for job advancements, but they lose their jobs more frequently than other bureaucrats, especially when the administration changes hands. As they also have greater possibilities of arranging work elsewhere, I conducted surveys in several ministries to determine whether they left Brasília at the end of their jobs.[17] The results show that their choice was overwhelmingly to remain in the capital and that they did so by arranging a similar appointment in another institution of government. Their reluctance to leave Brasília dispels the notion of a trapped bureaucratic elite. Rather, it suggests that the city's elite consists of a stable corps of those who circulate, rather "endogamously," through the upper-echelon positions of its bureaucracy.

However, the maintenance of this elite suggests a disturbing paradox: that when considered in relation to the poverty of the satellite cities, the privileges of the Plano Piloto contradict Brasília's founding premises. For the planners wanted to make Brasília an exemplar of development by negating the conditions of underdevelopment in the city's construction and settlement—not by displacing them from the coast to the interior, or by transporting them from the big cities to Brasília, or by transposing them into another scale. Yet, the very existence of satellite cities, in which almost three quarters of the population of the Federal District live, subverts this intention profoundly: it reproduces the distinction between privileged center and disprivileged periphery that is one of the most basic features of the rest of urban Brazil, of the underdevelopment Brasília's planners wanted to deny in building their new world.

Moreover, if we look again at table 1.1, we see that it suggests that this subversion developed perversely: that the development of Brasiliense society not only reproduced the social orders of the realm in the exemplary capital, but that it did so in an exaggerated way. This exaggeration becomes apparent when we compare the proportions of middle- and upper-income earners. We realize that the Federal District's remarkable concentration of those earning over 5 minimum salaries is not due to its predominance in the middle range of 5–10 salaries. In this range, it fares no better than São Paulo, and the peripheral Sobradinho comes very close to representing the entire district. Rather, it is in the upper income range, above 10 salaries per month, that the Federal District dominates the comparisons: its proportion is double São Paulo's, two and a half times Brazil's, and three and a half times Sobradinho's. As we shall discuss in a later chapter, the spatial distribution of this high income is absolutely concentrated: it is overwhelmingly found in Brasília—that is, in the Plano Piloto and its lake residences—and not in the satellite cities.[18]

The important point to stress here is that as this concentration applies in all areas of the city, the social inequalities they entail are associated with an extraordinary spatial stratification between center and periphery. Moreover, the distribution of income only partially reveals the extent of this differentiation. In fact, the disparities between Brasília and its satellites are even more severe because the good life of the capital is based to a significant degree on the perquisites of office—called *mordomias* or 'butlerisms'—that garnish the incomes of the elite officials of all branches of government. Depending on their level, these officials receive residence, car, food, telephone, and servants—who, of course, come from the satellite cities.[19]

These disparities suggest that the successes of Brasília's order depend to a considerable degree upon keeping the forces of disorder out of the capital and in the periphery. Thus, its high standards of living appear to be supported by a kind of dual social structure. Part 3 analyzes the development of this stratified society and shows that it unequivocally subverted the government's founding premises. That Brasília is a bureaucratic city in which government planners have had both the power and the resources to carry out their plans suggests that the government's own initiatives in organizing the city promoted this subversion. Part 3 is devoted to demonstrating the force of this paradox in the development of Brasiliense society.

TWO

Blueprint Utopia

Brasília serves in this book as a case study of the modernist city proposed in the manifestos of the Congrès Internationaux d'Architecture Moderne (CIAM). It embodies in form and organization CIAM's premise of social transformation: that modern architecture and planning are the means to create new forms of collective association, personal habit, and daily life. This chapter outlines basic features of the CIAM model city and places the design of Brasília within the historical context of avant-garde modernism.

2.1 Brasília's Pedigree

Brasília is a CIAM city. In fact, it is the most complete example ever constructed of the architectural and planning tenets put forward in CIAM manifestos. From 1928 until the mid-1960s, CIAM remained the most important forum for the international exchange of ideas on modern architecture. CIAM's meetings and publications established a worldwide consensus among architects on the essential problems confronting architecture, giving special attention to those of the modern city. Brazil was represented in the congress as early as 1930, and Brasília's architects Lúcio Costa and Oscar Niemeyer have practiced its principles with renowned clarity.[1]

That Brasília's design derives from CIAM proposals is easily demonstrated. Its most significant manifesto, *The Athens Charter*, defines the objectives of city planning in terms of four functions: "The keys to city planning are to be found in the four functions: housing, work, recreation (during leisure) and traffic" (Le Corbusier 1957 [1941]: art. 77). The last function, traffic, "bring[s] the other three usefully into communication" (ibid., art. 81). A later CIAM meeting augmented these to include a "public core" of administrative and civic activities. Planners refer to the organization of these functions into typologies of social activity and building form as zoning. What distinguishes modernist zoning from its precursors is the conception that urban life may be understood for planning purposes in terms of these four or five functions and, more important, that they should be organized as mutually exclusive sectors within the city. Together with circulation, this organization determines both the internal order and the overall shape of the CIAM city.

Now consider the Plan of Brasília (figs. 2.1, 2.2): it is a perfect illustration of how the zoning of these functions can generate a city. A circulation cross of speedways determines the organization and shape of the city exactly as Le Corbusier (1971a[1924]: 164), the guiding hand of CIAM, proposes in an earlier publication: "Running north and south, and east and west, and forming the two great axes of the city, there would be great *arterial roads for fast one-way traffic*" (fig. 2.3). Residential superblocks are placed along one axis; work areas along the other. The public core is located to one side of the axial crossing. Recreation in the form of a lake and green belt surrounds the city. *Et voilà*—total city planning.

Next, compare views of Brasília with those of two ideal cities by Le Corbusier, A Contemporary City for Three Million Inhabitants of 1922 and The Radiant City of 1930 (figs. 2.4–2.13). These two projects became prototypes both for and of the CIAM model defined in *The Athens Charter*. Note the explicit similarities between the two and Brasília: the circulation cross of speedways; the dwelling units of uniform height and appearance grouped into residential superblocks with gardens and collective facilities; the administration, business, and financial towers around the central crossing; the recreation zone surrounding the city. Brasília's pedigree is evident.

I make these comparisons not to belittle either Costa's or Niemeyer's originality in giving final form to CIAM proposals. Every architectural project has its own history and anxiety of influence. Moreover, there are differences between Le Corbusier's projects and Brasília. For example, Niemeyer's architecture is distinctively lighter and more iconic than Le Corbusier's, and Costa's plan includes a public core—the fifth function which had not yet been identified when Le Corbusier designed his ideal cities. Nor are these comparisons meant to imply that Costa's Master Plan was not the most deserving of the 26 entries in Brasília's national design competition.[2] They are made simply to illustrate that the same model of urban order structures these cities; that this model is described in the CIAM rulebook; and that Brasília follows these rules with great clarity.

In addition to the formal evidence establishing Brasília as a CIAM city, there is the pedagogical: both Costa and Niemeyer are Le Corbusian progeny. Le Corbusier's (and therefore CIAM's) influence on the development of modern architecture

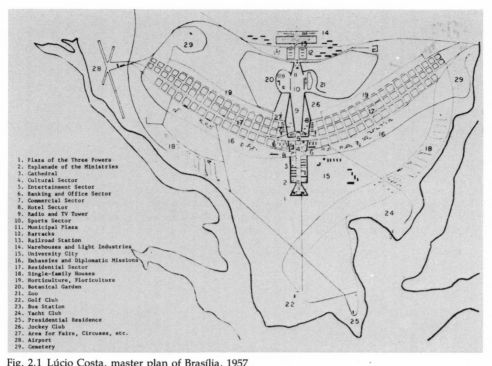

1. Plaza of the Three Powers
2. Esplanade of the Ministries
3. Cathedral
4. Cultural Sector
5. Entertainment Sector
6. Banking and Office Sector
7. Commercial Sector
8. Hotel Sector
9. Radio and TV Tower
10. Sports Sector
11. Municipal Plaza
12. Barracks
13. Railroad Station
14. Warehouses and Light Industries
15. University City
16. Embassies and Diplomatic Missions
17. Residential Sector
18. Single-family Houses
19. Horticulture, Floriculture
20. Botanical Garden
21. Zoo
22. Golf Club
23. Bus Station
24. Yacht Club
25. Presidential Residence
26. Jockey Club
27. Area for Fairs, Circuses, etc.
28. Airport
29. Cemetery

Fig. 2.1 Lúcio Costa, master plan of Brasília, 1957

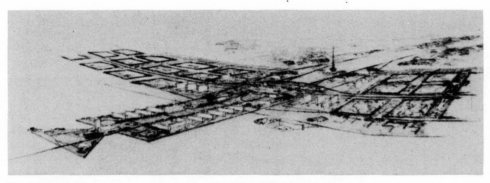

Fig. 2.2 Lúcio Costa, perspective sketch of Brasília, 1957. AU–Arquitetura e Urbanismo.

Fig. 2.3 Le Corbusier, A Contemporary City for Three Million Inhabitants, perspective sketch, 1922

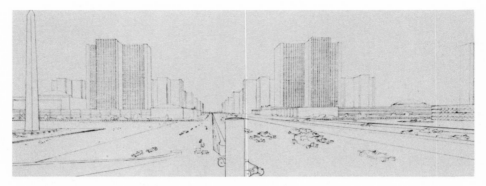

Fig. 2.4 Le Corbusier, A Contemporary City for Three Million Inhabitants, perspective, 1922
"The 'City' seen from the 'great arterial' freeway. To the left and right, the administration buildings. In the background, the museums and universities. One sees the ensemble of skyscrapers bathed in light and air." (Le Corbusier 1937: 36)

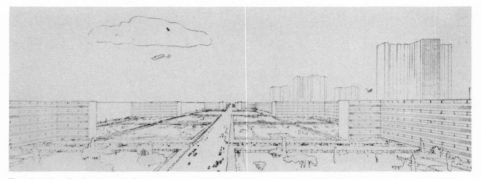

Fig. 2.5 Le Corbusier, A Contemporary City for Three Million Inhabitants, perspective, 1922
"A street running along an indented group of dwellings (6 double storeys). The indentations create a unique architectural impression, a far cry from the typical 'corridor streets.' Every window of each apartment (on both sides) opens out toward the park." (Le Corbusier 1937: 36)

2.6

2.7

2.8

Fig. 2.6 Aerial view of the South Wing, Brasília, 1981

Fig. 2.7 Aerial view of the crossing of the Residential and Monumental axes, Bus Terminal and platform, and Entertainment sectors, Brasília, 1981

Fig. 2.8 Monumental Axis, view of the National Congress and the Esplanade of the Ministries from the Supreme Tribunal in the Plaza of the Three Powers, Brasília, 1980

2.9

2.10

2.11

2.12

2.13

Fig. 2.9 Le Corbusier, model of the Radiant City showing residential sector, 1930. "In zones of habitation such as this, streets have no excuse for existing. The city has become a green city. Buildings used by children are situated in parks. Adolescents and adults can play outdoor games right outside their dwellings. Automobiles circulate somewhere else—where they are useful for something." (Le Corbusier 1939: 33)

Fig. 2.10 Le Corbusier, model of the Radiant City showing residential sector, 1930

Fig. 2.11 View of the Residential sectors of the South Wing, Brasília, 1981

Fig. 2.12 View of housing blocks and playground of Superquadra 108 South, Brasília, 1980

Fig. 2.13 Aerial view of South Wing Superquadras 308, 307, 108, and 107, Brasília, 1981

in Brazil was decisive (see Bruand 1981: 82–93). Between 1930 and 1945, Costa and his students systematically analyzed Le Corbusier's work and accepted it as the foundation of modern architecture in Brazil. Costa (1962: 202) called it "the sacred book of architecture." Le Corbusier's projects were available to Brazilians not only through architectural publications but, most important, through the lectures that Le Corbusier gave in São Paulo and Rio de Janeiro in 1929 and again in 1936. His second visit galvanized Brazilian architects into producing one of the most celebrated works of contemporary architecture in the world: the Ministry of Education and Culture in Rio, constructed between 1936 and 1943 (figs. 2.14–2.16).

Le Corbusier worked directly with a Brazilian team of architects on this project, headed by Lúcio Costa and including Costa's students Niemeyer, Reidy, Moreira, Leão, and Vasconcellos, all later to become prominent architects. Le Corbusier contributed two original schemes for the ministry building on alternative sites. Although he claimed paternity of the final project as well in his later publications, the constructed ministry is today attributed to the Brazilian team because of its adaptations of his second design. Nevertheless, it is a pure Le Corbusian building. It applies with great success the defining features of his public architecture, such as the *brise-soleil* (sun screen); the building raised on columns to free the ground for gardens and circulation; the functional yet sculptural massing of volumes; the synthesis of sculpture, painting, and architecture; the glass façade; the modern construction techniques of column support and non-weight-bearing partitions; and the location of structures within the building lot rather than along its edges to create an open plaza. These are exactly the principles of architecture, along with others in the Le Corbusian grammar, that Costa and Niemeyer later used in Brasília.

Considering Brasília's pedigree, therefore, I use the terms modernist architecture and city planning to denote the tenets of CIAM and its associated aesthetic, the International Style. Most specifically, I refer to Le Corbusier's formulations of them in *The Athens Charter* (1941) and *The Radiant City* (1933), and in his architectural and planning projects, A Contemporary City for Three Million Inhabitants (1922) and The Radiant City (1930). I also include as part of these denotations related architectural groups and styles which historians distinguish from CIAM but which share many of its basic principles. I must explain this inclusive view because it is important both in understanding CIAM doctrine and in determining the extent to which I can generalize from the analysis of Brasília to other examples of modernist planning.[3]

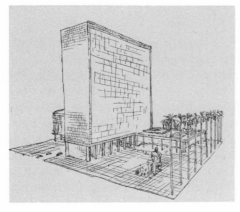

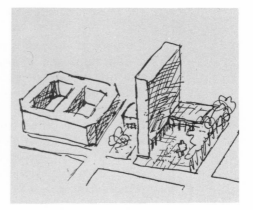

Fig. 2.14 Le Corbusier's second project for the Ministry of Education and Culture, Rio de Janeiro, 1936

Fig. 2.15 Le Corbusier's second project for the Ministry of Education and Culture. Note the differences between the conventional and the modernist city-block.

Fig. 2.16 North elevation of the Ministry of Education and Culture, Rio de Janeiro, 1937–43

Soviet modernism presents one case in point of a distinct architectural and planning tradition related to CIAM. I am referring to the Soviet avant-garde movements, especially the faction of constructivism known as the Association of Contemporary Architects (OSA) as it developed in the 1920s and 1930s, and to the so-called modern functionalism of the post-Stalin era. As Cohen (1981: 117) states: "Indeed, if there is any country where the rules set down in *The Radiant City* and codified in *The Athens Charter* have the weight of law, it is certainly the U.S.S.R." Although the Russians did not participate in CIAM meetings or manifestos, they maintained working relations with its leaders. Both groups shared many of the same basic principles in developing a critique of existing urban conditions, a comprehensive theory of the new city, and specific architectural solutions for the new institutions of industrial society, namely, for mass housing, factories, administration buildings, parks, and traffic systems.

In addition, members of the two groups shared basic social and political positions, such as a radical critique of private property and money relations; the development of new building types, which the Russians called "social condensers"; the conception of the dwelling unit as part of public services; the liberation of women from domestic servitude; and, the corporate organization of apartment blocks and neighborhood units.[4] However, they did have important differences, especially over the issue of "urbanization versus deurbanization" (see Kopp 1970: appendix 6 and Cohen 1981: 102–8), and their mutual criticism tended to be caustic. Nevertheless, their relationship was essentially one of siblings, though perhaps not of comrades. Although Le Corbusier was not a Communist, he was often mistaken for one by his western critics.

I draw attention to this relationship because of the influence of Soviet architecture on Brazilian architects. This influence has been particularly significant on the architects of the Left, notably Niemeyer who is a lifelong member of the Brazilian Communist party. The influence of Soviet architecture is due in part to its sibling relationship with CIAM but most especially to its explicitly revolutionary objectives. Thus, both Soviet constructivism and post-Stalinist functionalism provide more than just examples of specific architectural solutions for the Brazilians. They also provide the model of what Niemeyer (1980b [1955]: 55) calls "social architecture" in "the solution of collective problems": "While in so many countries [the architect] attends almost exclusively to the solicitations of a minority of the dominant classes, there [in the Soviet Union], to the contrary, his work is directed to the great projects of urban planning which have as their objective the common happiness and well-being."

Niemeyer (ibid., 53–54) argues that such a social architecture is impossible in Brazil. This is because Brazil lacks the "social base," "great collective plans," and "heavy industry" that are for him its necessary preconditions. Consequently, as a practicing architect, Niemeyer states that he has no choice but to serve either the elite classes or a "demagogic and opportunistic" government. As a politically radical modernist architect, Niemeyer claims that he is therefore forced to assume a basic contradiction in his practice between his necessarily "nonsocial" architecture and his political convictions—a dilemma to which we shall return. In this contradictory situation, Soviet architecture provides Niemeyer and others on the Left with a model of the desired alternative.

The broad consensus of issues between CIAM and constructivism raises an important point. Perhaps with the exception of total decontextualization, most of the features of the CIAM model city were developed by others earlier in this century and in the last. On the one hand, the various avant-garde movements contributed many elements. On the other, urbanists such as Haussmann (whom we consider later), reformist municipal governments, and French and British colonial administrations developed other features as the modern discipline of comprehensive spatial planning began to evolve with the need to manage the colonies abroad and the urban masses at home.[5] What distinguishes CIAM is that it expressly set out to build a common framework among such diverse contributors. In the words of Le Corbusier, its explicit purpose was to develop this consensus among groups of different architectural and political positions: "to express the maximum possible agreement between all the necessarily diverse tendencies represented by the very active members of such an international architectural conference: Catalan trade unionists, Muscovite collectivists, Italian fascists, and . . . sharp-eyed technical experts" (Le Corbusier 1967 [1933]: 188).[6]

Thus, CIAM was first and foremost an international congress whose members often linked mutually antagonistic social and political programs to the new architecture. As it was always divided into feuding groups, its manifestos can only be read as compromise statements.[7] These manifestos were based on resolutions (partially reprinted in Le Corbusier 1967: 187–89) that delegates from various national groups and avant-gardes prepared from extensive studies and then voted upon. For example, at the important 1933 meeting on The Functional City, eighteen nations were represented by over one hundred delegates.[8] They analyzed detailed studies of thirty-three cities from all parts of the world except Africa and South America. Problems of urbanization in these regions were addressed in Le Corbusier's (1967 [1933]: 220–61) presentations of his own master plans for Rio de Janeiro (1929), São Paulo (1929), Buenos Aries (1929), and Montevideo (1929) in South America, and for Algiers (1931–33) and Domaine de Badjara (1932) in North Africa.

In spite of its political and architectural diversity, however, the congress of 1933 established a dehistoricizing precedent: when in 1941 Le Corbusier codified its results in *The Athens Charter*, he presented his version of the congress. Not surprisingly, he eliminated the tensions between its divergent components and, most significant, any relation between architecture and political affiliation. What the real differences between communists, fascists, and technocrats might mean for the modern city proposed were covered over in the effort to present Le Corbusier's version as the one of consensus.[9] Thus, in considering the international consensus CIAM achieved on a model city, we must realize on the one hand that many of its features were developed by others in different contexts, and, on the other, that some of its most important manifestos are laundered of its own history.

The multiple decontextualizations of CIAM manifestos have several consequences for our analysis. They alert us to an approach to city planning which will reappear in the case of Brasília, both in its Master Plan (whose own myth-making we consider in the next chapter) and in its appeal to groups which in other ways are discordant: Brasília was planned by a Left-center liberal, designed by a Communist, constructed by a developmentalist regime, and consolidated by a bureaucratic-authoritarian dictatorship, each claiming an elective affinity with the city. Precisely because the CIAM model manages to unite such dissonant interests, its brand of modernism has come to dominate development projects worldwide. We shall have to consider the character and costs of the dehistoricizing consensus it achieves.

Moreover, we shall have to set the CIAM project within a historically broader architectural and social context than the one it claims for itself. This is a complex task, and I can only point to those major components that are directly significant for my study. For while it is important for historians to investigate the diversity of architectural movements related to CIAM, and the political contexts in which the science of city planning arose, I must as well grapple with the fact that CIAM's model city did come to dominate architectural and planning discourses about the modern city. This is the model that generated Brasília, and therefore the one on which I must focus my analysis.

2.2 The Modernist Project

> Take an airplane. Fly over our 19th century cities, over those immense sites encrusted with row after row of houses without hearts, furrowed with their canyons of soulless streets. Look down and judge for yourself. I say that these things are the signs of a tragic denaturing of human labor. They are proof that men, subjugated by the titanic growth of the machine, have succumbed to the machinations of a world powered by money. (Le Corbusier 1967 [1933]: 341)

The CIAM city is conceived as a city of salvation. It is proposed as a plan for deliverance from the "tragic denaturing of human labor" produced in and by the metropolises of industrialized society. According to CIAM doctrine, it constitutes a solution to the urban and social crises attributed to the unbridled domination of private interests in the public realm of the city, in the accumulation of wealth, and in the development of industry.

All of the avant-garde movements associated with CIAM were engaged in solving the crisis industrial capitalism had created in metropolitan organization and society. All shared a similar analysis of the situation: having been organized for private profit, the forces of production unleashed in the Industrial Revolution had reduced European cities to chaos by the turn of the century and had shattered their social fabric. The radical solutions proposed by CIAM called for the assertion of collective action and collective rights over private interests both in ordering the city and in managing the forces of industrial development. They proclaimed a new machine era in which the potential benefits of the Industrial Revolution would be extended to all classes and in which the city would be as orderly as an industrial assemblage.

As these egalitarian and functional prescriptions for the metropolitan crisis constituted a political critique of the development of capitalism in Europe, they therefore politicized architecture. As a result, most of the avant-garde movements adopted political parties as models of action. Nevertheless, as a critique calling for radical change, it was one amenable to different political affiliations among the "Catalan trade unionists, Muscovite collectivists, Italian fascists," and technocrats. Consequently, the avant-garde movements in architecture were distributed over the available political spectrum. Most affiliated with a radical Left—constructivism and cubo-futurism in Russia, utopianism and expressionism in Central Europe, the Bauhaus and Der Ring in Germany. It was the Ring organization of Gropius, May, Taut, Wagner, and others which represented the radical architects of Germany in CIAM (see Lane 1968: 127). Yet several members of this group and of de Stijl in Holland also associated with social-democratic coalitions of the Left center to build experimental residential quarters for the working classes in Amsterdam, Frankfurt, Hamburg, and Berlin (see Lane 1968: 87–124 and Tafuri 1976: 109–24). Still others of the Movimento Italiano per L'Architettura Razionale (MIAR) embraced Italian fascism before Mussolini himself turned away from modernism and adopted monumental classicism as the architectural style of his regime (see Benevolo 1977: 561–76).

It should be understood, however, that these political affiliations were often mercurial and ambiguous as radical architects appeared at the door of whichever authority, on the Left or Right, seemed capable of implementing total planning. "France needs a Father," Le Corbusier proclaimed. "It doesn't matter who. It could be one man, two men, any number" (cited in Fishman 1977: 265). Thus, hoping to find an omnipotent patron, he wrote on the title page of his major publication, *The Radiant City:* "This work is dedicated to Authority." The political history of the avant-garde movements in architecture has yet to be written.[10] For our purposes, what is significant is that all of these architectural avant-gardes shared certain fundamental premises in their evaluation of the crises of metropolitan society. In *Architecture and Utopia: Design and Capitalist Development,* Tafuri (1976: 50–124) establishes the unity of these premises in a persuasive, if dense, argument. One summary passage is worth quoting to reinforce this point:

> Free the experience of shock [i.e., the crush of the big city] from any automatism [i.e., passivity, alienation, anomie]; found, on the basis of that experience, visual codes and codes of action transformed by the already consolidated characteristics of the capitalist metropolis (rapidity of transformation, organization and simultaneousness of communications, accelerated tempo of use, eclecticism); reduce the artistic experience to a pure object. . .; involve the public, unified in an avowed interclass and therefore anti-bourgeois ideology: these are the tasks that all together were assumed by the avant-garde of the twentieth century. . . . And I must repeat, all together, and without any distinction between Constructivism and the art of protest.

From 1922 on, the various avant-gardes tried with apparent urgency to unify their positions on modern art and the metropolis (Tafuri 1976: 95 notes 61, 95). With an internationalism that they hoped would have political ramifications, they managed to synthesize such theories as dadaist anarchy, constructivist decomposition, and de Stijl order into a united front through joint manifestos, publications, exhibitions, and conventions.

These efforts eventually produced a convergence of propositions for a new kind of city. Principally through the writings of Le Corbusier and his followers, these in turn were synthesized (and dehistoricized, as I suggested) into the basic working model of CIAM. Once consolidated in this form, it became the almost universally recognized image of the planned modern city. In what follows, I shall briefly describe the major premises of this model. Although I set them within the historical context of nineteenth-century urban growth and of the development of city planning as a means of population management and political control, my principal concern is with the CIAM view of these developments and with its synthesis of planning propositions. I shall focus especially on its (1) anticapitalist and egalitarian basis, (2) machine metaphor and totalizing rationality, (3) redefinition of the social functions of urban organization, (4) development of building typologies and planning conventions as instruments of social change, (5) decontextualization and environmental determinism, (6) reliance on state authority to achieve total planning, (7) techniques of shock, and (8) conflation of art, politics, and daily life.

CIAM doctrine attributes the metropolitan crisis to the interactions of two factors. First, it points to the failure to plan cities according to the requirements and consequences of the machine and industrial production. Second, it attacks the institution of private property as the primary impediment to comprehensive planning. In analyzing the interaction of these two factors, CIAM propounded an argument based on the historical development of cities under capitalism to justify its planning proposals. Considering the way these proposals deny historical context in their own application, this is indeed a contradictory foundation.

CIAM argued that the cities of the Industrial Revolution were not planned as either the production units or the administrative centers that the development of industry required. They were organized neither by the needs of the production process nor by an efficient, taylorized cycle of industrial production, distribution, and consumption. If they have any organization at all according to CIAM ideology (Le Corbusier 1957: arts. 72–73), it is only that of the "ruthless rule" of private property. As a consequence, CIAM argued that the unplanned urban centers could not effectively manage the massive influx of migrants drawn to industrial employment and related services. Nor could they accommodate their own natural growth. Over the course of the nineteenth century, the population of major cities in Europe grew at an extraordinary rate (see A. Weber 1963). Both London and Paris quintupled in size. London swelled from 860,000 to 4.2 million and Paris from 550,000 to 2.5 million inhabitants. Berlin increased eightfold, from 200,000 to over 1.6 million. Manchester, Frankfurt, Hamburg, Lyons, Milan, and many other cities posted similar gains at the close of the century.

To describe the effects of this phenomenal expansion on the city, Le Corbusier developed a set of disease metaphors in an etiology of urban chaos. The monstrous growth of worker tenements created "cesspools" of tuberculosis and cholera. As the urban periphery of slums expanded "contagiously," the city spread into the countryside "like a disease." The sprawling metropolis lost the coherent physical structure of a "healthy organism" it once manifested. Instead, it showed all the symptoms of being in the final phase of a fatal malady: its circulation clogged, its respiration polluted, its tissues decaying in their own noxious wastes. As in a coroner's report, *The Athens Charter* concludes:

> All kinds of unpleasantness have come upon people who were unable to measure accurately the extent of technological transformations and their repercussions on public and private life. Lack of urban planning is the cause of the anarchy that reigns in the organization of cities and the equipment of industries. Because people have failed to understand the rules [of urban development], the countryside has been emptied, cities have been filled beyond all reason, concentrations of industry have taken place haphazardly, workers' dwellings have become hovels. Nothing was done to safeguard man. The result is catastrophic and it is almost identical in every country. It is the bitter fruit of a hundred years of the undirected development of the machine. (Le Corbusier 1957: art. 94)

The Athens Charter attributes this undirected development to the dominance of private interests in collective affairs. Private interests control not only the means of production (and thereby the development of industry) but, most important, the city's resources, principally land. In CIAM's view (Le Corbusier 1957: art. 72), the second and determining cause of the urban crisis is the control the interests of private property exercise over the development of the city.

CIAM argued that under capitalism, private ownership dominates land use and thereby determines the structure of the city. Its arguments are based on a consideration of the growth of nineteenth-century cities, and in this regard they seem justified.

Even in those cities that had numerous public squares and parks, the influence of private interests on public resources is evident when one considers how the public was defined in relation to the private—a relation we shall analyze in subsequent chapters. The dominant public spaces in these cities were streets and squares, defined both architecturally and legally by the buildings around them. Any attempt to widen a street or reorganize a square to accommodate heavier traffic, for example, had to confront the rights of adjacent property owners whose land would be affected. Furthermore, real estate speculation for private profit determined the land value of these lots and this in turn controlled building construction. Thus, the interests of private property in housing shaped the physical structure of these cities: they not only controlled those holdings that were in private hands but they restricted development in the public areas of the city as well.

It is at this point that the conflict between private interests and the public good engages CIAM. Without some form of land expropriation available to planners, CIAM argues that private ownership easily blocks attempts at urban reform, not to mention comprehensive planning for development. Therefore, *The Athens Charter* (ibid., art. 94) proposes that "the soil—the territory of the nation—ought to be available at any moment and at its fair value, estimated before plans have been drawn up. The ground should be open to mobilization when it is a matter of general interest." In an earlier rendition of this proposal, Le Corbusier (1967 [1933]: 189) characteristically exposes the radical implications of the more guarded version presented in *The Athens Charter*:

> Mobilization of private property, whether built on or not, [is] a fundamental condition of any planned development of Cities. . . . Destruction of the legal system! Modification of age-old truths! In order to provide liberty for the individual and all the benefits of collective action . . . contemporary society must have the entire land surface of the country at its disposal. "To have at its disposal" does not mean doing away with private property, or stealing, or depredation. It means improving the assets represented by our land for the benefit of mankind. Let the lawyers find a way!

As this statement makes clear, CIAM never espoused the abolition of private property, only its redefinition. While this redefinition is never fully specified (a lawyer's task), its outline is nevertheless apparent. It entails redefining the concept of ownership in land. Although residents in the CIAM city would have the right to buy and sell land, the state would hold the ultimate rights over land alienation. This right would be exercised by the planning authorities of local government in accordance with a national policy of land development. Land would be "redistributed" (Le Corbusier's term) from the private domain to the public in cases of conflict between public and private interests. Expropriated owners would receive payment at a value determined by the state and not real estate speculation.

Thus, in contrast to the capitalist view of land as disposable real estate, the CIAM proposals consider both urban and rural land as, ultimately, inalienable state patrimony. This redefinition does not abolish private property but it does remove the right of disposal in certain circumstances from the bundle of rights associated with land ownership. The other rights of ownership remain. CIAM doctrine also stresses that ownership is a right ultimately legitimated by the state as part of its collective organization. On the basis of this legitimation, CIAM proposals justify the right of planners to intervene in matters of land tenure when "the benefit of mankind" is at issue.

Thus, the mobilization of land is at the basis of several key objectives in CIAM planning. First, CIAM planners believed that it would abolish the ultimate power of private interests to block planning initiatives (Le Corbusier 1957: art. 73). Without property restrictions, planners would be able to assume, as the foundation of their plans, a position of unchallenged authority over the destiny of the city. CIAM planners argued that as a result, their urban plans would become blueprints for development, based on this presumed ability to control the future through action guided by rationality and centralized authority. Second, CIAM planners wanted to mobilize the land in order to establish a regional development policy, incorporating city and country into their comprehensive plans (ibid., art. 77). Third, they insisted that mobilization would curtail the pernicious effects of real estate speculation in the city (ibid., art. 72).

By controlling speculation, CIAM planners expected to be able to distribute urban resources on the basis of factors other than wealth. The basis of this distribution would in effect be the master plan of the city itself, which would allocate the advantages of collective organization—such as housing, recreation, education, and health facilities—to all classes of residents according to objective and rational criteria. As a result of this egalitarian distribution, CIAM argued that the modernist city would achieve an ultimate goal: it would be a city neither socially nor spatially stratified into money classes. It is therefore evident why mobilization was a key proposal of CIAM: not only would it supposedly establish the conditions for a classless city, but the planner's master plan would be the absolute basis of order in that city, and the planner its arbiter.

Land expropriation for public use was not, however, a new issue. It had its origins in the very beginning of urban planning legislation in England and France, and it is important to see how the CIAM proposals for urban reorganization both derive and differ from it. The phenomenal growth of unsanitary housing in both countries during the nineteenth century led to numerous legislative attempts beginning in the 1830s to regulate the private ownership and construction of tenements.[11] Social reformers and sanitation specialists pioneered these bills, seeking to make ownership in real estate accountable to minimum standards of health and welfare set by the state. Inevitably, these entailed a restriction of the rights of property ownership through government intervention in one form or another, and thereby urban planning—linked to the emerging social sciences—played an important role in the consolidation of centralized administrative and political powers in these European states.

Until the late 1840s, liberal bourgeois opposition to state intervention and, from a different perspective, defenders of the rights of citizens combined to defeat these proposals. But successive cholera epidemics in Paris and London during the 1840s necessitated immediate action on the governmental regulation of unsanitary housing. In England, the Public Health Act of 1848 was the first in a series of such regulations, culminating in the Housing of the Working Classes Act of 1890. These laws empowered a variety of government commissions to hold landlords responsible for the sanitary conditions of their dwellings. They established the right of health inspectors and planners to levy fines, taxes, and property improvement rates, to have free access to property to inspect and condemn, and finally even to requisition land. In France, the laws of 1841 on public works and of 1850 on slum housing went a step further. They gave the Municipal Council, through the courts, the necessary authority for the compulsory acquisition of land.

Devised for public works and slum clearances, these French laws were amended in 1852 to give the executive institutions of government the power to expropriate land without recourse to the courts. It was this ensemble of legislation, especially the acquisition of land by executive order, that enabled Baron Haussmann to realize his profound transformation of Paris in the following two decades. In the second part of the nineteenth century, laws similar to these were enacted in Belgium, Austria, Spain, Italy, and England, giving the state the power to carry out large-scale planning operations. From these executive powers came the spate of enormous public building projects that transformed European capitals. These involved massive demolition and construction in Paris (1853–69), Brussels (1867–71),

Barcelona (from 1859), and Florence (1864–77); the building of the Ringstrasse in Vienna (from 1857); and the installation of a main drainage system and foundations for the underground rail in London (from 1848).

It cannot be doubted that this Haussmannization of European capitals greatly influenced CIAM planning. Le Corbusier (1967: 209–11) admired the baron for bringing a measure of geometric order to Paris and for using a scheme of broad avenues to unite isolated areas of the city—two paramount principles in CIAM doctrine. Haussmann himself provided a model for the CIAM planner: technocrat, engineer, "surgeon"; incorruptible and autocratic. Furthermore, Haussmann established a rationale for large-scale planning that CIAM adopted. He justified his surgical incisions through workers' quarters as measures necessary to endow urban centers with "space, air, light, verdure and flowers, in a word, with all that dispenses health" (Haussmann 1890: quoted in Vidler 1978, p. 91). This justification is nearly identical, word for word, with CIAM's own explanation for its even more comprehensive "greening of the city" (Le Corbusier 1957: art. 12). Just as Haussmann had done, CIAM (ibid., arts. 8–17, 23–40) adopted the technical, technocratic, and moral justifications of public works legislation for its proposed transformations of the nineteenth-century city. Yet, both Haussmann's and CIAM's discourses on sanitation, housing, poverty, state intervention, and so on, may be seen to derive from the same need to grapple with the explosion of the urban populations of Europe during the eighteenth and nineteenth centuries. For this phenomenon had led to the understanding not only that the management of population was indispensible to the interests of capitalism but also that this management required the articulation of spatial planning, social science knowledge, and political power. If Haussmann and his contemporaries had not quite accomplished this articulation by the 1870s, CIAM inherited it by the 1920s as the already formed discipline of urbanism.

In this sense, CIAM's model city carries on basic aims of late nineteenth- and early twentieth-century public works legislation in developing a comprehensive program for urban organization, and in presenting it as an indispensable instrument of the good government of society. Nonetheless, CIAM planning goes beyond these intents in several significant ways. Under nineteenth-century legislation, building sites acquired and improved at public expense did not remain public property after improvement. Rather, they were restored to their original owners (Benevolo 1967: 135). As Haussmann himself protested, these improvements resulted in enormous capital gains for the original landlords at the expense of the city. In CIAM planning, expropriated sites would be purchased *before* improvements and would remain public property after redevelopment (Le Corbusier 1957: art. 94). Thus, as the government redeveloped the city, more and more of it would become public and less private. Eventually, a new kind of entirely public city would emerge as the end-product of CIAM development planning. In this situation (as in fact initially occurred in Brasília), citizens' rights to hold housing property need not be abolished because they simply become irrelevant.

In the second place, the Haussmannization or evisceration of the central quarters of numerous European cities did not solve the problem of mass housing or provide for the kind of egalitarian distribution of urban resources CIAM proposed. In fact, it had just the opposite intent and effect: that of securing the city for the rich by marginalizing the poor. These large-scale planning projects "solved" the housing problem of the working classes by exiling them to the periphery. The broad avenues cut through working-class neighborhoods were surgical incisions designed to remove "the dangerous classes" from the hub of the city. Engels (1872: 74–75) did not fail to recognize the true class intentions of Haussmann planning: "Breaking long, straight and broad streets through the closely built workers' quarters . . . turn the city into a pure luxury city. . . . The scandalous alleys and lanes disappear to the accompaniment of lavish self-praise from the bourgeoisie . . . but they appear again immediately somewhere else." Furthermore, while these avenues did bring a measure of fresh air into the city, their broad dimensions facilitated military maneuvers against the barricades of working-class rebellions—an urban planning lesson learned in the wake of successive Parisian revolts.

It is true that Le Corbusier's 1925 Plan Voisin for Paris (based on his first ideal city of 1922) proposes a Haussmannization on a scale not even Haussmann imagined. In this plan, the managerial elite of a new Paris occupy the center while the working classes have been removed to outlying satellite suburbs. Just as Engels had attacked Haussmannization as an instrument of class oppression, so French Communists condemned the Plan Voisin. They argued that it presupposed a centralized authoritarian government run by an elite corps of capitalists and managers and that its center-satellite organization reproduced stratified class distinctions. Between 1925 and 1930, however, Le Corbusier underwent a political *crise de conscience* (cf. Fishman 1982: 205–34). He became disillusioned with the kind of bourgeois rule such projects presumed. Instead, he proposed the Radiant City (1930–35), the prototype of *The Athens Charter*, which abolishes the satellite system and incorporates all classes within the city. In theory, it distributes its collective benefits to all residents. Thus, Le Corbusier (1967 [1933]: 13) could argue that the objective of urban planning is a city without classes: "I had created the prototype of a *classless city,* a city of men busy with work and leisure in surroundings that made these possible." We should remember that this radiant and classless model is the one adopted for the Master Plan of Brasília, which specifies that all classes of the federal bureaucracy must live within its residential units.

Thus, CIAM planning proposed to solve the urban crisis of capitalism by adopting the technical and rational arguments of public health legislation in the context of a comprehensive strategy of public works and good government. As we have seen thus far, it expands this strategy in two ways. First, it considers the entire planned city as a state-sponsored public domain. Second, it proposes to distribute to all residents the benefits of this collective organization on the basis of a master plan for development.

In yet a third way, CIAM reconceived the strategy of public works. The discourse of urban reform in the eighteenth and nineteenth centuries was often presented in terms of a metaphor of disease in an analogy between cities and the human body: the city was a diseased organism that required radical surgery in the form of planning operations to cut open its afflicted parts, to make incisions with broad avenues through congested quarters, to rehabilitate the city's lungs with new parks, and so forth (see Vidler 1978: 38–42, 68–96 on these medical analogies). As we have seen, Le Corbusier also adopted this rhetorical device of describing cities as malignant growths. However, CIAM based its planning prescriptions not so much on a model of the organism as on a model of the machine.

In CIAM's analysis, the solution to the crisis of the machine is to be found in the machine itself. If the machine had destroyed the cities of the first machine age (1730–1930), so called, it would be the salvation of the cities of the second. Nearly all of the avant-garde movements viewed the machine as a potential source of liberation: "The machine, that vast modern event, will be seen [in the Radiant City] for what it really is, a servant and not a ruler, a worker and not a tyrant, a source of unity and not of conflict, of construction and not of destruction" (Le Corbusier 1967: 176). In this prognostication, the machine would liberate society from the drudgery of manual labor, freeing women especially from domestic slavery and giving both men and women a new measure of humanity. Moreover, it would destroy national and class boundaries. It would create international and interclass communication; it would equalize. For society to realize the benefits of this vehicle of social progress, cities would have to be planned in harmony with its development and use.[12]

The simplest way to do this, CIAM proposed, would be to treat the new city itself as a machine, that is, to plan it as an engineer plans an industrial process by conceiving of the city as an industrial product. This new city would be organized not as a metaphor of the machine but quite literally as a machine, a "machine for living in" (as Le Corbusier once described the house). In this organization, the city would be broken down into its essential functions. These would be taylorized, standardized, rationalized, and assembled as a totality. Thus, the totalizing scope of modernist planning derives from its conception of the city as a machine. For a machine is never partially designed or partially constructed; only its completeness guarantees its functional, working order.[13]

In these machine-cities, the architect no longer designs individual objects. Instead, the architect organizes these objects into processes—into functions, interrelations, and communications—and plans their future development. Only through this kind of total planning in which the city is ordered as an industrial assemblage, could its complexity be controlled and could the potential benefits of the machine be extended to all classes of residents. Thus, unlike premodernist planning, the CIAM city took as its organizational model the very event which had destroyed preindustrial cities: the machine itself.

The purely technical arguments that the modernists developed to justify their planning proposals thus derive in part from public health and administrative concerns and in part from the model of the machine in industrial production. However, this constellation of technical arguments is linked to a comprehensive reassessment of the functions of the city. The model of the machine entails not simply breaking the city down into its essential functions of housing, work, recreation, and traffic. More significantly, it demands reorganizing and at the same time reconceptualizing these functions. It proposes to relate them through a master plan which will ensure that each one performs its assigned tasks in harmony with the others, as the gears of a machine do. The modernist model, however, does much more than just provide a blueprint of functional order. It cannot simply accept the identity of these functions as they had developed in the chaos of nineteenth-century cities.

The new architecture therefore set out to redefine systematically the social basis of each function. It does not simply redesign apartment buildings; it proposes to restructure domestic organization and the family as an economic unit.[14] In completely separating pedestrian and vehicle, it not only abolishes streets, it also eliminates the type of urban crowd and public activity that streets support. In planning a city in a park of playing fields and gardens, it does not simply "green" the city; more significantly, it proposes a new focus on sports for the displaced public activity of streets. The design of modern factories, commercial facilities, and superhighways reconceives the relationship between residence, work, and commerce, and between market and marketplace. Together, these redefinitions constitute a program of social change in which the institutional structures that had previously characterized each function are radically transformed.

Corresponding to these redefinitions, architects developed a set of equally revolutionary building types and urban structures. They were motivated by the central idea in architectural modernism that the creation of new *forms* of social experience would transform society, and they viewed architectural innovation as precisely the opportunity to do this. The new units of habitation, buildings sited in the middle of continuous open spaces, transparent glass façades, gardens on rooftops, avenues without intersections, and the free plan, are all, in this modernist doctrine, means to create new social practices and thus instruments of social progress. They are designed to transform society by forging new forms of collective associations and personal habits, and by precluding those considered undesirable.[15]

One of the clearest statements on the new architectural typology as a medium of social transformation is found in the OSA constructivist manifesto of 1928:

> We are opposed to such prerevolutionary building types as the speculative apartment house, the private residence, the "noblemen's club," etc., all products of prerevolutionary social, technical, and economic circumstances, but still serving as a model for buildings now being erected in the U.S.S.R.: [instead we propose] new types of communal housing, new types of clubs, palaces of labor, new factories, etc., which in fact should be the conductors and condensers of socialist culture. (Kopp 1970: 94)

Architecture as the conductor and condenser of a new way of life—this is a metaphor drawn from the model of the machine. These social condensers would transform human nature as electrical condensers transform the nature of current, turning the bourgeois individualist and the denatured laborer of capitalist society into fully developed members of the socialist collective. Modernist architecture therefore is not only or even most fundamentally an argument for a new technology in building construction. Its new building typologies and planning conventions were developed as instruments of social change on the basis of this central premise: that they would function as subversive set pieces within existing cities to regenerate the whole surrounding fabric of denatured social life. "The introduction of new building types into the old fabric of the city affects the whole by transforming it" (Lissitzky 1970 [1929]: 52).

In this theory of architectural condensation and radiation, the assemblage of condensers produces a *total* environment for a future society. It is a doctrine characterized by a type of environmental determinism in which there can be no half measures or partial solutions to the crisis of industrial or industrializing society. One of the most distinctive and original features of modernist architecture is that it refuses any accommodation whatsoever to existing urban and social conditions. The break with the past must be absolute. This total decontextualization is evident in *any* modernist building project. If we take, for example, Le Corbusier's 1925 Plan Voisin for the reconstruction of central Paris or Hilberseimer's 1927 project for central Berlin, we see that in both an enormous area of the city has simply been leveled to make room for the insertion of a new and complete environment (figs. 2.17 and 2.18). The contrast between the new city and the old is one of total antagonism—a turning inside out which we shall analyze in chapter 4.

With the few exceptions of cities actually built de novo, however, the modernists rarely had the opportunity to carry out their projects on such an apocalyptic scale. Most of their built work exists in the form of single buildings. Nevertheless, it is clear that each of these is but a fragment of a total vision, of an unrealized totality. Each is to function as an enclave of subversive social practices which will eventually transform the whole. This principle of total decontextualization is therefore fundamental to the modernists' project of creating social condensers because the very totality of these new environments permits no escape from what is essentially a forced conduction to radical changes in social relations.

How is this conduction possible? In large measure, it relies on the techniques of shock. The elements or conventions that compose the new architectural order constitute what I have already referred to as a strategy of defamiliarization. This strategy was central to all of the avant-garde movements in the arts during the formative period of modern architecture. It is essentially a concept of perceptual renewal and change (cf. Jameson 1972: 50–91 and Bürger 1984: 80–81). The Russian formalist, Viktor Shklovsky (1965), defined defamiliarization in art as the technique of making objects strange (*ostranenie*) so as to renew perceptions of them. It is a means of breaking through the deadening and mechanical habits of daily routines in order

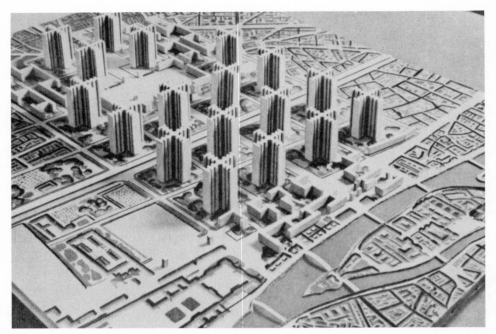

Fig. 2.17 Le Corbusier, Plan Voisin for Paris, 1925

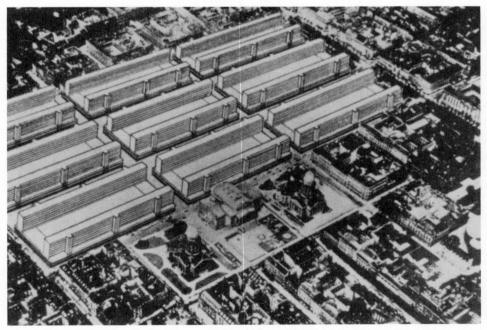

Fig. 2.18 Ludwig Hilberseimer, project for central Berlin, 1927. From Colin Rowe and Fred Koetter, *Collage City* (Cambridge: MIT Press, 1978). Copyright 1978 by The MIT Press.

to desacralize unquestioned values, to restore conscious experience, and to generate a critical reappraisal of the objects and institutions around us. Furthermore, Shklovsky characterized modern art as precisely that which deliberately draws attention to its own techniques of defamiliarization. As he put it, modern art forms deliberately "bare" or reveal their own devices for making the world strange so as to call attention to the processes of constructing and changing meaning. Brecht (ibid., 58) developed a similar notion in his theory of the "estrangement effect" (*Verfremdung*). The purpose of this estrangement and of baring its devices in art is to show us that society is not a natural given but itself the result of historical change and therefore changeable.[16]

The techniques of shock which the avant-gardes developed to raise critical consciousness include inversion, arbitrary juxtaposition, montage, decontextualization, decomposition, and deconstruction. The theories of shock abound: dadaist anarchy, surrealist objective chance (*le hasard objectif*), de Stijl decomposition, constructivist deconstruction, and Le Corbusier's objects evoking poetic reaction (*objets à réaction poétique*). As modern architecture is a synthesis of several art forms (e.g., sculpture, painting, and graphics), it drew from a large repertoire of such theories and techniques of shock—a combination brutally effective on the inhabitants of avant-garde projects; viz., *brasilite*.

The modernist strategy of defamiliarization intends to make the city strange. It consists in the attempt to impose a new urban order through a set of transformations that negate previous expectations about urban life. The modernists viewed the capitalist city as both socially and architecturally organized by discriminations between the public and the private, and by distributions of wealth, which had to be totally changed. In response, they developed proposals to produce both a new type of city and a new type of urban public for it in which such discriminations would disappear. Their new urban order was based on two sorts of transformations, the one institutional and the other architectural. The first consists in what we might call a displacement of social institutions traditionally centered in the private domain of social organization—such as property, residence, domestic organization, child and health care, and education—to a new state-sponsored public sphere of collective services, residences, associations, social clubs, and administrative councils.[17] This displacement redefines the institutional basis of the four functions of urban order by maximizing the role of the state's corporate domain and minimizing that of the familial domain in social organization. Its objective is to restructure the institutional relationships between the public and the private domains of social life so that they are both entirely regulated by a comprehensive, state-sponsored master plan. This project amounts to a proposal for transforming the social structure of capitalist society itself. For as the master plan eliminates private property as an institutional basis of both domestic organization and public order, the old distinctions between the public and the private disappear.

At the same time, these distinctions become architecturally illegible. This effacement constitutes the second strategy for creating a new urban public. It consists in transforming the nature of the capitalist city through building types, urban forms, and architectural conventions that negate its systems of representation. For example, the curtain wall of glass is such a convention of defamiliarization. An all-glass façade exposes the private domain, previously concealed behind walls, to public scrutiny. Glass transparency dissolves an opposition between private and public and between inside and outside, which had in the past been fundamental to the concept of façade in the representation of social order. In the modernist city, such conventions would impose a totally planned environment, and therefore a totality of perceptions, in which the targeted social distinctions would no longer be discerned simply because they would no longer be the focus of architectural design. Thus, by rendering them architecturally illegible, modernism sought to render them socially irrelevant.

In this double negative, CIAM modernism links architectural innovation, perceptual change, and social transformation in a utopian mode. Although it considers that innovation develops through a search for architectural forms that "condense" new types of social experience, it views the relationship between architecture and society as transitive: change the architecture and society will be forced to follow the program of social change that the architecture embodies. In this transitive prescription for the metropolitan crisis, CIAM doctrine becomes decidedly utopian. The utopian factor in the model of the city-as-machine rings clearly in the words of the grand master, Le Corbusier (1967: 143): "On the day when contemporary society, at present so sick, has become properly aware that only architecture and city planning can provide the exact prescription for its ills, then the time will have come for the great machine to be put in motion." The great machine of modern architecture is utopian because it proposes to regenerate the present by means of an imagined future, which is posited in built form as the beachhead of a new society within the existing order of things. As the means to this new society is built form, modernism argues that radical social change can and indeed must occur without social revolution. This utopian sidestep is precisely the challenge and the appeal of the final sentences of Le Corbusier's 1923 manifesto: "Architecture or Revolution. Revolution can be avoided" (Le Corbusier 1974: 269).

In the following chapters, we shall analyze the techniques and consequences of making the city strange in Brasília. There, the Master Plan achieves its total and totalizing order precisely by translating its objectives of institutional displacement into conventions of architectural defamiliarization. The investigation of the CIAM model city has drawn our attention to a number of issues in evaluating this order. One concerns history and context. CIAM doctrine doubly undercuts the importance of context in the making of history. On the one hand, in achieving consensus on a model city which can be built anywhere, its manifestos eliminate the tensions, specificities, and diversities of their own production. On the other, in its critique of the development of cities under capitalism, it studies history only to place it in the service of its own project: it constructs a historical narrative in which its own manifestos, prescriptions, and solutions are the outcome. It uses the past as an endorsement of its particular projection of the future—after which the past is swept away. We shall therefore give careful consideration to the role of history in the legitimation of Brasília; and, moreover, to the way we may use historical analysis to undermine any self-serving search for precedents.

Furthermore, I have suggested that modernist decontextualization rests on a theory of transformation in which the radical qualities of something totally out of context colonize that which exists around it. This something may be a single building conceived as an enclave of radical aesthetics and social practices within an existing city, or an entire city designed as an exemplar for the nation. The question for critical analysis is whether such an architectural set piece does not come to represent merely its own monumental disconnection. Do its innovations order the landscape around it, or do they just refer to themselves in sculptural isolation? These questions suggest two types of investigations in Brasília: one focusing on the semantic conventions of modernism's radical system of architectural representation and the other on whether the social values embodied in this system have generated new social practices.

The latter point relates to a second set of issues concerning the identification in modernist doctrine of the aesthetic and the political in the organization of social life. As Bürger (1984: 35–54) argues, a basic aim of all the European avant-garde movements was to reorganize social practice through the innovations of art, and thus negate "the status of art in bourgeois society as an institution that is unassociated with the life praxis of men." There are various ways to interpret this intention in modernist architecture as our study of the CIAM model city suggests. It seems to involve an expansion of the concept of the political to include daily life and especially the home since the experience of revolutionary kinds of residential space and organization is seen as the primary means of effecting a transformation of the whole field of social relations. On the one hand, such an expansion might open new arenas for political action, involving issues related to residence (those of housing, women, family, neighborhood, the poor, and ecology, for instance)—issues marginal to the traditional political arena of men, labor, the state, and parties but issues which have of course been crucial to the notion of cultural revolution and grassroots social movement in recent decades. In this possibility, the modernist city generates new and subversive political identities among those usually excluded from power. On the other hand, one could view state-sponsored architecture and master planning as new forms of political domination through which the domains of daily life, previously outside the realm of politics, become targets for state intervention. In this sense, the defamiliarizations and decontextualizations of the modernist city are but attempts to replace the chaos of the capitalist city with a new, predictable, and controllable beginning from which planners could realize the dream of a rational domination of the future. In Brasília, we shall find both possibilities; and often, it is the tension between the two that drives its development.

THREE

The Plan's Hidden Agenda

The search for origins is typically a subversive activity. Its usual purpose is to discover precedents that justify claims of one sort or another, inevitably at someone's expense. One has the suspicion that if such justifications were not needed, the search for precedents in the form of pedigrees, genealogies, myths of origin, and the like would be of no great interest. But the discovery of eminent ancestors, divine heroes, and first principles is an enterprise of serious consequence precisely because it can debunk as surely as legitimate pretension. Inquiries into the origins of regimes may lead to a god who begot a royal house and thus may legitimate claims of divine kingship. However, they may also uncover a fratricide that can substantiate the cause of counterclaimants. Not only do people use genealogies to validate existing social relationships, they use these relationships to prove the genealogies, modeling the form of the latter on the former.[1] This genealogical argument is a type of *petitio principii*, an illicit use of causality, a mechanism of managing and often reordering history to find support for present purposes. In whatever form, the search for origins is usually an illicit mode of justification because it always sends us back to itself as its own first principle.

In the last chapter, I established Brasília's pedigree as a modernist city. This was not an illicit enterprise because I was not attempting to justify its design but rather to place it within the historical and ideological tradition of CIAM manifestos. It was, however, a subversive one. I established Brasília's historical derivation to challenge, in this chapter, Costa's (1957) account of its origins as related in the city's foundation charter, the Master Plan of Brasília. This account is itself a subversive search for legitimation: rather than justify the city's design as a means to radical social transformation, it presents the founding of the city as if it had no history, as if it were not a response either to socioeconomic conditions in Brazil in 1957 or to modernism in architecture. Rather, it dehistoricizes its idea of Brasília, hiding its agenda for social change in a mythology of universalizing design principles, ancient cities, and sacred planning techniques. In the first part of this chapter, I deconstruct this mythological account. My purpose is to restore the Master Plan's subversive character as a modernist critique of Brazilian society so that, in the second part, I can examine the hidden agenda of radical intentions which motivate its specific proposals.

I analyze the Master Plan in detail because it is more than just a city blueprint. Rather, it is a foundation charter, an account of primordial origins with the status of law which establishes precedents for all subsequent development in Brasília. Moreover, it presents the architects' stated point of view, and in this study the reader should remember that the architects of Brasília are "most eminent natives." Furthermore, as a foundation charter, it is a masterwork of narrative construction in its own right. It is one of this century's most influential documents of city planning, especially in developing countries, and as such deserves careful consideration. Finally, although the architects' view is not ultimately what it appears to be as stated in the plan, this statement nevertheless illuminates their real intentions.

3.1 Plan Mythology

The linking of a plan for urban design with a program for social change is a fundamental feature of master planning in modern architecture. In general, this link is forged in two ways. First, the architecture of the plan consciously embodies new and desired forms of social life. For example, Soviet modernist prototypes for residental organization are based on a concept of collective domestic life rather than on a concept of private dwellings for nuclear families. In these schemes, the role of the private dwelling unit is drastically reduced as its functions, such as child care and cooking, are taken over by planned public services and displaced to common facilities. Because it is planned for a different type of domestic organization, this modernist residential unit is radically different in architectural design from a unit of private apartments for nuclear families (figs. 3.1–3.4). Second, the modernist link between architecture and society is conceived instrumentally. Modernists propose that people inhabiting their architecture will be forced to adopt the new forms of collective association and personal habit the architecture represents. In this way, architecture is considered an instrument not only of social change, but also of good government, rational order, and the renovation of life through art.

In these respects, the Master Plan of Brasília presents a paradox as a plan for a modernist city. Its program for social

Fig. 3.1 Example of a speculative apartment building constructed by an insurance company, St. Petersburg, 1913. The site is developed to yield maximum rentable floor area. From Kopp 1970.

Fig. 3.2 L. Alexander and V. Vesnin, *dom-kommuna*, 'communal house', Kuznetsk, 1930 (proposal). The apartments are located in the wings and the collective facilities in the central structure. From Kopp 1970.

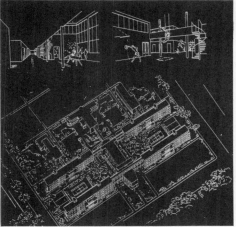

"If one accepts the premise that private dwellings should strive to operate on the basis of the greatest austerity, then by contrast, public dwellings should provide the maximum of available luxury accessible to all." (Lissitzky 1970 [1930]: 44)

"The creation of collectivized dining halls, nurseries, kindergartens, dormitories, laundries, and repair shops will really break radically with the existing family attitude toward property, and this will provide the economic premises for the extinction of the family as an economic unit." (Miliutin 1974 [1930]: 81)

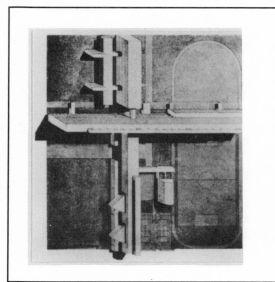

Fig. 3.3 M. Barshch and V. Vladimirov, axonometric drawing of *dom-kommuna* proposed by Stroikom, the Building Committee of the Russian Soviet Federated Socialist Republic, 1930. From Kreis 1980.

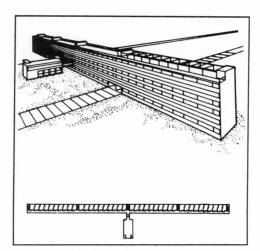

Fig. 3.4 Perspective drawing and plan of *dom-kommuna* type F developed by Stroikom. This was the prototype of the influential housing block designed by M. Ginsburg and I. Milinis for the employees of the Finance Commissariat (Narkomfin), Moscow, 1929. From Kreis 1980.

change and management constitutes a hidden agenda: while the plan suggests some of its aspects, its basic assumptions remain unstated. Neither its instrumentality nor its socioeconomic organization is discussed. Moreover, the plan offers no justification for why the new federal capital should have an architecture radically different from other Brazilian cities. Nor does it outline either the intentions or anticipated effects of building such a city in Brazil. Furthermore, the plan lacks any explicit description of the intended social structure of Brasília. It is not unreasonable to suppose that a comprehensive plan for a new city would include at least some discussion of its social organization, especially if this is to be the product of planned social change. Yet, there is little indication in the plan of how Brasília is to be settled or of what forms of social organization correspond to the obviously and profoundly different forms of urban organization presented in the design.

How are we to interpret this paradox? To begin with, it is revealing to note how Costa presents the plan and defines his role as planner of the federal capital. The Master Plan originated as Costa's entry in the national competition that the federal government sponsored in September 1956 to select a pilot plan for Brasília. The competition was organized at the insistence of Oscar Niemeyer, who had been chosen previously by President Kubitschek as the principal architect of the capital, responsible for designing its major public buildings and residential prototypes. The terms of the competition required only two documents from each contestant: a basic layout of the city indicating its major structures and spatial organization, and a supporting report.[2] Although the competition program listed numerous other subjects for consideration—such as agricultural planning in the Federal District, natural resource management, water and power supply, land tenure, employment opportunities, and investment requirements, it indicated that first consideration would be given to "the architectural idea of the form and character of the New Capital" (Holford 1957: 397). The program called for a competition of design ideas and not of organizational details, emphasizing the *form* most appropriate to express the city's fundamental character as the capital of Brazil, "to express the greatness of a national wish" as the jury report put it.

One of the jurors, Sir William Holford (ibid.), classified the twenty-six entries into two groups: those that concentrated on "the ideology of the design," best represented by Costa's entry, and those that gave additional attention to the details of city organization, best represented by the entry of the firm M. M. M. Roberto. In March 1957, the jury awarded first prize to Costa's plan.

From the moment it was unveiled, Costa's presentation created controversy as a masterful *brincadeira*, a kind of 'jest', almost a 'joke'. Although it received highest praise from five of the six voting members of the jury for "its unity of artistic conception" and for the clarity, elegance, and simplicity of its "Idea for a National Capital" (Holford 1957: 398), it presented merely the sketch of this idea and practically nothing else. Costa submitted his proposal on five medium-sized cards containing fifteen freehand sketches and a brief statement of twenty-three articles (fig. 3.5). His presentation featured not a line of mechanical drawing, no model, land-use studies, population charts or schemes for either economic development or administrative organization—in short, nothing other than the idea of a capital city.

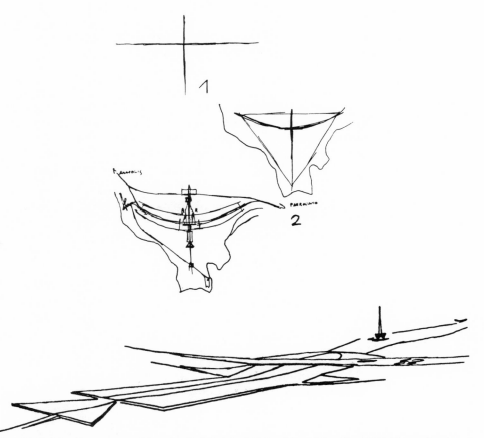

Figs. 3.5 Lúcio Costa, competition sketches for the Master Plan of Brasília, 1957. These sketches present the three essential elements of the plan: the crossing of two highway axes on which is superimposed an equilateral triangle to define the area of the city, two terraced embankments, and a platform.

Its contrast with the proposal of the M. M. M. Roberto firm could not have been greater. The latter presented scores of blueprints, voluminous statistical projections of population and economic growth, and detailed plans for regional development and administration. This contrast led the member of the jury representing the Brazilian Institute of Architects to dissent from the judgment, complaining that Costa's minimal presentation was "hardly worth consideration by a serious jury" (Holford 1957: 398). The Brazilian press captured the sense of combined outrage and admiration with which the public perceived Costa's proposal as a *brincadeira* when it commented that Costa had spent twenty-five cruzeiros on materials to win two million in prize money.

While this monetary *malandragem* ('roguery') may have captured the public's imagination, it was the extraordinary literary quality of Costa's plan that immediately persuaded the jury that here was a poetic voice suited to the epic task of founding a national capital. The extent to which this quality seduced the jury is evident in Holford's evaluation:

> At the first reading of his report, one realized that here was a thinker, an urbanist, of the first order. On second reading one realized that there was not a single unnecessary word in the report, and not a single unnecessary line in the sketch plan or diagrams: yet everything essential was said. . . . Even to me, who am no Portuguese scholar, the original version was immediately lyrical and striking. (Holford 1957: 398)

Thus, the rhetorical artifice of Costa's presentation persuaded the jury that everything essential was said when in fact it presented very little. This paradox suggests that a closer look at the rhetorical structure of the plan will reveal more about its *brincadeira*.

Costa begins his statement in epic fashion with an apology for his "unworthiness." He acknowledges the "sketchy manner" of his presentation and then defends it, unexpectedly, by disclaiming any professional or even personal responsibility for the proposal:

> It was not my intention to enter the competition—nor indeed, am I really so doing. I am merely liberating my mind from a possible solution which sprang to it as a complete picture, but one which I had not sought. I therefore come forward, not as a properly equipped expert, since I do not even run an office of my own, but as a mere *maquisard* of town planning who does not even mean to continue working out the idea offered in this

report, save perhaps as a consultant. And if I speak with such candor, it is because I base my reasoning on this simple assumption: if my idea has any validity, my data, although given apparently in such a sketchy manner, will prove quite sufficient, showing that despite its spontaneous origin, I subsequently gave it a great deal of thought before reaching this solution. And if the suggestion has no validity, then the Jury will find it easy to eliminate, and I shall not have wasted my time, nor that of anybody else. (Costa 1957: preamble)

By all accounts, this apologia of rhetorical self-effacement was considered a brilliant opening. Its elegant and ironic dissimulation of intentions conveyed to the jurors, and to Brazil, that Costa himself possessed that very "dignity and nobility of purpose" with which, as he claimed in the following paragraph, "the town planner must be imbued . . . [to] confer real monumentality on his urban scheme."

It is apparent from the rhetorical structure of this introduction that Costa presents the problem of founding a capital city as if it had no history. He does not justify the Master Plan as the outcome of a consideration of either historical conditions in Brazil or of a history of ideas in architecture. Rather, he dehistoricizes it by presenting it in the terms of a foundation myth, divinely inspired. Using classic conventions of mythic narrative and epic poetry, Costa begins the Master Plan with the suggestion of an annunciation. The text implies that Costa is playing the role of an improbable bard who is visited by the muse, in this case of architecture and city planning. His invocation is of the epic type "Sing in me O Muse," in which the narrator does not claim authorship of the work to follow. Rather, he portrays himself as a reluctant participant, an unlikely and even unqualified recipient of a vision he "had not sought." Claiming to act as a mere conduit for this vision, he is "merely liberating [his] mind" of the inspiration "which sprang to it as a complete picture." Thus, Costa asserts that the idea of the plan had a "spontaneous origin." Unpremeditated, unstudied, and self-generating, it is in this sense presented as if without human labor and therefore without historical origin or influence.

Rather, Costa's self-effacement as creator of the plan appears to let the "idea" speak for itself. As a pure creation of spirit, Costa suggests that the plan has its own inherent logic, one beyond the judgment of history and based on whatever universal authority this spirit may have. The effect of Costa's rhetorical strategy is thus to dehistoricize (in terms of Brazilian history and the history of modern architecture) both the act of founding the city and his own foundation role. Instead, the rhetoric mythologizes both, establishing the rudiments of a foundation myth for Brasília.

By foundation myth, I mean a genre of narrative characterized by its content, form, and social function. I suggest these attributes not as a comprehensive definition but rather as one to help us understand the intentions of the Master Plan. Foundation myths provide precedents for the orders of lived experience. They justify why things are the way the are—such as the universe, a city, a group of people, a ceremony, rights in land and citizenship, or a set of class privileges—by relating the precedents which, from the teller's perspective, brought these things into being and gave them their defining attributes. Such myths both state the precedent as an ideal and constitute a charter, as Malinowski said, for its continued observance. In addition, they often include a set of instructions for the reiteration of the precedent in present practice, as in city foundation myths in which such instructions serve as guides for subsequent planning decisions.

Myths of origin use specific types of narrative devices and rhetorical conventions, the definitions of which are a matter of endless debate but the existence of which is a matter of general agreement. They may use a convention such as "once upon a time" to signal the ahistorical epoch of primordial events, and a device such as the mediation of opposites like right and left, human and animal, terrestrial and aquatic, civilized and barbarian to establish the orders of experience that are given discrete form through the events of the story.

Following the analysis of Roland Barthes (1972: 109–59) and other mythologists, we may in addition consider a myth as a system of representations which speaks about another, already formed system of representations. It constitutes a second language, a metalanguage, which defines the other in its own terms and for specific purposes. In the case of the Master Plan of Brasília, we have several systems of representations speaking about each other. There is first the architectural, graphically presented. Then there is the doctrine of modernist architecture and the project of building a modernist city in Brazil, both of which are called to mind by the drawings and by the context of the design competition, but neither of which are related as such in the plan. Finally, there is the plan's written account of the origins and intentions of the architecture.

As a system of representations about precedents for lived experience, foundation myths function as a means of legitimating (or, conversely, overturning) existing distributions of social relations and practices, especially distributions of privilege and power. This is as true of the dream-time myths of the Australian aborigines as it is of the myth of Romulus and Remus in the founding of Ancient Rome, or the myth of the Russian Revolution, which, as it is told today, all but eliminates the role of Trotsky. As a means of legitimation, foundation myths represent the interests of specific social groups and persons, usually of those who tell them, as against the interest of others. The relation between the representation and its social context—that is, how it demonstrates or hides that it validates specific interests and that what it is speaking about has a specific social history in relation to other interests—may take many forms, the identification of which is an empirical problem of textual and contextual analysis.

Nevertheless, it is possible to generalize that in relation to historical events, foundation myths have the function of transforming history into nature for their tellers: they present as naturally given or received, as sacred, eternal, ideal, or universal, events and relations which are in fact the products of history. As Malinowski (1954: 125) concludes, "myths serve to cover certain inconsistencies created by historical events, rather than to record these events exactly." As a mechanism for reworking the historical record, they generally fulfill a certain sociological function which is to interpret the present by recourse to precedents beyond the bounds of history. Such validations involve a complementary process: on the one hand, a recapitulation of the past in present practice such that historical circumstance is experienced in terms of received categories and relations and, on the other, a naturalization of the present by projecting it as an always-has-been past. Ultimately, it is this attribute of giving a natural justification to what is historically motivated that identifies the Master Plan of Brasília as a kind of foundation myth.

The suggestion that Costa dehistoricizes the plan with elements of foundation mythology is worth pursuing because it illuminates the nature of his *brincadeira*. The plan's literary sense is sophisticated and self-conscious. It does not achieve its mythical qualities by presenting a just-so story, as for example the founding of Rome is related in the myth of Romulus and Remus. Rather, it associates itself with such foundation myths by alluding to them and by using their rhetorical conventions.

The mythic elements of the plan are many, and I need not detail every one to make the point. I have already observed that the plan begins with the rhetorical self-effacement of the narrator and the introduction of a mythic narrative voice. Following the pattern of other foundation myths, the plan suggests that the founding of a capital city is a civilizing event. It gives form and identity to an uncivilized geography (the Central Plateau), which is tamed and settled by a race of heroes who are at the same time reliving their past: "For this is a deliberate act of possession, the gesture of pioneers acting in the spirit of their colonial traditions" (Costa 1957: preamble).[3] As in a creation myth, the capital's construction functions as an ordering event for an entire region and, by extension, for the nation. In the almost universal tradition of founding myths (see Wheatley 1969, 1971), the plan presents the ordering event itself through ideal geometries and through mediations of opposed categories of order (the latter more fully demonstrated in chap. 5 when we discuss the plan's zoned typologies). For the present, my principal concern is with the way Costa eliminates the history of Brazil and of modern architecture from the idea of the plan—only to reinvest it with a mythology of ancient cities and their sacred planning techniques.

If Costa portrays himself as a somewhat reluctant recipient of a vision, he (1957: preamble) also states that he is "a mere *maquisard* of urban planning" in contrast to "a properly equipped expert." This distinction signals Costa's intention to give the plan a mythical rather than a historical foundation. A *maquisard* is a member of the French underground organization, the *maquis*, that fought against German occupation forces during World War II. As a militant supporter of a cause of liberation, the *maquisard* is a guerrilla who fights in an irregular and unofficially organized body of partisans. A characteristic feature of this guerrilla fighter is that he uses makeshift and devious means to achieve his objectives compared to those of the professional soldier. In a creative and synthetic way, he uses whatever resources are at hand. However, both his repertoire of tactics and his resources tend to be repetitive regardless of the task because he has little else at his disposal. By virtue of this ad hoc, but necessarily limited and repetitious activity, the *maquisard* is, in Lévis-Strauss's terms, a *bricoleur* at warfare.

In calling himself a *maquisard* as opposed to a "properly equipped expert," Costa is drawing the same distinction Lévi-Strauss (1966: 17–22) makes between "the 'bricoleur' and the engineer"—here in the relevant context of architecture, engineering, and city planning. I am not, of course, suggesting that Costa had any inkling of Lévi-Strauss's distinction or visa versa, but simply that the parallel is evident and striking. Moreover, if we accept Lévi-Strauss's analogy between *bricolage* and mythical thought, then Costa's identification of himself as a *bricoleur* is consistent with his role as the founding father of a city who consciously mythologizes its foundation.

Lévi-Strauss (1966: 17) describes the difference between the *bricoleur* and the engineer in terms of the application of a closed versus an open set of instruments to the solution of tasks. As the *bricoleur* possesses only a closed set, he applies it to all tasks: "His universe of instruments is closed and the rules of his game are always to make do with 'whatever is at hand,' that is to say with a set of tools and materials which is always finite and is also heterogeneous because what it contains bears no relation to the current project, or indeed to any project, but is the contingent result of all the occasions that have ever been to renew or enrich the stock or to maintain it with the remains of previous constructions or destructions." Costa proposes that the Master Plan is just such a closed universe when he (1957: preamble) asserts that it "sprang to [his mind] as a complete picture . . . [of] spontaneous origin." The notion of a spontaneous completeness implies that the plan should be viewed as a totality (a closed universe) which is self-generating and self-contained and therefore not susceptible to additions or deletions. If we consider how Costa justifies the essential elements of this totality, it becomes evident that they are given exactly the character that Lévi-Strauss ascribes to the *bricoleur's* instruments: they are presented as bearing no relation to the project of building Brasília in Brazil in 1957 or indeed of constructing a modern city. To the contrary, they are presented as the most ancient, eternally valid members of the world's stock of city planning conventions.

Costa (1957: art. 23) states that the plan consists of three essential structural elements: the crossing of two axes, two terraced embankments, and a platform (fig. 3.5). The axial cross defines the area of the city, contained within the figure of an equilateral triangle that is superimposed on the cross. It also defines the city's orientation as the axes are aligned with the cardinal directions. The equilateral triangle marks the area of urbanized land called the Plano Piloto. This term is used both as the name of Costa's plan and as a place name to distinguish the modernist city of the plan from the originally unplanned satellite cities around it. The Plano Piloto's public buildings are set along one axis and its residential buildings along the other (fig. 2.1). These organizational spines also function as superspeedways, providing access to their respective "sectors" of activity. The two terraced embankments form the Monumental Axis of government buildings. One establishes the Plaza of the Three Powers for the principal buildings of the three branches of the federal government. Raised above the first, the other creates a mall or esplanade for the buildings of the ministries of state. The platform is a multilevel structure at the point of axial crossing. It spans the intersection of the Monumental and Residential axes at one level, and contains the Entertainment and Transportation centers on two additional levels. Thus, Costa's scheme utilizes the same three design components to organize the city spatially as well as to differentiate its social functions into discrete sectors of activity. Through this structural homology of architectural-spatial organization and social-functional organization, Costa claims to provide a "complete picture" of urban order.

Let us consider how Costa derives these components. Of the three, the crossing of the axes is the most important. As it defines the area of the city and organizes the other components, it may be considered the generator of the plan. In the first article of the Master Plan, Costa uses the "sign of the Cross" to signify the primordial act of founding not only Brasília but any city: the plan "was born of that initial gesture which anyone would make when pointing to a given place, or taking possession of it: the drawing of two axes crossing each other at right angles, in the sign of the Cross." Costa's intention not to give the plan a historical origin is clear from this initial statement. To dehistoricize the origins of the city, he employs three simple rhetorical devices: the plan's generation is naturalized (i.e., presented as unlearned, "a gesture anyone would make"), universalized (i.e., valid for anyone and any place) and idealized (i.e., embodied in ideal geometric forms). With this rhetorical strategy, Costa accomplishes what I earlier described as a principal objective of myth-making: to give a natural justification to that which is historically motivated.

Costa's naturalization of the origins of the plan stresses the symbolic significance of the figure of the cross. As a sign, the cross functions in the plan as both an index and an icon, to use Charles S. Peirce's distinction.[4] It points to a spatially defined place (but in this case, any place), indicating the presence of human beings and their attributes of property, settlement, and civilization. It is an indexical sign because it indicates the presence of a city and its civilization as the source of the crossing axes in the same way that smoke indicates fire as its source. The cross of the plan is also an iconic sign in that it geometrically resembles several other well-known symbols, and this resemblance of form calls their meaning to mind. In a graphic medium, the cross of the plan resembles the cross of Christianity. This formal, iconic association evokes the idea of a sacred site for the city of Brasília and a divine benediction for the founding of the capital, an evocation based on the conventional association in the Christian world of crosses and things sacred.

In addition, Costa's cross iconically represents two archetypical symbols of city founding and planning widely if not universally known to urban planners and architects. The first is considered one of the earliest pictorial representations of the idea of city: the Egyptian hieroglyph of the cross within the circle, itself an iconic sign standing for 'city', *nywt*. The second is the diagram of the *templum* of ancient Roman augury, a circle quartered by the crossing of two axes.[5] It represents a space in the sky or on the earth marked out by the augur for the purpose of taking auspices. Hence, it signifies a consecrated place, such as a sanctuary, asylum, shrine, or temple. As Rykwert (1976: 44–71) explains, auguration over the *templum* was an essential part of the ritual foundations of Roman cities and military camps. It appears that the purpose of drawing the *templum* during foundation ceremonies was to transfer the order of the sky (i.e., of the cosmos) to its representation (the *templum*), to locate the augur at the center of this order (at the crossing of the axes), and then to project by ritual incantations this cosmic plan onto the proposed site of the city. Thus situated, the augur took auspices to determine if the site was propitious and, if so, consecrated the settlement, divined its secret names, and uttered its public one.

If the *templum* worked by analogy to incarnate the order of the cosmos in the foundation and destiny of the city, the same diagram of the cross in the circle provided the *axis mundi*, 'world axis', for its subsequent planning by surveyors. The frontispiece of the oldest Roman treatise on surveying features a starry circle, representing the sky, quartered by cross axes (Rykwert 1976: 49–51, figs. 6, 11). This *templum* appears to have been represented in the sheet-metal cross of the surveyor's instrument which, with affixed plumb lines, was used to establish the principal cross axes of the settlement and its subsequent orthogonal or checkerboard divisions. Thus, Roman surveying techniques complemented the belief that the city was organized according to divine laws. Surveyors reiterated these laws in the planning of cities, which were therefore their terrestrial embodiments, and planners and builders were guided in the production of form by ritual procedures to ensure this embodiment.

Without delving further into the ritual foundation and planning of ancient cities, my point is that just as the augur's diagrammatic *templum* worked by analogy, so Costa's claim that the plan of Brasília "was born of that initial gesture . . . [of the] drawing of two axes crossing each other" also establishes an analogy between the value of his plan and the value of the most ancient devices of city planning. The effect of this analogy is to legitimate the plan in terms of the prestige and sanctity of these devices. The order of Costa's presentation indicates that he intends such an analogical legitimation. The plan begins, in article 1, with the *initial* gesture of the crossing of two axes. As in the foundation of Roman cities, we have first the cosmic sign and then the application of (the surveyor's) technology: it is not until article 3 of the plan that the cross axes become super-speedways—"*Finally*, it was decided to apply the free principles of highway engineering . . . to the technique of urban planning" (emphasis added).

That Costa intended to invest by analogy the founding of Brasília with the power of sacred symbols and ancient, ordained planning procedures has been widely perceived by planners, architects, poets, historians, and journalists, both Brazilian and foreign. I shall limit myself to two examples. During Brasília's inaugural ceremonies on 21 April 1960, the Brazilian poet laureate Guilherme de Almeida inaugurated the Commemorative Monument of the Installation of the Federal Government in Brasília with a poem which focused on the symbolism of the cross. One passage reads: "Now and here is the Crossroad Time-Space, Road which comes from the past and goes to the Future, road from the north, from the south, from the east and from the west, road traversing the centuries, road traversing the world: now and here all cross at the sign of the Holy Cross" (cited in *Diario de Brasília*, 21 April 1960).

The second example comes from the work of Brasiliense pioneer Ernesto Silva. He (1971: 7) opens his *History of Brasília* with the Roman analogy to suggest the historical destiny of Brasília: "On 21 April, 753 B.C., Romulus founded, on the Palatine Hill, a city that would be the mark of a new era in the Pagan World—the Rome of the Caesars—the cradle of Christian Civilization. On the same day, 27 centuries later, Divine Providence willed that a pleiad [i.e., a group] of valiant men should give Brasília to Brazil."[6] Of course, Brasília is not literally like an ancient Roman city. Beyond its cross-axial structure, the plan does not utilize the orthogonal planning that Roman surveyors would have used in laying out a new city or military camp. But its literalness is not the point. Rather, Costa's rhetorical construction of the plan establishes analogies with the *idea* of the ancient city (especially Roman and Egyptian) and the idea of the Holy Cross and the *templum* as sacred planning devices.

Similarly, Costa (1957: arts. 9 and 10) explains his use of the two terraced embankments and the platform as instrumental selections from the world's ancient stock of city-planning techniques. He chooses those "best suited" to incarnate in stone the idea of the national capital. In justifying the triangular terraced embankment of the Plaza of the Three Powers, Costa begins with the idea that the public buildings of Brasília house the fundamental powers of government. "These are three [the executive, judicial, and legislative], and they are autonomous: therefore the equilateral triangle—associated with the very earliest architecture in the world—is the elementary frame best suited to express them. For this purpose, a triangular, terraced embankment (terreplein) [of unfaced stone] was designed." Costa (ibid.) legitimates the application of this planning device to both the plaza and the esplanade saying, "to transfer to present-day usage the ancient technique of the terreplein lends a certain harmony to the pattern and creates an unexpected and monumental strength."

If Costa is, in fact, seeking to make an architectural statement about democracy in this design for the plaza, we may legitimately wonder whether or not there is something of a symbolic confusion in its pseudo-historical derivation. For the earliest states supposedly associated with the "earliest architecture" were hardly democratic. However, Costa's association appears to be another example of his *bricolage* technique. While the forms of the equilateral triangle and the terreplein are legitimated architecturally in terms of their antiquity, their contemporaneous symbolic association with theocracy is discarded in favor of the Enlightenment association of these forms with democracy— an example of earlier ends called upon to play the part of new means, to paraphrase Lévi-Strauss's (1966: 21) definition of *bricolage*. Of course, any solution makes use of old ends as means. But in the case of *bricolage*, these ends are laundered of the historical conditions that determined them.

In another publication, Costa (1962: 344) amplifies the multiple, dehistoricized associations of this architectural *bricolage* when he argues that "if the Plaza of the Three Powers corresponds in terms of space and intention to Versailles, its majesty is other, it is the *people*—it is the Versailles of the People." Here, it is obvious that Costa's "symbolic confusions" are politically motivated.[7]

To complete his derivation of the essential elements of the plan in terms of a miscellaneous anthology of reappropriated, decontextualized architectural devices and planning conventions, Costa (1957: art. 10) claims that the Entertainment Center of the platform "has something in it of Picadilly Circus, Times Square and the Champs-Elysées . . . with arcades, wide sidewalks, terraces and cafés . . . in the traditional manner of Rio's Ouvidor Street [and] Venetian alleys." All this—the architectural ideas of the ancient, medieval, and modern worlds, of Egypt, Rome, Versailles, Paris, London, Venice, Rio, and New York— incarnate in a plan (lest we forget) for the city of tomorrow. In sum, if we are to believe Costa's myth of legitimation, the plan contains all the world's architecture, past, present, and future.

The ecumenical scope of this legitimation is indeed extraordinary. With great skill, Costa manages to give the plan of a new city the suggestion of a legendary foundation, to give technical planning devices the aura of sacred symbols, and to invest Brasília with a world mythology of cities and civilizations. My point is not to dispute the artistry of this achievement. It is rather to show that in claiming to provide one kind of origin for Brasília, Costa disclaims another: in providing Brasília with a mythological pedigree, he disguises its historical one by eliminating the history of Brazil and of modern architecture from the stated idea of the plan. As in a story of mistaken identities, he switches the city's birthrights. Costa uses such rhetorical devices as naturalization, universalization, idealization, reiteration, and *bricolage* to impart a sense of an organic, logical, eternally valid, ideal, and mythical origin for Brasília. In this creation story, the planner is poet and augur. However, the problem with Costa's explanation is that the idea of Brasília derives directly in both form and organization from the modernist model cities of Le Corbusier and CIAM manifestos—as I demonstrated in the preceding chapter. Thus, if Costa's legitimation invents one origin in the plan, in giving a "complete picture" it conceals the other—the origin of Brasília as a modernist city for Brazil. This switch of birthrights is the essence of Costa's *brincadeira*.

3.2 The Hidden Agenda

Why should Costa disguise the historical origin of the Master Plan as a modernist city? The answer is that within the context of the state-sponsored design competition, it was impolitic to make explicit his (and Niemeyer's) political and social presuppositions about Brasília. It is significant to note in this respect that the competition jury rejected the M. M. M. Roberto plan in large measure because it was *too* explicit about its assumptions. It presented such detail that the jury had little difficulty assessing its full implications:

> I can only say, for my part, that I have never seen anywhere in the world a more comprehensive and thoroughgoing master-plan for a new capital city on a cleared site. We all realized, at the same time, that if the Development Corporation adopted this plan they would take on board more than a pilot [as in pilot plan and ship's pilot]. They would have purser and quartermaster and bo'sun, a complete ship's company from cabin boy to captain, and a Director of the Line as well. . . . After admiring this

scheme for several days, my own feeling was that everything in it was worthy of admiration, except its main objective. It was not an Idea for a capital city. (Holford 1957: 397)

In contrast, Costa's presentation revealed neither the assumptions nor the implications of the modernist ideology of his design. Rather, its principal strategy was not merely to argue that the project of Brasília was fundamentally about national renovation, but more to pose the problem of new beginnings as a matter of mythology rather than of history. In avoiding the details of sociopolitical reorganization, it effectively disguised the revolutionary objectives of the plan and its planners in proposing a specifically modernist capital for Brazil.

At the same time, however, Costa's concealment did not eliminate these intentions from the plan. To the contrary, they became its hidden agenda, smuggled into the plan in a cloak of mythology about ancient cities and sacred planning techniques. For, as I have argued, modern architecture *concretely* embodies ideas for new forms of social experience. Therefore, Costa's plan remains instrumentally utopian however rhetorically legitimated because, prior to any verbal justification, it is a plan for a modernist city. By convincing the jury through his brilliant presentation of the mythology of his idea—of what was in fact the antithesis of the plan's historical identity and derivation—Costa succeeded in having his thesis of modernist planning accepted as the foundation of Brazil's national capital.

To understand the objectives and implications of the plan's hidden agenda, we must therefore set out this thesis of modernist planning and architecture. To do this requires establishing both Costa's and Niemeyer's conception of the role of the architect and of architecture in changing Brazilian society. In addition, we must establish as basic to this conception modernism's ideology of social and political development. Finally, to understand the significance of this ideology for the project of Brasília, we must also relate the architects' intentions to President Kubitschek's commitment to both modernism and modernization.

We can begin to analyze the plan's hidden agenda by seeing how Costa's intentions for social change are concealed in its specific proposals. Let us consider those for residential organization. In the plan, Costa (1957: art. 16) proposes his solution, the *superquadra* ('superblock'), without mentioning that it derives in form and function directly from numerous experiments with collective housing in the history of modern architecture. It especially derives from Le Corbusier's unit of habitation (*unité d'habitation*) and the communal house (*dom-kommuna*) of the Russian Constructivists. As I noted earlier, such modernist housing units are designed for a different concept of domestic organization, in which the role of private property is radically reduced in favor of collective facilities. Costa does not mention in the plan that the *superquadra*, as a building type, therefore carries with it a related set of social objectives for the transformation of social life.

However, not only was Costa aware of these objectives, but he has been, since 1930, the leading theorist in Brazil for "the new architecture," advocating its practice precisely because it presupposes such a program of social change. In many of his articles both before and after the plan, Costa focuses on the architectural justification, historical necessity, and social benefits of the collective residential organization of modernist design. To take one example, Costa (1962 [1952]: 230) describes this organization as "the modern concept of the unit of habitation [Le Corbusier's term] conceived and constructed not in function of real estate profit, but in function of the harmonious and better life of man and his family." Throughout his writings (e.g., 1980 [1930]: 15; 1962 [1952]: 230–39), Costa situates this "modern concept" in an explicit critique of capitalism, involving such issues as the problem of social justice in a context of rapid industrial development, the chaos of uncontrolled urban migration, and the need for a system of mass housing.

Nevertheless, the Master Plan of Brasília does no more than merely caution against the evils of real estate speculation (Costa 1957: art. 22) and claim that the architectural grouping of the *superquadras* will itself prevent "any undue and undesired stratification of society" (ibid., art. 17). These two proposals barely indicate the kind of social organization which Costa's other writings suggest for a city featuring "units of combined dwelling." What the key phrase "undue stratification" could possibly mean in Brasília is never explained in the plan. And yet, considering Costa's other writings, it is clear that Brasília's *superquadras* are designed to embody the benefits of collective residential relations (however these are defined) as opposed to capitalist relations of profit and property, which Costa considers detrimental to domestic life. In this design, the architect is clearly committed to creating a collective residential organization and thereby to restructuring relations between the private and public domains of social life.

This revolutionary architect is hardly the *bricoleur* of the Master Plan. How does Costa conceive of the role of this radical architect—the ghost writer of the plan? In CIAM theory, the architect is the master planner not just of cities but of all aspects of the social life that cities comprehend, "of the functions of collective life" as its first manifesto in 1928 defined the task (Conrad 1970: 110, sec. 2, art. 1). Le Corbusier (1957 [1941]: art. 87) writes with all seriousness in *The Athens Charter* that the CIAM architect is qualified for this task because he "possesses a perfect knowledge of man." However ludicrous this assertion may seem, *The Athens Charter* defined the field of modernist urban planning in Brazil after its publication. While more modest than its author, Costa (1962 [1952]: 235) recapitulates his claim when he states that the architect is "a technician, a sociologist and an artist," exercising "a primordial function in contemporary society."

What is this "primordial function" of the modernist architect according to Costa? In "Reasons for the New Architecture" of 1930, he (1980: 15) sets out the crucial argument: "there exists, already perfectly developed in its fundamental elements . . . an entire new constructive know-how, paradoxically still waiting for the society to which, logically, it should belong." In 1930, as in 1957, Costa believed—as did the Brazilian political Left in which Niemeyer was an influential member—that the social, political, and economic preconditions for this society did not yet exist in Brazil. However, what did exist was "the new constructive know-how," the new architecture. As this was conceived in terms of the new society, embodying its imagined principles of organization, the primordial function of Costa's architect was to build the exemplar. For in modernist theory, this would eventually colonize the social order around it and create the society to which it would then "logically belong."

3.3 Brasília's Development Inversions

Such exemplary change inverts usual notions of social development. The inversion is of two types. First, modernist theory challenges the common, one could say archaeological, understanding of the relations between cities and society. In that view, cities are seen as the products or artifacts or passive habitats of their societies, and thus changes in urban form are understood as ultimately dependent upon changes in social organization. Inverting this view, the modernist idea is of an exemplar, or enclave, or beachhead, or blueprint of radiating change which creates a new society on the basis of the values that motivate its design.

The second type of inversion projects the first into the future. If planners could control social development through the implementation of a new type of city, and if this city could be taken as an exemplary capital, as a model of national development, then they believed it possible not only to generalize its innovations throughout the nation, but moreover to propel society into a planned future, causing it to skip predicted but undesired stages in its historical development. Such a projection of development has particular relevance to the practice of modernist planning in third-world countries, for it suggests that the implementation of modernist urban and regional plans could cause the most backward of nations to jump directly into the most modern of worlds.

This two-step inversion was fundamental to the architects' intentions in Brasília. They viewed the state's project to build a new capital as an opportunity to construct a city that would transform, or at least strongly push the transformation, of Brazilian society—a project, moreover, of social transformation without social upheaval. Let us take an example of how the first type of inversion, concealed as it is in the plan, nevertheless motivates its proposals.

The plan (art. 17) suggests that "the social structure of [the] housing zone can be graded by setting a greater value on specific *superquadras*." This suggestion is posed as an *option* in view of the fact that earlier in the same article the plan stipulates that *all* inhabitants of Brasília are to live within the same type of residential unit, and *all* within its planned residential zone. Moreover, the kinds of architectural markers of status that the plan (ibid.) mentions are limited to those of view, variations in the size of otherwise similar apartments, and quality and finish of building materials. These status markers are essentially interior, private features. They are markers of an inconspicuous consumption in comparison with the dramatic leveling of status that results from having all residents live in residential units that are standardized both in plan and in form (figs. 2.11–2.13). The intent of this residential standardization is to preclude any differential distribution of urban amenities, of rights to the city we might say. On this objective, the plan (art. 17) is clear, although it is presented almost as an afterthought: "And, in any case, variations in the standard of living from one *superquadra* to another will be offset [*neutralizados*, in original] by the organization of the urban scheme itself, and will not be of such a nature as to affect that degree of social comfort to which all members of society have a right" (emphasis added).

Underlying the plan's use of the *superquadra* is therefore the argument that the lowest echelon employees of the government residing in Brasília (like janitors, guards, custodians, and drivers) ought to have the same rights to the city as the highest officials. Both are entitled in the plan to apartments and living conditions (such as neighborhood social clubs) of similar type.

Thus, the plan contains no special provisions for the lowest echelon functionaries. Any other residential arrangements for groups that in other Brazilian cities constitute the lower classes, such as satellite cities or a different type of housing unit, is explicitly prohibited in the plan (art. 17). The reason for this prohibition is obvious: such solutions would only reproduce existing Brazilian social conditions in Brasília, a situation which the planners wanted to avoid at all costs.

When one considers that in other Brazilian cities the social classes are spatially stratified, that possession of and access to urban amenities are differentially distributed by social class, and that differences in residential organization and building type are primary markers of social standing, we must conclude that the plan's standardization of residential organization is an attempt to transform Brazilian society through architectural design and urban planning. Thus, when the plan presupposes that lower echelon employees have the same rights to the city as higher officials, it is not because this egalitarianism exists as a social value in Brazilian society or government guidelines. It does not. It is rather based on the intention of the architects to create this value both for the state, sponsoring the city, and for its resident population.

Moreover, just as the plan insists on establishing new values as the foundation of its urban order, its intent is also to eliminate from Brasiliense society the unjust values the architects associate with capitalist social-spatial stratification. In this plan for societal development, the creation of a new city-society entails the destruction of the older urban-social order. We can grasp this dual intention in terms of a medical analogy often advanced by the European modernists, especially Le Corbusier, to justify their plans. As it is possible to treat a disease by suppressing its symptoms, so by architecturally denying both the effects and the symbols of social stratification, the intent of the plan is to eliminate, or at least render ineffectual (i.e., "neutralize"), the principles of this stratification insofar as they might possibly effect the government's provision of and the population's use of the city's public benefits. In the utopia of the Master Plan, the unequal distribution of advantage due to differences in class, race, employment, wealth, and family would have little place or efficacy in organizing urban life. And as the state would control, through the plan, the development of the entire city as a public benefit, the plan's proposals appear as an inescapable inversion of social evolution in which architects design fundamental features of society.

As an attempt to preclude the stratified distribution of rights to the city associated with capitalism, the Master Plan's most encompassing intention is to create the foundations of an egalitarian urban organization. We shall examine the fate of this intention in subsequent chapters when we analyze the implementation and impact of the plan's specific proposals. At this point, we may note one fundamental contradiction. While the Master Plan attempts to neutralize previous patterns of residential stratification, it makes no attempt to change the occupational stratification of the bureaucracy, of the place of employment. As Brasília is a city of government employees, the plan would appear to accept, and to be confronted with, a dual mode of organization, one at the place of work which is opposed to that proposed for the place of residence.

What then is the basis of the plan's egalitarian intent? It seems plausible to conclude that it can only be based on the possibility of neutralizing the hierarchies of work in the place of residence. This possibility can itself only be based on the expectation of a role reversal in which patterns of authority and deference established at work are not transferred to the home. Thus, for the plan's residential scheme to operate successfully, it requires of the bureaucrat who commands at work that he forgo the prerogatives of office in his relations with neighbors who may well be distant subordinates in the bureaucracy. Similarly, it assumes that subordinates can transcend at home and at the neighborhood social club the deference which separates them from high officials at work. As we shall see later, the plan did create a residential system which for a few years imposed a mixing of the various social classes in the same *superquadra* and club. But, as common sense would suggest, its egalitarian intentions soon floundered on the impossibility of such role inversions.

There is a second sense in which the architects' intentions for Brasília can be interpreted as a project for inverting the process of development. In the 1950s and 1960s most theories of modernization assumed that developing countries would follow the course taken by the economic, political, and social systems of Western Europe and the United States. Accordingly, for developing nations, the development process would consist in completing or reproducing the various stages that characterized the social transformations of industrialized nations. From an orthodox Marxist perspective as well, development entailed a predetermined historical sequence of modes of production, in which the bourgeois urban revolutions established the preconditions of Communist revolution.

In contrast to these theories of development based on the European experience of bourgeois social transformation, Soviet leaders argued for an inversion of the process. Lenin proposed that in the Soviet Union it would be possible to have, as he put it, "electrification plus soviet power"—centralized industrial development, incorporating American notions of taylorism and machine-age rationality, but directed by a party appartus which represented organized proletarian rather than bourgeois interests. His inversion replaced the development function of a national bourgeoisie with that of a vanguard party in order to transform conditions of backwardness in countries like the Soviet Union into those of socialism, while bypassing the stage of industrial capitalism.[8]

Modernist architecture advocated the possibility of a similar leap in the development process through the construction of modernist cities. This idea was sustained by several factors. Many seminal modernists were directly influenced by Lenin's theory of revolutionary change. As we saw in the last chapter, these included members of the Soviet avant-gardes who conceived of architecture as a "conductor and condensor of socialist culture"—as a means to turn the denatured life of peasants and workers into the collective life of Communist society. Throughout Europe and Latin America, many leading modernists shared this conception and affiliated with Leninist organizations of the radical Left in their own countries. In Germany, for example, these included May, Meyer, Hilberseimer, and Bruno Taut— leaders of the modernist movement who eventually fled to the Soviet Union to escape the Nazi regime.[9] That the concept of architecture as conductor and condensor of change entails the idea of a development leap is evident from the 1930 directive of the Central Committee of the Communist party against modernism. This directive discredited and ultimately disbanded the Soviet modernist groups by officially criticizing as utopian "those semi-fantastic and extremely dangerous attempts of certain architects, who wanted to clear *at a single leap* the obstacles barring the way to the socialist transformation of life" (cited in Frampton 1968: 238–39, emphasis added).

Although Stalin's directives had put an end to Soviet modernism by 1933, its idea that architecture could conduct a leap in social development influenced the creation of a common theory of radical change among the architects of the international modern movements. As discussed in chapter 2, it was this theory of change that ultimately justified the prescriptions of the CIAM city. However, this model city was not simply a "trojan horse of bolshevism," as one critic denounced the work of Le Corbusier. It was adopted both as a critique of capitalism and as an instrument of social transformation by architects of the radical Right as well, for example, by those of the pro-Fascist Syndicalist movement in France and the Group 7 in Italy. In this respect, the original CIAM city was a model of radical political consensus, for the idea that architects could and should change society by building a new urban environment appealed to the desires of both the radical Right and Left for a complete beginning anew. Thus, while for many architects the idea of a development leap derived from the application of Leninist ideology to architecture, we may also conclude that it became an inherent feature of modernist proposals to reorganize cities in terms of the "functions of collective life"—however defined—as prescribed in the CIAM manifestos.

The development inversions of the modernist city became most evident in proposals for new cities in developing countries, in those lacking a national industry and an established bourgeoisie, first in the Soviet Union and later in the third world. In confronting the deleterious effects of capitalism on urban life in both metropolitan and colonial cities, modernists addressed the issue of urban development in Africa, Asia, and Latin America. Through their plans for building new cities in these regions, rebuilding the old ones, and reorganizing the countryside, they proposed in effect that developing countries could jump directly from the stone age to the machine age, from colonialism to a new collective social order (however specifically defined), from isolation to regional and worldwide integration—without having to imitate the development (i.e., chaos) of urban Europe. As examples, there are Le Corbusier's master plans of 1931–42 for Algiers. He proposed that the superimposition of his modernist city on the colonial one would transform Algiers into the capital of the southern Mediterranean, establishing it as the cynosure of exchange between European and African civilizations and the hub of a vast plan for regional and international development.[10]

The key point of modernist internationalism—often linked in the minds of both modernists and their critics with Soviet internationalism—was that the theory and technology of the modernist city provided an already developed means of saving the underdeveloped world from the chaos and inequities of Europe's Industrial Revolution. Salvation required implementing a national policy of urban development in which modernist cities would serve as the models and nodes of regional development. If the governments of third-world countries could exercise their authority to impose this policy, they would bring their nations into the machine age in an orderly and rational fashion. The construction of new cities, especially capitals, would stimulate technology, establish networks of communications, integrate vast and backward regions of untapped resources, and organize social relations collectively to maximize the potential benefits of the machine.

In this modernist scheme of development, the construction of new cities functions in the same way that electrification does in Lenin's formula. It requires massive state intervention and obviates the necessity of market-led development on the part of a consenting or pioneering bourgeoisie. Salvation depends on state will. Thus, after an initial flirtation with the "captains of capitalism" to implement their plans, modernists tended to reject the role of the bourgeoisie in development and instead to place their faith in regimes of authoritarian capacities (viz., those of Lenin, Stalin, Mussolini, Franco, and Vichy). Ultimately, however, these regimes proved "unworthy" of the modernist project, for not one engaged modernist architects to build or rebuild cities at the required national scale.

After their disillusionment with authoritarianism at home, many European modernists turned to developing nations as offering greater opportunities for the realization of their urban and regional plans. In their view, most of these nations possessed, already, the prerequisites of modernist urban development: governments (national or colonial) not especially bothered by the constraints of democratic consensus in carrying out their directives, no embedded bourgeoisie to block the nationalization of land necessary for regional development, a plentiful supply of cheap labor, and vast, empty regions to populate and integrate in a project of nation-building. Thus, it was precisely because these nations were "backward" that they appealed to the modernists as a tabula rasa ready for their radical inscriptions. Consequently, modernists believed that by implementing their urban and regional plans these nations could leap over the mistakes of Europe into the glittering future of a second machine age.

President Kubitschek presented his architects with just such a development opportunity in the construction of a new capital for Brazil.[11] His intentions for Brasília coincided in three key ways with the objectives of the development inversions inherent in the modernist city. First, Kubitschek conceived of the building of Brasília as the cause, not the result, of regional economic development in the central west of Brazil. Second, in shifting the axis of economic development from the coast to the center, he planned to construct a network of communications—of highways, railways, and "teleways"—radiating from this center to all of Brazil's regions in a grand project of national integration. This instrumental conception of Brasília "coincided exactly," as he (1975: 62) said, with the development inversion Costa (1957: preamble) stresses at the beginning of the Master Plan: "In the case of Brasília, the city will not be the outcome but the cause of regional planning: its foundation is that which will give occasion to the subsequent planned development of the region."

These objectives of regional development and national integration were central themes of Kubitschek's own master plan, the Target Program, intended to propel Brazil into sustained economic growth. It was designed to achieve "fifty years of progress in five years of government" as Kubitschek's 1955 campaign slogan proclaimed. The Target Program established thirty-one development objectives, grouped into six categories: energy, transportation, food, basic industries, education, and the construction of Brasília.[12] Kubitschek gave Brasília top priority because he believed that the construction of the capital and subsequent regional growth would stimulate fundamental research and development in the other five areas. Brasília was also the metasynthesis of his program because as a means of development, it was its most exciting symbol. He believed that Brasília's construction would generate a new mentality in the country, one of accelerated optimism, achievement, and confidence in Brazil's own abilities to make "the big push" toward self-sustaining growth. Just as Costa used the crossing of two axes both to organize and to ordain Brasília, so Kubitschek (1975: 88) took its axial plan as both epicenter and symbol of his program for national development: "The quest for integration had begun with Brasília. And it would have to be pursued. It was to unite forcefully the country from the inside, extending, ultimately, the axes of [Brasília's] highway cross, which would link one to the other the four cardinal points of the national territory."

However, it was the third point of consensus between Kubitschek and his architects on Brasília that placed the objectives of regional development and national integration into a specifically modernist development inversion. This point was a consensus of *utopian* intentions. It was that Brasília should constitute an innovation in all aspects of development, such that not only would it cause the central west to catch up to the level of development of the southeast, but more significantly it would cause the rest of Brazil to catch up to the innovations of Brasília.

As modernism was the innovative force in the field of architecture, Kubitschek consequently envisioned Brasília as a modernist city and therefore asked Oscar Niemeyer, Brazil's leading modernist, to be the architect of the project. In Kubitschek's vision, Brasília was intended as an innovation in all areas of development, in highway construction, housing, technological research, education, medical services, techniques of state planning, and the like. In all of these projections, Brasília functioned as a blueprint utopia in two senses: it was intended to serve both as a means to achieve these innovations (the first type of inversion) and as a desired end in itself. In the latter sense, Brasília was conceived as a model city, a constructed image, not of existing Brazilian conditions, but of the future of Brazil. Kubitschek (1975: 62–63) typically expresses this utopian conception of the new capital in the following passage recording his reactions to Costa's Master Plan: "Owing to the need to constitute a base of radiation of a pioneering system [of development in all areas] that would bring to civilization an unrevealed universe, [Brasília] had to be, perforce, a metropolis with different characteristics that would ignore the contemporary reality and would be turned, with all of its constitutive elements, toward the future."

In portraying this imagined and desired future, Brasília represented a critique of existing conditions, of what was inadequate and unrealized in Brazil. Brasília was thus proposed as both a rational and a critical utopia. It was a rational utopia as a means and a process of development. Its realization would reveal the as yet unknown riches of the interior, the unknown strength of national integration, and, ultimately, the "unrevealed universe" of Brazil's greatness. It was also a critical utopia as an image of a future radically different from the present. Thus, Brasília's planners called it "the capital of the twenty-first century" not because they thought its design futuristic in any phantasmagoric sense. Rather, it represented for them a set of solutions to immediate development objectives that constituted a blueprint of how to get to a possible future.

3.4 The Exemplary Center

As Kubitschek's statement above suggests, his insistence (and that of the competition jury) that Brasília possess singular attributes as a capital city is intelligible as a logical implication of its utopian premise. For if the basic premise of Brasília's foundation is that it should produce a new Brazilian reality, then it is precisely Brasília's uniqueness among Brazilian cities that defines it as a blueprint of development. From the perspective of a development inversion, Brasília "had to be, perforce," radically different.

This utopian difference lies at the heart of "the idea of a capital city" that figures so prominently in Brasília's initial conception. It is an idea that we may also understand by reference to the theory of the exemplary court, a theory that is, paradoxically, both modernist and quite ancient as a conception of the nature and function of capital cities. In Wheatley's analysis of the symbolism of the ancient Chinese city and Geertz's of Indonesian statecraft, the exemplary court is defined as that center of authority which mirrors, in its own social and architectural organization, the structure of the cosmos and which in turn conveys this structure to the countryside.[13] The court is laid out as a diagram of cosmic order (as in the Roman *templum* discussed earlier). At its center (in a two-dimensional image) and at its apex (in three dimensions) is the king; around the king and at his feet is the palace; around the palace is the capital; around the capital, the obedient realm; and, around the realm, the outside world. The order radiating from the capital city is that of a configuration of concentric circles and nested spheres, depicting not just the structure of society or of a political mandala, but that of the whole universe.

In this scheme of statecraft, the court is both exemplary and mimetic: it should be an icon or copy of the cosmos, and the realm a copy of the court. Through its architecture, crowns, and coronations, it marks the center of authority as center—a charismatic center (to use Shil's [1965: 200–201] notion of charisma as an extraordinary quality that derives from being associated with "animating centers of the social order").[14] As exemplary center, the capital city conveys an aura of importance, legitimation, and inherent sacredness about what goes on there and also gives a sense of a reciprocal connection between its order and the way the universe is made.

In more symbolic than iconic terms, Brasília's founding fathers intended it, as a capital city, to function something like such an exemplary court. The principle of this court, its reflection of order to the realm, captures an essential aspect of Brasília's intended development inversion. As we have seen, Kubitschek viewed Brasília, in its innovations, as mirroring a comprehensive plan of development to the rest of Brazil that Brazil would imitate. In this scheme of inverted reflection, Brasília's exemplary innovations are intended to inspire a new beginning for the nation. This reflection constitutes an inverted exemplar because Brasília was imposed de novo as a revolutionary invention upon the old realm and its capital, rather than built following the old order of things. Nevertheless, it is a complex inversion which both evokes the past and denies it: its proposed new order is advanced as the realization of the promises of first beginnings—of Cabral's discovery of the New World of Brazil in 1500, and of Tiradentes's failed independence movement in 1789, for example—as it also breaks with the legacies of colonial rule and underdevelopment.

At this animating center of a new Brazil, Kubitschek augmented his own charisma by regularly holding much publicized "open-air courts." As in a royal progress, he visited construction sites with his retinue of officials. He laid foundation stones, inaugurated commemorative plaques, snipped ribbons, posed with shovel in hand, and immersed himself without apparent police protection in throngs of laborers. From the steps of half-built buildings, he made visionary pronouncements and pointed to the horizons of the Central Plateau. In his makeshift but paradigmatic headquarters, he constructed an image of himself as president as he appeared in the mass media to direct the construction of the capital and, through it, the nation's future. For Kubitschek, Brasília was an arena of creativity, and it was his involvement as ruler with this arena that conferred upon him an undeniable charisma. Even though Kubitschek invented rather than inherited his capital city, his use of it represents an exercise in the symbolics of power that follows in the tradition of statecraft of the exemplary center.

The principle of an inverted reflection of order and innovation also characterizes Brasília's status as a modernist capital city for Costa. It is the capital city as exemplar for the nation that motivates Costa's central idea in the Master Plan that Brasília should be conceived of "not as a mere organic entity, able to function effortlessly and vitally like any modern [i.e., contemporary, existing] town; not as an 'urbs,' therefore, but as a 'civitas,' having the virtues and attributes appropriate of a true capital city" (Costa 1957: preamble). Like Kubitschek, Costa is not simply appealing to the idea that a capital city is a center of administrative power. This feature would not in itself sufficiently distinguish Brasília from other Brazilian cities, for in Brazil all settlements with the legal status of city (*cidade* and *vila*) are by definition (and not by size) centers of administrative decisions and therefore capitals of their designated regions. To be a "true" national capital, Brasília would have to occupy the apex of a hierarchy of regional capitals more by being a model of their future development than by, and in addition to, being the ultimate source of their political legitimacy in the federal system.[15]

It is through this idea of the national capital as exemplary city that Brasília's agenda of social change is conceptually projected to regional capitals and to the country as a whole. As a two-step inversion, therefore, Brasília is intended both as a crucible of transformation for the local population and, in its role as exemplary capital, as a means of inspiring national development.

3.5 Niemeyer's Social Architecture

Oscar Niemeyer goes to considerable lengths to disassociate such political intentions from his architecture. Though he is a student of Lúcio Costa and ultimately of Le Corbusier and a lifelong member of the Moscow-oriented Brazilian Communist party, his typical statement is that, given the nature of Brazilian society, "solutions to social problems escape the drafting board, requiring, outside of the profession [of architecture], a coherent attitude in support of progressivist movements" (1980c: 58). Thus, he rejects calls for a more "social architecture," arguing that his analysis of the contradictions of capitalist society in Brazil leads him to focus rather on formal and technical innovations. While of biographic interest, such rejection should nevertheless not be taken at face value in the analysis of his work. As I have argued, the problem is that the modernist project is inherently a social one: in its forms and spatial organizations, it identifies the political and the aesthetic, the processes of social transformation and its own formal processes of production. This intent is historically given in modernism and quite independent either of its successful realization or of the architect's pronouncements. It is therefore the case that modernist form has a cultural and social history independent of any one practitioner—although this is what the cult of genius in modernism tends to deny.

Moreover, throughout his writings and interviews, Niemeyer candidly describes his architecture as being built on a base of contradictions specific to conditions of Brazilian underdevelopment. He argues that these contradictions are themselves responsible for the possibilities of technical, formal, and experiential innovation for which his architecture is renowned. In effect, he stresses an inversion of development in his architecture: that which is most advanced arises, paradoxically, from that which is least.

In 1955, before the beginnings of Brasília, Niemeyer (1980b) described modern Brazilian architecture as having to confront the same kind of contradiction that Costa had previously emphasized: that Brazilian modernists were technically capable of producing an architecture which "logically belonged" to social, economic, and political conditions not yet developed in Brazil. This contradiction was especially acute for the politically committed modernists because the paradigmatic society of modernist architecture was hardly realized (or realizable) in the advanced societies where it had originated, and yet it was relatively easy to construct individual modernist buildings in Brazil. For Niemeyer, these buildings remained isolated fragments of the vision because Brazil lacked the basic societal preconditions that would permit modernist architecture to "serve the collectivity" as an instrument of social renovation. He categorized these preconditions in 1955 as state- or party-directed initiatives for urban development on a massive and national scale; heavy industry to support these initiatives through the prefabrication and standardized production of building materials; and, an "evolved" (i.e., Communist) social organization to provide the program and rationale for the new building types of modern design. In addition, he emphasized that Brazil's dominant classes, the patrons of the new architecture, were simply not interested in solving the urban problems of the masses:

> [Our modern architecture] had arisen in a country [the Soviet Union] socially organized and evolved, where it could have reached its true objective—which is to serve the collectivity—and therefore, there, it would find in the nobility of collective plans and in the heavy industry that supported them, a human significance and an architectonic unity that is today lacking [in Brazil]. Directed by dominant classes little interested in problems of architectural economics—because what they really desire is to show off wealth and luxury—or by government initiatives that are not based on plans of a national character or of mass constructions, it has found, as the obligatory basis of its themes, vanity, demagoguery and opportunism. (Niemeyer 1980b: 53).

From these conditions, however, Niemeyer derived a startling inversion:

> From the lack of an effective social base, and of great collective plans that would complement it, derive, however, the versatility of our architecture, the lack of preoccupation with economic constraints and the variety and richness of forms . . . which the absence of heavy industry with systems of prefabrication is accentuating even more. Thus, what is in it, for some, false and secondary, is for us the imposition of given conditions that it faithfully expresses (ibid., 53–54).

Niemeyer therefore justified the practice of modernist architecture in third-world countries like Brazil in terms of their backwardness precisely because this condition established the possibility of leaps in architectural innovation.

This argument may appear to have been little more than a self-serving attempt to make a virtue of necessity. However, seen from another perspective, it was congruent with the idea in modernist theory of a development inversion—but here restricted, in the absence of heavy industry and state initiatives on an urban scale, to the formal and technical innovations of individual buildings. Thus, Niemeyer argued that although the position of Brazilian modernists was fundamentally compromised and contradicted, a candid acceptance of this Brazilian reality paradoxically yielded a freedom to experiment which advanced Brazilian architecture—at the limited scale of individual buildings—to the forefront of modern design.

Given this assessment of the contradictions of modern architecture in Brazil before the construction of Brasília, how did the state's initiative not only to build the new capital but moreover to make it the centerpiece of a national development program affect Niemeyer's argument? At least for the Federal District, the project of Brasília resolved three of Niemeyer's four basic contradictions. It was a state-directed enterprise of "national character" at the scale of "great collective plans"; it was planned for and supported by developments in Brazilian heavy industry; and, it did not depend on the sponsorship of the bourgeoisie to achieve its intended objectives. In fact, as the state expropriated as much land as it wanted, exercised absolute juridical authority over the Federal District, appropriated (and printed) the funds it needed, and restricted the emergence or expansion of private capital markets of all kinds in the planned city, it limited from the beginning any legitimate role that a national or local bourgeoisie might play in the urban development of the capital.

Niemeyer's reaction to the changed circumstances of practicing architecture in Brasília is most clearly stated in the article "Form and Function in Architecture," published in 1959 after his major public buildings and *superquadra* prototypes had been designed and were well under construction. The change in his argument is one of emphasis and effect. In the practice of modern architecture, he (1980c: 57) now stresses the paramount significance of "almost unlimited plastic freedom, freedom that is not servilely subordinate to the demands of technical determinants or of functionalism." To the contrary, Niemeyer begins his search for sculptural expression through an investigation into the possibilities of a building's skeletal structure, "through a plastic speculation about the structural elements of architecture." (ibid., 58).

Niemeyer emphasizes, however, that the use of unlimited expressive freedom should be restricted to public buildings of monumental character on the one hand and to individual houses on the other. This point deserves further attention. Both types of buildings are conjoined in Niemeyer's typology because they share the following feature: they are "isolated or separate buildings, surrounded by open spaces" (ibid., 57). Thus, it is as buildings seen in the round, separated from other buildings, that he considers the house and the public building as appropriate structures for sculptural elaboration. This ordering of open space and sculptural object is key to Niemeyer's design methodology. Moreover, it is fundamental to the theory of modernist architecture in general and will be discussed fully in the next chapter. For the present, we should note three characteristics that reveal the social and political agenda of Niemeyer's architecture.

First, if private houses and public institutions are similarly conceived—planned as detached structures, surrounded by open spaces, and designed as figural objects—then that which is private is not typologically distinguished from that which is public. Thus, in an architectural system in which monumentality is conferred in large measure through sculptural elaboration in open space, the private building is not less monumental than the public because they are both considered as sculptural objects within a field of sculptural objects. This design methodology has a radical impact on the nature of the city: it erodes—deliberately and systematically I shall argue later—traditional, architecturally drawn distinctions between the public and the private domains of social life.

Second, with specific reference to Brasília, Niemeyer (ibid., 57) argues that while monumental types of buildings should be conceived with complete plastic freedom, this freedom should be regulated by the "harmony of the whole" in designing "collective residences," that is, the *superquadras* and neighborhood units of Brasília. The buildings of these areas are, therefore, standardized in their volumes, open spaces, heights, finish materials, and other basic features. Niemeyer thus appears to organize the architecture of the modernist city through a typological contrast between exceptional, figural objects that are monumental, and repeated, serial objects that are quotidian. However, for reasons I shall set out later, in both theoretical and ethnographic terms the housing blocks are, in fact, perceived as being as monumental as their supposed contrasts. As a result, this formal design typology further serves to break down traditional architectural-urban distinctions between public and private, civic and domestic, collective and individual. In these terms, Niemeyer's architecture is seen to have a radical effect both on the physical organization of social life and on the codes by which people interpret that organization.

Finally, if these distinctions are eroded (*neutralizadas* was Costa's term) in the modernist city, what does the new architecture signify instead? Compared with conditions in other

Brazilian cities, the "freedoms" of Brasília's modern architecture remain grounded in the paradoxes of Brazil's underdevelopment. However, from within the totality of Brasília itself, it is the state, its policies, programs, and authority, which guarantees Niemeyer's architectual innovations. As the vast majority of Brasília's buildings are state property and all the product of state planning, the state emerges as the ultimate reference of Niemeyer's architecture and typologies. It is the ultimate meaning of a "public" domain now no longer defined either in relation to the civic domain of citizens or to the institution of (bourgeois) private property. As a totality, Brasília thus presents the viewer with a concretized image of the state and its collective plans.

In terms of the impact of its individual buildings, however, Niemeyer has in mind an additional effect. His architectual innovations in Brasília are explicitly intended to shock: "the new forms . . . surprise [the viewer] by their lightness and freedom of creation, forms that do not support themselves rigidly and statically on the ground, as an imposition of technology, but which hold the palaces suspended, light and white, in the nights without end of the Central Plateau" (ibid., 60). What is the value of this architecturally induced shock? For Niemeyer its purpose is to subvert everyday experience: "Forms of surprise and emotion that, principally, alienate [*alheassem*] the visitor—for however short an instant—from the difficult problems, at times invincible, that life offers to all" (ibid.). This is an interesting, loaded, use of the word *alienate*. In effect, the architectural freedoms of Brasília are designed to alienate the individual from his alienations, from that which, in a Marxist sense, alienates him from society. Thus, as the double negative suggests, the new architecture is intended to present a positive alternative to the alienating society and denatured life of other cities. As the buildings are designed to produce an "estrangement effect," there is behind the poetry of Niemeyer's architectural play the intent to shock into being a new social and psychological moment.

In sum, it is the formal creativity of Niemeyer's architecture and its underlying design methodology that are intended to produce real social, political, and psychological transformations. Although in the above quotation Niemeyer describes the defamiliarization of the visitor to Brasília as ephemeral, the implication is that the impact of the totally modernist environment on its permanent residents will be anything but brief. In these terms, the architecture of the city is itself a prescription for change, and thus we find in Niemeyer's architecture the same development inversion that characterizes Costa's plan.

Although Niemeyer disavows the practice of social architecture, claiming that solutions to social problems "escape the drafting board," a closer analysis of his own arguments reveals that a program for social change is inherent in the very nature of his modernist project. Moreover, Niemeyer's disavowals are not altogether innocent. In an interview he gave me in August 1981, he made a statement (published in a slightly different form in Niemeyer 1980a: 38) that summarizes, in a self-critical way, the extent of his utopian intentions in Brasília: "I see now that a social architecture without a socialist base leads to nothing—that you can't create a class-free oasis in a capitalist society, and that to try ends up being, as Engels said, a paternalistic pose that pretends to be revolutionary." Although we should question the implication that in a socialist society the modernist project would succeed as intended, the statement indicates that for Niemeyer Brasília was just such an oasis of utopian development in the backlands of Brazil. Thus, when he (1983) attributes the subsequent corruption of the oasis to the invasion of capitalist society, he is actually pointing to the failure of the conflation of the political and the aesthetic that underlies the inversion of development he intended.

3.6 Modernism and Modernization

Two final questions remain for us to consider concerning the government's relation to this utopian agenda: to what extent did Kubitschek advocate or even acknowledge his architects' intentions for social change in the planning of the capital? And, if the government's intentions were different, even opposed, to those of the architects on this basic point, why did the government accept the modernist Master Plan and the architecture of a notorious Communist?

Kubitschek's own writings contain little to suggest that he explicitly considered social innovation, either for Brasilienses or for the nation, as among the innovations he envisioned for Brasília. In fact, he (1975: 60) admits that before reading Costa's Master Plan at the time of the design competition, he "did not have a formed idea about the type of city I was going to construct." Instead, he appears to have left the details of the city and its innovations to his architects and to the various planning commissions he convened to organize and supervise the many different aspects of the project. According to a director of one of the most important of these commissions, the Working Group of Brasília, such experts had a very free hand in drawing up detailed proposals for eventual implementation.[16] These proposals included the Organic Law of the Federal District, the distribution of government-owned apartments, the scheme to eliminate real estate speculation, a proposal of representative councils based on the *superquadras,* and the systems of education and health services. Kubitschek does not appear to have participated to any great extent in either the conceptualization or elaboration of such proposals.

This is not to say that Kubitschek's devotion to Brasília was not decisive for its realization. To the contrary, he focused his efforts on advancing acceptance of the basic idea of Brasília in surmounting political and financial obstacles to its construction. However, in the extent to which he shared his planners utopian intentions, he emphasized the technical and symbolic importance of Brasília as the target-synthesis of his Target Program and especially of the possibilities of national integration. When I asked Niemeyer whether Kubitschek had been committed to the social innovations of the Master Plan and other proposals, he replied "We never discussed politics, either his or mine" (interview, August 1981). Be that as it may, it seems that for Kubitschek, Brasília was a charismatic center of round-the-clock animation which he used to augment his own charismatic leadership. From the available evidence, it appears that he may have been uninterested or even somewhat naïve about the social intentions of his planners and architects. Or, more shrewdly, he may have been convinced that once Brasília was built and inhabited those intentions would quickly become irrelevant.

If Kubitschek's relation to Brasília's architects may be described as a basically harmonious and occasionally inconsonant orchestration of intentions, this complex and at times contradictory relation reveals why the government should have wanted a modernist city rather than one based on baroque or neoclassical principles of planning and architecture typical of other Brazilian state capitals. The explanation essentially depends on the affinity between modernism and modernization. In the case of Brasília, we may suggest the nature of this affinity by explaining how it is that the same symbols can appeal to those who hold differing, even at points opposing, interpretations of those symbols.

Earlier, I discussed how the developmentalism of Kubitschek's administration led it to value innovation for its own sake. As modernism was the innovative force in architecture and planning, developmentalists found an elective affinity between modernist design and their own project of modernization. As an aesthetic, modernism was the style that best symbolized the innovative spirit of their programs; as a doctrine of development, it appealed to their desire to transform society radically through an exercise of state power at its center. But the fact remains that if modernism symbolized the innovations of both the architects and the government, their objectives of innovation, especially on the point of social change, were fundamentally different and even contradictory. The question to explain then is how both "communists and capitalists" can find their views signified by the very same set of symbols. Or, to turn the question around, why does modernism in Brazilian architecture signify change toward egalitarianism, collectivism, and socialism for one group, and toward nationalist development for the other?

The answer lies in the polysemous nature of the architectural symbol, in how it can have several distinct but related meanings and uses. Although the primary symbolic significance of modernist architecture for both groups is that it represented a break with the colonial past and a leap into the future, each group *uses* it to signify a leap in a different direction and therefore invests it with a different reading. As I have already presented the architects' agenda for Brasília's modernist design, I shall briefly suggest what the new style meant to the political elite of the Brazilian state, a meaning established during the Vargas years of the Estado Novo and still in force.

We may take as paradigmatic of this meaning one example from the history of modern architecture in Brazil discussed in the last chapter. Between 1936 and 1943, a team of Brazilian architects, led by Costa and Niemeyer and tutored by Le Corbusier, constructed the world renowned Ministry of Education and Culture in Rio de Janiero. The enormous international success of this building had two important consequences for Brazilian architecture. First, it launched Brazil's fledgling modern architects into international prominence. Second, perhaps more than any other cultural expression in Brazil, modern architecture became for the government the symbol of Brazil's emergence as a modern nation.

This symbolic association developed essentially because modernism in Brazil simultaneously broke with the past as it posited a radiant future. It expressed both a rupture with the colonial legacies of underdevelopment and a future of industrial modernity. The new architecture attacked the styles of the past—the Iberian and neoclassical architecture that constituted one of the most visible symbols of a legacy the government sought to supersede. Instead, it demanded industrial-age building materials and an industrial aesthetic appropriate to "the new age." In planning, it privileged the automobile and the aesthetic of speed at a time when Brazil (especially under Kubitschek) was embarking on a program of industrialization especially focused on the automobile industry. Moreover, it required centralized planning and the exercise of state power, which appealed to the statist interests of the political elite. For many in this elite, modern architecture's break with history came to symbolize and, in the important sphere of public works, to constitute Brazil's own efforts at modernization.

Thus, in the government's rhetoric of development, modern architecture was trumpeted as a most visible symbol of Brazil's progress, industrialization, independence, and national identity as a modernizing nation. The most influential proponent of this ontological relation between the development of modern architecture in Brazil and the rise of modern Brazilian society was Kubitschek himself, first as mayor of Belo Horizonte (1940–45) for whom Niemeyer built his famous Pampulha complex (cf. Braund 1981: 107–15), then as governor of Minas Gerais (1951–56), and finally as president:

> I have long been aware that modern architecture in Brazil is more than a mere aesthetic trend, and above all more than the projection into our culture of a universal movement. It has in fact put at our service the means with which to find the best possible solution of our city planning and housing problems. . . . It is, furthermore, a strong affirmative expression of our culture, perhaps the most original and precise expression of the creative intelligence of modern Brazil. (Cited in Papadaki 1960: 7)

On the basis of this "affirmative" relation between modern Brazilian architecture and modernizing Brazilian society, governments at municipal, state, and federal levels consistently used modernist architecture and planning as one of the most important symbols of their commitment to creating a new Brazil—an affirmation culminating in the construction of Brasília.

For both the architects and the government, therefore, modernist architecture signified a break with the colonial past and a leap into the future. For the architects, immersed in the political history of modernism in Europe, this symbolic rupture was interpreted as the opportunity to break with the capitalism of that past. For them, the anticolonialism of modern architecture signified anticapitalism as well. For the government, modernist architecture also meant the effacement of the colonial past from public building projects. But for its leaders, this symbolic anticolonialism was associated with modernization and nationalism and not socialist revolution. When I asked Niemeyer how it was that a notorious Communist could be consistently employed by notoriously anti-Communist regimes, he retorted "Why is it me that has to answer? Those who hire me know of my ideas, and when they ask me to do a project, it is the architecture that interests them" (interview, August 1981).

In 1942, a certain general condemned the modernist building of the Ministry of Education and Culture as an affront to the Estado Novo, the military, and Brazil because he claimed that its site plan was designed as a "hammer and sickle" by a bunch of "Communist architects." The minister of education, Gustavo Capanema, dismissed the charge as a fantasy of interpretation.[17] He argued that the design was abstract and that, like any abstraction, it was susceptible to countless figurative readings. If the general saw a hammer and sickle, this was because he projected onto an abstract design his own hostility toward the political sympathies he attributed to Costa, Niemeyer, and Le Corbusier. As the design was "in fact" abstract, Capanema assured the military that its "correct" reading was as a symbol of Brazil's commitment to a modernizing future.

Significantly, the same charge of "hammer and sickle" was leveled a few years later against Niemeyer's famous Church of São Francisco de Assis at Pampulha in Belo Horizonte. And, in 1981, it was raised, by a different general, against Niemeyer's mausoleum and commemorative column for Kubitschek in Brasília. Once again, representatives of the government responded with an official interpretation of the monument's abstract symbolism to allay the military's suspicion that a Communist plot had disgraced the national capital.

Multiple interpretations of an architectural sign are, of course, fundamental to the history of architecture. One has only to think of the use of the Parthenon (and classicism generally) to symbolize the radically different political beliefs of Jefferson, Colbert, Hitler, and Stalin to realize that an architectural sign may remain constant while its denoted meanings shift dramatically with changes in use, context, and intention. Moreover, at any one moment, it may be the object of competing claims about its "correct meaning." Yet, fundamentally, there is no preestablished priority among such claims. Thus, in Brasília, one finds multiple interpretations of the meaning of the city's architecture and planning distributed among the various actors in the city's history: the architects, government leaders, military commanders, pioneers, and workers in the satellite cities, among others. Each version is valid insofar as it is vitalized and sustained by the interests of these social groups. For each group attempts to make known (if not dominant) its interpretation and in so doing to assert its role in (if not control over) the history and mythology of the city.

3.7 The Counter-*Brincadeira*

In this chapter, we have analyzed the Master Plan as an account of new beginnings. This analysis has answered a number of questions raised at the outset. We have seen first that the plan's mythology disguises a subversive agenda for the transformation of Brazilian society. This agenda explains why Brasília had to be radically different from other Brazilian cities, and why this difference had to be one of modernist design. It also explains why this modernism symbolized the intentions of both the architects and the government, even though these intentions were at points contradictory. Finally, the analysis of Brasília as an instrument of development inversions suggests both the motivation and the intended effect of building a modernist city in a developing country such as Brazil: to produce not only regional and national development based on its innovations, but also leaps in the development process itself, maximizing the project of modernization for industrializing nations.

Although Brasília was conceived to create this modernized society, it was built and occupied by an entirely different one. In the differences between the two lies the basic contradiction with which the history of constructed Brasília begins. This history constitutes a Brazilianization of the city, a counter-*brincadeira*, so to speak, to Costa's *brincadeira* in the Master Plan, because the dynamism of Brazilian society unequivocally destroyed the plan's utopian hopes.

The contradiction of Brasília's history is more complex, however, than one simply between the imagined utopia and the existing order. The dichotomy of "plan and reality" usually advanced to explain the failures of modern urban planning simplistically assumes that planners' intentions are more or less perfectly realized in their plans—only to be sabotaged by external forces beyond their control.[18] However, a careful analysis reveals that there are really two sets of issues here. On the one hand, we have the social program modernist planners *thought* they were concretizing with their architectural-urban proposals. This program they tend to characterize with such terms as egalitarian, socialist, collectivist, and communitarian. On the other hand, we must now consider whether the planners were mistaken as to the nature of the imagined social order to which their proposals refer. In spite of their claims to being "sociologists," we must determine whether a more profound analysis of their proposals for redefining the urban functions of traffic, housing, work, and recreation reveals that they contradict the designers' own intentions, and further, that once constructed they constitute something very different from their imagined city.

PART TWO

THE CITY DEFAMILIARIZED

FOUR

The Death of the Street

The discovery that Brasília is a city without street corners produces a profound disorientation. At the very least, the realization that utopia lacks intersections means that both pedestrian and driver must learn to re-negotiate urban locomotion. In a larger sense, it may signal that "the man multiplied by the motor"—to use a shibboleth of futurism—has at last realized his utopia. In other Brazilian cities, the pedestrian strolls to the corner of almost any street, waits for the light, and with some security ventures to the other side. In Brasília, where the *balão*, or traffic circle, replaces the street corner and where there are therefore no intersections to distribute the rights of way between pedestrian and vehicle, this passage is distinctly more dangerous. The resulting imbalance of forces tends, simply, to eliminate the pedestrian: everyone who can drives. The absence of the rite of passage of street corners is but one indication of a distinctive and radical feature of Brasília's modernity: the absence of streets themselves. In place of the street, Brasília substitutes high-speed avenues and residential cul-de-sacs; in place of the pedestrian, the automobile; and in place of the system of public spaces that streets traditionally support, the vision of a modern and messianic urbanism (figs. 4.1–4.5).

At the scale of an entire city, Brasília thus realizes one of modern architecture's fundamental planning objectives: to redefine the urban function of traffic by eliminating what it calls the corridor street, the street edged with continuous building façades. In its critique of the cities and society of capitalism, modern architecture proposes the elimination of the street as a prerequisite of modern urban organization.[1] It attacks the street for a number of reasons. On the one hand, it views the corridor street as a cesspool of disease. On the other, it considers the street an impediment to progress because it fails to accommodate the needs of the machine age.

Yet, modernist planning derives only in part from public health concerns and technological innovations. More profoundly, modern architecture attacks the street because, as we

Fig. 4.1 Largo do Pelourinho with a view of the museum of the city and the former slave market, Salvador, 1980

Fig. 4.2 Plaza of the Three Powers with a view of the Planalto Palace and the museum of the city, Brasília, 1980

Fig. 4.3 Praça Tiradentes with a view of the former Palácio Municipal and jail and the monument to Tiradentes, Ouro Preto, 1980

Fig. 4.4 Plaza of the Three Powers with a view of the National Congress and the statue *The Warriors*, Brasília, 1980

Fig. 4.5 Aerial view of the Plaza of the Three Powers and the Esplanade of the Ministries, Brasília, 1981

shall see in this chapter, it constitutes an architectural organization of the public and private domains of social life that modernism seeks to overturn. In the type of city modernism attacks, the street is both a particular type of place and a domain of public life. The architectural organization of this domain structures the entire cityscape in terms of a contrast between public space and private building. In sustaining this contrast, the street embodies the concept of the public defined in relation to the private. Thus, the street is not simply a place where various categories of activity occur. It also embodies a principle of architectural order through which the public sphere of civic life is both represented and constituted.

That the street embodies such a discourse between the public and the private will become clear when we examine its structure in the preindustrial city and its elimination in the city of modern architecture. Accordingly, in this chapter we shall consider the street (and what has replaced it) in two contrasting types of urbanism, that of preindustrial Rio de Janeiro and Ouro Preto and that of Brasília. We shall ask what the design and planning of streets in these examples may tell us about the structure of urban organization in different types of cities. In addition, we shall ask what this organization may tell us about the nature of ruling political regimes and about their relations to society. For I shall suggest that to compare the structure of public space in the preindustrial cities of a colonial empire and in the administrative capital of a modern bureaucratic state is to reveal different types of urban order as concretizations of contrasting political regimes. Furthermore, it is to expose very different conceptions of what constitutes the public and the private in the relations between civic authority and civil society.

I contrast modernist with preindustrial urbanism in Brazil because Brasília was designed to transform, both architecturally and socially, an urban way of life established in preindustrial cities. Thus, European modernism attacks the nineteenth-century city in large measure because its preindustrial physical foundations, dominated by the "ruthless rule" of private property, does not meet the requirements and consequences of industrialization. In Brazil as in Europe, we must therefore assess the structure of preindustrial urbanism to understand the significance of modernist transformations.

Preindustrial urbanism in Brazil crystallized into a national pattern during the late eighteenth and early nineteenth centuries, and I focus on Ouro Preto and Rio de Janeiro because they were capitals, respectively, of these centuries. During this period, Brazil's large cities emerged as dominant, radiating centers of cultural, social, and attitudinal influence, establishing regional (in the case of Ouro Preto) and national (in case of Rio) patterns of urban form as well as of urban society.[2] As urban life crystallized and expanded in Ouro Preto around its gold production and in Rio around the arrival of the Portuguese court from Lisbon, both capitals became exemplary centers for their respective domains. They served as vehicles for change in the hinterland and projected their patterns of urban organization to other cities. Thus, in the periods in which we shall look at them, Ouro Preto and Rio express dominant patterns of preindustrial urbanism in Brazil. These patterns are the final result of three centuries of colonial endeavor. They reveal a synthesis of the most characteristic and fundamental features of preindustrial urbanism, one no longer dependent either socially or culturally on rural patrimonial society and one not yet transformed by industrialization.

While industrialization certainly changed this synthesis, it continues to represent a basic pattern of social life and spatial organization in many if not a majority of small Brazilian cities. This pattern remains important because although it is often assumed that urbanization is a product of industrialization, there is in fact a lack of correlation between the two processes in Brazil.[3] Since 1940, cities in the nonindustrial regions have been growing about as fast as cities in the industrial regions. Essentially, these cities remain pre- or nonindustrial, expanding on the foundations of the early nineteenth-century urban pattern. Thus, the contrast I shall draw between modernist and preindustrial urbanism is not simply an exercise in historical analysis but is addressed to the issues of urbanization in contemporary Brazil.

The corridor street is basic to these issues because it constitutes the architectural context of the outdoor public life of Brazilian cities. In its preindustrial form, this context is defined in terms of a contrast between the street system of public spaces and the residential system of private buildings. It is this relation between the public and the private, with its consequences for social life, that Brasília subverts.

To understand how the street orders the public and private domains and how its elimination in Brasília affects this order, we must first determine how the street can mean anything at all. One way of doing this is to identify the architectural conventions that architects and planners use in designing urban spaces—of which the street is the principal type—and that are experienced in everyday life as an architecture already built. If we analyze these conventions in preindustrial Rio de Janeiro and Ouro Preto, the significance of the death of the street in Brasília will become apparent.

4.1 The Architectural Context of Street Life

One of the most profound shocks of migrating to Brasília is the discovery that it is a city without crowds. It is not the absence of crowding that migrants complain of, but rather the absence of the social life of crowds that they expect to find in the public places of a city. In interview after interview comparing Brasília with hometowns of all sizes, Brasilienses register this basic difference: in Brasília "there are no people in the streets," the city "lacks crowds" and "lacks the bustle of street life." The absence of an urban crowd has earned Brasília the reputation of a city that "lacks human warmth."

Brasilienses consistently attribute this lack of street life to several factors, such as the enormous distances separating buildings, and the segregation of activities into discrete urban sectors. But the most common explanation is at the same time the most profound. It is that Brasília "lacks street corners." This observation refers to the absence in Brasília of the entire system of public spaces that streets traditionally support in other Brazilian cities, to the absence not only of corners but also of curbs, sidewalks edged with continuous façades of shops and residences, squares, and streets themselves. It is an explanation that uses the corner as a metonym for the street system of exchange between people, residence, commerce, and traffic. It is one that explicitly draws a connection between the public spaces of a city and the public life streets support (figs. 4.6–4.9).

The nature of this connection is suggested in the following typical comparison of a hometown and Brasília, given by an official of the capital's development corporation (Novacap). This civil engineer was born in a small city in the interior of the northeastern state of Ceará. He moved to the state capital, Fortaleza, for his university studies and remained there for many years after completing his degree. For reasons of better employment, he moved to Brasília in the mid sixties. Describing his first year in the city as a period of *brasilite*, 'estrangement', he attributed his "allergy to Brasília," as he called it, to the absence of the kinds of "traditional public places of encounter" he was used to, especially the neighborhood street corner. He defined the social importance of corners by calling them "points of sociality" in the neighborhood (*pontos de convivência social*). These were the most important places of (generally male) encounter and public activity in the residential community. In his neighborhood in Fortaleza, for example, he described "X's corner," named after a store-restaurant-bar that occupied a corner building site, as the place to go whenever he wanted to

Fig. 4.6 Residential street in the neighborhood Barra Funda, São Paulo, 1988

Fig. 4.7 Residential Access Way L1, Brasília, 1980

Fig. 4.8 Rua Boa Vista, downtown São Paulo, 1988

Fig. 4.9 West Residential Highway Axis, Brasília, 1980

meet a friend, pass the time, find a neighbor, or hear the news. This corner was his neighborhood's information nexus, its outdoor living room so to speak.

In Brasília, however, he found that the lack of corners (i.e., of the street system of public spaces) had an interiorizing effect; it forced people to remain in their apartments and replaced the spontaneity of street encounters with the formality of home visits. "To meet a friend I practically had to go to his house or he to mine." As people are often more reluctant, he claimed, to receive friends in their homes than to meet them in a public place, this interiorization of social life had the effect of restricting and ultimately constricting his social universe. To one accustomed to an outdoor public, to the sociality of the corner, its elimination produced not just an interiorization of social encounters, but also a profound sense of isolation. In planned Brasília, there are no urban crowds, no street corner societies, and no sidewalk sociality, largely because there are no squares, no streets, and no street corners.

Brazilians expect to experience the daily life of crowds in cities not only because they anticipate a larger population in cities than in the country, but even more because they expect to find streets in a city and because the street is the customary arena of *movimento*—of the public display and transactions of crowds. This expectation is based on the distinction that the very existence of *ruas*, 'streets', makes between urban life and rural life. Rural communities (*aldeias, povoados, fazendas,* and *roças*) do not have *ruas*; rather they have *estradas*, 'roads', and *caminhos*, 'paths'. Only cities—those settlements officially classified, regardless of their size, as *cidades* and *vilas*—have *ruas*. Thus, one of the urbanite's expressions for going downtown, to the commercial center of the city, is *vou à rua*, 'I'm going to the street', and the peasant's expression for going to town from the hinterland is exactly the same. Therefore, the word "street" signifies "city" because it refers to a particular type of place that only cities have.

This type of place has a distinctive physical form that constitutes a fundamental difference between urban and rural architecture. This difference is most clearly perceived in preindustrial Brazil, but it applies equally to the physical foundations of industrialized, though not modernized, communities. In rural settlements, the basic pattern of land use is one of detached buildings separated from each other on all sides by open space, some of which is used for circulation (fig. 4.10). In contrast, the preindustrial city is, from an architectural perspective, a solid mass of contiguous buildings out of which the spaces for circulation are carved. The buildings are not freestanding (with

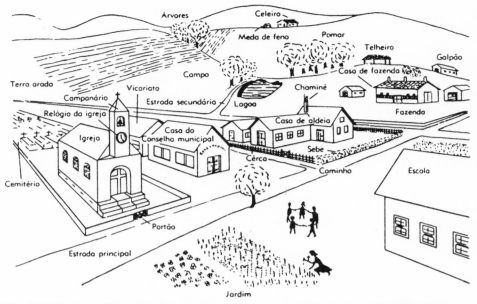

Fig. 4.10 Dictionary illustration of stereotypical pattern of rural land use and building (*Novo Michaelis* 1979: 49)

Fig. 4.11 View of the Largo do Pelourinho, Salvador, 1980 (see fig. 4.1)

significant exceptions discussed later), and the bounded spaces are streets used primarily for circulation (fig. 4.11). Moreover, the preindustrial city generally expands by enclosing the open, rural space around it with buildings. Even where city space is progressively filled in, new buildings usually maintain this spatial sense of enclosure which defines the street.

The street is not, however, just a passage for traffic. Its space is only one element of a complex form. As an architectural configuration, the street is comprised of a space open to the sky and the physical frame that contains and shapes it, that is, the façades of the buildings, and a floor. The latter is usually paved and differentiated into two or more levels: the base level of the buildings and the roadway proper, at a lower level, the two being mediated by a third level of curb, sidewalk, and steps which differentiates the street into distinct but interpenetrating zones of activity (see especially figs. 4.6, 4.8, 4.19, and 4.28). The interplay of the expansion of this floor and the height and character of the surrounding buildings gives the impression that the sky has a defined height. The street system of public spaces comprises all the elements of this architectural configuration.

The urban square is a special case of the street defined in these terms.[4] Jean Baptiste Debret's 1839 plan of Rio de Janeiro (fig. 4.12) reveals that squares developed in relation to streets in several distinct architectural morphologies: as a widening or lateral expansion of thoroughfares, generally called a *largo* and frequently originating as a parvis (the area in front or to the side of a church) which was widened to accommodate a relatively permanent street activity, such as a market (fig. 4.12, e, f, g, h, and A); at the intersection of radiating streets, a type usually distinguished by the term *praça*, (fig. 4.12, D, e, and V); or, as an outlying piece of land that the city eventually absorbs and frames into a square, called by the now archaic term *rocio* (fig. 4.12, d). In all of these cases, the square is defined by the same architectural features as the street (compare figs. 4.1, 4.3, and 4.13).

To see how these features constitute the architectural context of street life in the preindustrial city, we may look at Debret's illustrations of nineteenth-century Rio (figs. 4.13–4.18). But for obvious changes in such things as dress and transport, these scenes of the street and square present a remarkably contemporary view of street life in Rio and especially in smaller cities throughout Brazil. With great ethnographic accuracy, they depict the life of Rio's outdoor public domain—the daily and ceremonial activities of its crowds, the habits of its strollers, shoppers, vendors, and paupers.[5]

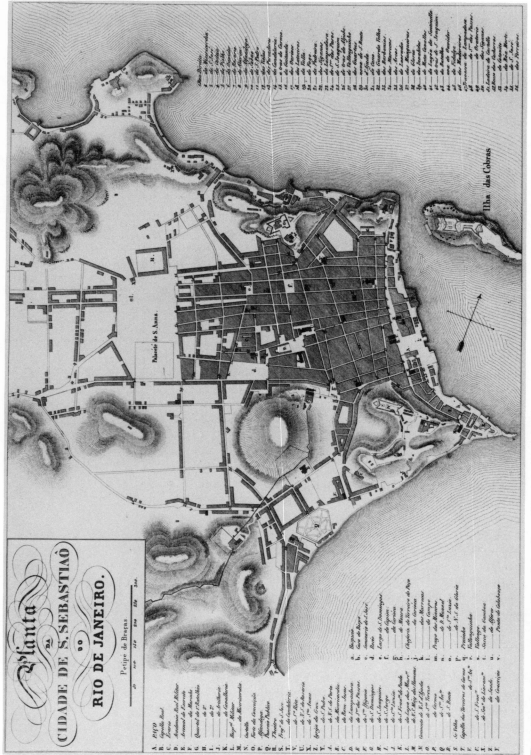

Fig. 4.12 Jean Baptiste Debret, Plan of the City of Rio de Janeiro, 1839

Debret's illustrations portray Rio during its initial period of cultural and political primacy, after the relocation of the Portuguese court from Lisbon in 1808 had transformed it from a sleepy colonial city of 60,000 inhabitants into Brazil's most influential city and the capital of an empire. What is especially important for our purposes is that the presence of the court engendered an urban crowd unlike any previously found in Brazilian cities—a vast body of all classes of people permanently residing and working in the capital. By the time Debret arrived nearly a decade after the royal hegira, Rio's population had doubled. The afflux of 24,000 Portuguese and numbers of other Europeans metamorphosed the life of the capital. The Crown embarked on a project of institution building. It created numerous institutes of higher education (including those of military science, engineering, medicine, and fine arts), a national library, and a myriad of government bureaus, all of which were new to Brazil. These institutions required new buildings, and the resulting public works gave a definitive character to the civic, commercial, and residential domains of the city. As the titles and offices of the court attracted wealthy Brazilian families to the capital, Rio became in turn a condensor and relay of an idealized pattern of urban life, its physical form serving as a recognizable setting for its crowds, customs, fads, and peculiar synthesis of European and African sensibilities.[6]

If we compare Rio's principal civic square, a street in the downtown area, and a street in a residential neighborhood (figs. 4.13, 4.16, 4.17), we see that a limited number of factors define and mediate the contrast between the street's solids and voids. These establish a characteristic pattern of forms and massings throughout the city. The appearance of the architectural frame of public space is similar in each case. Its most significant feature is the street's lining of contiguous façades: each building adjoins the next, and each is built exactly in line with its neighbor in relation to the sidewalk. Thus, the public space of the street and square is contained by a solid front of buildings. Although most buildings have a backyard, or *quintal*, which serves as a *private* outdoor space (not visible in the illustrations), there are no front yards of any kind to separate their façades from the public outdoor space. Rather, their aligned façades are built flush with the sidewalk, and their doorways give out immediately onto the public street.[7]

A number of architectural elements mediate this opposition between the street's wall lining of façades and its passage of space. These elements relate the private domain behind the wall to the public domain in front of it. The first such elements that come to our attention are doors, windows, and balconies. It is

(*text continues on p. 118*)

Fig. 4.13 Jean Baptiste Debret, View of the Largo do Palácio, Rio de Janeiro (1816–31)

Fig. 4.14 Jean Baptiste Debret, The Acclamation of Dom Pedro II, Largo do Palácio, Rio de Janeiro, 1831

Figure 4.13: View of the Largo do Palácio. An inventory of the buildings customarily erected around a city square gives an initial picture of its social life. Figures 4.13, 4.14, and 4.15 show different views of Rio's palace square, the Largo do Palácio, (also known as the Largo do Carmo and today the Praça XV de Novembro). The perspective view, figure 4.13, shows the following buildings. Formerly the residence of the viceroy and before that the mint, the royal palace occupies the entire left side of the square. It was primarily used for royal receptions and other court affairs. Its long façade served as a customary place of communication between the court and its subjects: the royal family and officials used its windows and balconies to air important pronouncements to the public (represented by those gathered in the square below) and to receive, on festival days, the processions that toured the square before entering the imperial chapel. As one side of the square is occupied by the court, another is taken by the church. The entire back side of the square houses the church, chapel, and cloister of Carmo, with special passageways constructed for direct communication between the buildings of church and state. By convention, one wall of the Brazilian square—in this case the right one—is given over to the establishments of civil society. Here, we find the houses of Portuguese merchants, luxurious shops, and a number of units rented by French entrepreneurs who converted them into cafés, elegant billiard parlors, and fashionable hotels. At a remove from the square along the side of this block facing the sea is a customhouse and shipping depot. Finally, a quay and a monumental fountain form the seawall of the square.

The inventory of buildings around the city's principal square reveals that it is the domain of the city's most important collective institutions, and for this reason the locale of enterprises that depend on their patronage. It is the domain of institutional power, both religious and political—the lack of their spatial distinction being significant. Church and state always share the principal city square in Brazilian cities (and throughout Latin America). To suggest the significance of this pattern, we may note that in many European cities (Spain and Portugal excepted) these institutions are customarily found on different squares. They are spatially segregated around a municipal square of government institutions, a church square, and a square for the transactions and associations of the market. The physical separation of the institutions of church, state, and market became a prominant pattern of urban organization during the High Middle Ages in the type of city Weber (1978) describes as the city-commune, the city of burgher democracy. In this pattern and its contrast in Latin America, we have examples of how the physiognomy of a city suggests the nature of its political organization.

Figure 4.14: The Acclamation of Dom Pedro II. Figures 4.14 and 4.15 illustrate two types of activities that characterize the crowd of the civic square. Both types are noncommercial activities and both relate to the concentration of institutional power around the square, but in different ways. Figure 4.14 commemorates the "acclamation" of five-year-old Pedro II on 7 April 1831. It marks his father's abdication of the Brazilian throne in his favor and his presentation to the public as future emperor. This celebration is an example of an officially sponsored ceremonial congregation of the outdoor urban crowd. The crowd assembles both as spectator and actor in the rituals of church and state during which these institutions use public displays to reiterate their authority. It is the display of order, both of the sponsoring institutions and of the crowd, that is ritually important. The crowd is organized according to the most important divisions of civil society (however few these may be in the Brazilian case), and it functions as a public body to represent these divisions and their articulation in ceremonies that emphasize the order and legitimacy of society's hierarchical structure. The spatial order of these divisions reproduces their social order, and thus participation in such ceremonies teaches the ruled about the orders of rulership and involves them in an act of veneration.

Thus, figure 4.14 shows the following spatial organization of the participants which is itself a representation of their social and political relations. The young emperor occupies the left side of the central window, standing above and to the right of his brothers, behind whom are the members of the Regent Council. Facing the Crown and encircled by its military force are the officially designated representatives of the crowd: a deputation of justices of the peace on horseback, each representing a different residential neighborhood and carrying its colors and emblems. Behind a company of artillery that separates the crowd from both the Crown and its appointed representa-

Fig. 4.15 Jean Baptiste Debret, The Refreshments of the Largo do Palácio, Rio de Janeiro (1816–31)

Fig. 4.16 Jean Baptiste Debret, The Barber Shop, Rio de Janeiro (1816–31)

tives, we find the multitudes waving the yellow and green branches of the coffee tree, these being the imperial colors. Face to face with imperial authority, this Brazilian crowd of April 1831 is obviously not the crowd of the French Revolution. It is not one poised on the edge of insurrection, nor does it even suggest the possibility. Its lack of political organization in the public square of the city—the fact that the people are not organized into popular constituent groups—is an indication that traditionally the Brazilian square is less a forum for the protests of civil society than one for the ceremonious reiteration of legitimate authority. Its political monologue between state and society suggests the nature of Brazilian political structure.

Figure 4.15: The Refreshments of the Largo do Palácio. As much as the square is a stage for formal ceremony and political assembly, it is also the city's *sala de visitas*, its public visiting room. It is a realm of informal encounter and congregation, a place for leisure-time socializing, a place to see and be seen. In this aspect, the square's activities are informal, quotidian, and essentially noncommercial. People gather to socialize away from the restraints of the home. Their activities consist principally in the varieties of conversation: in discussion, exchanges of opinion, news, and information, anecdote, and flirtation. The former are, of course, indispensable to the political life of citizens, and the square provides the setting for the formation and exercise of public opinion. These informal activities occur among and between all classes of people as all have free access to the square. It is the heterogeneity and voluntarism of the square's encounters that distinguish the social activity of its room from that of the house.

As figure 4.15 illustrates, the square's conversations are usually abetted by some form of refreshment and entertainment, services that make the social hour of the square pass agreeably but that do not constitute business. The square is not the domain of the economic; it is the domain of informal and extradomestic sociality, of conversation and pastime. In this illustration, Debret portrays the habits of one of the groups that frequents the square every day: the "middle class of little capitalists," as he (1978: 202) calls them, those who own one or two slaves whose daily earnings, collected weekly, are sufficient income for their masters to enjoy leisure time. The afternoons of this leisure time are spent in the square. After the midday siesta, these "little capitalists" habitually gather in the square from 4 o'clock until the Ave Maria at 7. By 4:30, every seat along the quay wall (street furniture) is taken. Debret (1978: 202–3) relates that the conversations of this leisured class are punctuated by "a little ritual" of purchasing a sweet and a swig of fresh fountain water from the street vendors. The game is to become widely recognized as a big spender on sweets, a favorite and flirtatious client, and so become fêted by all the vendors of the square. Just as the "little capitalists" have their corner of the square, other groups have by informal agreement and by habit marked out their areas of congregation. Thus, the background of the illustration reveals merchants, shopkeepers, street vendors, ship captains, ship brokers, sailors, foreigners, court officials, dock workers, and a policeman whose responsibility it is to maintain the peace of the square.

Figure 4.16: The Barber Shop. The area surrounding the civic square in Brazilian cities, the *centro*, is the commercial domain of the city, its downtown. It is a warren of streets devoted to commerce, shopping, and services, and its street-life revolves around the economic. In Debret's time as well as today, an illustration of one of Rio's principal downtown streets, such as the Rua do Ouvidor, would show wall-to-wall commercial establishments at street level, and warehouses, manufacturers, hotels, and residences on the floors above. Figure 4.16 portrays the mixed residential and commercial use of the ground level typical of its side streets. In the *centro* of the city, many people earn their living on the pavement: the peddlers, musicians, knife-sharpeners, bootblacks, beggars, and the like. Literally one step removed from this economy of the pavement are the stallholders, exemplified in the illustration by the barbers. The stall is little more than a hole-in-the-wall, and its activities invariably spill out onto the pavement. Even today, stalls are rarely shut off from the pavement by a barrier, such as glass. Rather, the activities of the street flow into and out of them through a permeable building façade, which thus creates a liminal space neither precisely public nor private.

The barber shop of the illustration is a typical stall of many services. Its signboard reads "Barber, Hairdresser, Blood-letter, Dentist, and Applier of Leeches." The barbers are shown preparing

Fig. 4.17 Jean Baptists Debret, The *Folia* of the Emperor of the Holy Ghost, Rio de Janeiro (1816–31)

Fig. 4.18 Jean Baptiste Debret, A Bureaucrat Promenades with His Family, Rio de Janeiro, 1820

for the day's labor. They are former slaves who have purchased their freedom. One is sharpening the razors with his helper; the other is mending the stockings of their clients. He is seated on a bench that straddles the threshold, where the clients will wait for their turn in the barber chair inside the stall. At the end of the day, the barbers will bring their street furniture inside, lower the curtain over the doorway, and sleep on straw mats at the back of the stall. Thus, the illustration portrays an essential feature of the Brazilian downtown street: it is a domain of mixed, and mixed-up, use; one of commerce, residence, and work.

Figure 4.17: The Procession of the Emperor of the Holy Ghost. Figures 4.17 and 4.18 present scenes of streets in residential neighborhoods. The activities of these streets correspond to those of the civic square in several ways, but their referents are different. As in the square, their congregations are not based on commercial interests, though they are often aided by the refreshments of the local bar and restaurant. They can be of a formal and organized nature, as in processions of the neighborhood patron saint, political assemblies of neighborhood residents, or even street games of neighborhood children. They are also informal and spontaneous, as in sidewalk conversations between neighbors. Their points of reference, however, tend to be different: they involve their actors less as citizens of the city as a whole than as community residents and neighbors. They refer to the neighborhood as a space within the city having a distinguishing set of identities, and to the family household as providing both the unit of residence and the identity of residents.

Figures 4.17 and 4.18 illustrate two kinds of street processions. The organizational basis of the first is the community and that of the second is the household. Figure 4.17 portrays a *folia,* one of the many kinds of religious celebrations that peregrinate through the streets of Brazilian neighborhoods. Debret depicts a *folia do divino* in Rio de Janeiro during the week prior to the festival of Pentecost, which occurs on the seventh Sunday after Easter to celebrate the descent of the Holy Ghost upon the Disciples. Traditionally, a *folia* comprises a group of men, generally neighbors, who form an association or fraternity to raise money for the annual festivals of the Holy Spirit. Carrying devotional symbols and singing popular songs adapted for the purpose, they parade through neighborhood streets weeks and even months before each festival seeking contributions from the faithful. A typical day of alms collecting ends with a special dinner for the group at a neighbor's house in which each course is accompanied by song. In these circumstances, the *folia's* scared charge may overflow into profane revelry. Such *folias* are quite different from the civic and religious processions which city and church officials promote. Those processions originate at official places like city squares and churches, represent the hierarchy of officialdom in their processional order, and require an audience. In contrast, the *folia* is a popular fraternity/festival, organized by the people of a neighborhood, in the space of their own community, solely out of their voluntary contributions. As in many other instances of popular religious life, *folias* usually celebrate parody as much as anything else. Their revelries and reversals mock social, political, and ecclesiastical orders although, as parody, they ultimately reaffirm these norms. Debret suggests this intention in his illustration. As everyone knows that the Holy Ghost has no emperor, the supposed election of the latter by popular vote serves to emphasize the former's sublimity. Moreover, in *carnaval* fashion, this emperor often plays the fool, in every respect a mock ruler. In Debret's rendition there is the additional factor that the emperor is shown as a child (a reference to Pedro II, perhaps) led about the streets by adult revelers who constitute his court of page, standard-bearer, musicians, alms collectors, and knights—a parodic image of the royal court made popular and of the king supported by his people. Thus, the illustration reveals an important aspect of Brazilian street life. It identifies the context in which the *vox populi,* with its complex orchestration of parody and norm, is most often heard: the neighborhood street.

Figure 4.18: A Bureaucrat Promenades with his Family. Thus far, we have discussed the street as a domain of extradomestic public life for both the city and the neighborhood—as one in which the restraints, conventions, and mores of the home are relaxed if not removed. But at times the neighborhood street is also an extension of the domestic order of the houses that form its physical frame. The street's façade provides for the interpenetration of public and private spaces at selected points (doors, windows, balconies, etc.), and its space is conceived of as a room like the living room of a house. Just as the façade wall constrains, both literally and especially symbolically, domestic relations from disrupting the freedoms of the street, the immediacy of its contact with the sidewalk facilitates their continuation into public space.

Figure 4.18 illustrates the extension of domestic order and authority into the public space of the neighborhood. It also portrays the space of the street (as well as its façade) as a place for the public display of family fortune. Such extensions of the household into the street occur at specific times: after work, on holidays, and especially on Sundays. Here we see a bureaucrat of "medium fortune" leaving his house with his family for a promenade through the neighborhood. The promenade is a highly ordered affair. Its spatial arrangement is based on, and publically reiter-ates, the domestic ranking of its members. Of course, the size and elegance of the procession are all-important to the family's prestige. "According to the ancient custom observed in this class," Debret (1978: 182) relates that the head of the family "opens the march." In single file, he is fol-lowed by his children, ordered by age (youngest first) and by his wife. After the master's family come the household servants, ranked according to their own authority relations: the bureaucrat's wife is followed by her maid (a more prestigious light-skinned slave), who is followed by the nursemaid, the nursemaid's slave (i.e., the slave of a slave), the master's valet who keeps order at the rear of the column, and two young slaves in their "apprenticeship" phase. Little conversa-tion transpires in single file as the purpose of the procession is a display of family status and not pleasantries. Although such formalities are no longer in fashion, the family promenade and other forms of conventionalized strolling remain important social activities in Brazilian neighborhoods —especially on Sunday afternoons in small cities when the family as a group makes the rounds to the houses of neighboring relatives and close friends. Such extensions of domestic relations into the public space of the community familiar-ize the neighborhood street. They bring into its room the propriety and morality associated with kinship relations. They set limits to the kinds of public behavior the community will tolerate, and these limits serve to distinguish the street life of the residential neighborhood from that of the downtown and the civic square.

important to note that because the façades are flush with the sidewalk, these openings provide a means of direct visual, vocal, and even tactile communication between the two do-mains, as is evident in the exchanges of conversation, food, service, money, and gestures (figs. 4.14, 4.16, 4.17). Thus, the street façade's function is complex: it defines by containment and separation interior and exterior, private and public, house and street (and all that is associated with these contrasting domains of social life) and yet provides for numerous kinds of passages between them.

As a selectively porous divider, therefore, the street façade constitutes a liminal zone of exchange between the domains it holds apart. It not only serves the need to negotiate boundaries, but also stimulates our fascination with liminality in that its passageways are usually marked for special public attention. Apertures are distinguished by the ornaments of carved lintels, entablatures, window frames, and balustrades; by the sign-boards of places of business; and by escutcheons displaying coats of arms and other emblems that announce family status in the public world. As a liminal zone, the street façade is on the one hand the exterior wall of the private domain and on the other the interior wall of the public.

In the latter sense, it defines the space of the street as a room, akin to the living room of a house, which is marked as such by what we might call street furniture. Thus, not only the wall's apertures but also its surfaces are ornamented—by volutes, rosettes, stone drapery, and the like which appear as wall hangings of the public room. A feature typical of interior design that appears on the façade is the wainscot, the lower three feet of an interior wall finished differently from the upper part (figs. 4.16, 4.17). At waist height, the wainscot generally distinguishes the level of sitting in a room from that of standing. On the exterior façade, it functions to emphasize the street's character as a room and also to establish the zone where benches, seats, and tables are either built into the wall or placed on the pavement. The quay wall of the civic square (figs. 4.13, 4.15) was constructed as a two-tiered bench for sitting in the city's most public outdoor room.[8]

Thus far, we have discussed a number of architectural attributes that characterize the street as a domain of public life. The most important attribute is the opposition between the street's frame and its space which the others mediate in a variety of ways. This opposition is itself the basis of a fundamental convention of architectural order that structures the entire cityscape into a coherent and predictable pattern of solids (buildings) and voids (spaces). What is important about this convention for the study of cities is that it organizes the perception of solids and voids into a system of information, a legible code, about what the relations between them signify. In the case of the preindustrial city, this is a system of information about the meanings of public space and private building, and more generally about the articulations between the public and the private domains of city life. This architectural codification of the "brute facts" of perception occurs in two situations: in design, when architects make spaces and objects, defining one in relation to the other; and, in the everyday experience of an architecture already constructed. In both cases, the same perceptual categories are brought into meaningful relation through the conventions of architecture.

4.2 The Solid-Void/Figure-Ground Convention

Conventions are culturally recognized and socially sanctioned relationships between expressions and what these expressions stand for.[9] The conventions of architectural design are the elements of composition codified into norms and prescriptions of information. For example, the plan of a building is a conventional representation in two dimensions of a three-dimensional structure. To knowledgeable readers it contains a code of building instructions and aesthetic relations. The use of classical pediments and columns on building façades is an easily recognized convention: that of quoting from the past as a way of indicating affinities with the idealized virtues of ancient republicanism. In each case, the convention is essentially a principle of difference—two dimensions opposed to three; the past opposed to the present. Architectural legibility, like any other, pivots on this principle: opposition creates a structure of signification capable of being invested with contrasting values, the identity of which history and prevailing ideology determine.

The principal convention of difference ordering the street in both perceptual experience and architectural composition is the organization of its solids and voids into figure and ground relations.[10] We perceive the city street as both a void and a volume of space contained by surrounding solids (fig. 4.19). As a void, it reveals these solids; as a volume it takes the shape of its container. The street thus constitutes a special kind of empty space; it is a void that has a defined shape, usually a rectangular volume. From the context of its containing solids, the street emerges as a distinct and recognizable figure, one which is empty but which has form. We may therefore consider the corridor street as a figural void.

The recognition of a figure requires the presence of a context, its ground, from which it appears to stand out. As studies in Gestalt psychology have shown, the figure stands out because it appears to possess a contour that separates it from the ground (fig. 4.20). As a common boundary between two fields, a contour can appear to shape one field more than the other. The field most shaped by the contour is perceived as the figure; the other is the ground. A figure is therefore a noncontinuous field against which the ground is perceived as a continuous field.[11] In the case of the street, the ground consists of the buildings—or any other visual boundary, such as trees—that give shape to the void. For example, imagine figure 4.20b as a city plan in which the street shown in three dimensions in figure 4.19 is represented in two dimensions as one of the white stripes. From these examples, the pattern is evident: where streets are perceived (and designed) as figural spaces, the buildings surrounding them function as ground. This pattern organizes the experience of urban space in three dimensions and in two, that is, both from the perspective of the person in the street as in figure 4.19 and from that of the plan as in figure 4.20b.

These figure-ground relations present a visual paradox that confirms the character of the street as a room. When buildings are ground to the figural space of the street, their walls must end at the space but paradoxically can have no boundary because the

Fig. 4.19 Giuseppe Zocchi, Uffizi, Florence, 1754

Fig. 4.20 Figure-ground
relations

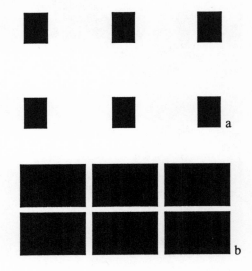

contours belong visually to the figure (the space) and not to the
ground (the wall). In other words, the plane of the façade (its
surface and edges) belongs visually to the space and not to the
wall. The space of the street "steals" the façades of surrounding
walls for its contours. This paradoxical condition creates the
impression that the building façades are the interior walls of an
outdoor room. The traditional architectural solution to this
paradox of the wall that must stop but that has no boundary is
to create a border around it that acts as an area of transition
between figure and ground. This is done by applying ornament
to the wall surface and by framing its edges and openings with
a sidewalk along the bottom edge, a cornice along the top,
pilasters at the sides, and window and door frames around the
apertures (as in figs. 4.17–4.19). In addition to serving as
decoration for the outdoor room, these framing elements have
an important perceptual function: they confirm the figural
character of the street and provide raised surfaces behind which
the wall can comfortably end. They create a border condition in
which their inner edges will be perceived as belonging to the
ground (the wall) and their outer edges to the figure (the street)
as its defining contour.

One of the most significant architectural features of the
solid-void/figure-ground convention is its reversibility: figures
may be either solids or voids, as one is but the negative of the
other. In figure 4.20, consider the blacks as solids and the whites
as voids, and compare figures 4.20a and 4.20b. In the former, the
solids are figural and the voids ground, whereas in the latter
these relations are reversed. Thus, buildings may be perceived
and indeed designed either as ground (as in our previous

example) or as figure (consider a cathedral standing in a square for instance). In sum, solids may constitute the perceptual ground in contrast to which voids emerge as distinctive figures, or voids may constitute the ground in contrast to which solids appear as distinctive figures. There is in all of this a discourse of perception, if you will, between solids and voids and figures and grounds. Each exists only in its relation to the other, forming a structured set of perceptual differences. As the analysis of the street in Ouro Preto will demonstrate, it is the possibility of reversing these differences that give the solid-void/figure-ground convention great semantic utility in distinguishing architecturally the public and the private domains.

The analysis of this street convention has special relevance to the study of the city for a simple reason. Insofar as a circulation system of streets forms the anatomy of a city, its representational structure characterizes the urban order as a whole. This is so because the organization of the city's solids (buildings) and voids (principally streets and squares, but also courtyards) into figure-ground relationships promotes a perceptual order of these relations among the totality of architectural elements (figs. 4.23 and 4.24). Thus, the semantic structure of the street organizes the entire cityscape into a coherent and predictable order. This order serves both architects and inhabitants alike as a system of simple oppositions for elaborating aesthetic, political, and social values, as the comparison of Ouro Preto and Brasília will show.

Architects study this order through an analytical device known as the figure-ground plan. It represents the three dimensional solid-void structure of the city in two dimensions, and architects use it both in evaluation and in design. The plan consists of a blackening or hatching of either the solids or the voids—but typically the solids—to reveal their organization into figure and ground relations (figs. 4.21–4.27). Considering this analytical use, we may say that the solid-void/figure-ground convention has a special status in our investigation: based in the physics of perception, it is both fundamental to the everyday experience of objects and spaces and a convention that specialists use as a means of analysis and design.

When we compare, in approximately the same scale, the figure-ground plan of a typical preindustrial city with that of a modernist city, we make a startling discovery: these simple figure-ground relations produce strikingly *inverse orders of solids and voids* (figs. 4.21 and 4.22). As Rowe and Koetter (1978: 62–63) observe in their study of these Gestalt patterns, the preindustrial city is almost all black in the plan; the modernist almost all white. The former presents a manipulation of defined

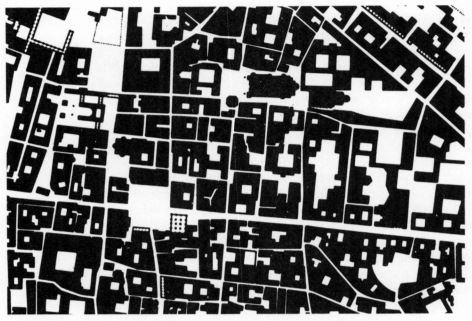

Fig. 4.21 Figure-ground plan of Parma, 1830. Figures 4.21 and 4.22 show approximately the same area (350m × 530m) in the same scale (1:3460). Copyright 1983, The Cornell Journal of Architecture.

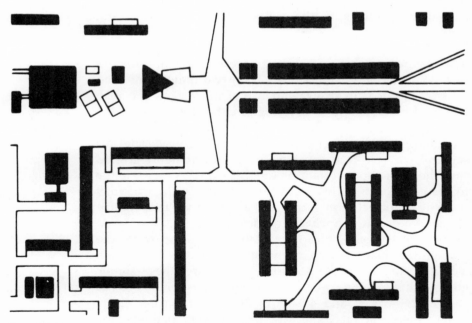

Fig. 4.22 Figure-ground plan of an east-west section of the South Wing, showing residential *superquadras* and commercial sectors, Brasília, c. 1960

voids (streets, squares, and courtyards) in largely unmodulated solids; the latter a manipulation of solids (buildings) in largely unmodulated voids. Each features an entirely different category of figure: in one, space; in the other, object. In the preindustrial city, streets read as figural voids and buildings as continuous ground (figs. 4.21, 4.23, 4.24, and 4.25). In the modernist city, streets appear as continuous void and buildings as sculptural figures (figs. 4.22 and 4.27). In the former, bounded spaces are defined by a solid mass. In the latter, isolated buildings stand free in boundless space.[12]

These comparisons are enormously suggestive about the principles of urban order. They demonstrate that even in supposedly unplanned cities, object-space relations are not produced haphazardly. Rather, they manifest a coherent order, a constructed logic, which is to say, an architectural convention worked out in different historical contexts. Like any other domain of cultural activity, architecture is never in this sense unplanned. There is no such thing, therefore, as the so-called organic or spontaneous city. Those cities which do not result from planners' decisions are only in the most narrow sense unplanned. They are not unordered or even unthought.

Moreover, it should now be evident that the formal conceptualization of the preindustrial city as a solid mass in which the public spaces of streets and squares are figural voids is not unique to the Brazilian cases we are considering. This elemental urban form of solids and voids has had an enduring presence in the occidental experience of city life. The figural street system developed its recognizable Western character as the arena of public commerce and congregation in Greece and her colonies from the fifth century B.C. onward, when especially the square— as an elaboration of the street—appeared as the outdoor forum for the ritual and political affairs of citizenship. It was formalized and carried to Northern Europe by the Romans and, after the eclipse of urbanization during the Dark Ages, again became the prominent form of urban organization as variously embodied in late medieval, Renaissance, and baroque interpretations. During the sixteenth century, the Spanish and the Portuguese transported their colonial version to Latin America, where they established the principal city square as the domain of the most important institutions of church and state (see discussion of fig. 4.13). Thus, in various incarnations and with somewhat different but related political meanings, it has been basic to the physical structure of Mediterranean, Northwestern and Central European, and Latin American cities.[13]

We are, therefore, considering a conception of urban order and a system of representing it that have dominated the Western

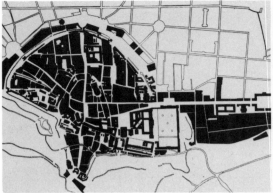

Fig. 4.23 Figure-ground plan of Munich, 1840.
Copyright 1983, The Cornell Journal of Architecture.

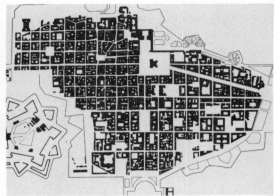

Fig. 4.24 Figure-ground plan of Turin, 1840.
Copyright 1983, The Cornell Journal of Architecture.

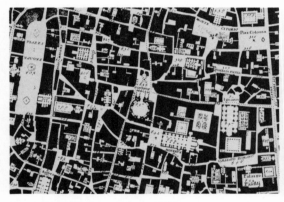

Fig. 4.25 Nolli plan of Rome, 1748

Fig. 4.26 Figure-ground plan of New York, 1930.
Copyright 1983, The Cornell Journal of Architecture.

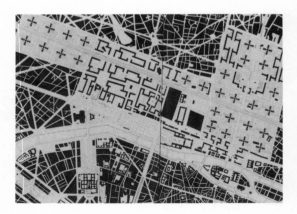

Fig. 4.27 Le Corbusier's Plan Voisin for Paris, 1925.
Figure-ground plan shows existing and proposed
city.

experience of cities without serious challenge for twenty-five hundred years. I am not claiming that this system is somehow a generalized, ahistorical structure of perceptual experience. Rather, I suggest that it is a structure of signification maintained over a very long period of time by professional education and practice in architecture, one with a history of use and value (especially as reinterpreted in early modern Europe) prevailing in the institution of architecture until twentieth-century modernists advanced a radically alternative conception. In the following discussion, therefore, the cities of Ouro Preto and Brasília serve as representative examples, and their comparison as a contextualized instance, of a more global antagonism between opposing conceptions and representations of urban order.

Most important for our purposes, the striking inversions of the modernist and preindustrial figure-ground plans suggest a way of studying the transformation of city and society in terms of the order architecture creates. They suggest that this perceptual order is also an ordering of social relations and practices in the city. As such, architecture constitutes a system of conventions that may be used to stand for something else. What it stands for can only be determined through an ethnographic and historical study of how it is used.

4.3 The Street in Ouro Preto: Private Property and Public Display

During the eighteenth century, the city of Ouro Preto emerged as a center of fabulous gold wealth 600 miles inland from Rio de Janeiro (figs. 4.3, 4.28–4.31). As a result of its riches, it became the capital of Brazil's mining economy in the present-day states of Minas Gerais, Bahia, Goiás, and Mato Grosso. The settlement of the city parallels the growth and decline of its gold production.[14] In 1700, pioneers from São Paulo established a mining camp called Vila Rica de Ouro Preto, 'The Rich Town of Black Gold'. By 1750, the population reached its peak of 95,000 inhabitants, 25,000 of whom lived in the city center and 70,000 in the immediately surrounding *comarca*, 'county'. Slave labor powered the mining economy. In 1796 there were 5.2 nonwhite inhabitants for every white, a ratio giving a rough idea of the master-slave coefficient in the economy. Its major social groups consisted of entrepreneurs with large-scale mining operations, city officials representing the Portuguese Crown, wildcat prospectors and merchants, indentured servants, and slaves.

According to Furtado (1971: 79–82), the Brazilian mining economy afforded people of limited means unusual prospects for wealth and status because it was not an economy based on large mines, but rather on the less capital intensive system of alluvial panning. It was a lucrative situation for all, including the slaves, many of whom managed to work for their own account. As a result, migrants flocked to the new Eldorado. At mid-eighteenth century, gold production and population peaked. Gold output reached 1,770 kilos of refined ore. By 1777, however, production was down to 1,050 kilos, by 1811 to 360 kilos and by 1820 to a mere 120 kilos. From the mid-century high of 95,000 inhabitants, the population declined drastically to 8,000 by 1816, at which level it remained for the next hundred years. With Ouro Preto's mines exhausted, the inhabitants regressed into subsistence agriculture or simply abandoned the city for other promised lands, leaving behind a gold-plated testament to mercantile enterprise.

In its glory, the city displayed its riches in classic fashion: through grand architecture. By the end of the eighteenth century, thirteen major churches, a palatial city hall, state capital, and treasury had been constructed in a blaze of public building projects that—considering the size and isolation of Ouro Preto—rival those of Periclean Athens in conspicuous consumption of vast resources, liturgical splendor, and elaborate celebration of civic accomplishments. Yet, for all its monumental opulence and political prominence, Ouro Preto was also a residential and working city for all classes of inhabitants. How, then, were these two elements of the urban order, the public and the private, architecturally related?

If, in a most general sense, political discourse is about such things as private gain and public good, how does the urban order represent the relationship between the public and the private in a city dominated by the politics of capital accumulation? A detailed analysis of this urban order would have to relate its architectural evolution to the various phases of capital accumulation and consolidation of power: from the collective settlement of a pioneer camp, to the main-street free-for-all of many individual competitors, to the grandiloquent public display of political and financial elites. I shall focus on this final grandiloquent phase of Ouro Preto's development to consider the following question. In Ouro Preto, as in most occidental cities, the private accumulation of wealth is paramount in defining both the physical and the political structure of the city. In what specifically *architectural* ways is private property the source of public order in such a city, and in what ways is wealth represented as civic display in public buildings and monuments?

In cities such as Ouro Preto the solid mass of buildings constitutes the perceptual ground in contrast to which the voids of streets and squares emerge as figures (figs. 4.28 and 4.33). As most private activity occurs inside buildings and most (but not all) public activity occurs in streets and squares, the figure-ground conventions of the street provide a means of distinguishing the two domains. In such cities, the experience of a figural void predictably signals that one is in the public domain, in a street or square; this in turn cues certain kinds of behavioral expectations (figs. 4.28 and 4.31). Similarly, when perceiving an anonymous ribbon of street façades, one knows that these are private properties, unless otherwise informed by a flag or a signboard, for example. The public and private domains are thus distinguished by a simple and legible architectural convention:

$$solid = ground = private$$

$$void = figure = public$$

But, of course, not all buildings are private. How then are public buildings and monuments recognized in terms of this convention? The semantic solution is remarkably simple: the opposition between figure and ground is reversed to signal buildings that are in fact public. These buildings (churches, government institutions, museums, monuments, and the like) are designed not as continuous ground but as sculptural figures (figs. 4.29 and 4.30). They are broken away from the context of private buildings (the solid fabric of the city) through a combination of design strategies. They are generally set in the void of a square or a green that serves as the ground against which they are perceived as monumental figures. Often they are also heavily ornamented, sculpturally massed, and massively scaled. Thus, civic buildings stand out as great public gestures, figures in space, against the surrounding field of more uniform, contiguous, and in this case whitewashed façades. The repetitive forms and massings of these everyday structures constitute the ground out of which monuments to city, nation, God, and private wealth literally arise. The reversal of figure and ground thus provides the architectural means of transforming wealth into public display. In this way, the street code of figure-ground and solid-void conventions systematically relates civic architecture and the architecture of everyday life. In doing so, it presents an extremely simple and legible ordering of the public and private domains.

We can summarize the fundamental architectural structure of public display and private property in Ouro Preto as follows.

Fig. 4.28 Rua Coronel Alves, looking toward the Igreja de Nossa Senhora do Carmo (see figs. 4.29 and 4.30), Ouro Preto, 1980. The street and church are shown in plan in the lower left of figure 4.33.

Fig. 4.29 West elevation of the Igreja de Nossa Senhora do Carmo, Ouro Preto, 1980

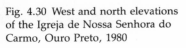

Fig. 4.30 West and north elevations of the Igreja de Nossa Senhora do Carmo, Ouro Preto, 1980

Fig. 4.31 Rua Tiradentes, Ouro Preto, 1980

Fig. 4.32 *Superquadra* apartment block, SQS 108–Block E, Brasília, 1980

In this preindustrial baroque city, both space and building are reversibly both figure and ground. Although space is consistently figure and building ground, these relations are easily reversed to signify public monuments and civic institutions. This reversal of figure and ground is the key rhetorical principle of the architectural discourse—literally a "running back and forth," as the etymology of the word *discourse* suggests— between the public and the private. The ambi-valence of the system loads each element of the figure-ground convention with alternating values:

$$solid = ground = private$$
$$\times$$
$$void = figure = public$$

4.4 The Modernist Inversion

Modernism breaks decisively with this traditional system of architectural signification. Whereas the preindustrial baroque city provides an order of public and private values by juxtaposing architectural conventions of repetition and exception, the modernist city is conceived of as the antithesis both of this mode of representation and of its represented political order. By asserting the primacy of open space, volumetric clarity, pure form, and geometric abstraction, modernism not only initiates a new vocabulary of form, more radically it inverts the entire mode of perceiving architecture. Recognition, the activity of perceiving meanings and relationships, is turned inside out—as if the figural solids of the modernist city had been produced in the mold of the figural voids of preindustrial urbanism (compare figs. 4.31 and 4.32).

Basic to modernism's doctrine of salvation is the elimination of the figural street. This it condemns as the bastion of a corrupt civic order of stagnant public and private values, imposed on the city through an architecture of antiquarian monuments, chaotic streets, decadent ornament, and unsanitary dwellings. Modern architecture eliminates the corridor street by inverting the baroque planning convention of figure and ground and by rupturing its discourse of reversals. A comparison of the figure-ground plans of Ouro Preto and Brasília reveals this inversion clearly (figs. 4.33–4.36). In the modernist city, vast areas of continuous space *without exception* form the perceptual ground against which the solids of buildings emerge as sculptural figures. There is no relief from this absolute division of architectural labor: space is always treated as continuous and never

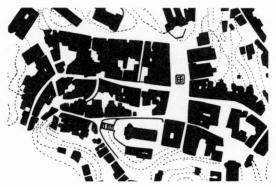

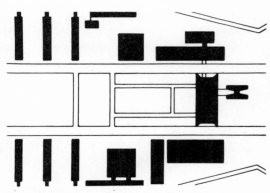

Fig. 4.33 City center, Ouro Preto, 1980. The figure-ground plan of Ouro Preto and the plans of different sectors of Brasília (figs. 4.34–4.36) show approximately the same area (470m × 710m) in the same scale (1:8000).

Fig. 4.34 Monumental Axis, Brasília, 1981

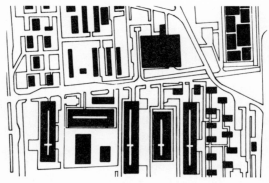

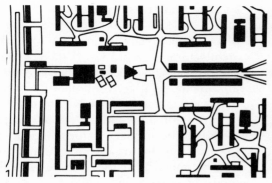

Fig. 4.35 Commercial Sector South, Brasília, 1981

Fig. 4.36 Residential Axis South, Brasília, c. 1960

as figural; buildings always as sculptural and never as background. In the modernist inversion of the figure-ground convention

$$solid = figure\ (never\ ground)$$

$$void = ground\ (never\ figure)$$

The consequences of this inversion are profound. It eliminates the reversals of the traditional code by insisting on the immutability of the terms: by establishing the absolute supremacy of continuous nonfigural void, it transforms the ambivalence of baroque planning into a monolithic spatial order. Reversals are now impossible. In effect, it abandons the discourse of reversals in favor of an uncompromising clarity of function. The perceptual structure of the street in Ouro Preto has thus been doubly

134

inverted in Brasília. On the one hand, the broad avenues of the new city are unsubordinated to any other spatial or volumetric entity. Without architectural containment and without visible destination, they rush past the monumental buildings they isolate in space. On the other hand, as isolated sculpture, *every* building now vies to be recognized as a monument. Each competes for attention, each immortalizes its creator, and each celebrates the "beauty of the speedway" leading people and machines to apparently limitless horizons.

The motivations and consequences of these polemical inversions are essentially of two types. One involves the conventions of architecture, addressing the process of signification itself. The other involves a reevaluation of the social and political values signified. Modern architecture institutes its distinctive mode of recognition by refashioning old conventions into new conceptual devices. The success with which modernism breaks with the past in advancing its claims is in large part due to the simplicity of these formal solutions. By inverting the poles of the traditional oppositions between figure and ground, and neutralizing their reversal, it brings a radical unfamiliarity to an architectural code *the terms and values of which we already know.* It retains the terms of the baroque "argument" (i.e., solid, void, figure, ground) but presents them with a different logic so as to bring their established values (i.e., public, private) under new scrutiny. By holding the terms constant but defamiliarizing their relations, the modern code explicitly exposes the process of architectural signification, that is, the process of investing empirical categories (the terms) with significance. In the strange steel-and-glass landscape of the modern city, the inverted figures and displaced voids call attention to themselves as convention. They shock us into an awareness of the process of saying something about something in stone, of inscribing social values in an architectural code. Thus, through inversion, neutralization, and defamiliarization, modern architecture deliberately lays bare its own devices and intentions for restructuring our perception.

Yet, it does more than just unmask convention. Having exposed the process of inscribing social discriminations in architecture, it attempts to efface the inscription and to write a new one in which private property in real estate is no longer a source of public order, and traditional discriminations between the two no longer the focus of architectural comment and convention. If architectural inscription in capitalist cities constitutes a discourse (in the sense of a going back and forth) between "public figures" and "private ground," the modern project is therefore nothing less than the total transformation of this civic discourse in which the very distinctions between the public and the private disappear.[15]

How is such erasure possible? Modernism's power as a conquering vision results from its ability to translate its objectives for a new institutional order into simple conventions of architectural defamiliarization. These conventions impose a totality of perceptions in which identification of the public and the private cannot be made, and in which—in theory—a way of life based on such discriminations is therefore negated. In large measure, this semantic erasure is a direct and unavoidable consequence of eliminating the figural street through the inversion of the figure-ground convention. In the ideal modern city where *all* buildings are figures, the code of recognizing public institutions as *exceptional* figures in the common ground is rendered irrelevant. Public institutions are reduced, paradoxically, to sculptural anonymity: as sculptural objects in a vast field of sculptural objects, they are indistinguishable. Thus, the efficacious reversals of the traditional code have now become a semantic impossibility. If we know that all buildings are not private, yet cannot distinguish which are public, the old architectural convention for discriminating between the public and the private is effectively invalidated.

4.5 Transforming Civic Discourse: The New Public of Brasília

The modern city that emerges from these transformations is in theory an entirely public city. Its utopian design eliminates private property in real estate as an institutional basis of urban order for both family and civic life. However, as the public is defined in relation to the private, the elimination of the latter does not leave the former unchanged. Therefore, the modernist city features a new kind of public domain. The example of Ouro Preto suggested that the type of urban order whose basic unit is an opposition between public street and private building expresses a type of political order that is grounded in preindustrial capitalist relations between public affairs and private interests. If, in this sense, urban order is a concretization of political order, what kind of public city is the one that eliminates private realty?

In Brasília's Master Plan, the city's architecture and organization constitute an argument for egalitarianism:

> The four-by-four grouping of the superblocks will, while favoring the coexistence of social groups, avoid any undue and undesired stratification of society. And, in any case,

variations in the standard of living from one superblock to another will be offset [*neutralizadas,* in original] by the organization of the urban scheme itself and will not be of such a nature as to affect that degree of social comfort to which all members of society have a right. (Costa 1957: art. 17)

The egalitarian discourse thus maintains that the architectural conventions themselves ("the four-by-four grouping," "the urban scheme itself," and others developed in the Master Plan) will produce a communitarian political order. The city is to belong "to the people" (a category which originally included ministers of the government and their chauffers living in the same superblock) regardless of socioeconomic differences. As an inscription in space, all of the city's buildings and all of its spaces are to signify the public good. By eliminating market competition and profit from architecture, state-sponsored total design intends that collective and not private enterprise will generate this public good. Where there is to be little profit from city-building and where all construction must be referred to a Master Plan, an inequitable distribution of urban amenities will not occur. Moreover, where all buildings are monuments to this plan, class domination will not be able to mystify itself in the form of individual monuments to profit and privilege which dissimulate the private conquest of the public realm.[16] Instead, the totality of Brasília will be a monument to the collective efforts of master planning and to the state, which sponsors it. Thus, the Master Plan—"the urban scheme itself"—stands behind the new secular order as its motivation and ultimate reference. As the plan speaks through architecture, the city itself becomes the oracle of its egalitarian intentions.

To understand the nature of Brasília's new public, we shall look at what has taken the place of the old street and its public domain. The modernist alternative is the "local commercial sector," intended to provide the same commercial services as the traditionally mixed residential-commercial street and square (examples of which can be seen in figs. 4.1, 4.8, 4.16, and 4.31). We shall consider the initial concept of the commercial sector, its evolution, and, most important, its reception by Brasilienses since the city's inauguration in 1960.

Nowhere in Costa's plan does the word *rua*, 'street', appear. We can, therefore, assume that its absence is deliberate and corresponds to the elimination both of the concept of the street and of the physical fact itself.[17] The Plano Piloto (map 5.2) is organized around the crossing of two "radial arteries": super-speedways called the Residential-Highway Axis and the Monumental Axis. The former encompasses 14 contiguous traffic lanes. These are divided into center lanes for fast traffic and side lanes for local traffic. The side lanes connect to the residential units on either side through ramps, underpasses, and cloverleaf interchanges. While somewhat less symphonic in traffic flow, the Monumental Axis features 8 lanes, 4 in each direction, separated by the enormous Esplanade of the Ministeries.[18] Neither axis has a single traffic light or stop-and-go intersection, for the objective of this circulatory scheme is the "unimpeded flow of traffic through the central and residential sectors" (Costa 1957: art. 7). That this objective will result from the elimination of streets is a basic contention of the plan: in article three, Costa defines its *idée maîtresse* as the application of "the free principles of highway engineering—*including the elimination of intersections* [i.e., street corners]—to the technique of urban planning" (emphasis added).[19]

On either side of the Residential Axis, Costa (ibid., art. 16) interpolates a ranked series of *vias*, 'ways', today numbered L1 to L5 and W1 to W5, to serve the residential superblocks. The plan calls for *faixas*, 'bands', of community facilities and local commerce, alternately intersecting these service ways, to be developed between the *superquadras*. Each band of commerce, called a "local commercial sector," is reached by a *via de acesso motorizado*, 'motorized access way'—a choice of terms carefully and consistently avoiding any reference to "street."

In fact, Costa's original proposal (art. 16; fig. 4.37) assiduously denies any reference to the old marketplace: store entrances and display windows are to front onto the *superquadras* and not the accessways. Thus, the scheme links commerce and residence by way of the arcadian park of each superblock and not the "dirty, hazardous street." The latter is architecturally segregated and restricted to functions of vehicular supply, access, and parking. With unflappable faith in the power of words and architecture to change the world, the Master Plan transforms the age-old institutions of the marketplace and the market street into a "commercial sector" and a "motorized service way."

The absence of the word *street* in the plan is thus prophetic: it reveals an attempt to dismantle the traditional urban market by reordering relations of commerce and residence, pedestrians and transport. However, it is more than simple lexical proscription which eliminates the market street from Brasília. The street has also been transformed architecturally from a figure carved out of a solid mass into an unbounded throughway. It is no longer recognizable as a figural void in a discourse of figure-ground relations. The serviceways of Brasília can only be perceived as asphalt strips catering to the needs of machines in motion. They bear no relation to the street as a socializing space for pedestrians. Similarly, the marketplace has been architecturally reconceived as a single building, a sculptural block, which is to say, a figural object in the void—or, in the words of Lúcio Costa (1957: art. 16), "a single body only" set out starkly against the trees on one side and against the service access on the other. This reconceptualization of the commercial street effects a fundamental change in the relationship between urban commerce and residence. For Costa's plan accomplishes a radical functional differentiation of commercial space and thereby of exchange: streets have become entirely identified with the functions of transport and supply; distribution with detached buildings.

Having considered the prehistory of the "street" in Brasília, it is revealing to see how Brasilienses have responded to its elimination. The commercial sector developed in three phases. These correspond to the major division of the city into Asa Sul (South Wing) and Asa Norte (North Wing), the former constructed well before the latter, which still remains incomplete. In the first phase, the commercial sectors of the South Wing were built according to plan (figs. 4.37 and 4.38). However, the antistreet conception of these sectors proved untenable: in defiance of the Master Plan, the residents rejected it. Some planners argue that because the city was unfinished at the time of its inauguration, the total vision could not be implemented, let alone appreciated. However, the true explanation for the plan's failure is perhaps less apocalyptic. The first inhabitants of Brasília's *superquadras* simply rejected the antistreet because it contradicted social practice. Constituting a cross-section of the bureaucracy, these settlers were predominantly from urban Brazil, where the street is the focus of public activity.[20] As people accustomed to the bustle of the street, they quickly grasped and repudiated the radical intentions of the Master Plan. They refused the proposed garden entrances of the commercial units and converted the service backs into store fronts (fig. 4.39). Associated with sidewalks, traffic, and *movimento*, the original backs were perceived as customary areas of exchange and sociality. As a result, habit reproduced the street in practice where it had been architecturally denied.

To this day, the garden sides of most of the commercial units in Asa Sul remain undeveloped (fig. 4.40). The result is what one might call a front-back problem. Reversal has returned but in the form of confusion. Façades obviously designed as fronts are masked by storage crates, locked gates, and general neglect. Although some stores "solve" the problem by constructing two entrances, the one on the "street" always reads as the front door. The reinversion has thus been complete. Although the

Fig. 4.37 Lúcio Costa's original proposal for a prototypical local commercial sector, from the Master Plan of Brasília, 1957

Fig. 4.38 Local Commercial Sector 102 South, Brasília, 1980

Fig. 4.39 Store "fronts" of Local Commercial Sector 108 South, Brasília, 1980

Fig. 4.40 Store "backs" of Local Commercial Sector 308 South, Brasília, 1980

street itself had been architecturally denied and remains legally proscribed in Brasília (as city ordinances based on the Master Plan establish uniform heights, setbacks, openings, displays, etc.), the inhabitants of Asa Sul resuscitated its semantic code. They put their shops back on the street in contact with curbs and traffic. Not surprisingly, the signs of the popular street reappeared: mixed-up functions (cars and people), uncoordinated signs, colors, and displays, window-shopping, sidewalk socializing, loitering, and even littering. The riot of urban codes reasserted itself in spite of the best attempts yet devised to prevent it.

However, both the extent and the effectiveness of this rebellious revival are limited at best. First and most important, Brasília does not have a genuine system of streets. Therefore, any attempt to recreate one is doomed to relative isolation within the totality—in this case, limited to the older commercial sectors of Asa Sul. Second, officialdom was not pleased with this turn of events. One administrator claimed that the popular street code reemerged because the central planning agency, Novacap, was unable to effect total control over commercial development (interview, October 1980). He argued that because of an initial lack of financial resources, Novacap could not develop the commercial sectors as coordinated wholes. Instead, it was forced to contract individually. The absence of a "guiding hand" led to uncontrolled development and competition among proprietors, with the resulting street riot of signs and symbols. Faith in "total design" was not easily discouraged, however, and the government resolved to give it a second chance in the construction of Asa Norte.

The design of commercial units in the north appears as an attempt to preclude by architectural and legal means a recurrence of the kind of street behavior that "deformed" the southern units (fig. 4.41). Each local commercial sector is now broken up into separate pavilions standing 30–50 feet apart. Each pavilion is composed as a two-story cubic loggia having two or three shops per side below and offices above. The second story protrudes over the first, creating a perimeter arcade tucked well into the body of the building. Their square plan somewhat resolves the front-back problem of Asa Sul by allowing shops to occupy all sides of the structure. Equilateral symmetry thus solves the problem by turning each side into a front.

In the new solution, however, the pavilions have also been pulled back about 25 feet from the curb and constructed several feet above street grade. One must now traverse a flight of stairs to reach each one. The sidewalk, that traditional ribbon of social exchange, has now been irretrievably severed from the street, broken into discrete lengths, and wrapped around each pavilion as an arcade. While it might be argued that these arcades simply replace the sidewalk with a protected passage, their effects are quite different. On the one hand, protection is actually minimal. On the other, this design precludes the possibility of street life by severing the street from the place of exchange. It eliminates sidewalk contact between the two and considers each separately, demoting the street to the single function of transport and sequestering all commerce into self-contained, detached mini-malls. In the absence of a continuous sidewalk edged with façades, not only is "strolling down the avenue" impossible, but moreover the urban *flâneur* is now confronted with extinction.

Recently, city officials unveiled the "final solution" to neighborhood shopping in the modern city, inaugurating the third phase of local commercial development in Brasília (fig. 4.42). Twenty years late, Local Commercial Sector 205/206 North finally and totally realizes the ultimate projections of the Master

Fig. 4.41 Local Commercial Sector 204 North, Brasília, 1980

Plan. Conceived as a totality and constructed as a single megastructure, it represents "the way all of Brasília was supposed to have been built" in the words of one city administrator (interview, March 1981). Not surprisingly, the official media presents it as a model of urban development. As the architects and planners of the building explained, it represents a "return to the principles of the Master Plan" (interview, March 1981). It is deliberately designed to pull all shopping activity away from the "street" and "return" it to the sides facing the *superquadras*. No longer conceived as a simple block of stores or even as discrete pavilions, the project engulfs the entire site, on both sides of the road, into one palatial structure.

Locally referred to as Babylonia, 205/206 North is a veritable palace of consumption: a ziggurat *qua* mall complete with arched windows, roof terraces, scissor ramps, labyrinthine corridors lined with expensive shops and play areas for the toddlers of Brasília's new elite. As a final solution, it eliminates beyond doubt, recall, or even memory all traces of the traditional shopping street. With its stores internalized into the bowels of the building, the mall's façades appear as high, blank white

Fig. 4.42 Local Commercial Sector 205/206 North, called Babylonia, Brasília, 1980

walls, above and behind which the arched windows of the internal corridors rise. To let the road pass through it, the structure divides in half, turning the public accessway into a speedway connector. Parking is no longer available along the accessway but is relegated to the sides of the structure. A landscaped mini-lawn replaces the sidewalk, leaving hazardously little space for pedestrians to walk between the building's flanks and the road. Perhaps having realized that there are so few pedestrians in Brasília, architects have simply ceased making traditional gestures to them—like store windows and sidewalks.

As if to confirm the architectural elimination of the street in Brasília, Brasilienses do not use the word *rua* in address terminology. Using the city's impeccably rational address system, they say, for example: *na Comercial 103 Sul*, 'in the Commercial [Sector] 103 South', and *na SQS 407*, 'in Superquadra South 407'. The one exception proves the case: Local Commercial Sector 107/108 South is commonly referred to as the Rua da Igrejinha, 'The Street of the Little Church' (fig. 4.43). It is named after the only recognized landmark in the residential areas of the city, the

Fig. 4.43 Local Commercial Sector 107/108 South, called the Street of the Little Church, looking toward the Little Church of Fátima, Brasília, 1980. Compare with figure 4.28.

Igrejinha de N. S. de Fátima, 'The Little Church of Our Lady of Fátima'. Designed by Oscar Niemeyer, it was the first church constructed in the city. Although there are many other churches, two striking Buddhist temples, and other exceptional structures (like mammoth supermarkets) in other commercial sectors, only the Igrejinha is considered enough of a landmark to be immortalized as a street name in the public memory.

The reason for its commemoration is obvious in light of our analysis of the preindustrial street: from the perspective of the shopping sector (as in the illustration), the church is perceived in relation to its context according to the rules of traditional and not modern urbanism. It is in fact the only instance in Brasília of a traditional figure-ground relation between a public monument and a public street. Urbanistically, it follows the model of churches in cities like Ouro Preto (compare figs. 4.43 and 4.28): it crowns the street leading to it as a figural object set in a defined void. Thus, in relation to its commercial sector, the design of the Little Church of Fátima recapitulates the monument-street complex of preindustrial cities, and, for a moment, the public memory of it.

FIVE

Typologies of Order, Work, and Residence

To those familiar with the apparent disorder of other cities, in Brazil or elsewhere, Brasília presents the radically unfamiliar view of total urban order. The Master Plan creates order by organizing city life in terms of several basic proposals. I analyzed one of these proposals in the preceding chapter, that of replacing the street and its system of public spaces with a new system of traffic circulation. The all-figural city that results features a new and total order of parts, one comprehensively structured by the bureaucratic state. How does the Master Plan, on behalf of the state, organize this city of objects? In this chapter, I shall evaluate its proposals to structure Brasília in terms of the modernist functions of work and residence. These proposals are three: (1) to organize the city into exclusive and homogeneous zones of activity based on a predetermined typology of urban functions and building forms; (2) to concentrate the function of work in relation to dispersed dormitory settlements; and (3) to institute a new type of residential architecture and organization based on the concept of the *superquadra*. My objectives in this evaluation are several. They are first to question the conceptualization of city life in terms of functions and zones; second, to provide an ethnographic description of the organization of zones, focusing on those of work and residence; and third, to analyze the motivations and consequences of this organization.

These objectives necessarily entail somewhat different methods of analysis for each proposal. The concept of zoned functions needs to be evaluated both in terms of the organization of the preindustrial city it replaces and in terms of its own logic in relating form and function. The spatial organization of work must be understood in terms of the local economy of the Federal District. This contextualization demands a survey of the type and distribution of available jobs in order to reveal the consequences of separating the place of work from the place of residence in the modernist city. While this examination focuses on actual conditions of work in the Federal District, the analysis of the concept of the *superquadra* first requires that we focus on the ideal model of residential organization developed between 1957 and 1960. It further requires that we differentiate between various components of the ideal: between the architectural model as proposed in Costa's Master Plan and initially embodied in Niemeyer's buildings, and the government's model of how the *superquadras* would be occupied. In this chapter, we shall consider the architectural model and in part 3 the government's. Although I use various methods to analyze these proposals, I evaluate how the people of Brasília interpret each.

5.1 Zoning the City: A Typology of Form and Function

The preindustrial Brazilian city is typically organized into three or four domains of institutional influence, that is, areas of the city in which the affairs of one institution or another dominate daily activities. These domains are distinguished by a customary spatial distribution of urban institutions, one established at the outset of colonization and based on Iberian models. Thus, the principal institutions of church and state occupy a pivotal square (*a praça*), those of commerce, finance, and light manufacturing are in a central area around it (*o centro*), and those of residence surround these (*os bairros residenciais*). Sometimes, an additional domain of recreation is important in the spatial conception of the city, such as the municipal park or the beach in Rio de Janeiro (but here the beach is less important as a preserve of nature within the city than as a domain of sociality similar to that of the public square). Thus, the municipal square, the downtown, and the residential neighborhood are both spatial categories and domains of predictable social activities, distinguished in both instances by virtue of their landmark institutions.

Although these categories are conceptually distinct in terms of the characteristic institutions to which they refer, they are not mutually exclusive in terms of either activities or institutions. Fundamental to preindustrial urban organization is the heterogeneity of functions, activities, and institutions in all areas of the city. Thus, municipal squares and downtowns are also places of residence for certain classes of people. Similarly, residential neighborhoods are usually organized around small squares which reiterate on a local scale the institutional organization of the municipal square: they feature parish churches, headquarters of neighborhood social and political associations, and houses of prominent members of the community. Moreover, residential neighborhoods always support a variety of commercial establishments—typically on the ground floor of houses—for the everyday needs of the community. Although small cities often do not have a commercial center distinct from a municipal square, the terms *o centro* and *a praça* are, nevertheless, used in different situations to refer to different aspects and expectations about the same place.

Similarly, in those cities where spatial distinctions based on industrial class relations have arisen, the actual experience of the city is still one of a mixing of classes in most areas. Thus, although such oppositions as "center and periphery" (São Paulo), "city and suburb" (Rio de Janeiro, Recife), and "South Zone and North Zone" (Rio de Janeiro) differentiate areas of relative wealth and poverty, all classes have neighborhoods *within* these cities. Moreover, wealthy neighborhoods are often immediately contiguous with poor ones, and in the most dramatic examples of the spatial proximity of socially distant strata, the poorest (illegal but often permanent) squatter communities are found inside middle-class districts. While Brazilian cities are historically differentiated into several domains of institutional influence, the experience of each, and the quality of its daily life, are a heterogeneous mix of functions, activities, institutions, and classes.

Unlike its precursors in the nineteenth century, modernist planning homogenizes this preindustrial heterogeneity into exclusive "sectors" of "urban functions." It achieves uniformity in the structure and configuration of its sectors by reconceiving city organization in a number of ways. To rethink the city, to destroy the past and begin anew, it turns preindustrial urban order inside out by eliminating the street system of circulation. Producing a new type of cityscape with this inversion, it attempts to preclude class-based spatial differentiations through the agencies of total planning and architectural standardization. Having eliminated discriminations between public space and private building as a basis of urban order, it organizes its city of objects on the basis of a concept of zoned functions.

We may define zoning as the correlation, or typologizing, of social activities, building forms, and planning conventions. Modernist architecture redefines each of these elements and develops their classification as an instrument both of social transformation and of the rational organization of daily life transformed. It classifies urban social activities into the four functions of housing, work, recreation, and traffic, at times adding a fifth function termed the "public core of administrative and civic affairs." However, the fifth is never well defined, and its problematic status will become significant in our evaluation of modernist planning. Correlated with this typology of urban social life is a classification of building types and spatial conventions—the apartment block raised on columns, the office building, the transparent façade, the free plan, and the like—a correlation motivated by the idea that a new physical environment will create new types of association and habit. Thus, the typologies of modernist master planning are not only total in the sense that they impose a totally planned city. They are also totalizing in the sense that the new architecture always refers to some aspect of the new society; that is, the classification of form always refers to the classification of function.

The purpose of a master plan is therefore to achieve a rationally structured homology between social-functional and architectural-formal organizations. The zone is the basic unit of such a structure and is conceived of as a single correlation of function and form, for example, of housing and the *superquadra*. As the zone is its conceptual unit, the sector is its unit of spatial organization. Ideally, each zone is comprised of a single sector, or area, of the city. Thus, the place of work is separated from the place of residence. Where zones must mesh, as with traffic circulation, every effort is made to keep the activities of each as independent as possible. Therefore, pedestrians are given one system of circulation and cars another. As each of the basic urban functions comprehends numerous types of activities, each zone is subdivided. Each subdivision of activity, with its assigned architectural form, is given a separate, self-contained sector within the encompassing zone. Thus, within the housing zone, there is one sector for actual residence (the *superquadra*) and one for local commerce. Ideally, each sector within the city has a unitary definition, based on a single correlation of form and function. It is this uncompromising rationality in the planning of its parts that gives the modernist city the quality of total and totalizing order.

When we turn to the case of Brasília, there is an additional factor that increases its totalizing aspect: all of its sectors are organized into a single architectural and schematic image, that of a great cross of speedways. The cross is the most encompassing correlation of form and function. It serves both as the organizational spine for the distribution of social functions and building forms and as the symbol of the city's total organization. Thus, Brasília's planning achieves total order through two types of totalizations: by typologizing social functions, building types, and spatial conventions, and by subsuming the distribution of social and architectural typologies into a single urban form.

Advocates of this kind of total urban order commonly argue that its rationality increases the legibility of the city's plan and thus inhabitants' knowledge of the city. We may therefore note at this point the way in which Brasília's typologies of order affect both abstract and practical orientation. As we might expect, its total order inverts the problems of orientation associated with other cities. It increases the legibility of the whole but decreases that of its parts, producing a peculiar set of navigational dilemmas. Most cities are not identified with a total shape. They present a nonfigural conglomeration of sprawling districts within which, however, individual neighborhoods are identified by distinctive landmarks of one kind or another (including place names which are temporal markers of personages and events in the collective memory). The idiosyncracies of place are memorable in these cities and therefore crucial in one's knowledge of them. In contrast, Brasilienses understand Brasília as a single, legible image—commonly read as a cross, an airplane, or a bird—composed of neighborhood units that with very few exceptions they find uniform, undistinguishable, and land-markless.[1]

When one asks them for directions, for example, they will inevitably reckon by the whole first, describing the cross in some fashion and then locating the desired point within it. Or, they will simply give the address, which again depends on a knowledge of the whole. Both modes of reckoning are entirely abstract. Indeed, it is almost impossible to give practical directions because there are very few memorable reference points. Moreover, people can't say "go to the corner and turn at the light." In such a situation, even long-time residents regularly have difficulty finding the location of a place even though they grasp it in their mental map of the whole city and have been to it many times. Thus, while the typologies of total order produce an unusual, abstract awareness of the plan, practical knowledge of the city actually decreases with the imposition of systemic rationality.

This disjunction between abstract knowledge and practical experience is exacerbated by the impeccably rational address system, which confronts people with an entirely new vocabulary to describe urban location. What was once a street address in Rio de Janeiro like Rua Montenegro 87 becomes in Brasília an apartment address of such complex denotation as SQS 106–F–504. Even after one knows what it means, which in the abstract depends on seven different discriminations of information, it helps very little in correlating a sense of real place with its position on the mental map of the whole, or even in actually finding the apartment. The address system is especially disastrous in the commercial sectors. Not only do Brasilienses have difficulty remembering the exact location of shops in look-alike blocks (what is the memorable difference between CLS 403–A–33 and CLS 405–A–33?) but the merchants, too, exhibit their ambivalence toward the system by idiosyncratically using different versions of the code in their advertisements.[2]

Further investigation into this new vocabulary of orientation reveals that Brasilienses also encounter a bewildering array of sector abbreviations: the telephone directory lists 70 unpronounceable acronyms such as SQS, CLN, QL, HCGN, and MSPW (fig. 5.1). These are universally used in place names and address codes, for there are no other available designations short of writing out the entire phrase. In sum, Brasilienses confront not only a correlation of form and function based on an unfamiliar logic, but an equally strange language to describe it. As a result, the total order of Brasília may increase their abstract knowledge of the plan, but it also alienates them from their own experiences of it.

Map 5.1 illustrates the functional organization of this total order in relation to the axial plan: the function of work concentrated in sectors along the Monumental Axis, that of housing along the Residential Axis, and that of recreation surrounding both axes.[3] Corresponding to this typology of functions, the Master Plan (arts. 9–11 and 23) proposes to give each axis, and each major sector within them, distinguishing architectural and spatial characteristics. According to Costa (1962: 343–45), these are determined by a typology of shapes and by a set of scales— the residential, the monumental, the gregarious, and the bucolic. The planner's intention is to differentiate the functions of the city's figural buildings by assigning different shapes and patterns of shapes to each sector. In the previous chapter, I demonstrated that in terms of the basic logic of the plan (i.e., the solid-void/figure-ground relations) such differentiation is semantically inefficacious: regardless of their sector, the buildings are all freestanding objects, and as such they are all monumental. At most, we may say that the sectors of the Monumental Axis are designed to make some of their monumental objects appear even more monumental (in the sense of being the most conspicuous, dramatic, and exceptional gestures in a field of exceptional gestures), while the sectors of the Residential Axis are only less so. This paradox of anonymous monumentality suggests that Costa's intended correlation of form and function is spurious if its purpose is to differentiate function in terms of form.

What it suggests instead is that the correlation modernism makes between form and function is most fundamentally based on equivalence rather than difference. It applies the same formal conception of object as figure to buildings destined for different use and applies the same strategies of defamiliarization to different functions (such as the use of the transparent façade in both the office building and the apartment block). This uniform application reduces the perception and the experience of differ-

Abreviaturas de Logradouros

CH	– Chácara		SCS	– Setor Comercial Sul
CLN	– Comercial Local Norte		SDN	– Setor Diversões Norte
CLS	– Comercial Local Sul		SDS	– Setor Diversões Sul
CRN	– Comercial Residencial Norte		SEN	– Setor de Embaixadas Norte
CRS	– Comercial Residencial Sul		SEPN	– Setor de Edifícios Públicos Norte
EPCL	– Estrada Parque Ceilândia		SEPS	– Setor de Edifícios Públicos Sul
EPCT	– Estrada Parque Ceilândia Taguatinga		SES	– Setor de Embaixadas Sul
EPDB	– Estrada Parque Dom Bosco		SGAN	– Setor de Grandes Áreas Nortes
EPIA	– Estrada Parque Indústria e Abastecimento		SGAS	– Setor de Grandes Áreas Sul
EPTG	– Estrada Parque Taguatinga Guará		SGO	– Setor Garagens Oficiais
EQN	– Entrequadras Norte		SGTC	– Setor de Garagens de Transportes Coletivos
EQS	– Entrequadras Sul		SHIN	– Setor Habitacional Individual Norte
HCE	– Habitacional Coletiva Econômica (Cruzeiro Novo)		SHIS	– Setor Habitacional Individual Sul
HCGN	– Habitacional Coletiva Geminada Norte		SHLN	– Setor Hospitalar Local Norte
HIGN	– Habitacional Individual Geminada Norte		SHLS	– Setor Hospitalar Local Sul
HIGS	– Habitacional Individual Geminada Sul		SHN	– Setor Hoteleiro Norte
IAS	– Indústria e Abastecimento Sul		SHS	– Setor Hoteleiro Sul
MLN	– Mansões do Lago Norte		SHTN	– Setor Hotéis de Turismo Norte
MSPW	– Mansões Suburbanas Park Way		SHTS	– Setor Hotéis de Turismo Sul
MUDB	– Mansões do Lago Sul		SI	– Setor Inflamáveis
PLL	– Posto Lavagem e Lubrificação		SIA	– Setor Indústria e Abastecimento
QI	– Quadra Interna		SIG	– Setor Indústrias Gráficas
QL	– Quadra do Lago		SMHN	– Setor Médico Hospitalar Norte
RES	– Residencial Econômico Sul (Cruzeiro Velho)		SMHS	– Setor Médico Hospitalar Sul
RESCL	– Residencial Econômico Sul (Comércial Local)		SMU	– Setor Militar Urbano
SAAN	– Setor Armazenagem e Abastecimento Norte		SPMS	– Setor de Postos e Motéis Sul
SAAS	– Setor Armazenagem e Abastecimento Sul		SPN	– Setor Policial Norte
SAIN	– Setor Áreas Isoladas Norte		SPS	– Setor Policial Sul
SAIS	– Setor Áreas Isoladas Sul		SQN	– Super Quadra Norte
SAN	– Setor Autarquias Norte		SQS	– Super Quadra Sul
SAS	– Setor Autarquias Sul		SRES	– Setor Residencial Econômico Sul
SBN	– Setor Bancário Norte		SRIA	– Setor Residencial Indústria
SBS	– Setor Bancário Sul			e Abastecimento (Guará)
SCEN	– Setor de Clubes Esportivos Norte		SRTN	– Setor Rádio e Televisão Norte
SCES	– Setor de Clubes Esportivos Sul		SRTS	– Setor Rádio e Televisão Sul
SCN	– Setor Comercial Norte			

Outras Abreviações Utilizadas

acamp	— Acampamento	Entr	— Entrada	Planalt	— Planaltina
Aer	— Aeroporto	Escr	— Escritório	Pç	— Praça
ap	— Apartamento	Espl Minist	. Esplanada dos	Proj	— Projeção
Av	— Avenida		Ministérios	Q	— Quadra
bca	— Banca	fds	— Fundos	Res	— Residência
bl	— Bloco	Gal	— Galeria	r	— Residencial
Brazl	— Brazlândia	lj	— Loja	s	— Sala
c.	— Casa	lt	— Lote	Sobr	— Sobradinho
Ceil	— Ceilândia	merc	— Mercado	slj	— Sobreloja
Ch	— Chácara	mód	— Módulo	s/s	— Subsolo
cj	— Conjunto	NB	— Núcleo	Tag	— Taguatinga
Ed	— Edifício		Bandeirante	Tr	— Trecho
		Pal	— Palácio		
		Pq	— Parque		

Fig. 5.1 Listing of place names and abbreviations from Brasília's telephone directory, 1981

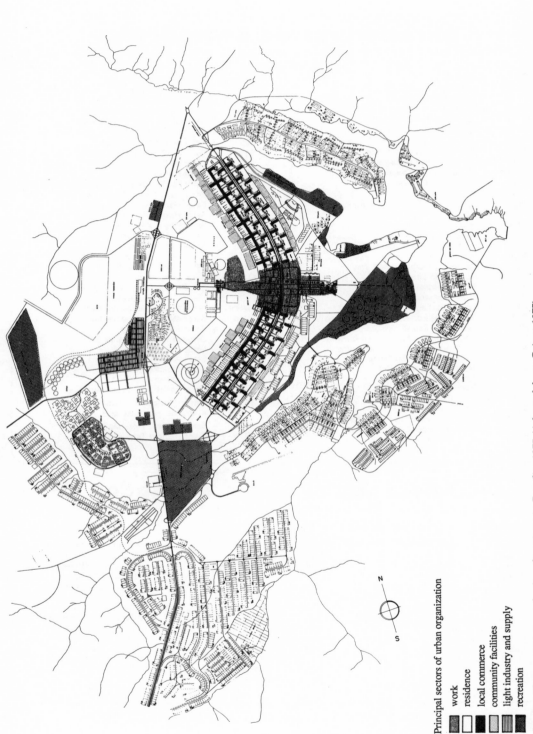

Principal sectors of urban organization

work
residence
local commerce
community facilities
light industry and supply
recreation

Map 5.1 The organization of urban functions in Brasília, 1975 (Adapted from Geipot 1975)

ence in form and, significantly, in function: the formal equivalence of all the buildings in the various sectors implies an
equivalence among their functions as well. It is the merging, the
homogenization, and not the differentiation, of function that
residents experience in the city's architecture. Brasilienses especially note, and dislike, the merging of the functions of work
and residence—a complaint directed primarily at the *superquadras* that Congresssman Ulysses Guimarães, president of the
opposition party during the years of military rule, epitomizes
when he observes that "no one likes to sleep in the office" (*Veja*,
18 April 1984, p. 37).

This reduction of difference derives from two sources. On the
one hand, as we have seen, modernist ideology sets out to
reduce architectural discriminations as a means of reducing
social discriminations. This correlation is based on the vision of
an egalitarian society in which status differences traditionally
associated with the private domain of family and residence do
not determine an individual's rights to the city and in which
these rights are instead determined by new collective identities
based on work—which is to say, ultimately on affiliation in the
institutions of the bureaucratic state. This transformation entails
a collectivization of residence that we shall discuss later. As this
collectivization is in turn based on work, it is not surprising that
Brasilienses experience a deep penetration of the roles and
identities of work into residential life (hence Guimarães's observation). As we shall consider in the next chapter, the federal
government's initial organization of residence in Brasília actually accomplished what modernist theory proposed: it distributed the apartments on the basis of work affiliations. Thus,
there appeared in Brasiliense society an *equivalence* of the principles on which the functions of work and residence were
organized—that the architecture both helped create and also
reflected and reinforced. While the functions remained spatially
separate, their organizational principles appeared similar.

This formal and functional equivalence reveals a number of
basic contradictions both in the planners' intentions and in the
means by which they sought to realize them. On the one hand,
if the intention of the modernist concept of zoned functions is to
differentiate function by form, then we must conclude that in a
city of figural objects the concept fails. It remains an illusion
created on paper, on a blueprint in which different sectors are
drawn in different colors and labeled "residence," "work,"
"recreation," and so on. In terms of the most basic object-space
relations, there is in fact nothing different in the treatment of
these sectors. Hence, the overwhelming sense of monotony and
sameness that Brasilienses experience in the city.[4]

On the other hand, if the intention of the concept of zoned functions is to reduce differences between the principles on which various functions are organized—which amounts to equating the functions of urban life uniformly for all residents in terms of the principles of a collectivized, egalitarian social structure—then we must conclude that the generalization of work relations to the other functions may not accomplish this end if work is based on a stratified hierarchy of command and status relations. This is precisely the contradiction faced in Brasília between the actual organization of work and the intended organization of residence that I raised in chapter 3. If residential relations are established on the basis of work relations and the latter are based on the occupational stratification of the bureaucracy, then hierarchic work relations are bound to contradict egalitarian attempts to allocate the same residential conditions to different occupational strata. This problem is not unique to Brasília because the kind of collectivization that the ideology of the modernist city entails depends on the centralization of authority at the level of the state. Rather, it reflects the merging of state and society that the modernist model presupposes: the identification of the state as the organizer of social life, through work, in every sector of society. Thus, even though "the functions" are spatially separated into homogeneous zones, they are each motivated, organized, and regulated by the same planning agent—the state. With this identification in mind, let us now consider the organization of work.

5.2 The Monumental Work Sectors

The 28 sectors located along the east-west Monumental Axis organize the function of work in the bureaucratic capital (map 5.2). In so doing, they constitute the axis around which nearly everything in Brasília ultimately revolves. As a domain of bureaucracy and related services within a capital city, however, they are unique in the organization of Brazilian capitals: they entail a complete separation of the place of work from the place of residence. No one lives in the sectors of the Monumental Axis. Rather, they are entirely assigned to the functions of federal and municipal administration and to the services they require.

What is the significance of this concentration of jobs in the Monumental sectors, not only in relation to the organization of work in the city and the Federal District as a whole, but also in relation to the organization of the other functions, especially that of residence? A survey of the type and distribution of jobs

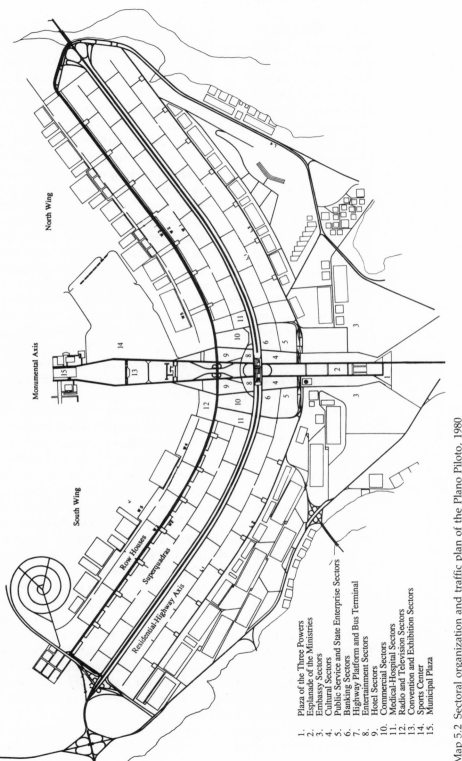

North Wing

South Wing

Monumental Axis

Row Houses

Superquadras

Residential-Highway Axis

1.   Plaza of the Three Powers
2.   Esplanade of the Ministries
3.   Embassy Sectors
4.   Cultural Sectors
5.   Public Service and State Enterprise Sectors
6.   Banking Sectors
7.   Highway Platform and Bus Terminal
8.   Entertainment Sectors
9.   Hotel Sectors
10. Commercial Sectors
11. Medical-Hospital Sectors
12. Radio and Television Sectors
13. Convention and Exhibition Sectors
14. Sports Center
15. Municipal Plaza

Map 5.2 Sectoral organization and traffic plan of the Plano Piloto, 1980

in these sectors will provide a framework for understanding the significance of this spatial organization of work. Tables 5.1–5.4 present data on the demand for manpower in the Federal District in terms of the actual jobs available by sector of employment and by locality (see pp. 188–89).[5] They also evaluate in this respect the relative importance of the Plano Piloto in comparison with the satellite cities.[6]

We must first characterize the concentration of jobs in the Monumental sectors in terms of the structure of the economy of the Federal District. Since Brasília was designed as an administrative capital, without heavy industry, it is not surprising to find that this economy is overwhelmingly based on employment in the tertiary sector of service activities. With an ever increasing share of the economy, these activities comprised 71%, 77%, and 80% of all jobs in the Federal District in 1970, 1975, and 1980, respectively (table 5.1). By comparison, 38% and 46% of Brazil's economically active population were in tertiary-sector activities in 1970 and 1980, respectively (Faria 1983: table 14). Table 5.2 gives the occupational structure of this sector in the Federal District. It is revealing to note the level of employment that the government maintains in its own corps in relation to the other categories of the tertiary sector that this corps supports. The proportion of those directly involved in public administration was 18% over the decade. As the total employed population in the district increased 157% in all sectors during this period, this percentage reflects an enormous (but proportional) growth in government jobs. It is extraordinarily high in comparison with the 1980 average for Brazil of 4% (of all those economically active), with that for the state of Rio de Janeiro of 7%, or even with that of 11% for the former federal capital, Rio de Janeiro, in 1970 before the transfer of many government agencies to Brasília (IBGE 1981a: 6, 412; Geipot 1975: 20). While this category has remained proportional, the others in the sector have grown markedly, essentially reflecting increased services for those in the vast administration and their dependents.

The dominance of the Plano Piloto in the Federal District is clearly expressed in the fact that it offered 60% of all jobs and 75% of jobs in the tertiary sector of employment in 1975, the most recent date for which comparative figures are available (table 5.3). Within the Plano Piloto, the role of the 28 Monumental sectors is similarly expressed: they contained 56% of all jobs and 58% of those in the tertiary sector (tables 5.3 and 5.4). In relation to the Federal District as a whole, they contained 33% of all jobs and 43% of tertiary-sector jobs.[7]

Our first conclusion about this concentration of jobs is that the Monumental sectors constitute the place of work for a majority of those holding jobs in the Plano Piloto and, perhaps even more significantly, for one-third of those working in the Federal District. The other jobs in the Plano Piloto are distributed in the remaining 44 types of spatial sectors as follows: 27% in the Residential sectors and the remaining 15% in sectors surrounding the axes (table 5.4). Those in the Residential sectors are dispersed throughout the city in approximately 60 local commercial sectors, none of which has over two thousand employees and most of which have only several hundred (Geipot 1975: 158). Those in the other sectors are mostly concentrated in three isolated sectors: the Embassy sectors (2%), the University of Brasília (2%), and the Industry and Supply sectors (7%), which store and distribute materials brought into the Federal District but which produce very little in the way of manufactured goods. With the exception of the Industrial Sector jobs, the remaining employment, 35% of the total, is therefore dispersed throughout the Plano Piloto in zones primarily characterized by residence. As the Monumental sectors offer the majority of jobs, in an area devoid of residence, it is evident that the Monumental Axis constitutes a remarkable concentration not merely of the single function of work, but essentially of one type of work—that patronized by the state.

The overwhelming importance of state patronage is further revealed by the income structure of the three sectors of economic activities for the decade 1960–69. Graphs 5.1–5.4 illustrate not only the importance of the tertiary sector in the generation of total income in the Federal District (graph 5.3) but also the heavy dependence of this sector on the government (graph 5.4). The dependence and therefore vulnerability of these sectors to government activities is so great that the evolution of their income over the decade corresponds closely to the state's participation in the tertiary sector (graph 5.4). Thus, the peak observed in 1967 in primary income (graph 5.1) corresponds to the nadir of government participation in the tertiary sector. The withdrawal of the federal government from the local economy in this sector in the years immediately after the 1964 coup forced a significant number of people out of the market altogether and into both subsistence and wage-labor agriculture in the rural zones of the Federal District.

The role of the government in the income evolution of the industrial sector of the local economy is similarly decisive. This sector is strongly influenced by fluctuations in the construction trades (table 5.2). As the government is the principal client in these trades, the entire industrial sector is dependent on government contracts in civil construction (graph 5.2). Thus, after the inauguration of Brasília, when construction practically

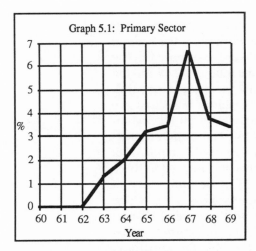

Graph 5.1: Primary Sector

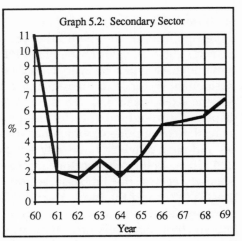

Graph 5.2: Secondary Sector

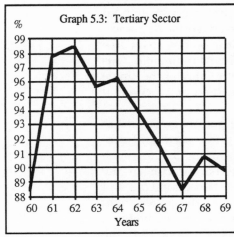

Graph 5.3: Tertiary Sector

Graph 5.1 Primary sector share of Federal District income, 1960–69

Graph 5.2 Secondary sector share of Federal District income, 1960–69

Graph 5.3 Tertiary sector share of Federal District income, 1960–69

Graph 5.4 Government share of tertiary sector income, Federal District, 1960–69
(Source: Geipot 1975: 24–25)

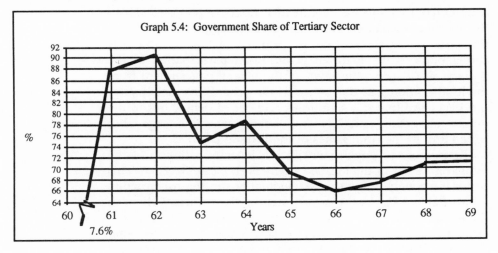

Graph 5.4: Government Share of Tertiary Sector

7.6%

ground to a halt for lack of commitment from Kubitschek's successors to consolidate the transfer of the capital, there was an immediate and sharp decline in the performance of the overall industrial sector. This performance did not begin to recover until after the coup in 1964, when the military regime renewed the process of consolidating the capital in Brasília and therefore initiated a new cycle of construction to accommodate institutions transferred from Rio de Janeiro. During the decade following the coup, the dynamism of the sector was directly linked to decisions by the government to accelerate the transfer of its agencies to the capital, resulting in a second flurry of public building projects. Since then, the dynamism of the sector has slowed considerably but continues to be linked to government decisions to expand its operations in Brasília.

It is evident from these data that work in the Federal District is both concentrated in one area of the Plano Piloto, the Monumental Axis, and overwhelmingly dominated in all economic sectors by government activities. The dependence of the local economy on the state derives, of course, from the fact that Brasília is an administrative capital. In Brazil, however, cities such as Rio de Janeiro, Recife, and Salvador are also administrative capitals of their respective regions and yet have far more diversified economies. The nearly total dependence of Brasília's economy on the government derives from a principle of planning which these other cities do not share: Brasília was conceived in the modernist paradigm of settlements in which cities are solely administrative in function. From these data, we have a measure of the overwhelming degree to which the economy of this type of city (and regional development) is regulated by the modes of organization—the occupational structure, needs, resources, initiatives, political decisions, and the like—that characterize the bureaucratic state. In subsequent chapters, we shall consider the ways in which these modes of bureaucratic organization have decisively affected the development of social and residential organization in Brasília. For the moment, it is important to see how the concentration of one type of work at the planned center of the exemplary city creates an empty center for other than work- or consumer-related activities.

The concentration of work in the Plano Piloto makes it a commuter city in a double sense. First, its satellites are dormitory settlements, with the partial exception of Taguatingua (tables 5.5 and 5.6). Second, the axes reproduce this commuter relationship within the city itself, because the Residential Axis is a dormitory for the work sectors of the Monumental Axis. These commuter patterns are described in tables 5.6–5.7 and require little additional comment. Suffice it to say that the transportation costs that arise from this kind of urban organization are phenomenally high, including costs for buses, cars, fares, fuel, road work, and maintenance.

It is also significant that this kind of organization places the poor at a distinct disadvantage both in finding and in keeping a job. We have already discussed how the modernist city glorifies the beauty of speed and its machine, the automobile. Among the population of the Plano Piloto, a far greater percentage (46%) drive a car to work than in any other Brazilian city. In Rio de Janeiro, only 15% of the working population drives to work; in São Paulo, 18%; in Belo Horizonte, 19%; in Porto Alegre, 25% (Geipot 1979: 38). These comparisons give an idea of the dominance of the automobile in Brasília. In contrast, only 17% of those living in the satellite cities of Brasília drive a car to work, while 75% ride the bus (a proportion similar to those who take the bus in the other cities). This distribution of car and bus transportation corresponds to the income stratification between the center and the satellites of Brasília that we shall discuss later.

The important point is that in separating the places of work and residence, and in concentrating the former while dispersing the latter, modernist planning leads to the stratified use of the city along class lines, especially for purposes other than work. For those who can least afford it, transportation to work in the city is most expensive. For example, bus fares are based on the total cost of service and are therefore proportional to the distance traveled. Thus, fares are highest for people living farthest away. As almost no one in Brasília lives near work, household transportation costs are among the highest, if not the highest, in Brazil. The average bus fare in the Federal District in November 1975 was almost double that in Rio de Janeiro (Geipot 1979: 29). Since the poorest people live farthest from the Plano Piloto, it is obvious that commuter costs take a large portion of the working poor's family income. Thus, the burden falls heaviest on those who can least afford to travel to the principal source of employment. Furthermore, these high costs mean that the popular classes will only come to the Plano Piloto when absolutely necessary, that is, for work. During off-work hours, transportation costs and distance combine to keep the working poor out of the city. For these people, the Plano Piloto has essentially an instrumental value, that of employment.

Thus, the separation of work and residence (in combination with the concentration of the former and the dispersion of the latter) contributes significantly to the development of a centrifugal pattern of class segmentation following work-dormitory transportation lines. Within the Plano Piloto itself, it also produces an empty city center during off-work hours. The use of the Monumental Axis is characterized by the rhythms of the commuter work schedule: it is full during the work day; empty at night, on weekends, and on holidays. It witnesses an enormous flux of commuters four times a day: into work at 8 and 2, back home for lunch and dinner at 12 and 6 o'clock. Thus, it is only occupied for instrumental purposes: primarily for work, and secondarily for consumer needs and services. For other purposes, it is an empty center, without a single place that could be characterized as a domain of off-work conversation and public opinion, a space for the noninstrumental gathering of citizens, in short, a public square.

The fate of the three sectors at the center of this instrumentally valued space—the Entertainment sectors north and south and the Bus Terminal—illustrates why modernist planning precludes the existence of the mixed-use, mixed-class space of the square. With the Entertainment sectors, Costa's intention was no doubt to provide a place for the kind of heterogeneous social activities associated with the life of streets and squares. The Master Plan describes these sectors as areas of "arcades, wide sidewalks, terraces and cafés . . . in the traditional manner of Rio's Ouvidor Street [and] Venetian alleys" (art. 10)—as a concentration of the kind of entertainment and conversational spaces that one finds dispersed throughout other Brazilian cities. We have already discussed both the architectural and the social contradictions of this intention for a city that does not and cannot have streets or squares. The very isolation and self-conscious concentration of "entertainment" into homogeneous sectors precludes the possibility of creating anything other than an instrumentally used space, something like a shopping mall of the North American suburban variety. The shopping mall is an instrumental space that differs from "Venetian alleys" (even though both have corridors) essentially because, dissociated from all other functions, whatever sociality it has is ultimately based on the intention of making a purchase. It is therefore no surprise to find that, as realized, the Entertainment sectors are not a "little Venice" but two shopping malls on either side of a highway. Rather than an oasis of sociality within the work sectors of the city, they are islands of retail commerce. This development is therefore not a deformation of the plan as some consider, but must be seen as a logical consequence of its design principles.[8]

The Interurban Bus Terminal of the Highway Platform is one of the liveliest places in the city and certainly the most popular in the sense of being the domain of working-class commuters from the satellite cities. Its exchanges between cars, buses, and taxis on the one hand and between commuters, vendors, hustlers, and proselytizers of all kinds on the other display an array of almost streetlike activities that tend to carry over into the fringes (but no farther) of the Entertainment sectors. Although it is located in the middle of speedways and nearly impossible to walk to except from these sectors (which are themselves nearly impossible to walk to), it is the space closest in popular use to a typical Brazilian city square (though of the least hospitable sort).

Its popular character depends on its being the hub of Brasília's commuter and interurban bus system. Thus, it is the point of disembarkation for migrants riding the bus to Brasília. More important, it is the point of transfer for all buses, both for those from the satellite cities and for those traveling within the Plano Piloto. Therefore, all buses—even those making a loop around only one of the Residential wings—make an obligatory stop at the Highway Platform to pick up and discharge passengers. From the perspective of the commuter, his or her journey to any point within the city requiring a change of buses means waiting for some time at the platform for a transfer. As "only the poor ride the bus in Brasília," and as the poor who work in the Plano Piloto live in the satellite cities, the Bus Terminal is the domain of the peripheral, popular classes commuting to and from work. It is recognizably their place, with the sights and smells and activities of another Brazil.

The Bus Terminal, however, does not have the sociality of a public square as we defined it in the last chapter. Its conversations take place between buses, just as those of the Entertainment sectors are between purchases. Its users never go there except to take a bus or to sell something to someone taking a bus. Its sociality is, therefore, incidental to its primary function as a transportation center. As in airports, train stations, and bus terminals everywhere, its gatherings follow commuter patterns, which are single purposed and usually class based. Thus, these sectors at the center of the city have only instrumental value in the organization of space in Brasília. This instrumentality produces an empty city center in a double sense: the central sectors are cyclically empty of people whenever their respective functions (consumption, transportation) are not being utilized, and they are always empty of possibility for one income group or another; that is, for those who lack money for anything but work necessities, the Entertainment sectors are excluded from their experience of the city, while for those who have extra money, the Bus Terminal is the last place to visit.

In conclusion, the organization of work in Brasília in terms of the modernist paradigm of urban settlements leads to: (1) a nearly total dependence of the local economy on the modes of organization of the bureaucratic state; (2) a concentration and centralization of jobs in relation to dispersed dormitory settlements; (3) a use of urban space based primarily on the commuter shuttle between work and dormitory areas; (4) an exorbitantly expensive commuter transport system; (5) a centrifugal pattern of class segmentation following work-dormitory commuter lines; and (6) a city center segregated by income class that for anything but work or consumer activities is empty.

The organization of function in terms of space in Brasília is perhaps best summed up by the following Brasiliense aphorism: "In Brasília, there is only *casa e trabalho*, house and work." This aphorism consciously and sarcastically points to what is missing in a social life that is circumscribed in the oscillation between home and office. It refers to a missing "third term" that is variously described by Brasilienses as *a rua* (the street), *a praça* (the square), or *a praia* (the beach). What is missing is the outdoor public life of the city, a public sphere of encounters based on *movimento*, conversation, play, ceremony, ritual, pageantry, as well as political congregation. These are no longer meaningful dimensions of civic life for those who have moved to Brasília. The center of the city, where the square should be, is empty of other than instrumental encounters. Lacking "public encounters of the third kind," social life oscillates unremittingly between work and residence.

5.3 The *Superquadra* Solution

Just as the function of work is organized into homogeneous sectors, so the function of residence is allotted special sectors within the Plano Piloto and the satellite cities. Table 5.8 gives the distribution of the Federal District's resident population over two decades, and table 5.9 summarizes the change in this population by decade. Tables 5.10 and 5.11 present an inventory of the residential sectors of Brasília and give basic data on their population, number of dwellings, density, green areas, and income distribution (the last to be discussed later). Each sector is identified in these tables with their respective traffic zones, which may be located on map 5.3 (p. 194).

The residential sectors are differentiated into four subtypes, each associated with a different form of housing but all ultimately related in their planning to a concept of zoned, "collective" dwelling. Sectors of Collective Dwelling (*Habitação Coletiva*) are those that consist exclusively of apartment blocks. These blocks share residential facilities and are arranged in groups within green areas (*áreas verdes*) of public land. The word collective refers to this sharing of common facilities (one of which is the green area itself) and not simply to the existence of apartment blocks as opposed to houses. Within the Federal District, these sectors are found predominantly in the Plano Piloto where the apartment blocks are organized into units called *superquadras*. Thus, the *superquadra* is a specific type of collective dwelling and is unique to the Plano Piloto. Within the Plano, *superquadras* house approximately 66% of the population and contain approximately 70% of the total number of dwelling units. Apartment blocks of the collective type are also found in Cruzeiro Novo, where they house all residents, and in small numbers in the satellite cities.[9]

The principle of collective, zoned dwelling is applied to the house as a form of residence in the organization of the second subtype, the sectors of Individual Paired Dwelling (*Habitação Individual Geminada*). These are row houses organized in such a way that each pair of rows defines a "local way" giving access to the service backs of the house units, while their main façades front onto a green area shared with the row on the other side. In the Plano Piloto, they now contain about 7% of its population in a strip along the southern length of W-3. In Cruzeiro Velho they constitute the only form of housing and are distributed in a uniform manner around an area planned for such community facilities as shops, schools, theaters, churches, and athletic and social clubs. The third subtype, the sectors of Collective and Paired Dwelling (*Habitação Coletiva e Geminada*), is a combination of types one and two and features both apartment blocks and row houses. They are found exclusively in the Plano Piloto, along the northern edge of W-3 and account for about 4% of its population.

Finally, the sectors of Individual Dwelling (*Habitação Individual*) contain freestanding houses, each with its own plot of land. Within the administrative region of Brasília, they represent a middle- and upper-income suburban development around the Plano Piloto and are found in the Lake and Mansion sectors. Within the other administrative regions of the Federal District (i.e., in the satellite cities of Taguatinga, Ceilândia, Gama, Sobradinho, Planaltina, and Brazlândia), they are the predominant, and in some cases the only, type of residential development. In these satellites, they are planned almost exclusively for lower-income families. Even in these sectors of individual houses, both rich and poor, an effort has been made to incorporate the notion of collective living: the land is subdivided so that each house plot fronts onto a green area of public property which each resident is supposed to share and tend collectively with his neighbor.

In what sense do these sectors constitute a redefinition or reconceptualization of the urban function of residence? Modernist master planning is a comprehensive approach to restructuring urban life precisely because it advances proposals aimed at both the public and the private domains of society. Its proposal for the private realm centers on the concept of a new type of domestic architecture and residential unit, the most basic embodiment of which is, in Brasília, the *superquadra*. Therefore, we shall focus our discussion on its organization of residence in the Plano Piloto, where it is the principal mode of dwelling. Moreover, even though it is found as such only in one area of the Federal District, it is the prototype for the principle of collective, zoned dwelling that is the basis of planning for the other residential types.

To understand the nature of this prototype, and the way in which it presents a new vision of residential organization, we must disaggregate a number of interactive factors, differentiating between the architects' and the government's model of the *superquadra*. The model that Lúcio Costa developed embodies fundamental modernist ideas of autonomy and community in residential organization crystallized into architectural form by Soviet and Western European architects. Costa's *superquadra* derives directly from the Soviet Constructivist prototype for collective residence, the *dom-kommuna* (compare figs. 3.2, 3.4, and 2.11–2.13). In this prototype, the role of the private apartment is greatly reduced as the social functions of the nuclear family it traditionally houses are taken over by planned collective services and physically displaced to common facilities.[10] In this displacement lies the basic objective of transforming the nature of the family both as a unit of socialization and as a unit of domestic economy. In this reorganization of the home, there is as well the important objective of freeing women from domestic servitude and more generally, especially for the Soviets, of transforming relations between the sexes, as well as between parents and children. The planned residential unit that emerges from these objectives is that of a self-sufficient community providing a full range of collective services for its residents (e.g., schools, day-care centers, kitchens, clinics, shops, etc.); and that of a unit linked with similar units into a larger community, the articulation of which is based on each unit's affiliation with a government institution or production group like a factory or a farm.

As derived from these intentions, Brasília's *superquadra* system of residence has the following overall organization (map 5.2). The function of residence is typologically opposed to that of work by the arms of the axial cross of speedways: the Monumental Axis of work sectors divides the Residential Axis into its South Wing and its North Wing. In mirror image, these organize the quotidian and domestic domain of residential functions. Each wing is divided into nine bands (*faixas*), numbered 100 to 900. The band's number indicates its position to the east (even) or to the west (odd) of the axial speedway. It also indicates its function. Bands 100 to 400 contain the *superquadras*, two bands on each side of the speedway. Band 500 is a commercial strip called W-3 that also contains community facilities and services (such as libraries and clinics) at the entrances to the 300 band of *superquadras* between W-3 and W-2; bands 600 and 900 contain higher-order community services such as schools that draw students from all of the residential sectors; band 700 contains the sectors of row houses in the south and those of mixed row house and apartment blocks in the north; band 800 remains undeveloped.

Each band in the 100 to 400 series contains 15 *superquadras*, yielding a total of 60 in each wing and 120 in the entire city. These are identified by a three-digit code, beginning with those on either side of the axial crossing. The first digit indicates a *superquadra's* position in the east-west sequence of bands, and the last two digits its position along the north-south continuum of dwelling units. The sequence begins with "the twos" so that an east-west slice through the city on either side of the highway platform cuts through *superquadras* (south or north) 402, 202, 102, and 302. This numerical order repeats sequentially 15 times along the Residential Axis until the sixteenth series is reached at the extremities of the wings.

An individual *superquadra* is an area of residence of approximately 240 by 240 meters. It contains no fewer than 8 and no more than 11 apartment blocks which house between two thousand and three thousand people. The apartment blocks are of two basic types. In bands 100, 200, and 300 they are uniformly rectangular blocks six stories above supporting columns. A typical block has 36 apartments grouped into three sets around entranceways (elevator, stair, and service core), in which 150–250 people reside. In band 400, the blocks are uniformly three stories above grade, some with and most without columns. However, as the apartments in this band are much smaller than those in the others (and thus intended for lower-income residents), each block actually has more apartments and more residents. An apartment's address synthesizes the relation between the wings, the bands, the *superquadras*, the blocks, and the apartments such that the address SQS 406-C-304 means Superquadra South 406–Block C–Apartment 304. It relates no less than seven levels of information about the organizational system of the Plano Piloto I have just described. While there is some variation between the dwelling units in the arrangement of blocks, they all follow an essentially similar rectangular pattern. Moreover, this standardization of plan is reinforced in the standardization of form as the blocks are themselves all concrete slabs of uniform height.

The issue of variation within a standardized pattern, of what is most fundamentally that of identity and difference, is crucial to the architectural conception of the *superquadras* and is expressed in a variety of ways. On the one hand, they are conceived of as "an uninterrupted sequence . . . a linked series" (Costa 1957: art. 16) of like elements. As such, they express the modernists' machine metaphor of assembly-line process, order, repetition, regulation, growth, and equivalence. For the modernists, this assembly is ultimately an image of community, of the participation of parts in a greater whole. On the other hand, as parts, the *superquadras* are intended to be self-sufficient units, with an "autonomy" (as Costa put it) sufficient to produce individuating differences. Two of Costa's unrealized planning suggestions (art. 16) clearly reveal this intent to create a sense of individuality, uniqueness, and exception in the midst of process: he proposed that each *superquadra* should be symbolically differentiated by a "wide green belt" densely planted with a different species of trees. He also suggested that each quadrant of the city be distinguished by a different color applied in a variety of ways. One cannot help but imagine that there is in this combination of plant, color, and spatial codes something of a totemic logic for symbolically differentiating fundamentally identical residential units.[11]

At a functional rather than symbolic level, the *superquadra* is conceived of as a self-sufficient residential unit with its own facilities and as one linked to three of its neighbors by other, shared facilities (fig. 5.2). As an autonomous unit, each in principle offers its residents four kinds of basic services: those of commerce, child care, education, and recreation. As originally planned, these services were collective from the residents' perspective in the sense that all residents would have equal rights of use by virtue of their status as *superquadra* residents and regardless of individual disparities in income, education, social background, and the like. Each *superquadra* is associated with a local commercial sector consisting of two rows of shops separated by a service way that is supposed to provide for the shopping needs of its residents. As discussed in the last chapter, the original plan had the fronts of these shops facing their respective dwelling units. Thus, each *superquadra* formed a self-sufficient unit of residence and commerce with one half (i.e., one side) of a local commercial sector. This design was not

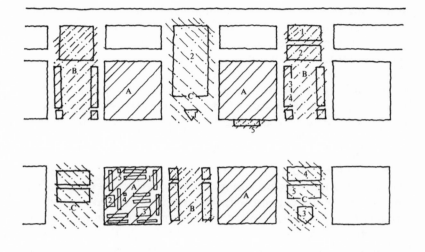

Fig. 5.2 Neighborhood unit of four *superquadras* (*unidade de viznhança*).
A. *Superquadras:* 1. Apartment blocks; 2. Nursery school; 3. Elementary
   school; 4. Administration building (planned); 5. Newspaper stand.
B. Local Commercial Sector: 1. Public services (library, art school, assistance);
   2. Neighborhood supermarket; 3. Retail trade (heavy); 4. Retail trade
   (light); 5. Service station.
C. *Entrequadras:* 1. Church; 2. *Escola parque;* 3. Cinema; 4. Social club; 5. Sports

supposed to prevent residents of one *superquadra* from using the
local commerce of another, but it was intended to emphasize the
individual identity of each unit of residence and commerce.
Although the Master Plan does not specifically state what kind
of economic relations should characterize this unit, a system of
special discounts for residents at their local commercial sector
(and only at some types of shops and services) was later
proposed and partially implemented.[12]

Within the model *superquadra* itself are located two institutions
of child care and elementary education: a *jardim da infância,*
'nursery school', to provide a full day of child care services, and
an *escola-classe,* 'classroom school', for academic instruction at
the elementary level. These schools and their associated playground facilities are built in the green area of the *superquadra.*
This area is the open space in which the housing blocks are set
and makes up about 60% of the total area of the *superquadra.* It
is designed as a kind of residential park, free of traffic for the
recreational and social use of residents. There are about 25
square meters of green area per resident, a measure considered
ideal by UNESCO standards. (By contrast, there are 4.5 square
meters of green area for each inhabitant of Metropolitan São
Paulo.) In addition, as developed in blueprint form by Novacap,

dwelling units provide parking facilities, newspaper stands, and small administration buildings (these latter were never built).

While each *superquadra* is considered a self-sufficient residential unit for certain purposes, every four constitutes a *unidade de vizinhança*, 'neighborhood unit', for purposes of sharing a number of common facilities and administrative affairs. Each neighborhood unit in bands 100 to 300 has an area of land reserved for its collective affairs called an *entrequadra*, 'interblock'. This is a traffic-free area located either directly above or below the local commercial sectors. The plan calls for each interblock to have a neighborhood club to provide the unit's eight to twelve thousand members with meeting halls, restaurants, snack bars, and sports facilities including a swimming pool and tennis courts. The club is supposed to function as the social and cultural center of the neighborhood unit and also as its representative organization. In addition, the model interblock features a church, a theater-cinema, a playing field (essentially for unit soccer matches), and an *escola-parque*, 'park-school', to complement the elementary education offered in each *superquadra* with activities in arts, crafts, and audio-visual communications.[13] Finally, each neighborhood unit is provided with a service station for cars located along W-1 or L-1, a post office, and a police and first-aid station.

If, in these ways, the concept of the *superquadra* is aimed at achieving a sense of residential identification and neighborhood affiliation, we may ask at this point how Brasilienses perceive it. Their first observation is often that it confronts them with a completely unfamiliar type of residential organization. Although isolated examples of its architectural and planning principles (e.g., Alfonso E. Reidy's Unidade Residential de Gávea [1952] in Rio de Janeiro) exist in many Brazilian cities, the *superquadra* itself is unique to Brasília. Moreover, although most cities have been affected by modernist architecture, the organization of an entire city in its terms is something new. Brasilienses generally perceive that the *superquadra* represents an experiment in residential organization—that it is more than just a collection of apartment buildings in the modern style. But what this organization means, and what their affiliation is with it, remain ambiguous.

Most Brasilienses evaluate the *superquadra* in terms of their experiences with the residential organization of other Brazilian cities. The *bairro* is the most encompassing level of organization within a city that Brazilians are likely to identify with as a place of residence. The *bairro* has a much stronger residential identity in Brazil than the gloss 'quarter', 'district', or 'ward' implies to Anglo-American readers. As a unit of residence, the *bairro* is clearly defined as a spatial, political, and symbolic organization of residents. Within its geographical boundaries, the typical urban *bairro* is politically incorporated as a unit of municipal administration with officials elected to city council. It is often further organized by a representative *bairro* association (*associação de bairro*, sometimes called *associação de moradores*, 'residents association', or even *associação dos amigos do bairro*, 'association of friends of the *bairro*'). In addition, as discussed in the previous chapter in relation to Debret's illustrations of Rio de Janeiro, the *bairro* may be symbolically organized around patron saints, popular festivals, and sport teams, featuring festival groups and sports clubs that meet throughout the year and often provide a context for political action as well. With some exception, membership in these groups is restricted to *bairro* residents.

Within the *bairro*, there are commonly several other types of residential identifications that extend beyond the household. These identities relate to the extension of domestic order into the *bairro*'s public space, an extension we discussed in reference to Debret's illustrations (figs. 4.17 and 4.18). Thus, we find the ideas of *minha rua*, 'my street', *minha vizinhança*, 'my neighborhood', *meu quarteirão*, 'my block', and *minha vizinha de porta*, 'my next-door neighbor', important in establishing identities of place. While "neighborhood" is a difficult term to define precisely, it is used to delimit an area of face-to-face contact, usually physically reckoned in terms of streets and squares, in which personal relations are established on the basis of such things as the extension of credit from shopkeepers, gossip, and the proximity of related families. In most cases (and only somewhat less so in Brazil's large cities), a Brazilian is likely to consider it an area of kin relations, in which an extensive number of families related to him resides. Often, neighborhoods incorporate into associations (*associações da vizinhança*). While these associations do not send representatives to municipal political organizations, they frequently take on symbolic attributes that represent "the neighbors" to the *bairro* and to the city. The city block and street corner are especially significant domains of everyday social life as we have seen. On festival occasions, such as *carnaval*, block residents (either of one street or of a square block) may "go to the streets" as an organized group of revelers—an organization that for all of its apparent spontaneity often has bylaws of incorporation and meets throughout the year as the need arises to consider *bairro*-related issues.[14] Finally, the next-door neighbor (who is often a relative, especially in smaller cities) represents a most localized institution for the exchange of services, favors, and of course gossip.

The point I wish to make is that none of these residential identities and categories is applied to the *superquadra*. Out of 24 residents interviewed for extended life histories at one of Brasília's social clubs, for example, 21 stated unequivocally that they did not consider the *superquadra* to be a *bairro*, a neighborhood, or a city block. Furthermore, all 24 stated that the apartment blocks did not function either as what one might call vertical neighborhoods or as city blocks and that they did not know their next-door neighbors on any more than a formal basis. These responses are typical of many other interviews.

In addition to confronting an unfamiliar type of residential organization, most residents are perplexed about the quality of social life in the apartment blocks. No doubt, many experience apartment living for the first time upon moving to Brasília. Except in São Paulo and Rio de Janeiro, the apartment building is a relatively new form of mass housing in Brazil. It did not appear to dominate the skyline of even large Brazilian cities until the mid-1950s. What is significant is that even for those who have previously lived in apartments, the house remains the ideal residential type, especially among families. It is interesting in this respect to note that when I asked a class of nine-year-olds in the Classroom School of SQS 308 to "draw a picture of home," not one gave me a drawing of a *superquadra* apartment block. In fact, even though most of these children lived in *superquadra* apartments, no one drew an apartment or apartment building of any kind. They all gave me pictures of freestanding houses with the stereotypic human face façade of two windows, a central door, and a pitched roof. Not one had the flat roof characteristic of Brasília's modern style.

In comparisons between houses and apartments, as between *bairros* and *superquadras*, an important component of this residential ideal emerges—that of the family's social life within the domestic sphere. What is most salient in these comparisons is the reported absence of a public life of the family, that is, of its sociality within the dwelling units. I am not here referring to the important fact that children generally find the *superquadras'* recreational spaces very accessible and to their liking. The security and accessibility of these spaces give them a sense of camaraderie and independence throughout childhood that parents tend to value as the most positive and desirable feature of *superquadra* residence.[15] Rather, I am referring to the social life of the family as a household in its relations to neighboring family households and to that of adults and teenagers. In these respects, the *superquadra* is considered a very limiting environment. It is characterized by what residents call a *fechamento*, a 'closing in or shutting up'.

The following statements, spliced together from many interviews, should give the reader a sense of this "shutting up" or interiorization in contrast to the public life and sociality of the *bairro*. In the latter, "people have more contact with each other"; "people, especially relatives, help each other"; "ties of friendship are more easily formed"; "there is more friendship, more sociality (*convivência*), more gossip"; "there is corner talk"; "in the *bairros*, people arrange to meet on the corners, but in Brasília there are no corners." In contrast, the *superquadra* "lacks its own life"; "lacks individuality and personality"; "lacks a sense of community"; "lacks residential organization." In the *superquadra*, "people close themselves in"; "people are withdrawn"; "people don't know each other, not even their next-door neighbor"; "people find making friends difficult"; "people die alone." A similar set of opinions contrasts the house and the *superquadra* apartment: houses "facilitate friendship between neighbors and relatives"; "the door is always open." However, in the apartments "the door is closed"; "people live locked up"; "there is little reason to go outside."

These reactions amount to a significant condemnation of the *superquadra* as a residential concept. To what extent are they attributable to its architectural design? The sense of isolation in the *superquadra* results in large measure from a similar kind of defamiliarization of public and private space in the residential domain that the elimination of the street creates in the extradomestic domain of the city. The prototypical modernist housing block, as developed for example by the Soviet Constructivists, diminishes the space allotted to each private apartment in order to give it back to the residential unit as a whole in the form of collective spaces and facilities. This quid pro quo derives from the application of the twins of modernist ideology, rationalization and standardization, to the problem of creating a new type of residential community as the building block of a new social order. In part, the rationalization of construction techniques and the development of a standard minimum housing unit are aimed at making the most out of limited resources. But this optimization serves a process of social change in which the ultimate objective of redefining the relation of individual and community is approached by restructuring the relation of private needs and public goods. Thus, the first CIAM manifesto declares that

> Rationalization and standardization . . . expect from the consumer (that is to say the customer who orders the house in which he will live) a revision of his demands in the direction of a readjustment to the new conditions of social life. Such a revision will be manifested in the reduction of certain individual needs henceforth devoid of

real justification; the benefits of this reduction will foster the maximum satisfaction of the needs of the greatest number, which are at present restricted. (Conrads 1970: 110)

The most radical conception of the housing block that such a "revision" generates is that of a dormitory of sleeping rooms disposed around common rooms. There is good evidence that Le Corbusier's residential prototypes developed this basic plan in forms inspired by the monastic ideal of a group of individuals whose private lives are restructured in terms of a new collective persona (see Serenyi 1967). This ideal is expressed in the typical monastery plan by the reduction of individual apartments to sleeping cubicles and the corresponding elaboration of community spaces. While I am not suggesting that the *superquadra* derives directly (though perhaps indirectly) from this plan, it does in fact attempt something similar. In plan, the housing block embodies an attempt to gain in collective spaces what it diminishes in private; in elevation, its gridded glass façade negates the expression of individual status and personality in an attempt to communicate an egalitarian, rational social order. What the *superquadra* plan reduces is the social spaces of the private apartment. What its façade negates—at the scale of an entire city—is the expression of individuality. Together, they constitute a profound defamiliarization of residential life as Brazilians are accustomed to it.

5.3.1 The Apartment Plan

We may bring out the defamiliarization of the model *superquadra* apartment by comparing it with the conventional organization of the Brazilian middle-class apartment. That the middle-class apartment follows a conventional organization of space will become evident in a moment. To illustrate the *superquadra* apartment, I shall use the plan designed by Niemeyer for SQS 108 (fig. 5.4). This plan served as the model for many of the blocks in bands 100–300 that Novacap's Department of Architecture and Urbanism, of which Niemeyer was director, designed and built in the early years of Brasília's construction. To illustrate the conventional middle-class apartment plan, I could use almost any middle-income apartment building in a major Brazilian city (e.g., fig. 5.3b). However, I refer the reader instead to the plans for SQS 308 in Brasília itself (fig. 5.5). This *superquadra* was among the several assigned to the Bank of Brazil for its employees. The bank was responsible for its design and construction, for which it hired its own team of architects. While this team followed the general patterns established by Novacap

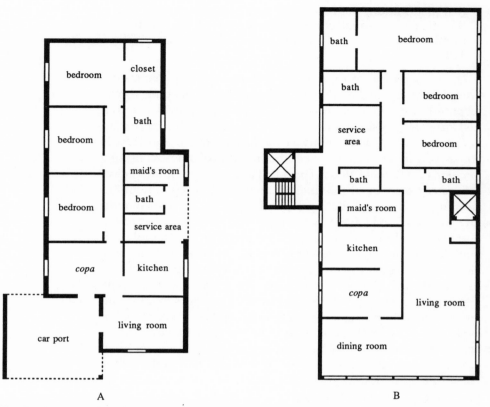

Fig. 5.3 Two examples of *copas* and kitchens: (a) plan of an urban house in Campinas, showing a typical arrangement of *copa* and kitchen (redrawn from Lemos 1978: 194); (b) plan of a middle-class apartment in São Paulo, showing typical distribution of *copa*, kitchen, servant quarters, and service area, 1981.

for the *superquadras*, it designed a floor plan typical of the conventional organization of space in middle- to upper-middle-income apartments. In this respect, it was fundamentally different from Niemeyer's plan. The advantage of making this comparison—beyond introducing intentions other than Niemeyer's—is that the circumstances surrounding the design and construction of these plans were identical. Both were put forth at the same time and both confronted the same technical resources in their construction. Moreover, both housed upper- and lower-level bureaucrats and thus similar income groups.[16] Therefore, their differences are ideological; that is, the one reproduced the status quo (albeit within a radically different façade), while the other introduced changes in residential planning as a means of changing residential organization.

The family apartment building first appeared in Brazilian cities, and specifically in São Paulo, in the 1920s to meet the

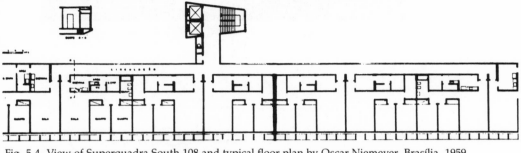

Fig. 5.4. View of Superquadra South 108 and typical floor plan by Oscar Niemeyer, Brasília, 1959. From *Brasília: Ediçao Arquitetura e Engenharia* (1960).

changing residential circumstances of middle-class families who had been accustomed to living in their own houses in or near the city's center and near the place of work of the head of household. Increases in the urban population and the resulting saturation of city centers at this time confronted the middle-class family in search of accommodations with a dilemma: to continue to live in a house, it would have to opt for one in peripheral *bairros*, far from the center and from work; to continue to live near both, it would have to accept the apartment building, which it had previously viewed as a warren of the promiscuous poor, or at best as a barely respectable dormitory for single men working away from home, but certainly not as an abode fit for family life. To attract these families, therefore, building speculators developed an apartment plan that could reproduce what was most important to the middle class about the house: its social organization of space. According to the architect and historian Carlos Lemos (1978: 147–62), this plan became a national standard during the interwar period as family apartment buildings sprang up in major city centers throughout Brazil.

175

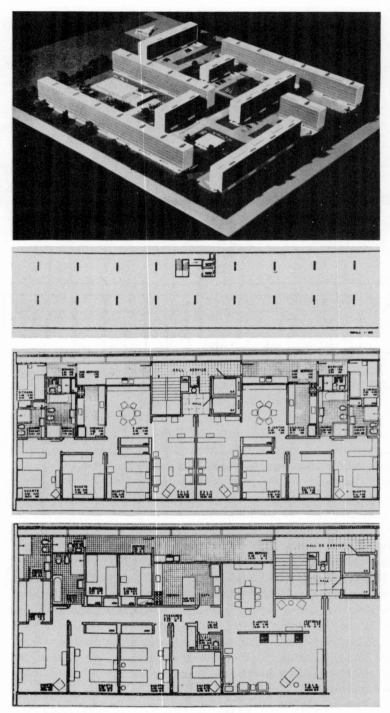

Fig. 5.5 Model of Superquadra South 308 and plans of entrance level and typical apartments, Brasília, 1959. From *Brasília: Ediçao Arquitetura e Engenharia* (1960).

Based on the organization of the comfortable middle-class house, the family apartment is divided into three functionally independent zones: the social area, the intimate area, and the service area.[17] As a reflection of the social structure of the middle-class Brazilian household, this plan is based on a division between masters, who occupy the social and intimate areas of the apartment, and servants who work and live in the service area. This division is a norm of middle-class life, for it is standard practice for even modestly middle-income families to employ cheap domestic labor to cook, clean, wash, and tend to children. I have not space here to describe the history of servant quarters in Brazilian residential architecture. I want to suggest, nevertheless, that it was the problem of bringing these quarters from the grounds of the slave-owning estate into the middle-class house, and more pressingly, into the apartment, that gave rise to the tripartite organization of domestic space into social, intimate, and service areas.

In the typical apartment, the social area consists of a visiting room, a dining room, a *copa*, and a balcony. To these social spaces, the house adds a backyard and, especially in older houses, a veranda or porch. In most households, both the visiting room and the dining room are little-used and formal spaces, the former reserved for the reception of visitors and other stately social events and the latter for the main meal of the day when the head of household is home from work. One may argue that the balcony is a high-rise version of the veranda—a bit of outdoor space for the apartment dweller, a front façade extension of interior space into that of the street below, a zone of exchange between the two domains. However, in the traditional organization of the house, the veranda functioned as a large outdoor living room: it was the heart of the informal social life of the family. In the apartment, this place of daily, informal gathering is the *copa*.

There is no adequate English equivalent to describe this room. The term *copa* began to appear on house plans at the turn of the century to identify the large cupboard in the passageway between the kitchen and the veranda that was used to store utensils, cooking spices, tea, biscuits, ripening fruit, vials of medicine, needle and thread—in short, the infinite trivia of household life. Gradually, the area of the cupboard became something of a pantry, something of a breakfast nook, a place to make cheese, darn a sock, and have a snack. It brought together both the informal social life of the veranda and the work activities of the backyard and kitchen. In the apartment as in the house, it became the place to serve all but the main meal of the day, and, as the saying goes, "where the family eats, the family stays." Thus, the *copa* is a multipurpose room associated with the kitchen (fig. 5.3). It is what one might call the democratic space of the household, equally accessible to every member, to masters and servants, males and females, adults and children. Its importance lies in the fact that it unites the activities of the three zones that nowhere else intersect. It is the space in which the household superimposes the relations of leisure and work, of socializing and service.

In the rest of the apartment, the three zones are kept entirely separate. In fact, municipal building codes usually require that a corridor isolate the intimate area of family bedrooms and baths from the other areas. This principle of separation becomes most highly elaborated in the planning of the service area, though it is not just a question of separating functions but, more important, of separating classes. The service area consists of two components: the circulation system of the apartment building and the service area proper to each apartment. The organizing principle of both components is that, with the significant exception of interaction in the *copa*, the service class of the household should have as little contact as possible with the master class as members of each circulate through the building, and as the servants perform their work tasks in the kitchen and tend to their own affairs in their living quarters.

This principle has given rise to the convention—which several of the architects I interviewed claimed to be unique to Brazil in Latin America—that every apartment building except those for the lowest classes must have two completely independent circulation systems. (Such dual circulation systems are, of course, standard features of the *houses* of the upper classes in many countries.) The system begins with two entrances at street level, a "noble" entrance and a service entrance, each with its own elevator and each preferably on a different side of the building. If only one street access is possible, then the circulation paths must diverge to their respective elevators as quickly as possible in the entrance hall. The use of the service and noble elevators is asymmetrical. While the service class (domestics, doormen, janitors, repairmen, etc.) may not use the noble elevator, "nobles" should use the service entrace and elevator according to the rules of etiquette; that is, when carrying large packages, when leaving for or returning from the beach or athletics, when walking the dog, when less than properly attired, when "dirty," or when engaged (however rarely) in manual labor. I should say that there is something of a game and a good bit of paternalistic humor in the class relations that this circulation system embodies. But I am here concerned with its formality in design and less with its contravention in practice.

Corresponding to each elevator, the apartment should have separate entrances for its two classes of inhabitants: a noble door off a front hall and a service door off a service corridor. Just as in the house plan, where the service area is linked to the backyard, the reigning convention in apartment planning is that the service area must have independent and external access. In economically constructed middle-class buildings, where the service corridor has been eliminated to save space, the absolute necessity of maintaining double entrances produces a somewhat overdetermined situation: the two elevators and the two apartment doors are incongruously placed side by side.

The service area of the apartment consists of the kitchen, the maid's bath and bedroom(s), and the laundry facilities. The latter include a basin for washing clothes, lines for drying, and an ironing board, all of which are located in the service corridor for reasons of ventilation. Bordered by two corridors, the service on the one side and that of the intimate zone on the other, the service area is effectively isolated from the noble areas of the apartment. Unmediated access to the kitchen from the dining room is rarely tolerated.

In both design and use, this service area appeals to the most atavistic of middle-class values: the apartment kitchen is still the kitchen of the *casa-grande* at a remove from the living space of the *patrão;* it is the domain of servants, rarely of the mistress of the house; the maid is still a slave of unwelcome presence in the family areas; and her little room with its door opening onto the wash basin in the service corridor is still the *senzala*, the slave shanty. Lemos (1978: 97) observes that in the nineteenth century "the mark of status of the head [of household] or of the rich was precisely the distance to the kitchen"—a distance which signaled superiority because only the rich could live separate from the work spaces of their houses while the poor were obliged to live close to or in such spaces. Perhaps because of its profound appeal to these entrenched class values, the contemporary, middle-income house or apartment, even a modest one, is according to Lemos (1978: 145) "proud of its *edicula* [the technical term for the service area], the construction that increases its property value, that can define or suggest a lot about social position. By the size of the *edicula*, one knows the wealth of the resident."[18]

I have gone to some lengths to describe the apartment's social organization of space because its profound influence on domestic life makes the changes—some radical, some restrained—of Niemeyer's *superquadra* plan all the more significant. The first thing to note is that the plan of SQS 108 (fig. 5.4) does not challenge the conventional tripartite separation of functions. It does not use the modernist free plan that stresses the flow and interrelation of functions, especially of the living areas. Rather, it reproduces the customary divisions of social, service, and intimate areas. When I asked a high official of Brasília's most important planning commission how a communist architect could have designed apartments with servant quarters and service elevators, he simply replied—as if the question required no further discussion—"In Brazil, it has to be that way." If a direct assault on the fundamental divisions of domestic space was not feasible, Niemeyer's plan nevertheless makes some significant alterations within the tripartite scheme itself.

Niemeyer's treatment of the service area and circulation system is certainly less remarkable for what it does than for what it does not include. Unlike that of SQS 308 (fig. 5.5), Niemeyer's plan does not provide separate entrances for the two elevators. They stand side by side in the same hall. Thus, the circulation of masters and servants is identical until the elevators. After the elevator ride, both classes again converge on the same door: Niemeyer has provided only one entrance to each apartment which both masters and servants must use. Furthermore, as there is no service corridor, all the apartments are self-contained units along a common corridor. As a result, each service area is accessible only from inside the apartment. The kitchen is thus internal and not external to "noble" space, into which moreover the kitchen door leads without mediation. Finally, the maids' rooms are so small as to discourage habitation. In fact, when an international congress of architects and planners visited the newly constructed blocks in 1959, these rooms were shown as pantries (no doubt out of embarrassment but nevertheless to suggest the alternative).

Admittedly, these modifications of the conventional organization of the service area are almost trivial in light of maintaining its existence. Nevertheless, I think that they can be viewed as attempts to sabotage customary practices in the stratified divisions of domestic space and social relations. By leaving out crucial elements of the system, the plan "bares the devices" of taken-for-granted social practices and tries to make people recognize these devices through the experience of inconvenience and absurd juxtaposition. However, these intentions, like so many others in Brasília, have had a somewhat perverse outcome. Although *superquadra* residents generally agree that the service areas are poorly planned, they have not given up servants. The result for maids is that the reduction of space has simply made a bad situation worse. While it appears to be the case that fewer middle-income families in the *superquadras* have live-in maids than might be expected (perhaps because of the size of the quarters, but perhaps also because of a general trend away from this practice as a result of increased costs and changes in the familial sensibilities of the middle classes), nearly all have day maids who must spend an inordinate proportion of their pay and time traveling the great distances to and from the satellite cities. In Brasília, they work for miserable wages without the benefit of at least bed and board. If they should happen to live in the apartments, then they do so, perhaps with a child, in quarters no bigger than a large closet. And while the juxtaposition of twin elevators may make class structure and social contradiction more visible, they do not discourage discriminatory practice. From the maid's perspective, they merely increase humiliation.

The most radical change in the model apartment plan is not, however, in the service area but rather in the social area: the plan eliminates the informal social spaces of the *copa* and the balcony. This elimination, combined with the impossibility of having either a veranda or backyard, leads Brasilienses to complain that the apartments are "cold" and inhospitable. Moreover, the lack of a balcony precludes the familiar exchanges between interior and exterior, between public and private, that balconies facilitate. As a result, people feel "shut in" their apartments. Once inside, however, they find only one social space, labeled *sala* or 'living room' on the plan, that must combine the functions of visiting room, dining room, and *copa*. In a sense, this combination is consistent with the objectives of "free planning." However, families find it awkward, strange, and inconsistent with customary social practices. Just as the elimination of the street corner defamiliarizes the public space of the city, more than anything else the elimination of the *copa* defamiliarizes the public space of the apartment.

This reduction of family public space is, of course, consistent with modernist objectives of reducing the role of the private apartment in the social lives of residents, and correspondingly of encouraging them to use the collective facilities of the new dwelling units.[19] However, in Brasília, the outcome of this design seems to be both a sense of isolation inside the apartments and yet an abandonment of the green areas of the *superquadras*. With the elimination of the public space of the city, what this *superquadra* plan seems to encourage instead is a further retreat into the privacy of the intimate areas of the apartment. As a result, many Brasilienses view the model *superquadra* apartment as "antifamily," as against the traditional social solidarities and structures of the Brazilian household.

ienses view the model *superquadra* apartment as "antifamily," as against the traditional social solidarities and structures of the Brazilian household.

No doubt, this retreat corresponds to deep middle-class needs for the construction of an interior world, as Walter Benjamin (1973: 167) suggests in his essay on nineteenth-century Paris and the fetishism of its middle classes: "The private citizen who in the office took reality into account, required of the interior that it should support him in his illusions." Modernist architecture does not, of course, create this need—it responds to it. Even though the modernist city was intended as an antidote for this bourgeois fantasy world, as a means to forge a newly invigorated collective realm, the elimination of the public spaces of the city street on the one hand and of the informal social spaces of the apartment on the other has in fact left little "room" for anything but the construction of private, interior worlds.

5.3.2 The Apartment Façade

In addition to isolation, the most consistent criticism that *superquadra* residents voice is their condemnation of the uniformity of the residential architecture. As expressed, this criticism is in the first instance directed against the look-alike style of modern architecture. Residents reject what they call the *arquitetura padronizada*, 'standardized pattern architecture', of all building types and forms. While few deny the innovative quality of Brasília's monumental sectors, the uniformity of the residential *superquadras* outweighs this evaluation, producing a general condemnation of the city's "monotony," "sameness," and "standardization." One Brasiliense originally from a small colonial town in Minas Gerais put this rejection quite clearly: "I never felt the 'enthusiasm of Brasília' very strongly because Brasília is very standardized, up to and including the gravestones in the cemetery, standardized."[20] Brasilienses simply object to having to live (and die) in uniform concrete boxes that by law they cannot change.

At the heart of this criticism of modern architecture is the perception that it is fundamentally anti-individualistic. The uniform buildings do not express, simply, that people strive to develop individuating characteristics and that they like to display their differences. The absence of individuating differences is most keenly felt where people live, and it accounts for the frequent use and significance of the criterion of 'personality' (*personalidade*) in evaluations of Brasília's residential architecture. Brasilienses consider that the *superquadra* blocks lack personality not only because their architecture is monotonous, but more basically because it denies the individuality of residents. They feel that the architectural uniformity represses their personality in favor of the totality. It is, therefore, perceived as "fundamentally against people's right to be different, to evolve, to innovate," as one wealthy entrepreneur explained. And this free-market sensibility is often contrasted with the "communist look" of a city that "obeys a pattern."

The criterion of personality reveals what residents consider to be one of the important functions of architecture: to mark status distinctions. Generally, it is the façade of a building that signals through its modeling, size, scale, ornament, and materials such distinctions as wealth, class, family, fashion, and ingenuity. It marks the privileges of private property and the attributes and aspirations of class membership. Façades are used as status markers because they are obviously public presentations of the self within. However, the modern architecture of Brasília denies residents this use. Instead, the standardized, reticulate fenestrations present façades that are rational, abstract, unornamented, and uniformly scaled. Such façades are, of course, no less symbolic, as their many condemnations attest. However, as far as Brasilienses are concerned, they signify very little about their individuality and very much about their anonymity in a bureaucratic city.

There is no doubt that in modern architecture the use of the non-load-bearing glass curtain wall arises from advances in building technology and hygienic concerns. It is an example of the introduction of new building materials and of the industrialization of construction techniques. From the architect's perspective, it expresses the fact that in the new construction systems, the façade is no longer a weight-bearing element; it is rather a light, thin wrapper that lets air, sunshine, and a view of nature into the interior spaces it encloses. However, one cannot argue that its use in the modern construction industry, at least in Brasília, represents an economy of scale. According to the technical director of Encol, one of Brasília's largest construction firms, a glass curtain wall is about 50 percent more expensive to build than a load-bearing masonry wall (interview, Sept. 1981). If it is more expensive, and in this sense less rational, why use it in a situation of limited resources, as was especially the case during Brasília's construction? The technical director's response to this question was that it was used in Brasília's housing blocks because it was specified in the Master Plan and then legislated into the city's building codes that provide a typology of possible patterns and regulate their architectural details. What then motivates the Master Plan?

It has been my intention throughout this work to demonstrate that the specific forms of modernist technological innovation (and even that which motivates the search for innovation) are ideological creations as well. They are developed as instruments of social change, rational order, and political power, and they constitute a set of techniques for defamiliarizing the taken-for-granted, submitting life to the renovations of art, and eliminating the "undesirable." Thus, the ideological objective of standardization is to evoke standardized responses to the agenda of a new way of life embodied in the architecture of the modernist city. The unornamented, transparent façade is a prime example of such an ideological instrument. Just as the elimination of ornament from the façade denies the public display of individual status in architecture, and thus achieves a leveling of private individuals in relation to the public sphere of representations, so the transparency of glass exposes the private domain—previously concealed behind ornamented walls—to a new public scrutiny. The glass transparency turns the domestic domain inside out, so to speak, by the simple technique of dissolving the architectural barrier that prevents one from seeing what goes on inside.

It is an extremely effective technique. Thus, with malicious irony, Brasilienses have nicknamed the glass boxes in which they live "the *candango*'s television set"—meaning that they provide a form of free public entertainment, that the poor man (*candango*) who doesn't have a TV can nevertheless watch the nightly soap operas of middle-class life just by staring at the illuminated façades of the *superquadra* blocks. Brasilienses react to this exposure as an assault on their privacy, which they resist by putting up every kind of visual barrier—curtains, blinds, potted plants, even bird cages. But this resistance matters very little in their evaluation of the intentions and effects of the glass façade because, especially at night when families are at home and apartments are ablaze with light, the sense if not the fact of transparency remains. What matters is that the idea of the glass façade constitutes an attack on the very concept of the private, in which a new arena of morality is created in the display of private lives for possible public censure. The sense that people have about this kind of "public TV" is that it displays individual differences only to eliminate them.

The way in which the transparent façade challenges accepted values of public and private is directly related to the way these values are represented in architectural design. Therefore, it remains for us to analyze this representational structure. The transparent façade constitutes a tactic of defamiliarization in the modernist arsenal of such tactics because it defamiliarizes the conventional values signified by the wall, especially the load-bearing wall, as a prime architectural element. Moreover, it transforms these values in exactly the same way that the modernist city of figural objects transforms the preindustrial city of figural voids: through the inversion of design conventions. The design of the transparent façade thus complements that of the city of objects—the one achieves in elevation what the other achieves in plan. Together, they produce a powerful and elegant harmony of intentions, expressed in both plan and elevation, to transform the idea of the preindustrial city and the experience of the social values its architecture embodies.

We may analyze the structure of the preindustrial (load-bearing) façade, and the modernist transformation of it, in terms of the same solid-void/figure-ground conventions that we used in the analysis of the street. The load-bearing façade is composed of solids and voids like the city on a larger scale. The voids are the openings (windows, doors, and balconies) and the solids the wall surface itself. In perceptual terms, the openings generally have a figural character while the surface functions as ground (fig. 4.20a; consider the blacks as openings and the white as wall).[21]

Not only does a wall support weight, it also establishes a division between inside and outside and thus between private and public. Unless we are told otherwise, by ornament for example, we interpret a wall's opaque surface as signifying what is private. Even if paper thin, its opacity symbolizes both the load-bearing function of the entire wall and its function as barrier, neither of which is symbolized by its openings.[22] By the same token, we look to the openings for some form of access to the spaces within. As places of exposure and exchange, they signify that which is public about the domain inside, and for this reason their frames are often highly ornamented. The perceptual structure of the façade thus provides a simple, legible architectural code for relating the public and the private symbolically—in exactly the same terms as the street code we analyzed earlier:

$$\text{solid (wall surface)} = \text{ground} = \text{private}$$
$$\text{void (wall opening)} = \text{figure} = \text{public}$$

As with the street code, however, it is obvious that not all such solids are private. Sometimes a wall surface is designed to attract public attention, for example, a church façade where the wall surface presents biblical stories in bas-relief or the walls of a city hall where murals, sculptures, or texts describing important events display the city's history. In such façades, the opposition between figure and ground has been reversed so that

185

the wall surface becomes figural. Thus, as in the case of the street, the logic of the façade's perceptual design is semantically efficacious: when the wall surface becomes figural, we know to read a public statement of one sort or another. Once again, the reversal of figure and ground is the key rhetorical principle: the load-bearing façade carries an ambi-valent code for relating public and private values.

Modern architecture produces the transparent façade by inverting the terms of this code, and this inversion in turn ruptures its discourse of reversals. In semiotic terms, the inversion is identical to the one of the street code. Modernist design inverts the figure-ground relation between the wall surface and one type of wall opening, the window, to produce a façade in which the windows are continuous ground and the wall, or what is left of it, is figural. In curtain wall construction, the façade is no longer load-bearing. The wall surface can therefore be reduced to a minimal grid of vertical and horizontal bars (the mullions and spandrels). These function as thin supports for the glass panes, and the windows expand in dimension to fill the entire space between them. Perceptually, this façade is a continuous sheet of glass marked by a network of crossing bars. The sheet of glass (i.e., the void) now serves as the ground whereas the reduced wall surface (i.e., the solids) now possesses the contours and is thus figural (compare figs. 4.20a and b).

This inversion has several consequences. First, the reversals of the ambi-valent preindustrial façade are now impossible. The ground (the windows) cannot become figural, nor the figures (the bars) become ground, without reverting back to the preindustrial type of façade. Moreover, the windows cannot carry any form of ornament without becoming solid (i.e., opaque), which would defeat the intentions of modernist transparency. Nor can the minimal bars carry ornament without greatly expanding their surface area and thus becoming like a traditional wall surface. It should therefore be clear that the elimination of ornament so decried by the *superquadra* resident, and so applauded by the modernist, is inherent in the architectural logic of the transparent façade itself.

Second, if façades say something about public and private values, then the modernist intention to transform these values is clearly expressed in the transparent façade: the customary symbol of the private domain, the wall, is reduced to a minimum, while that of the public, the window, is expanded to a maximum. However, the nature of this public window is not the same as that of the figural window, or that of the balcony or veranda. The end result is a new kind of all-public façade, in which the private plays almost no role—precisely the kind of public TV Brasilienses object to.

Over the years, in fact, the people of Brasília have found this symbolic reduction of the private intolerable: the more recent apartment blocks have returned to an opaque wall architecture. In one sense, the rejection of the transparent façade corresponds to the rejection of the antistreet plan discussed in the previous chapter. They are both negative reactions to the social agenda of the modernist city. In another, more important sense, however, these rejections have different motivations. The first represents an attempt to reconstitute the popular life of the street as a social domain accessible to all. The second represents something more than just an attempt at greater privacy. More significant, it is a result, and a symbolic manifestation, of the privatization of the Plano Piloto itself by an elite group of residents. It represents their rejection (and therefore the failure) of the collectivity of the *superquadra* and the neighborhood unit; it is the product of real estate speculation, of the creation of a housing market after the government sold its *superquadra* apartments, of market forces at work to marginalize the lower-income groups to the satellite cities and to consolidate the center for the upper strata. Thus, to understand further the evolution of residential organization in Brasília, we must examine these processes of social stratification.

For the present, we can conclude that Brasília's modernist design achieves a similar kind of defamiliarization of public and private values in both the civic and the residential realms. On the one hand, it restructures the public life of the city by eliminating the street. On the other, it restructures the residential by reducing the social spaces of the private apartment in favor of a new type of residential collectivity in which the role of the individual is symbolically minimized.

This design, harmonized in plan and elevation, created a kind of new world for the government to populate after the architects unveiled the built city. As one migrant explained about her experiences in this newly inaugurated world: "Everything in Brasília was different. It was a shock, an illusion, because you didn't understand where people lived, or shopped, or worked, or socialized." The architects' responsibilities for planning Brasília effectively terminated when they turned an inhabitable city over to the government in April 1960. They had posed the problem of a new capital for a new Brazil in radical terms and had given it a form that possessed its own agenda of social change. We must now examine how the government planned for the city it commissioned, and how it responded to the contravention of its plans.

TABLE 5.1
Distribution of Employed Population by Sector of Activity,
Federal District, 1970, 1975, 1980

Year	Primary		Secondary		Tertiary		Total
1970	6,996	3.9%	44,401	24.9%	126,914	71.2%	178,311
1975	9,594	3.4	55,407	19.8	215,409	76.8	280,410
1980	11,245	2.5	81,924	17.9	364,676	79.7	457,845

Sources: Derived from Geipot 1975: 21; *PEOT* 1977: vol. 2, 131; IBGE 1981a: 624.

TABLE 5.2
Structure of the Employed Labor Force by Subsector,
Federal District, 1970, 1975, 1980

Subsectors	Employed Population			Percentage of Employed Population		
	1970	1975	1980	1970	1975	1980
Agriculture, mining, fishing	6,996	6,929	11,245	3.9	2.4	2.5
Industry[a]	9,857	18,563	31,429	5.5	6.4	6.9
Construction	34,544	49,252	50,495	19.4	17.1	11.0
Commerce	16,857	34,397	50,956	9.5	11.9	11.1
Transportation, communications	—[b]	14,637	26,237	—[b]	5.1	5.7
Services[c]	(77,994)[b]	96,078	177,290	(43.7)	33.3	38.7
Public administration[d]	32,063	53,120	83,299	18.0	18.4	18.2
Other activities[e]	—[b]	15,821	26,894	—[b]	5.5	5.9
TOTAL	178,311	288,697	457,845	100.0	100.1	100.0

Sources: Derived from *PEOT* 1977: vol. 2, 129; Codeplan 1980: 62; IBGE 1981a: 624

[a]There is no heavy industry in the Federal District. Light industry includes, in order of importance, construction materials, food products and processing, publishing and printing, furniture, rubber products, clothing, shoes, fabrics, and paper products. Most of these are small-scale "cottage industries." In 1974, 44% of factories in the Federal District employed less than 5 workers while only 16% employed more than 20 (Codeplan 1974).

[b]The categories "transportation and communication," "services," and "other activities" are combined for 1970. The percentages for these combined categories for the years 1970, 1975 and 1980 are 43.7%, 43.8%, and 50.3%, respectively.

[c]The category "services" includes activities related to food and lodging, repair and maintenance, personal and domestic affairs, community welfare, entertainment, and to those of the "liberal professions" (architecture, engineering, medicine, law, etc.).

[d]This category also includes activities related to national defense and public security.

[e]"Other activities" is comprised principally of occupations related to institutions of credit and insurance, the real estate market, international organizations and foreign delegations, and others that do not fall into any of the above categories.

TABLE 5.3

Distribution of Jobs by Locality and Sector, 1975

| Locality | Economic Sectors, 1975 | | | | | | | |
	Primary		Secondary		Tertiary		Total	
Federal District	9,594	100.0%	55,207	100.0%	211,986	100.0%	276,787	100.0%
Plano Piloto	1,729	18.0	3,312	6.0	158,989	75.0	164,030	59.3
Satellite cities	7,865	82.0	51,895	94.0	52,997	25.0	112,757	40.7
Guará	543	5.7	3,624	6.6	2,597	1.2	6,764	2.4
N. Bandeirante	35	0.4	760	1.4	5,671	2.3	6,466	2.3
Taguatinga	2,138	22.3	12,194	22.1	21,305	10.1	35,637	12.9
Ceilândia	1,361	14.2	13,680	24.8	7,790	3.7	22,831	8.3
Gama	1,589	16.6	12,780	23.2	8,214	3.9	22,583	8.2
Sobradinho	395	4.1	4,221	7.7	4,929	2.3	9,545	3.5
Planaltina	819	8.5	2,984	5.4	2,491	1.2	6,294	2.3
Brazlândia	985	10.3	1,652	3.0	—	—	2,637	1.0

Sources: Derived from Geipot 1979: 52; *PEOT* 1977: vol. 2, 135.

TABLE 5.4

Spatial Distribution of Tertiary-Sector Jobs
in the Plano Piloto, 1973, 1975, 2000 (Summary)

| Locality | Jobs | | | Percentage of Jobs in Plano Piloto | | | Percentage of Jobs in Federal District | | |
	1973	1975[a]	2000	1973	1975	2000	1973	1975	2000
Federal District	197,034	211,986	790,623						
Plano Piloto	91,345	158,989	355,780	100.0	100.0	100.0	46.4	75.0	45.0
Monumental sectors	64,430	91,907	219,390	70.5	57.8	61.7	32.7	43.4	27.8
Residential sectors[b]	16,812	43,495	86,778	18.4	27.4	24.4	8.5	20.5	11.0
Other sectors	10,103	23,588	49,612	11.1	14.8	14.0	5.1	11.1	6.3

Sources: Derived from Geipot 1975: 97, 141–46, 156–60, 165–67; Geipot 1979: 54–55, 60–62.
Sector-by-sector data for 1975 may be found in Holston 1986: table 5.2.

[a]The 1975 data do not distinguish the employment along the commercial avenue of W-3 from that of the Local Commercial sectors of Bands 100 and 300 in the South Wing, or from that in the Public Building Sector (W-3 north) of the North Wing. To give a more realistic view of the demand for labor, the distinction between these sectors of the aggregate number of jobs is estimated. This estimation is based on a comparison with 1973 data which does distinguish between these various commercial sectors.

[b]Figures do not include informal market jobs. These are especially important for women from the satellite cities who work as domestics. The figures cited refer to jobs in the residential commercial sectors.

TABLE 5.5
Distribution of Businesses in the Federal District
by Locality, 1974

Locality	Type of Business													
	1		2		3		4		5		6		7	
PP	164	26.6%	3247	34.0%	53	68.8%	1184	69.7%	166	43.6%	1449	51.6%	71	34.0%
GU	9	1.5	109	1.1	—	—	12	0.7	6	1.6	290	10.3	10	4.8
NB	40	6.5	709	7.4	5	6.5	95	5.6	19	5.0	71	2.5	5	2.4
TA	275	44.6	2231	23.4	19	24.7	296	17.4	57	15.0	614	21.0	64	30.6
CE	—a	—	1104	11.6	—	—	33	1.9	51	13.4	66	2.4	17	8.1
GA	77	12.5	1041	10.9	—	—	37	2.2	54	14.2	151	5.4	26	12.4
SO	35	5.7	597	6.3	—	—	31	1.8	15	3.9	144	5.1	9	4.3
PL	15	2.4	368	3.9	—	—	8	0.5	7	1.8	18	0.6	6	2.9
BR	1	0.2	143	1.5	—	—	4	0.2	6	1.6	4	0.1	1	0.5
TOTAL	616		9,549		77		1,700		381		2,807		209	

Sources: Derived from Codeplan 1974; 1980: 77.

1 Industry
2 Commerce
3 Transportation and communication

4 Services
5 Social activities
6 Professional activities

7 Other activities

PP Plano Piloto
GU Guará
NB Núcleo Bandeirante

TA Taguatinga
CE Ceilândia
GA Gama

SO Sobradinho
PL Planaltina
BR Brazlândia

aCeilândia's industries are included with Taguatinga's.

190

TABLE 5.6
Relations between Work and Residence:
Commuting between the Satellite Cities and the Plano Piloto, 1970

Locality of Residence	Jobs in Locality	Residents Employed in Locality	Persons Working outside Locality	Persons Working in Plano Piloto	Attraction of Plano Piloto
Taguatinga	16,931	14,438	17,890	14,927	83.4%
Gama	5,165	4,715	11,884	9,939	83.6
Sobradinho	4,389	3,770	5,606	5,010	89.3
Planaltina	2,587	2,427	2,567	1,674	65.2
N. Bandeirante	5,173	1,598	2,325	1,654	71.1
Brazlândia	725	608	1,552	925	59.6
Squatter Settlements	4,648	4,507	17,521	12,781	72.9
Temporary	1,682	320	1,362	1,122	82.3
Total			60,707	48,036	
			100%	79.13%	

Source: Adapted from Barboza and Paviani 1972.

TABLE 5.7
Commuter Trips by Motive and Locality,
Federal District, 1975

Locality	House to Work	House to School	House to Other	Nondomestic Origin	Total	Percentage of Federal District Commuter Trips
Plano Piloto	553,389	195,157	227,749	76,023	1,032,318	82.9%
Guará	6,895	3,944	7,158	1,543	19,450	1.6
N. Bandeirante	9,534	1,574	5,387	1,164	17,659	1.4
Taguatinga	44,328	18,110	48,345	5,948	116,731	9.4
Ceilândia	5,195	937	4,961	916	12,009	1.0
Gama	11,598	2,790	8,830	1,446	24,664	2.0
Sobradinho	5,832	2,493	4,499	779	13,603	1.1
Planaltina	1,426	164	1,093	158	2,841	0.2
Rest of FD	3,669	614	1,585	182	6,045	0.5
Total	621,861	225,783	309,607	88,159	1,245,410	100.1%

Source: Geipot 1979: 48.

TABLE 5.8
Urban Population by Locality, Federal District,
1960, 1970, 1975, 1980

Locality[a]	Resident Population							
	1960		1970		1975		1980	
Federal District	141,742		546,015		859,187		1,177,393	
Urban	127,204	89.8%	524,315	96.0%	827,419	96.3%	1,139,480	96.8%
Rural	14,538	10.3	21,700	4.0	31,768	3.7	37,913	3.2
Plano Piloto	68,665	48.4	156,668	28.7	198,579	23.1	246,360	20.9
Cruzeiro	—	—	—	—	29,696	3.5	44,197	3.8
Satellite Cities	58,539	41.3	367,648	67.3	599,135	69.7	848,923	72.1
Guará	—	—	24,864	4.6	69,100	8.0	97,057	8.2
N. Bandeirante	21,033	14.8	11,268	2.1	17,926	2.1	23,691	2.0
Taguatinga	26,111	18.4	107,347	19.7	165,124	19.2	217,154	18.4
Ceilândia	—	—	84,205	15.4	117,761	13.7	256,207	21.8
Gama	(16,472)		72,406	13.3	121,036	14.1	132,726	11.3
Sobradinho	8,478	6.0	39,458	7.2	56,432	6.6	62,980	5.4
Planaltina	2,917	2.1	18,508	3.4	35,361	4.1	39,964	3.4
Brazlândia	(355)	—	9,592	1.8	16,395	1.9	19,144	1.6

Sources: Adapted from IBGE 1959: 79; *PEOT* 1977: vol. 2, 47; Codeplan 1980: 53; IBGE 1981c: 5.

[a]The rural areas of Paranoá and Jardim are not included. In 1980, the population of the former was 3,483 and of the latter was 4,552. The populations of Brazlândia and Gama are given for May 1959 and September 1961, respectively.

TABLE 5.9
Urban Population Change by Decade, Federal District, 1960–80

Locality	Percentage of Population Change	
	1960–70	1970–80
Federal District	285.2	115.6
Urban	312.2	117.3
Rural	49.3	74.7
Plano Piloto	128.2	57.3
Cruzeiro	—	—
Satellite Cities	528.0	130.9
Guará	—	290.4
N. Bandeirante	(−46.4)	110.3
Taguatinga	311.1	102.3
Ceilândia	—	204.3
Gama	337.6	83.3
Sobradinho	365.4	59.6
Planaltina	534.5	115.9
Brazlândia	2,602.0	99.6

Source: Table 5.8.

TABLE 5.10
Residential Sectors:
Population, Dwelling, Density, Green Areas, Income

	Traffic Zone[a]	Percent of Population 1975	Dwellings	Density (residents per hectare)	Green Area[b] (meters^2 per resident)	Number of Minimum Salaries[c] (per dwelling per month)
Federal District[d]		[100.0][e]	141,192	1.6	—	7.2
Plano Piloto		100.0	43,957	2.6	—	14.0
		[29.1]				
Superquadras		66.3	29,921	276	23.3	15.6
SQS 100/300 ⎫		(36.1)	(10,753)	244	24.7	19.4
⎬ 37–55						
SQS 200/400 ⎭		(36.0)	(11,286)	256	22.7	14.1
SQN 100/300 ⎫		(14.0)	(3,937)	314	18.7	14.3
⎬ 58–76						
SQN 200/400 ⎭		(13.9)	(3,945)	289	21.7	11.0
SHIGS 700	41, 48, 51	7.0	2,980	154	30.1	14.6
SHCGN 700	64, 69, 74	3.5	1,400	114	52.8	15.4
Isolated mansions	23	0.1	74	—	—	20.5
Vila Planalto	22	1.6	602	—	—	4.3
South Lake	84–87	3.2	1,277	21	278.8	20.5
North Lake	88–89	1.8	665	—	—	—
SHIN	88	(25.6)	(170)	21	278.8	19.3
SML	89	(74.4)	(495)	10	—	3.2
Military sectors	30, 79	1.2	499	—	—	10.0
Cruzeiro Velho	56	4.2	1,544	160	—	6.6
Cruzeiro Novo	57	7.4	3,538	305	—	7.1
Parkway	78, 90–91					
mansions	93–96	1.4	502	1	5,086.0	5.2
Industrial sectors	80–81	0.4	179	—	—	3.0
SPMS	82	1.4	555	—	—	3.7
Granja do Torto	83	0.2	80	—	—	4.1
Octagonal	92	—	—	—	—	—
Miscellaneous		0.3	141	—	—	5.8
Satellite Cities		[70.9]	97,235	125	—	4.2
Guará		[9.6]	13,501	206	11.1	6.0
N. Bandeirante		[1.2]	1,580	187	—	5.2
Taguatinga		[21.1]	31,254	138	18.4	4.5
Ceilândia		[12.7]	16,986	136	23.5	3.0
Gama		[15.2]	19,115	112	—	3.5
Sobradinho		[7.0]	9,519	81	87.9	4.5
Planaltina		[4.0]	5,280	145	25.1	2.8

Sources: Derived from Geipot 1975: 15, 80–87, 96, 167; Geipot 1979: 22, 57; *PEOT* 1977: vol. 2, 225–26, 240; Codeplan 1980: 60.

SQS   Superquadra South
SQN   Superquadra North
SHIGS   Sector of Individual Paired Dwellings South
SHCGN Sector of Collective and Paired Dwellings North
SHIN   Sector of Individual Dwellings North (Lake)
SML   Sector of Lake Mansions
SPMS   Sector of Gas Stations and Motels South

^aSee map 5.3.

^b"Green area" refers to the planned recreational space within the *superquadras* and between rows of paired or single houses.

^cThe official minimum salary for the period May 1975 to May 1976 was Cr$532.80, which was equivalent to U.S.$58.74 at the 1975 exchange rate. The number of minimum salaries per dwelling per month was calculated from the Geipot survey of 1975. This survey found the average monthly income per dwelling for the total number of dwellings within each traffic zone in the Federal District (map 5.3). To arrive at an overall estimate for areas of more than one zone (e.g., for the satellite cities as compared to the Plano Piloto, or for the bands of *superquadras*), I adopted the following method. The average monthly income per dwelling of each zone was multiplied by the total number of dwellings in that zone. The resulting income subtotals were added to arrive at a weighted composite estimate that proportionately reflects the different income levels of each component zone. This income total was then divided by the total number of dwellings, and the resulting average monthly income per dwelling for the composite area was divided by the minimum salary for 1975.

^dData do not include Brazlândia or the rural areas of Paranoá and Jardim. Population figures vary somewhat from those given in table 5.8.

^eFigures in brackets are percentages of Federal District population. Figures in parentheses are subpercentages of their most proximate inclusive categories.

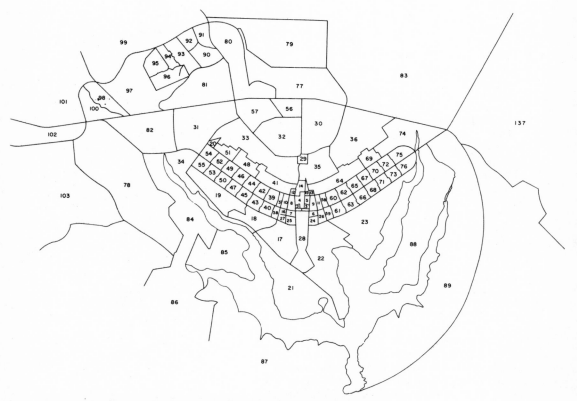

Map 5.3 Traffic zones and sectors of Brasília, 1975 (Source: Geipot 1979)

TABLE 5.11
Spatial Distribution of Average Income,
Superquadras, 1975

Traffic Zone[a]	*Superquadras*	Number of Minimum Salaries[b] (per dwelling per month)
South Wing bands 100 and 300		
37	SQS 102, 302	19.2
39	SQS 103, 104, 303, 304	17.7
42	SQS 105, 106, 305, 306	20.7
44	SQS 107, 108, 307, 308	20.7
46	SQS 109, 110, 309, 310	19.4
49	SQS 111, 112, 311, 312	17.9
52	SQS 113, 114, 313, 314	20.7
54	SQS 115, 116, 315, 316	19.1
South Wing bands 200 and 400		
38	SQS 202, 402	16.8
40	SQS 203, 204, 403, 404	15.5
43	SQS 205, 206, 405, 406	17.0
45	SQS 207, 208, 407, 408	15.4
47	SQS 209, 210, 409, 410	11.9
50	SQS 211, 212, 411, 412	11.0
53	SQS 213, 214, 413, 414	11.6
55	SQS 215, 216, 415, 416	14.7
South Wing band 700		
41	SHIGS 702–707	17.5
48	SHIGS 709–712	11.6
51	SHIGS 713–715	15.5
North Wing bands 100 and 300		
58	SQN 102, 302	24.8
60	SQN 103, 104, 303, 304	15.7
62	SQN 105, 106, 305, 306	10.5
65	SQN 107, 108, 307, 308	22.8
67	SQN 109, 110, 309, 310	—
70	SQN 111, 112, 311, 312	12.7
72	SQN 113, 114, 313, 314	9.9
75	SQN 115, 116, 315, 316	—
North Wing bands 200 and 400		
59	SQN 202, 402	23.3
61	SQN 203, 204, 403, 404	11.2
63	SQN 205, 206, 405, 406	11.3
66	SQN 207, 208, 407, 408	9.1
68	SQN 209, 210, 409, 410	11.2
71	SQN 211, 212, 411, 412	9.4
73	SQN 213, 214, 413, 414	—
76	SQN 215, 216, 415, 416	—

(*continued*)

TABLE 5.11 (*continued*)
Spatial Distribution of Average Income,
Superquadras, 1975

Traffic Zone[a]	*Superquadras*	Number of Minimum Salaries[b] (per dwelling per month)
	North Wing band 700	
64	SHCGN 702–710	15.6
69	SHCGN 711–713	15.7
74	SHCGN 714–716	13.6

Source: See table 5.10.

[a]See map 5.3.

[b]See table 5.10, note c.

PART THREE

THE RECOVERY OF HISTORY

SIX

Rights to the City

If the fundamental premise of Brasília's foundation is that it should signal the dawn of a new Brazil, then it is precisely its exemplary uniqueness among Brazilian cities that defines it as a blueprint of development. This utopian difference between capital and nation meant that the planning of Brasília had to negate Brazil as it existed. Thus, the Master Plan presents the founding of the city as if it had no history. Similarly, the government intended to unveil the built city as if it were without a history of construction and occupation. On inauguration day, it planned to reveal a miracle: a gleaming city, empty and ready to receive its intended occupants. This presentation of an inhabitable idea denied the Brazil that the city had already acquired: its population of builders.

However, whereas Costa's narrative dehistoricized Brasília by mythologizing its first principles, the government's planners paradoxically rehistoricized it. This paradox in planning efforts follows from an inherent contradiction of utopia: to be different, an imagined utopia must negate the prevailing order that generates a desire for it and to be autonomous, it must remain dehistoricized. Yet, in so doing, it becomes powerless to achieve autonomy since whatever substance it might have comes from that very order. This contradiction is unavoidable in utopian projects because any attempt to use the prevailing order destroys the utopian difference that is the project's premise. The Master Plan defuses this contradiction by concealing the historical origins and intentions of Brasília in a cloak of mytho-poetics. Thus, as an imagined utopia, it remains silent about the details of the city's construction, settlement, and organization, for these would have negated its objective: freedom from existing conditions, from what was inadequate and unacceptable in Brazil. They would have violated the strictures of utopian discourse and compromised the idea of a capital city.

In giving this idea substance, however, the government could not avoid compromising its own intention to break with Brazilian history: it could not entirely negate the prevailing order that it had to use to construct the city. The solution it attempted to this paradox was to recruit a labor force for the purposes of construction, but to use its executive and police powers to remove that labor force from the built capital. By denying residential rights to the construction workers, it intended to keep the Brazil they represented from taking root in the inaugural city. The difficulty with this solution is that it destroyed the utopian project. The government planners necessarily and even unconsciously used the only means available to secure their objective: the mechanisms of social stratification and repression that constitute the very society they sought to exclude. In so doing, they introduced the principles and processes of this society into the foundations of Brasília.

This Brazilianization of the city is not, however, a simple reversal of the initial inversion. The counter-*brincadeira* in the story is not merely a reflection of the order of the realm back to the capital. Founded on a paradox, Brasiliense society developed from the interaction of its utopic and dystopic elements. This dialectic generated new administrative initiatives as planners tried to keep the actual in line with the imagined. These directives, however, only reiterated the initial paradox: for planners responded to the deformation of their plans by exorcising the factors they held responsible (such as illegal squatter settlements, chaotic growth, and subversive political organization) by the same dystopic measures (such as denying political rights, repressing voluntary associations, and restricting the distribution of public goods). Thus, in compounding the basic contradictions of Brasília's premises, they created an exaggerated version—almost a caricature—of what they had sought to escape. Their initiatives produced a unique city, but not the one they imagined. Rather, they turned Brasília into an exemplar of social and spatial stratification—one that clearly demonstrates, moreover, the role of government in promoting inequality.

In the following chapters, I analyze this paradoxical development and establish its initial conditions in the stratified recruitment of Brasília's inaugural population, the mobilization of pioneers to rebel against their exclusion from the built capital, and the consequences of their rebellion. Although these chapters are, therefore, partly studies in social history, I want to say at the outset that they have an anthropological motivation: my purpose is to account for the distribution of political relations that I found in the city during my fieldwork and that I could only understand by inquiring into the history of Brasília's settlement. Thus, the questions I ask of this past are those formulated to illuminate the ethnographic present, a configuration I seek to understand as a result of historical transformation—in this case, one constituted in the denial and paradoxical recovery of history.[1]

6.1 Populating an Idea: Differential Incorporation

President Juscelino Kubitschek celebrated the foundation of Brasília with a First Mass on 3 May 1957. In so doing, he ritually reenacted the founding of Brazil as marked on 3 May 1500 by Pedro Álvares Cabral's First Mass in the New World. Kubitschek's objective in reenacting a primordial moment of Brazilian history was not unlike Costa's in using ancient cities and sacred symbols to inspire his Master Plan. Both intended to legitimate their efforts by historical analogy. For Kubitschek, the analogy enabled him to claim that by marking the epicenter of national space, the foundation of Brasília signified nothing less than the refoundation of Brazil itself at a national rather than a colonial stage of development. Assuming the epithet of his imperial predecessor, King D. João III, the Populator, Kubitschek saw this act of founding a capital city as the means to establish a radiating sovereignty, as the means to consolidate, civilize, and populate his nation-continent.

However, in keeping with the kaleidoscopic appropriations typical of this kind of legitimation, Kubitschek's analogy was also with Brazil's first governor-general, Tomé de Sousa. In his memoirs (1975: 369), he describes Tomé de Sousa's mission as the avatar of his own development project. Both rulers, he suggests, arrived on the "shores" of an "empty" land with two plans in hand: one for the construction of the capital city (Salvador and Brasília); the other for the institutional organization of the polity (the Rules of Government of the colony of Brazil and the Organic Laws of Brasília). In Kubitschek's own terms, what united the destiny of both cases was their inversion of the usual ontological relation between a state and its people: the plans were intended to create the polities (in the sense of both the social units and the political systems) to which they would later belong. As Kubitschek (ibid.) observes, "In point of fact, there did not exist the Brazil that the governor-general had to govern." Rather, both rulers arrived before the populations for whom they built their cities, and both prepared models of their respective polities before these polities had citizens to organize accordingly. Neither considered the prior inhabitants, namely, the Amerindians or the construction workers of Brasília, entitled to full membership in their imaginary domains. Instead, both rulers viewed their capital cities as the means to mark the arrival of a civilizing order destined to rule an as yet unconsolidated territory. In this sense, both capitals were means to create an empire of signs in polities as yet without substance, in polities awaiting their predestined civilizations.

To construct his city and to recruit its legitimate population, Kubitschek created a number of federal agencies, enterprises, and commissions of a statutory type. Of these, there were two principal umbrella organizations, one for each fundamental objective. Part of his so-called indirect administration of government, the first was the state enterprise Companhia Urbanizadora da Nova Capital do Brasil (henceforth, Novacap).[2] It was launched in 1956 by legislative act under the directorship of Israel Pinheiro and charged with building the city and administering its affairs during the construction period. Having sponsored the national competition, which Lúcio Costa won, Novacap organized technical teams to develop and coordinate the realization of his Master Plan. These teams produced blueprints for the city's buildings, roadways, electrical power, water supply, communications, hospitals, schools, and the like. In addition, Novacap was responsible for the affairs of the vast construction camp itself—for the recruitment of personnel, for the supply of building materials, for the contractual obligations and overall supervision of the construction, for the organization of goods and services for construction crews, and for the maintenance of law and order. Between 1956 and 1960, Novacap exercised these functions as a ministate ruling an island of activity in the Central Plateau. For all practical purposes, it exercised absolute power over a frontier population of pioneers that had reached almost one hundred thousand by inauguration day.

The second organization that Kubitschek created was responsible for the recruitment of the population for which the capital had been built: the civil servants of the federal bureaucracy. Part of the Kubitschek's direct administration, the Grupo de Trabalho de Brasília (henceforth, GTB) was a task force founded in 1958 under the presidency of João Guilherme de Aragão in his capacity as director general of DASP.[3] Kubitschek charged the GTB with preparing suggestions, in the form of plans and schedules, for all matters concerning the transfer of the federal institutions of government and their employees. To accomplish this task, the GTB gathered representatives from all civilian and military ministries, from the various institutions of the legislative and judicial branches of government, and from Novacap. In addition to actually recruiting federal functionaries for the transfer, its various subgroups prepared proposals to organize the bureaucracy and its employees in postinaugural Brasília. These proposals included a constitutional reform covering all aspects of law affected by the transfer of the capital, the Organic Law of political organization, the Law of Judicial Organization, a budget, and a number of other projects that altogether defined the legal status of the Federal District, its administrative and political structures, and its residential organization. I shall use the term the Organic Laws of Brasília to refer to the combined intentions of these proposals including, in a wider sense, those of Novacap and the GTB for both the pre- and the postinaugural organization of the city.

To understand the nature of these intentions, it is necessary to focus on the organization of those people that the government included as full members in the bureaucratic polity in relation to those that it excluded, or considered to have less than full rights. We must focus on this differentiation because the government's project was to organize its own corps of employees into a localized corporate unit, a Federal District, with unique identities, determinate boundaries and memberships, autonomy in relation to other municipalities, presumptive perpetuity, and organization and procedures necessary to regulate its collective affairs. This project of incorporation therefore rests on a set of minimal criteria that constitutes and differentiates the population of Brasília. These criteria are expressed in membership rules and conditions that regulate the status of members, their participation in the public domain of their social units, and their obligations, privileges, and powers. For this reason, if we are to understand the government's intentions in populating Brasília, we must analyze the basis on which it incorporated the population of civil servants as full citizens of the city in contrast to those that it sought to exclude as having no such rights.[4]

The principal criteria of incorporation were those that regulated who would have rights to reside in the new city. These rights of residence referred to access to housing in the Plano Piloto, the only planned, permanent, and authorized new settlement in the Federal District. Specifically, they were expressed in the rules and conditions regulating access to the *superquadra* apartments and row houses constructed and owned by the government, as these were the only authorized residences available in the Plano Piloto at the time of its inauguration. As these residences were public property and constituted the major resource of Brasília's public domain, the rules relating to their distribution both reflected and established basic conditions of participation in this domain. Therefore, to expose the nature and consequences of the government's plan for incorporation, we shall focus on the distribution of rights to residence as revealing basic criteria that established different statuses among Brasília's inaugural population.

These criteria segmented the population into two recruitment units with differential access to the public domain: the one recruited by Novacap for the city's construction, which the government deprived of rights to reside in the city; and the other recruited by the GTB for the bureaucracy of the capital, which the government endowed with a variety of settlement rights, the most important of which was the right to reside in the apartments the construction workers had built. Moreover, although the Novacap unit was incorporated with unique identities, memberships, and boundaries, its members lacked the autonomous political organization and administrative procedures necessary for collective action or representation. In contrast, the GTB unit was organized as a corporate group through two types of representative councils. Thus, although all of the Brazilians recruited to Brasília were citizens of Brazil, not all citizens were equally enrolled in Brasília's public domain. This differential distribution of rights to closed sections of the population defined Brasília as a differentially incorporated polity within the federation of Brazilian states and territories.[5]

This stratified recruitment of Brasília's inaugural populations constituted the essence of the government's plan to settle and organize the new capital. It determined their structure and articulation, and therefore established the terms of their subsequent social and political transformations: on the one hand, the construction workers transformed themselves politically by mobilizing into representative associations to protest their lack of rights to the city; on the other, the bureaucrats lost their urban political organization with the dissolution of one of their representative councils. This demise left the Plano Piloto residents as a whole without legitimate means for collective action or representation in the city's public domain. Moreover, for that very reason, it freed the elite sectors of society from collective sanctions, allowing them to pursue their own interests in the city at the expense of the less powerful.

The significance of differential incorporation in understanding these developments is not diminished by the fact that the construction camp was planned as a temporary settlement. In the first place, while the government's plan assumed, however unwisely, that the majority of construction workers would go home after the inauguration, they did not. Second, this assumption was patently contradicted by the need, known from the beginning, for massive numbers of workers to continue building the barely inhabitable Brasília after its due date. These workers remained systematically excluded from the Plano Piloto. Finally, the very conception of a city dedicated to a single function necessarily presumes some form of differential incorporation of the population, if full access to its public domain is restricted to residents who exercise this function. In this case, the single function is administration. But the presumption applies equally to ritual and military cities, for example, ruled by status groups exercising authority over a more inclusive polity. Thus, Brasília's identity as a solely administrative city necessarily entails differential access to its public domain for those who either are or are not prior members of the bureaucracy. As we shall see shortly, this identity was clearly stated as a founding principle of Brasília's Organic Laws.[6]

Thus, even if planners intended that the disadvantaged population of construction workers should eventually disappear, the two recruitment units cannot be isolated from each other in understanding the development of Brasiliense society. Rather, our methodological challenge is to grasp this development as a relational process. For in fact, the government did not create a city *of* bureaucrats, unveiled on inauguration day to consist largely of a population of federal functionaries enjoying equal access to the public residences. Rather, it created a city *for* bureaucrats who were a minority population with privileged access to a public domain of resources which excluded the vast majority. Therefore, even before its inauguration, Brasília was a stratified city in which differential incorporation was the fundamental condition of social organization.

The basis of recruitment to this organization was occupation. Thus, among those recruited by Novacap for the construction project, we find engineers, architects, skilled and unskilled workers, merchants, agriculturalists, and administrative functionaries of the enterprise itself. Similarly, among those recruited by the GTB for the bureaucracy, we find ministers of state, department heads, technical advisors, clerks, stenographers, chauffeurs, janitors, and coffee-boys. It is thus evident that each group was composed of members occupying vastly different class and status positions. Nevertheless, by virtue of their recruitment and regardless of their backgrounds, all of them came to Brasília to find themselves in one of two situations with respect to their rights or lack of rights to the city. This recruitment defined what was peculiar and fundamental to Brasília's inaugural populations: both the Novacap and the GTB units were composed of people who usually belonged to different social groups and categories but who found themselves united in their status with respect to the distribution of rights to the city. It was the incorporation of such differences into the same recruitment group that established not only what was socially radical about the constitution of Brasília's collective domain, but also the terms of the social conflicts that destroyed it.

On the one hand, the GTB planners had as an objective the leveling of previous status differences by distributing the same rights to the city to different social classes; that is, they sought to create one status group out of several different ones in relation to residence in the *superquadras*. This "principle of equality," as the planners called it, established an egalitarian mixing of different classes in the same residential unit. However, the mixture proved explosive, igniting class and status conflicts among the residents. In turn, these conflicts led to the demise of the planned collective structure of the *superquadras*, to alliances between the privileged GTB class and their social counterparts among those not originally entitled to reside in the government apartments, and eventually to the marginalization of the lowest class of civil servants from the city. On the other hand, for most of the Novacap recruits, their collective disabilities established the basis for interclass alliances around demands for rights to reside in the Federal District. These demands led, rebelliously, to political mobilization, to violent confrontation with the state, and eventually to the creation of the satellite cities.

To understand the structure of these events is to grasp the way they developed as a field of possible actions and thus the way historical change is organized. The first step is to reveal the principles of Novacap's recruitment of pioneers and their internal differentiation in terms of (*a*) market relations (i.e., recruitment to construction or to commerce), (*b*) status relations (i.e., eligibility for settlement rights and housing privileges), and (*c*) power relations (i.e., political organization and capacity for collective action). In this chapter, our concern is with the constitution of these relations and with the structures of meaning that rendered them significant for the development of collective interests; in the next, with the actions, processes, and transformations that engage them.

6.2 The Recruitment of Pioneers

In early 1957, the Kubitschek regime began a national campaign to enlist people for the construction of Brasília. It sought volunteers for three purposes: to build the capital, to supply the construction, and to plan and administer the project. For these purposes, it recruited laborers and building professionals, entrepreneurs of various sorts, and functionaries of Novacap and other state agencies. All of these people lived at the construction site of the future capital and were called "pioneers." The recruitment campaign focused on popularizing the construction of Brasília as the means to forge a new national identity. Broadcast to the nation as a media event, the core of this campaign was an appeal for Brazilians from all regions and backgrounds to participate in a public works project intended to produce national integration. The participation of difference in the creation of a new national identity was thus the principle of its rhetorical legitimation. This discourse of participation was in turn reinforced by another concerning the frontier solidarity and democracy of the pioneers, a discourse propagated both in their own testaments about the construction era and in official publications on Brasília.

Both aspects of this legitimation were, however, in fundamental conflict with the actual instruments of national integration. The discourse of participation was contradicted by the regime's plan to incorporate the inaugural populations of Brasília differentially: it sought to recruit massive numbers of pioneers who would ultimately be excluded from the city they built. The discourse of frontier solidarity and democracy was contradicted by the labor conditions and recruitment processes of the construction project: these stratified the pioneers into various classes with different interests, privileges, and powers in relation to each other—establishing a structure of differences that generated struggles and alliances among these classes, one that we need to understand in order to account for the political destiny of the pioneers as a whole.

In the following discussion, therefore, I shall first analyze these discourses of recruitment and then the processes of stratification that contradict them. My concern in discussing the former is to show how the government presented its intentions to the nation rather than to look at the actual motivations of migrants. These motivations we shall examine in relation to the labor market of the construction project. In addition, I am concerned to show how the regime's discourses of participation—contradicted by its practices in establishing market, status, and power relations in the construction territory—structured subsequent collective actions by pioneers and the state's response to them.

6.2.1 Discourses of Participation: Reinventing the Nation

Kubitschek waged his recruitment campaign in the press, radio, and television. It was not as if this campaign was absolutely necessary to get the project underway. For that, he had only to conquer the opposition in congress. It was more that he made Brasília the metasymbol of his developmentalism so that in generating enthusiasm for it, he was at the same time justifying his entire administration and its enormous expenditures, his policies of economic development, and ultimately his vision of the future of Brazil. He made his case to the nation through a skillful media campaign which presented all aspects of the construction and inauguration of Brasília as a pageant of Brazilian progress, magnifying his own charisma by appearing at its animating center.

In this context, Brasília's legitimation involved three basic rhetorical strategies. The first is one we have already encountered in relation to the symbolic appeal of Brasília's modernism. It is the aesthetic of erasure and reinscription, of the possibility signified in modernist architecture and planning of effacing the old order and of inscribing a new one. This discourse of rupture with the past that simultaneously posits a radiant future was adopted by the industrial concerns that stood to gain from Kubitschek's policies. If we look, for example, at their advertising campaigns during those years, we see how important participants in the project of building the new Brazil interpreted Kubitschek's recruitment appeal and rebroadcast it. Thus, to take a sample of newspaper and magazine advertisements announcing the participation of firms in the construction of the capital, we find: "Here begins a new Brazil!—Rupturita Explosives Incorporated (a pioneer in the explosives industry)"; "Brasília: The dawn of a new era—Bimetal Incorporated"; "The decisive mark of national progress—Mercedes Benz of Brazil"; and "Brasília: A new path—Cobrasma Incorporated."[7]

While the past is being put aside in these texts, one also finds the equally dominant theme of legitimation by historical analogy. Thus, we find Phillips Petroleum announcing that in Brasília "Brazil sees realized the dream of the Inconfidentes [the independence movement of 1789] and the Ideal of the Republicans." Other common historical analogies found in such advertisements include "Brasília realizes the dream of Dom Bosco" and "fulfills the discovery of Brazil." In Kubitschek's brand of heady optimism for progress, these two types of legitimation— by historical rupture and by historical recapitulation—are complementary not contradictory. While the one breaks with the past as it leaps into the future, the other identifies that future as the true realization of Brazil's initial promise, which the intervening years had failed to achieve. The simultaneity of rupture and recapitulation in creating a second new nation is exactly the meaning of the declaration of *Manchete*, the popular weekly magazine, on the title page of its special inaugural edition, 21 April 1960: "The ringing of the bell that announced the death of Tiradentes [the executed leader of the Inconfidentes] proclaimed the inauguration of Brasília."

Of the many analogies linking Brasília to the glorious spirit of History, perhaps none received greater national attention than the denomination of all those who participated in the construction of the capital as "the *bandeirantes* of the twentieth century." As a manufacturer of building materials put it, "Eternit salutes the brave *bandeirantes* who with their courage and sacrifice drove in the foundations of the most modern city in the world, confirming the great technical and creative capacity of the Brazilian people." During Brazil's colonial period, *bandeirantes* were groups of armed adventurers who penetrated to the heartlands of South America seeking gold, diamonds, Indian slaves, African runaways, and the land of eternal youth.[8] They marched through the backlands of the continent, raiding Indian villages and procreating with Indian women. In addition to miscegenation, their most lasting legacy is an ideology of marching westward, of expanding the frontier, and above all of taming the land, known as *bandeirismo*. Although Vargas appealed to this frontier legacy throughout the Estado Novo to stimulate the agricultural colonization of the central west, it was rather to the columns of migrants on the road to Brasília in the late fifties that the popular press dedicated the epithet of latter-day *bandeirante*.[9] With this dedication, the term *bandeirante* came to mean not a frontier marauder but rather the builder of a new Brazil.

Initially, however, there were two distinct categories of Brasília *bandeirantes*. There were "pioneers" and there were *candangos* among those the government recruited during the years 1956 to 1960. At the beginning of this period, the term *pioneer* referred specifically to "the firsts" (another category of honor): to the first state officials, professionals, merchants, cultivators (Nippo-Brazilian specialists from São Paulo), and the like in the construction territory; to all, that is, except the construction workers from the interior (skilled or unskilled) who constituted the mass of *bandeirantes*. Those were *candangos*. While the term *pioneer* was used as an honorific, the term *candango* was derogatory, almost offensive. It signified a man without qualities, without culture, a vagabond lower-class lowbrow.

The etymology of this word encapsulates a good bit of the history of Luso-African and Luso-Brazilian class relations before it undergoes a fundamental but brief redefinition in the course of Brasília's construction. Until Brasília, it was for centuries an omnibus word of derogation. According to most authorities, it is a corruption of *candongo*, a word from the Quimbundo or Quilombo language of the Southwestern Bantu of Angola. It was the term by which the Africans referred, disparagingly, to the Portuguese colonizers. As such, it came to the New World with Angolan slaves. In Brazil, it first appears on northeastern sugar cane plantations where slaves applied it in derision to their Lusitanian and later Brazilian masters. However, at some point, the Brazilians managed to invert the referent of denigration: the word *candango* becomes a synonym of *cafuzo*, the offspring of an Amerindian and a Negro; or, more exactly in the congeries of Brazilian racial types, the offspring of a *mameluco* (Amerindian + Caucasian) and a Negro. As these racial mixtures constitute a great part of Brazil's backland population, the word *candango* became a general term for people from the interior as opposed to the coast, and especially for the poor itinerant laborers whom the interior has produced in such quantities.

With these laborers, the term came to Brasília. During the course of the capital's construction, however, both its sense and its referent fundamentally changed. Brasília's recruitment campaign identified the new nation-builder as "the common man." It placed at center stage, in the limelight of national attention and faith, those who had previously been excluded from principal roles in Brazil's development: the unskilled, uneducated, and itinerant laborers from the interior; the declassed and impoverished; the masses of northeasterners, Mineiros, and Goianos; the culturally and racially non-European; the miscegenated Brazilian (the *cafuzo, mulato, mameluco*); the unorganized laborers of both rural and urban origins who migrate seasonally to and from all regions of Brazil, known by such terms as *cabeça-chata* ('flat-head'), *pau-de-arara* ('parrot's-perch'), and *bahiano* (after the state of Bahia). The campaign declared all of these *candangos* to be key constituents in a new pact of national development. Claiming that Brasília would "mark the dawn of a people," as tire manufacturer Pirelli put it in a commemorative advertisement, it promoted the *candangos* as national heroes.

The change from pejorative to honorific was thus forged in the rhetoric of nation-building. It was promoted both as the intended effect of Brasília on the national will and as evidence of the generation of a new common man, the modern *bandeirante*, capable of achieving Brazil's great destiny. In the words of Kubitschek, it represented the construction of new national identities for the masses of forgotten Brazilians:

> Future interpreters of Brazilian civilization, in analyzing this period of our history, must dwell with astonishment before the bronzed figure of this anonymous titan, who is the *candango*, the obscure and formidable hero of the construction of Brasília. . . . While the skeptics laughed at the intended utopia of the new city that I prepared to build, the *candangos* shouldered the responsibility of re-

sponding to me, working day and night to accomplish, in my administration, the letter of the Constitution. . . . The sad appearance of a dejected invalid, with which Euclides da Cunha portrayed our *sertanejo* [backlander], is fading out of the Brazilian panorama. You will not find it in the fellow of the *candango*, to whom we owe this city. (Juscelino Kubitschek, *Diário Carioca*, 5 January 1960)

The emergence of this "anonymous titan" as nation-builder synthesizes all three of the rhetorical strategies of Brasília's legitimation campaign: that of historical rupture in the creation of the modern future, historical analogy in the reiteration of the patriotic past, and the participation of the formerly excluded in the construction of a democratic and charismatic present.

Figure 6.1, a full-page advertisement taken out by the Esso Oil Corporation of Brazil to celebrate the inauguration of the capital, captures all three legitimations in a typical image of the period. It also reveals a perhaps not unexpected development: as the *candangos* became heroes, everyone became a *candango*. The advertisement begins with the physical type and expressions of an "original" *candango*, a worker from the interior. But midway through the text, the term *candango* is used to refer to all pioneers, "from the administrators and technical experts to the workers." Thus, the pioneers declared themselves *candangos*, and the *candangos* were declared pioneers and the epitome of the modern *bandeirante*. From unskilled worker to the president of Novacap, the term was generalized as one of prestige to include all associated with the construction. During the construction years, this process of semantic transformation was promoted both by national elites and by local elites (i.e., "the firsts") who began to include themselves in the term's denotation. It proceeded to such an extent that *candango* became the unrivaled epithet of all those born in or adopted by Brasília, as *carioca* is the name for the people of Rio de Janeiro. We might consider this process as one in which the word *candango* was resignified by having its original class referent widened to include all classes of migrants. It was thus dehistoricized, depoliticized, and generalized to such an extent that its original class basis was eclipsed.

It is in this context of redefinitions that we may understand the *candangos'* own recollections of "frontier solidarity and democracy" during the construction of Brasília. Before I started to record this oral history, I supposed that the *candangos* would have internalized an ideal portrait both of their role and of Brasília's in building a new Brazil. I further imagined that this idealization would have strongly influenced their reaction to the disadvantages actually accorded them. However, I did not find that it was a significant factor in this reaction, or indeed that

"MÔÇO...
EU FIZ ESTA CIDADE!"

"Quer dizer, eu não fiz ela tôda, mas ajudei um bocado!" Assim como êle, milhares de outros "candangos"... milhares de novos bandeirantes se orgulham de ter feito Brasília. Cada um dêles contribuiu com o seu quinhão de técnica, de talento e de trabalho para tornar realidade êsse belo sonho brasileiro.

Hoje Brasília abre as portas para o mundo e canta a sua glória. Mas a glória que fica é a dos "candangos" brasileiros - dos administradores e dos técnicos aos operários. Êles gravaram na epopéia da construção de Brasília a marca do arrôjo brasileiro, o valor de sua inteligência e a fé inabalável no futuro dêste País.

A Esso Brasileira de Petróleo estêve ao lado dêsses homens desde o primeiro instante. E êles nos ajudaram a construir ali o primeiro pôsto de serviço de Brasília - pioneiro em terra de pioneiros - o Pôsto Esso Tiradentes, inaugurado a 21 de abril de 1959 pelo Presidente Juscelino Kubitschek.

ESSO BRASILEIRA DE PETRÓLEO (ESSO)

" 'Buddy . . . I built this city! I mean, I didn't build all of it, but I helped a lot!' Like him, thousands of other *'candangos'* . . . thousands of new *bandeirantes* are proud of having made Brasília. Each one of them contributed with his share of know-how, talent, and work to turn into reality this beautiful Brazilian dream. Today Brasília opens its doors to the world and sings its glory. But the glory that remains is that of the Brazilian *'candangos'*—from the administrators and technical experts to the workers. They engraved in the epic of the construction of Brasília the mark of Brazilian boldness, the worth of its intelligence, and the unwavering faith in the future of this country.

"Esso Brasileira de Petróleo has been at the side of these men since the first moment. And they helped us to build there the first service station of Brasília—a pioneer in the land of pioneers—the Tiradentes Esso Service Station, inaugurated on 21 April 1959 by President Juscelino Kubitschek."

Fig. 6.1. Advertisement for the inauguration of Brasília, Esso Oil Company, 1960. From *Brasília: Ediçao Arquitetura e Engenharia* (1960).

Kubitschek's recruitment campaign had motivated many pioneers other than those among the elite of Novacap. Most of the *candangos* I talked with claimed that they had come to Brasília in search of jobs and adventure and that they didn't pay much attention to what they called "the politicans' rap"—though most could recite Kubitschek's catchwords. And although most of them remain quite bitter about their displacement from the city, saying "the *candangos* were forgotten, thrown aside" and the like, it is surprising to find that without exception in my experience their bitterness is directed at the postinaugural period and not at Kubitschek or Novacap.

To the contrary, the construction years are recollected with great nostalgia as a golden era of fraternity among men and fraternization among classes. This recollection of a frontier solidarity and democracy, as both *candangos* and elites sometimes call it, is the pioneers' own idealized version of Brasília's recruitment. I say idealized because it had no foundation in the juro-political conditions of construction camp life and work, as I shall show in a moment—as baseless as Kubitschek's discourse of participation in relation to the policies of exclusion. Yet, from another perspective, its mystification of such conditions is significant because it represents for many, if not most pioneers their memory of participation in the construction of Brasília.

What is important for us to understand is the very specific context in which the memories of solidarity and democracy have meaning for the pioneers, for out of context they can lead one to mistake *sentiments* of human fellowship for specific political rights and institutionalized social relations which did not exist. We must be careful, as some have not, of accepting the folk view uncritically, without examining the actual distribution of class and status advantages either of the construction camps or of what we take to be democracy. One such folk view that has been reprinted many times is represented by Niemeyer's own recollection:

> We really did have a task to accomplish, and we wanted to accomplish it in the allotted time. And it is just this that aroused a fighting spirit, a determination we had never before encountered, striking a common denominator between chiefs and subordinates, workers and engineers, that brought us all to the same level, a natural and spontaneous affinity that the class differences still existing in our country make it difficult if not impossible to set up. (Niemeyer 1960: 22)

> That human solidarity . . . gave us the impression of living in a different world, in the new and just world we had

always wished for. At that time we lived as if in a great family, without prejudice and inequality. We lived in the same houses, ate in the same restaurants, frequented the same places of amusement. Even our clothes were similar. We were united by a climate of fraternization resulting from identical discomforts. (Niemeyer 1961: 64)

It is interesting to compare this elite version of "human solidarity" with that of a *candango:*

It was like this. There wasn't the club so to speak, you know. There wasn't high society [*soçaite*] either. However, there, the engineers lived in their own camps. That wasn't it [i.e., this residential segregation was normal in Brazil]. [What was unusual about Brasília was that] You saw that the engineer had the same appearance as the worker, dressed in casual pants, boots and all. Right? You didn't see him like this [well dressed]. (Bricklayer, recorded by Lins Ribeiro 1980: 114)

Although this workman contradicts the substance of Niemeyer's claims about a leveling of class and status in residential conditions (in housing, food, leisure, and family life, as I shall show below), it nevertheless confirms what seems essential about these two versions: that under a regime of very hard work, to which everyone was subjected, a set of symbolic exchanges occurred that generated a sense of fellowship across otherwise maintained class and status boundaries.

These symbolic exchanges were defined by two conditions that gave them transcendental meanings (i.e., of solidarity and democracy). For both classes, what counted was (*a*) accessibility at the workplace to the other, almost physical contact, under (*b*) similiar conditions of work. I am not referring to any leveling of status differences (which did not occur), but to a change in the usual pattern of encounters between members of different status groups and classes. Thus, the elite exchanged their usual attire for work clothes and, rubbing sweaty elbows with workers, felt a sense of class transcendence. The workers exchanged their usual workplace segregation for a sense of being important participants at the center of what the elite considered important, who therefore had to come to their "place" to get the job done and with whom they had daily informal contact. The context of these exchanges was an existence entirely devoted to building an inhabitable capital in only three and a half years, in other words, entirely devoted to work. It was the extraordinary work routine of an isolated camp that made these exchanges necessary and meaningful. Indeed, the ideology of hard work was so enshrined at the camps that its regime became the index of progress for Kubitschek's entire Target Program: it was known throughout Brazil as the "rhythm of Brasília," defined as "36 hours of work a day—12 during the day, 12 at night, and 12 for enthusiasm." This rhythm was an expression of the new time consciousness of modernity, one which believed in the possibility of accelerating history, of mobility in society, and of creating discontinuities in the classbound routines of daily life to generate a new human solidarity.

For the *candangos* especially, the notion of a new solidarity seems to rest on their having had a sense of direct access to elite persons and soon-to-be important places. Their sense of democracy had absolutely nothing to do with political rights or institutions, of which they were entirely deprived. Rather, it had to do with their being proximate to, in a visual, tactile, physical way, "things" elite and charismatic. That this relation should be considered democratic is perhaps perplexing, but also perhaps comprehensible when we consider that these were very poor workers suddenly in the presence of power—of people of power, especially Kubitschek, and of places of power which they were themselves building. Their interpretation of this experience as democratic rests in large part on the inherent charisma of power which touched them and made them feel special, as if they had special access to it, as well as on the fetishism that elites cultivate of their persons and places so that fraternizing with the plebs makes the plebs feel as if their rulers are just like them. These two democratic sentiments—of access to power (and its complement of being recognized by power) and of equivalence between rulers and ruled—are epitomized by the many stories *candangos* tell of Kubitschek's visits to the construction sites. Every *candango* has a "JK story" about his personal encounter with the president of the nation.[10] Similarly, *candangos* tell of the important buildings they built, like the Palace of the Dawn or the Supreme Federal Tribunal, which today they cannot even enter. These stories express the circumstantial nature of Brasília's frontier solidarity and democracy, illustrating their dependence on two sharply bounded conditions—the intense work regime and the opportunities it produced for access to the charisma of power. So great was this dependence that when these conditions ended with the capital's inauguration, the *candangos*' sense of solidarity and democracy immediately dissolved.

This dissolution is nowhere more concisely expressed than in subsequent changes in the meaning and use of the word *candango*. Just as the underclass *candangos* remained disadvantaged and ultimately excluded, the class basis of the term reemerged in common usage soon after the inauguration of the city. With the transfer of the capital, the government adopted the term *brasiliense,* not *candango,* as the epithet of the city for all official matters. Most members of the local elite followed suit in their public affairs as, for example, in Brasília's daily newspapers (even in the title of one, the *Correio Braziliense*), in other publications, and in the names of social clubs, professional associations, and enterprises. Thus, officially and socially correct usage began to undermine the terms of frontier solidarity. For the elite, a *candango* became, again, someone who was neither officially nor socially correct while those who were both were *brasiliense.* For the *candangos,* too, the term's meaning began to change. For those who lost their jobs in the construction industries after the inauguration, as so many did, the word came to describe someone who was unemployed and excluded from the city he built. In bitter self-descriptions, *candangos* told me that it meant at that time—and still means for them—"a socially declassed individual," "a poor person who is like a tree that has already given its fruit."

Today in Brasília, the sense of *candango* as a class term is firmly entrenched in popular usage: it primarily refers to those who live in the satellite cities, on the periphery of those who call themselves *brasilienses.* Thus, it still evokes unemployment and exclusion, but not so much with its original connotations simply because the number of pioneers is small among those who today consider themselves *candangos.* If one goes to the elite sectors of the Planto Piloto, to Lago Sul for example, and asks the children "Are you *carioca*?" they will way "No, we are *brasiliense.*" "Not *candango*?" "*Candango*? Never." But if one goes to the satellite cities and asks the same questions, the children will say without a blink, and their parents will confirm, that they are *candangos.*

The final twist in this story of semantic transformation involves the term *pioneer* itself. Immediately after the inauguration, it became clear to all the pioneers that they would be pushed aside by federal bureaucrats holding residential rights in the city. Having perhaps had greater expectations than the rest of Brasília's preinaugural inhabitants about the just rewards of dedication and sacrifice, the officials of Novacap and the Social Security Institutes became especially disillusioned about their declassé fate. To make matters worse, the "arriviste" bureaucrats took over their name, much as they had done to the *candangos* before: the bureaucrats began to call themselves pioneers, which was perhaps understandable as conditions were still primitive but the height of ingratitude and insensitivity to the earlier pioneers. To this appropriation of their hard won identity, the latter came up with a justly famous response: in mocking revenge, they reserved the term *pioneer* for the johnny-come-lately bureaucrats, but to highlight the theft of identity they referred to themselves and their cohorts of the construction era as *piotários*—a mixture of *pioneiros*, 'pioneers', and *otários*, 'suckers'.

For the common *candango*, the legacy of Brasília's rhetoric of participation is evident if we look at the city today for commemorations of its construction: we find not a trace memorialized of the once lionized "anonymous titan." Unlike so many of the post-World War II cities of Eastern Europe, for example, where one finds monumental representations of the construction worker as city-society-state builder, Brasília has not one such memorial among its approximately 25 official monuments.[11] The reason for this symbolic absence is obvious (if tactless): as a lot, the pioneers never had a place reserved for them in the capital of the future and thus could not be glorified there. While in the populist rhetoric of recruitment they were included in building this future, in plan, policy, and practice they were excluded. Yet, perhaps the more interesting aspect of Kubitschek's recruitment campaign lies elsewhere than in this contradiction—which is, after all, usual in Brazilian political life. Rather, perhaps it lies in one of those perverse and satisfying twists of history: having based his campaign on a charismatic legitimation that emphasized the values of participation in building a new Brazil, Kubitschek found himself especially vulnerable to these same arguments when made by rebellious workers demanding rights to settle in the capital. In effect, his legitimations provided them with the symbolic strategies of their rebellion.

Nevertheless, the contradictions of Brasília's discourses of participation reveal the underlying social forces of its recruitment. They suggest the actual market, status, and power relations that organized Brasiliense society.

6.2.2 *The Labor Market*

To initiate the epoch of construction, the directorate of Novacap did three things. First, it expropriated all land—with the exception of the two existing settlements, Planaltina and Brazlândia—within the area of the future Federal District. The fact that the Plano Piloto would occupy only 16% of this area meant that rights to reside within close commuting distance of the capital could not be sold through private transaction buy only through the government's concession of public land—a fact that gave the state complete control over the legal settlement of the region surrounding the capital. Second, in late 1956, Novacap divided the site selected for the capital into two zones of planned but temporary occupation based on a spatial organization of work. One zone was reserved for construction camps and one for commercial establishments providing services and supplies to the work force.

The construction zone was divided into three areas (table 6.1; see pp. 251–52). One was the central camp of Novacap. Another contained the lodgings, offices, and depots of the Social Security Institutes that were responsible—in an arrangement with the Kubitschek administration that I shall describe later—for building the city's residential units. The third area contained the camps of the various private construction firms hired to build the city. In the first two areas resided pioneers who constituted a group of public sector employees. Among this group, approximately 2,600 were employed by Novacap and lodged (some with dependents) in two encampments near the Free City (map 7.2). One, called Novacap Headquarters or Velhacap, contained the enterprise's central offices, a primary school, various installations of the Welfare Institute of Industrial Workers, and residences for about 850 of Novacap's administrators and professional staff. Next to this camp, Novacap built another called Candangolândia, or "Candango-land," to lodge its 1,200 workers. In addition about 100 pioneers were employed by the various federal autarkies (six Social Security Institutes, two federal savings banks, and the Popular Housing Foundation) which had to construct enough residences in the South Wing of the Plano Piloto to accommodate the transfer of the federal government from Rio by the capital's inauguration. The officials of these autarkies were distributed in ten camps, nine defining the sites of *superquadras* and one the site of W-3 row houses (table 6.2). In these and adjacent sites were found the camps of the private construction firms that the autarkies contracted to carry out the actual building.

In contrast to this construction zone of publicly underwritten activities, the commercial zone was an area temporarily reserved for the private initiatives of those who at their own risk would undertake to supply the personnel of the construction camps with goods and services. This zone became known as the Free City (Cidade Livre), though officially it was called the Provisional Pioneer Nucleus or Núcleo Bandeirante.

Novacap's third inaugural act of the construction epoch was the opening, with the initiation of road and airstrip construction in late 1956, of a national labor market in an area of the Central Plateau where one could almost say none had existed before. Its effect was immediately dramatic: in an area that contained only about 6,000 inhabitants, the first 6 months of construction brought a doubling of the population; 8 months later, it had quintupled; and by May of 1959, just over two years later, it had increased more than tenfold (IBGE 1959: 4). The structure of the labor market that attracted such a torrent of migrants is given for the year 1959 in table 6.3. It reflects an economy based on a gigantic public works project, with two-thirds of the population employed in the secondary sector of construction and related industrial activities. Almost completely focused on the needs of those building the capital, the primary sector of agricultural and mining activities employed 11% of the total while the tertiary sector of services occupied the remaining 23% of the population. Even though the relation between the secondary and the tertiary sectors in 1959 is almost exactly the inverse of what we find ten years later (see table 5.1), the structure of the construction economy evinces the same kind of overwhelming importance of a single sector of activity and nearly total dependence on the patronage of the state that is characteristic of Brasília's postinaugural economy.

The specialized nature of this public works regime resulted in several peculiar features that became important in conflicts over the rights to settlement. One was the anomaly of having more than an absolute majority of the total population gainfully employed. In fact, for every 10 producers there were only 8 dependents, a ratio significantly different from the national one of 10 producers for 20 dependents or, even more impressively, from that for the surrounding state of Goiás of 10 for 30 (IBGE 1959: 54). Brasília's high ratio of producers to dependents of course reflects the single purpose and consuming work of the enterprise. Yet, the high proportion of economically productive people also reflects the peculiar demographic structure of a construction camp itself: of the 23,000 adults living in the authorized camps, 56% were single and 85% male in contrast to the corresponding national indices of 39% and 50%, respectively (IBGE 1959). Moreover, of the married men, only 36% resided in the camps with their families, the remaining two-thirds either having left their families behind to work in Brasília or having found accommodations for them elsewhere in the construction territory. Therefore, 86% of the adult men in the construction camps lived without mates or families. These figures suggest two critical problems for the mass of laborers: the absence both of women and of families in the authorized construction camps where the work routines and barrack accommodations discouraged the presence of either. For men without women, whether single or married, sexual frustration could be allayed in the red-light district of the Free City. For men with families, however, the problem of finding legal and affordable accommodations for their dependents within the authorized temporary settlements was much less easily overcome.

The planning of the construction project thus established a number of features that were central to Brasília's subsequent development: government ownership of property, planned settlement, zoned functions, a local economy principally focused on one sector and one patron, and an abiding work ethic. It also generated a set of demographic anomalies that had the effect of a wild card within the constraints of this neat arrangement: in large measure they stimulated an unpredicted and rebellious growth of the commercial city, leading merchants and their working class allies into a classic struggle for a variety of rights, privileges, and powers against the forces of legitimate authority.

6.2.3 Recruitment

With the exception of Novacap's directors, very few pioneers were compelled to venture the hazards of the Central Plateau to fulfill a patriotic mission. Rather, men went to the frontier of Brasília for adventure, work, and wages. As the demand for labor was enormous and the supply limited, it became generally known—principally through networks among migrants—that workers in Brasília enjoyed a seller's market: not only were jobs available for the asking in all categories of construction, but also wages were high, hours practically unlimited, on-the-job training standard practice, and promotion on the basis of newly acquired skills rapid. Activities were so intense at the construction site that to keep pace with the schedule of building the capital in three years, both Novacap and the private construction firms encouraged a massive recruitment of even unskilled workers throughout Brazil until the end of 1958. At that time, the seller's market for unskilled labor collapsed: a drought devasted the entire northeast of Brazil, forcing tens of thousands of desperate people—called *flagelados*, 'scourged'—to the south, to wherever jobs were available, and especially to Brasília.

The impact of this drought on the population of the construction site is evident in the migration profile given in table 6.4 for the year 1959, the peak of preinaugural activities. It is worth pausing momentarily to note the regional affiliations of this profile, for these will become important in subsequent political developments. Overwhelmingly composed of workers and their dependents, 96% of the migrants were from three regions: from the northeast (43%), from the southeast (29%, principally from Minas

Gerias), and from the central west (24%, principally from Goiás). There are at least two ways to view their patterns of regional migration: in terms of place of birth or in terms of last residence. As table 6.4 illustrates, the former was demographically most significant, as 71% migrated directly from their place of birth to Brasília.[12] Of the three main regions of migration, 96% of those born in the central west, 67% of those in the southeast, and 59% of those in the northeast migrated directly. These direct migrations established strong regional ties which became the basis for social and cultural solidarities and for political organizations. It is also relevant to note that as a whole the pioneers were not rural migrants—at least not directly—as four out of five migrated to Brasília from an urban residence.

Pioneers were recruited in several ways. Nearly all of the executive, administrative, and professional staff members both of the private and of the public concerns were recruited in advance. They were either already employees of the companies, in which case they were transferred to Brasília, or they were contracted at the home offices for the assignment. In addition, the government, the private firms, and independent recruiters brought many construction workers to Brasília through advanced recruitment. The government utilized the services of the existing National Institute of Immigration and Colonization (INIC) to recruit, process, deliver, and even insert workers into construction jobs. INIC sponsored a network of placement centers, distribution posts, and transit lodges throughout Brazil which directed migrants, often providing free transportation, to the two centers in charge of "regularizing" Brasília's labor force: one center established in the neighboring city of Anápolis, a major distribution point for Brasília's supplies, and one center at Novacap headquarters in Brasília. Those who arrived in Anápolis were screened for their qualifications and given a letter of introduction to the authorities in Brasília to expedite their onsite induction into a specific job.

Although this network delivered a steady flow of potential construction workers, the private firms developed their own strategy for bringing them to Brasília. The firms were motivated by a simple market logic: the enormous demand for laborers had created a wage war. The firms reasoned that if they could recruit workers outside of Brasília, they could hire them at lower wages. Accordingly, they sent trucks to the cities and the hinterlands of especially the poorer states in search of laborers.[13] Often they worked in conjunction with a local politician who rounded up potential migrants with stories of an employment Eldorado. The migrants signed on almost as indentured servants, having to work off the always inflated costs of transportation at wages that were below market value in Brasília. The traffic in laborers became so profitable that a genre of independent and especially unscrupulous labor recruiters arose to meet the need—typified by the lone operator who went into business with a single truck converted for passenger transportation, in which he scoured the northeastern states for marketable young men.[14]

Whether or not already contracted in one form or another before their arrival, all those who wanted to work in the construction zone had to pass through INIC's recruitment center at Novacap headquarters. The recruitment process began with the presentation of an official work card that stated the applicant's qualifications and employment record; or, if he lacked the card, a series of tests to establish his skills and to procure the necessary papers. Next, the *candango* underwent a medical examination after which he received an identity card from Novacap's Department of Security. Finally, the *candango* was assigned a job from lists of openings that the private firms, the Social Security Institutes, and Novacap were required to register with the recruitment office. After this initial assignment, however, laborers were free to change jobs. Indeed, the construction firms encouraged them to do so as fierce competition motivated one to lure workers from another. After admission to this market, the *candango* found himself in something of a labor free-for-all: lists of available jobs and their competitive hourly wages were broadcast over a ubiquitous loudspeaker system in the Free City; they were even read to audiences before the screening of films and circulated among workers at the construction sites themselves by competitors who sent cars fitted with speakers to advertise jobs with higher wages and more overtime. In spite of this frenetic wage war (which no doubt delighted workers but which Novacap ended in 1959 by establishing a fixed wage scale for all categories of construction work), no employer with work in the construction zone was permitted to hire a worker who had not passed through Novacap-INIC's process of recruitment.

Thus Novacap strictly regulated the construction labor market by restricting jobs to those who had been inducted through its office. This regulation was effectively, and often brutally, enforced by Novacap's own and much feared army of security agents (the GEB, Guarda Especial de Brasília), who were themselves recruited from among the *candangos*. Novacap insisted on controlling accesss to the construction camps for a number of reasons. Although the private firms operated the camps, the government had built them at its own expense. In this sense, Novacap was policing its investment. Moreover, it was the authority responsible for maintaining order among a construction force of twenty thousand males living in close quarters under frontier conditions. In this respect, its security problems were logistical, for there were numerous camps (each firm organized its own) dispersed throughout the construction zone. But the most significant reason was simply that this zone was the site of the future capital, and therefore Novacap wanted to preclude the possibility that its labor force might take root. By strictly controlling access to and accommodations within the zone, it wanted to make sure that it would not one day find an enormous population of laborers and their families resolutely installed in shanties. Even after the avalanche of migrants in early 1959 made it impossible for Novacap's recruitment office to accommodate the volume of applicants, Novacap continued to enforce job regulations strictly. It merely decentralized its rule, allowing the firms and the institutes to hire directly, but continued to control job and housing quotas within the construction zone.

If this zone was marshalled as a boot camp, the Free City grew as its opposite under a laissez-faire policy. The government's plan was to encourage entrepreneurs to supply the construction effort at their own risk, and of course profit, and after the city's inauguration to become its commercial and service population. To this end, it reserved a small site at the intersection of the two main highways into the Federal District for "private initiative." It offered two incentives to entrepreneurs: free land and no taxes. In December 1956, Novacap ordered the concession of lots, for a period of four years, to those interested in the venture. The lots were made available under a type of contract known as a 'commercial accommodation' (*regime de comodato*), which guarantees the free loan of something nonfungible for a stipulated period of time.[15] The contract gave the entrepreneur the right to build his commercial establishment in the front part of the lot (in this case defined as the street side) and his own residence in the back. It specified that because all constructions were temporary, they had to be wooden. The combination of laissez-faire governance and temporary wooden buildings turned the Free City into something like a frontier town of the North American Wild West variety, to which it was often compared: it featured false-fronted buildings along the boardwalks of an alternately dusty and muddy main street, which was itself the arena of an overwhelmingly male culture of abundant cash, ambition, and pent up desire.

However, Novacap's commercial contracts stipulated that at the end of the four-year period its wrecking crews had the right to raze the entire city to the ground. With a turn of phrase still famous in the Free City, the president of Novacap declared: "In April 1960, I will send the tractors to flatten everything." Before that apocalyptic day, the entrepreneurs had the right according to their contracts, and were encouraged according to Novacap settlement policy, to transfer their businesses to commercial lots in the Plano Piloto. Among all the pioneers, only these entrepreneurs and their employees had a preestablished right, thus granted, to a presence in the inaugurated city. This right entitled the entrepreneur to purchase the building rights to one commercial lot in the Plano Piloto (which the state would own, as the land itself was inalienable) upon which to put up a building at his own expense in accordance with uniform planning regulations. I should emphasize that this was not a right to reside in any of the government residences, as the contract made no provisions for the entrepreneur's eventual residence in the *superquadras* of the Plano Piloto.

Although all interested parties were eligible for a lot in the Free City, applicants had to demonstrate the availability of sufficient capital to sustain their proposed venture. Having done so, entrepreneurs received a lot either from the administrator of the city, appointed by Novacap, or directly from one of Novacap's directors. As these enterprises involved no risk to Novacap, the selection of entreprenuers was a relaxed process, one less rigorous than the selection of construction workers. In fact, from the beginning, Novacap maintained little supervision over commerce in the Free City because its objective was to attract commercial enterprise to the new Federal District. To overcome the initial inertia of capitalists to invest in this project, Novacap therefore adopted an extremely laissez-faire attitude. However, this was merely a temporary tactic in its overall economic planning. For Novacap held fast to its trump card that at an already marked hour it would destroy the Free City and transplant its commercial activities into the decidedly un-laissez-faire economic regime of the inaugurated capital.

For a period of four years, therefore, a commercial city arose at the confluence of two transportation routes in classic imperial fashion: a ruling authority created a bazaar at the gates of its noncommercial capital. On the one hand, those whom it recruited in the construction trades were billeted in regimented camps as the work crews of a public building project. On the other, those whom it recruited for their capital investments in all activities except the actual construction of the capital populated the Free City and dominated its capitalist economy. It was called a Free City precisely because it grew in an area free of regulations that applied elsewhere. Its freedoms were rooted in the fact that its preeminent residents, the entrepreneurs, enjoyed free land grants and paid no taxes. However, for the laboring masses seeking to enter the frontier Eldorado of Brasília, the Free City was free in another sense. It was an open city. In contrast to the construction zone, it was immediately accessible to all: to those just off the bus, to those awaiting documentation for construction work, to those rags-to-riches dreamers, to those who preferred the routines of service sector employment to the rigors of construction, to those in the oldest of professions, to those whose husbands and fathers were laboring in the camps. All migrants could enter the Free City freely, could find a place to live freely, could find work freely—freely meaning, of course, in accordance with individual means.

Thus, the Free City was a capitalist city on the fringes of a planned economy, in which differences in privilege were based on individual differences in income which were not only allowed but encouraged to find their unequal expressions. This open city of difference, of individualism, of entrepreneurial ethic contrasted sharply with the controlled construction zone (as with the built capital after it) in which income differences found little opportunity to express themselves in life-style, and in which differences in social status—although in fact correlated with significant differences in camp privileges—tended to be negated ideologically in the fraternity of hard work.

6.3 Rights, Privileges, and Powers

Having examined the labor market and the recruitment of pioneers, we may now analyze the distribution of advantages that the interaction of class, status, and power relations among recruits engendered. The basis of my analysis is that the distribution of advantages concerning work and residence generated a set of collective interests specific to each subset of pioneers, around which it organized (or failed to organize) collective actions against the state. In this discussion, my main use for the concepts of class, status, and power is to explain the incidence and forms of these collective actions.

Table 6.5 presents an inventory of the various situations of pioneers in the labor market of the construction territory. I shall regard these situations as my criteria of class because they seem best to account for the kinds of interests that united their members as collective actors. The table's assessment is based on the government's *planned* occupation of the construction site. Therefore, it does not include the pioneers in the illegal squatter settlements listed in table 6.1. Later, we shall consider these illegal settlements as a reaction to this plan.[16] In what follows, I shall outline the rights, privileges, and powers that these class relations entailed, focusing on issues of (a) work: access to jobs, wages, employment security, work conditions, and, for the entrepreneurs, access to an open market; and (b) residence: access to authorized housing (both pre- and postinauguration), accommodations for dependents, and the quality of living conditions. Let us first consider the situation of the construction workers in the private sector camps, a subset constituting 63% of the total population of employees.

A worker recruited to construction had three basic advantages by virtue of his having passed through the recruitment process: he had the right to be hired for a construction job either by the private firms or by Novacap itself, and, once hired, he had the right for the duration of the job to free housing within the camps and to inexpensive meals at camp canteens. These rights devolved automatically from recruitment to construction. As they were not available to other workers(i.e., those in the Free City), they illustrate the significance from a working-class perspective of the predetermined differentiation between the market spheres of the construction camps and the Free City. Having gone through the recruitment process, the construction worker was virtually guaranteed employment and its advantages; for, as I have described, the demand for workers far exceeded the supply—at all times for skilled laborers, and until 1959 for unskilled. After that time, applications from the unskilled were either delayed or not processed. In addition, workers in the construction camps considered that they had two other types of advantages over other workers: the availability of practically unlimited hours of work at good pay and the possibility of rapid occupational mobility within the building trades, especially from unskilled to skilled categories.

The first advantage raises the issue of wages. According to those who have studied the construction industry in Brasília (Lins Ribeiro 1980 and Bicalho 1978) and to those workers I interviewed, the great eldorado of employment in construction was not so much in the actual hourly wage paid for the standard workday as in the availability of steady work at that wage and especially in the accumulation of overtime hours. The legal minimum monthly salary in effect for most of the construction period in the area of Goiás out of which Brasília was carved was among the lowest in the nation. It was Cr$2.4 (about U.S.$17 in 1958) as compared with Rio de Janeiro's high of Cr$3.8. Nevertheless, it was higher than any other area in the central western states and also higher than the minimums in the northern and the northeastern states with the exception of the metropolitan area of Recife. Therefore, as the vast majority of the work force was from the interior regions of these states, the hourly wages calculated on the basis of this minimum—between seven and eighteen U.S. cents depending on the job—were relatively attractive. Moreover, one of the great attractions of Brasília's construction work was that it actually paid these hourly wages, and on a regular basis. To give the reader an idea of the impact of such employment on the earnings of a poor man from the interior, I cite the not unusual example of one of my informants who in 1956 made about 10 "old" cruzeiros (U.S.$0.15) per day working as a butcher in his hometown in the backlands of Goiás. He migrated to Brasília as soon as construction started, signed on at the lowest level of unskilled labor, and was earning 10 "old" cruzeiros *per hour* for the regular 240 hour month (10 hours a day, 6 days a week). After several months, he became a timekeeper and doubled his hourly wage—also adopting, as seems to have been common among *candangos*, the nickname of his job so that he became and is still known as Zé Apontador or Joe Timekeeper. Considering that lodging was free and that a full midday meal could be had for 3 "old" cruzeiros, it is not difficult to see why *candangos* were drawn to Brasília for regular construction wages.

In addition to collecting regular-time wages on the 240 hour month, *candangos* were able to work an incredible number of overtime hours under "the rhythm of Brasília." Probably more than any other attribute, it was this frenetic, nonstop work pace that drew *candangos* to the capital. Often coming as close as humanly possible to the fabled 36 hours of work a day, *candangos* claim that they rarely worked a minimum of 12 and frequently a maximum of 22 hours of construction a day, according to Lins Ribeiro (1980: 103–12), who conducted a study of these work conditions. Both in his interviews and in mine, workers maintain that most were eager to work two and sometimes three 24-hour shifts a week in combination with regular ones of 12 to 16 hours. I confess that I remain skeptical about these upper limits. Perhaps the camaraderie of the all-out work effort, which *candangos* recall with such affection, has led to exaggeration.

Nevertheless, it does seem that through overtime *candangos* typically worked 90 hour weeks, a routine that boosted the median monthly income of the construction workers as a whole to what must have been for most of them the lordly sum of Cr$6.6 (U.S.$36). Moreover, we must realize that the "basket of market goods and services" that this income had to cover was exceptionally reduced: construction workers had free housing, transportation and health services, subsidized meals, little need for household goods, few dependents to support in Brasília, and little time for recreational expenditures.[17] When we consider that these items made up over 80% of the estimated budget of working-class families in São Paulo in 1958 (DIEESE 1974), it is clear that the amount of spendable or remittable income available to the unskilled laborer was extraordinarily high.[18]

The second great attraction of construction work in the new capital was the ease with which an unskilled worker could move into a category of skilled labor and higher pay. We can calculate from the 1959 census that approximately half of the construction workers were registered as skilled and half as unskilled laborers. Perhaps most of those in the skilled categories had started without qualifications. It is difficult to be more exact because the extreme shortage of skilled laborers made Brasília's work force extremely adept at improvisation. Its workers became famous as *quebra-galhos* (literally, 'break-branches'), meaning 'trouble-shooters', 'problem solvers', 'handymen',—in short, a type of *bricoleur* ready to tackle all tasks with limited assets but with great ingenuity; or, as one *candango* lampooned, "ready to undertake tasks for which he has not been sufficiently prepared." The shortage of skilled workers and exigencies of time therefore created abundant opportunities for job advancement. Such mobility occurred at two distinct moments in the work process, at the time of initial recruitment and through on-site promotion. Nearly every *candango* I interviewed told the same story of the illiterate and unskilled migrant who, upon arriving in the Free City, was instructed by his more knowledgeable cohorts to buy or borrow a hammer and saw before applying for work at the Novacap-INIC recruitment office. Then, during his job interview, he was to declare himself a carpenter, exhibiting his tools. Apparently, the qualifying tests administered did not in most cases prevent the daring but unskilled worker from being hired as skilled labor.

In the second instance, opportunities for advancement opened up within the work crews themselves. As the construction firms were always overextending their resources both to capture as many contracts as possible and to maintain the grueling work pace, they would typically organize their work crews—each under the direction of a job foreman (*encarregador*)—around a few skilled workers who would train a much greater number of inexperienced men while actually doing a job. If any of the unskilled workers showed talent for the assignment, they were soon promoted into skilled positions to allow the company to shift the original skilled workers to other projects. In addition, highly skilled workers were frequently lured away from their jobs by more lucrative offers from other companies, prompting the advancement of their less skilled assistants.

Considered altogether, these job and wage opportunities effected a profound economic transformation on the entire labor force. They turned impoverished, itinerant day and piece laborers into hourly wage workers, incorporating many for the .first time into an urban labor market as a distinct occupational class.

The preceding assessment of the advantages of construction work must be counterbalanced by the workers' lack of rights, privileges, and powers in other aspects of their relations to the production process. As regards work conditions, these aspects involve the legality of overtime, job safety, job security, and more generally the application of national labor laws and the availability of legally constituted mechanisms for mediating either individual grievances or collective demands. While there can be no doubt that most of the construction workers wanted all the overtime they could get, and that getting it, most thought that they had a good deal, it is also certain that the rhythm of Brasília was both extralegal and dangerous. Article 59 of the Consolidated Labor Laws of 1943 permitted two hours of overtime per day, at a 20% increase in pay, beyond the legal eight-hour work day—provided that this extension was the result either of a written agreement between employer and employees or of a collective labor contract. Under extraordinary circumstances, it permitted another two hours of overtime as long as this extension was communicated within ten days to the relevant labor authority. Considering these labor codes, Lins Ribeiro (1980: chap. 3) and Bicalho (1978: chap. 4) demonstrate that the extension of the workday beyond eight hours in Brasília was of dubious legality. The addition of two extra hours did not conform to the law because neither the firms nor Novacap secured the required written agreements. But even allowing for the accepted practice in the construction industry of a ten-hour day without explicit agreement, it seems evident that the mechanisms used in Brasília to extend the workday far beyond ten hours—such as additional extra hours and especially double shifts (*viradas*)—had absolutely no legal justification. These mechanisms were in operation as extralegal phenomena because they were neither negotiated between interested and represented parties nor subject to legal redress of any sort. Rather, Novacap's statelike powers over the construction territory enabled it to ignore inconvenient legal requirements, permitting it and the private firms to set the work pace and conditions they needed to get the job done within the three and a half year deadline. Under such circumstances, Lins Ribeiro and Bicalho argue that these manipulations of work time—including methods of subcontracting piecework for either fixed prices or fixed hours (*tarefa* or *empreitada*)—amounted to a pervasive exploitation of the labor force.

Whether or not we are justified in regarding the rhythm of Brasília as illegal—a question I cannot completely answer—or as exploitative if the workers themselves informally agree to it, we can nevertheless conclude that it had two indisputable effects on the labor force. First, it led to a progresssive and startling deterioration. The combination of exceptionally long hours, deadline pressures, and the lack of adequate training created serious job hazards. As a result, work-related accidents and deaths became a progressively common occurrence. Although the construction firms did not keep records of these job accidents, we can get an idea of their increasing frequency from the number of accidents requiring treatment at the hospital of IAPI reported for the entire population of preinaugural Brasília: 342 accidents in 1957, or 1 for every 36 people; 1,974 in 1958, or 1 for every 15; and 10,927 in 1959, or 1 for every 7 (cited in Lins Ribeiro 1980: 92). No doubt, most of these accidents were suffered by the smaller population of construction workers, making their rate of occurrence among these workers even more alarming.[19]

Second, the need to build Brasília at breakneck speed led Novacap to view the requirements of labor laws and institutions as obstructive. As a result, laborers were left for all practical purposes without legal recourse or collective representation. Novacap was content to govern the construction territory as a kind of juridical anomaly, one lacking the requisite institutions of regulation, mediation, and representation "on all sides of the table." On its side, Novacap deliberately neglected to establish any means of juridically regulating labor relations until after the inauguration.[20] On the side of the federal government, the executive and judicial institutions of state responsible for labor relations (i.e., the offices of the Ministry of Labor and the labor courts) were not instituted in the preinaugural territory. Thus, neither individual grievances nor collective demands could even be heard, except at the labor courts of neighboring municipalities in Goiás, which had questionable jurisdiction over the construction territory.

For their parts, neither the employers nor the workers of the construction firms were collectively organized during the construction period although the Consolidated Labor Laws permitted each to form its own association. Undoubtedly, the construction firms made no attempt to form an employers' association in Brasília because they found their interests adequately empowered by Novacap itself: as legal corporations contracted by the state enterprise, they had the requisite authority and power to regulate their own affairs. Although they employed their own guards and inspectors, their power ultimately rested on their authority to call in Novacap's security force to control workers—a tragic example of which I give below. By contrast, a very small group of construction workers did form an employees' association in July 1958. The labor laws allowed industrial or occupational groupings only at the level of the county (*município*). As preinaugural Brasília did not have municipal status (a juridical ambiguity Novacap used to advantage), their organization was obliged to establish its headquarters in the nearest municipal center, Planaltina. It was called the Professional Association of Workers in the Industries of Civil Construction and Furniture of Planaltina, Luziânia, and Formosa. Most members of the small group of association organizers were skilled workers with previous union experience, who thereby had an awareness of their labor rights under the law (cf. Bicalho 1978: 20ff.). Their immediate objectives were two: to inspect work and living conditions at the camps and work sites, and more important to arouse among their fellow workers an awareness of both the right and the need to organize.

However, in both efforts, the association had little success. In the first place, it encountered a dire problem of education: the overwhelmingly majority of *candangos* had little if any notion of their rights to organized representation. Moreover, most *candangos* were apathetic to the idea of a union: they thought "they were making a lot of money, and therefore they were under the illustion that the deal was good," as a former association delegate told me. In the second place, the association encountered stiff opposition from Novacap and the construction firms, who thought that union organizing would hinder the rhythm of Brasília. Not only were association delegates made to feel unwelcome on camp and work site inspections, but the association's petition to the Ministry of Labor for official recognition as a union—without which a worker organization cannot bargain, use the labor courts, or receive a share of the annual trade union contributions collected from all workers—took a full year to pass. In addition, its principal demand that the state create a conciliation board (the lowest level of labor court) in the construction territory to hear individual grievances was largely ineffective both because the board did not begin to operate until well after the inauguration of the city and because this change in settlement status automatically created a system of labor courts for the Federal District.

In conclusion, it is evident that not only did Brasília's construction workers lack basic rights as individual workers—rights stipulated in law and supposedly safeguarded by governmental institutions—but they also lacked the autonomy, organization, and procedures to undertake collective actions as a unit of recruited pioneers. Rather, both individually and collectively, they were subjugated without representation to the authority of Novacap and the construction firms. In contrast, their employers exercised essential class rights, privileges, and powers without the need for an officially constituted association: they monopolized the entrepreneurial management of the construction industry, and they protected their interests by influencing both the economic policy and the juro-political organization of the construction territory—an influence summarized in the concept of the rhythm of Brasília. Although workers considered that they benefited financially and professionally from this work regime, their private sector employers (and their representatives—the executives, managers, and liberal professionals of the firms) realized much greater benefits from these advantages as measured, for instance, in the income differences between the two (table 6.5) or in the suppression of labor conflicts. Therefore, we may conclude that the rigors of the rhythm of Brasília also reflected the great degree to which employers had consolidated their class position over employees.

This consolidation was moreover clearly expressed in status privileges that differentiated the living conditions of employees and managers in the constructions camps. (For convenience, I shall use the terms *managers* and *management* to refer to executives, administrators, and technical experts.) Among the pioneers as a whole, there appear to have been two distinct and named status groups, one of which successfully claimed and the other of which had effectively imposed upon it differentiating types of social esteem. By status group, I refer to those who share the same position in a hierarchy of defined positions, and therefore whatever attributes attach to the rank. As these groups encompassed pioneers in the Free City and in the public sector camps as well as those in the private sector camps, my discussion of the latter will hold in general terms for the other two.

The status groups were labeled by terms that served both for reference and for direct address: one was called the *candangos*, and the other the *doutores* ('doctors'). A former "doctor" of the period (by actual occupation an administrator of one of the institute camps) defined their differences in the following way: "The *candangos* were the workers, humble men, who called all those who worked in the office 'doctors,' whether they were engineers or not" (Mendes 1979: 87). An initial point to note about this definition is that throughout Brazil the use of "doctor" as a term of personal reference and address signals high respect. Among superior class equals, it signifies achieved status, usually based on university education of any sort. Among class unequals, it is used as a status marker of privileges ascribed to superior class positions. Its use establishes, in the act of addressing, all of the assumptions and requisites of class asymmetries.

These status groups were defined by conventions of expected behavior: managers expected their subordinates to treat them deferentially, an expectation that confirmed in daily life their superior class position both to their subordinates and to themselves, and that was backed up by employer powers. As appearances are crucial in status differentiation, this expectation was maintained by a series of assumptions about the obvious. The sign system of status affiliation for *candangos* included manner (humble), dress (poor), education (none), origin (interior), language (ungrammatical), and even mode of arrival (as *pau-de-araras*). Those who fit this description were labeled *candangos* and expected to behave deferentially to those who did not—as exemplified by having to address them as "doctors" in formal third person constructions, while the "doctors" in turn could use the familiar *você*, the second person pronoun, or the term *candango* itself. Certainly, such systems of class and status identification are rigorously practiced, with local variations, everywhere in Brazil. Nevertheless, perhaps we can say that in the new world of Brasília, appearances became paramount indicators of class, more important than the traditional family name or property.[21]

All of these indicators exemplify the circular indexicality of social stratification based on status, a circularity that makes such systems so hard to change: an effect (such as grammatical speech) of prior privilege (formal education, training, family background, and the like) is taken as justification of future privilege. While this circularity holds for all of the signs mentioned, there was a master index on which the basic perception of status rested as the pioneer's definition cited earlier suggests: the distinction between office and nonoffice work, that is, between manual and nonmanual labor. In the context of the work camp, the use of this distinction rather than any other on which to base the distribution of privilege was undoubtedly the most secure means of maintaining the relative exclusivity of elite status: while many workers experienced rapid occupational mobility, this experience rarely (if ever) amounted to a structural mobility between the status groups because their occupational advancements were confined almost entirely to categories of manual labor. Therefore, the distribution of camp privileges as fringe benefits to those with nonmanual technical expertise and managerial qualifications effectively maintained class positions in the daily life of the camps. No matter how hard a manual laborer worked, he could not purchase these privileges, for money alone could not procure them. So effective was this stratification that there are even indications of self-policing among the *candangos* to discipline those who attempted to usurp "doctor" privileges.[22]

What were these privileges, and how were they distributed? In the private construction camps, we are considering a universe of approximately 16,000 *candangos* and 600 "doctors." The camps exhibited an internal pecking order that followed the hierarchical organization of work: at the top was the owner of the company, followed by the staff of engineers, the administrators, the job foremen, the master tradesmen (*mestres de obra*), the skilled workers (*profissionais*), and finally the unskilled workers (*serventes*). The category of "doctor" comprised the first three while that of *candango* the last two. The foremen and master tradesmen occupied ambiguous positions, sometimes associated with the "doctors" (principally for housing privileges) but most of the time associated with the *candangos*. We are primarily concerned with the distribution of those privileges that ultimately generated a core of collective interests for each category of pioneer. It appears that status differentiations affecting the routines of daily life such as the means of transportation (*candangos* rode in open trucks, "doctors" in jeeps), inspections (*candangos* were searched at camp gates for alcohol, "doctors" were not), and etiquette (such as socially significant address terminology) never became issues around which class actions of either an organized or spontaneous nature occurred. Similarly, the unequal distribution of off-work privileges did not stimulate *candangos* to react collectively even though they had few options for their scarce free time beyond sports in the camps or the triad of alcohol, prostitutes, and films in the Free City. In contrast, the "doctors" in many camps had their own clubs and club facilities, and such recreational privileges as the use of company jeeps on the weekend and private screenings of films several times a week.

While neither work nor recreational conditions became issues of organized conflict, the differentiating privileges of what we may call reproductive conditions (i.e., food, housing, and family) did generate various measures of collective response among *candangos*. The least organized, most spontaneous response expressed worker discontent over the poor quality of meals served in the company canteens. This discontent periodically erupted into food riots, which Novacap's security forces severely repressed. Unplanned and leaderless, these riots lacked organizational consequences for collective demands. They focused on the poor quality of the food itself, erupting over an egregiously bad meal but temporarily defused by a good one. Thus, they did not address the differential allocation of company resources in which managers received better food, private cooks, and dining halls.[23]

Rather, it was the distribution of privileges concerning housing and family accommodations that sparked not merely collective responses to immediate problems but moreover organized actions for long-term rights. The private construction companies distributed camp accommodations according to the hierarchical organization of work. The basic class division between workers and managers was reflected in the allocation of housing types. Workers were assigned to barracks: the unskilled to those without internal subdivisions and the skilled to those divided into small rooms, each for two people. Both accommodations used the same type of outdoor, unroofed sanitary facility. On the other side of the great status divide, managers resided in individual houses with indoor bathrooms. Like the barracks, the houses were architecturally differentiated, principally by size and location, according to job rank. It was a gradation culminating in the house of the firm's proprietor, which in at least one case documented by Lins Ribeiro (1980: 64) was an enormous structure separated from the camp by a barbed wire fence. Thus, the hierarchies of company organization determined an allocation of housing privileges in which with few exceptions managers monopolized access to private, single-family dwellings.[24]

More than any other, this privilege differentiated the lives of managers and workers in the camps: for not merely did it give managers a sense of privacy and of daily life after work, it created an overwhelming difference between the two by allowing managers to live with their families while preventing workers from living with theirs. The significance of this status privilege becomes all the more evident when we look at the demographics of family life as related in the 1959 census. Although 34% of the almost 17,000 men in the private camps were married, 91% of them lived without mates. In all, there were only about 1,450 families in these camps, encompassing not more than 25% of the married men. If we assume that most of the managers exercised their privilege to reside with family, it would appear that in addition about eight to nine hundred master tradesmen and skilled workers were permitted access to family dwellings. It is intriguing to speculate that these privileged, skilled workers may have formed something of a "labor aristocracy" among construction workers, though their role in subsequent political confrontations with the state remains unknown. What is clear is that the rest of the married workers were not less likely than the managers to want to live with their families during the construction years. For them, there were only two options: to rent accommodations in the Free City for their families, or to build illegal dwellings for them somewhere in the countryside surrounding the camps. Of the two, the latter was the more common and, after 1958, the only viable option. After 1958, the supply of rentable accommodations in the Free City had been exhausted, and moreover their rents had been driven beyond the reach of most workers by a crisis of supply that I shall discuss in a moment. Therefore, workers who wanted to bring their families to Brasília had in fact little choice but to appropriate land for their houses, either by launching or joining land seizures, which by May 1959 contained over 28% of the territory's population (table 6.1).

As we shall see in the following chapter, both the initiation and the maintenance of these settlements required the development of autonomous worker organizations to counter Novacap's attempts to eradicate them. Therefore, we may conclude that whereas workers failed to organize around work or recreational disadvantages, they did so around those affecting conditions of residential life, especially of housing and family residence. As a result, residential associations and not labor associations became the important means of organizing collective interests and actions among the working classes of preinaugural Brasília.[25]

The stratified distribution of residential rights led workers not only to transform their own political identities but also to form alliances with the entrepreneurs of the Free City on whom they depended for goods and services. To understand the basis of this interclass alliance, we must briefly survey the situation in the Free City. Its population then consisted of about 5,500 economically active people (4,300 men and 1,200 women). Of this total approximately 500 were employers, 2,000 self-employed workers, and 3,000 employees. Class position in the Free City depended on access to and control over capital, commercial property, and their income-producing uses. In this respect, the residents of the Free City were divided into two classes, a division clearly reflected in their median monthly incomes (table 6.5): an entrepreneurial class, composed of employers with a median income of Cr$20.1 and of executives and self-employed liberal professionals with comparable incomes; and a working class, composed of employees and the self-employed with incomes of Cr$4.1 and Cr$5.9, respectively.

Advantage in the Free City depended solely on the economic power of this income.[26] Those whom the entrepreneurs hired had no rights other than those to wages as a condition of employment and no privileges other than those that their wages could purchase. Although the self-employed had no contractual obligations either with the state or with the entrepreneurs, they were the ones who primarily serviced the city itself, providing goods and services (such as shack repair and transportation) for its burgeoning internal market, which was increasingly independent of construction company patronage. They constituted a somewhat fluid subset insofar as some eventually became entrepreneurs while others became or continued as part-time employees. However, like everyone else, their ability to work and live in the Free City depended on their access to capital. In this crucial aspect, Free City workers differed from construction camp workers: while the latter were guaranteed free housing and inexpensive meals, the former had no subsidies of any kind. Therefore, as the incomes of Free City workers averaged 38% less than those of construction camp workers and had to cover a great deal more in the way of goods and services, the former constituted the lower strata of Brasília's preinaugural working classes. In the capitalist city, class advantage depended strictly on the naked power of money, and therefore its employees and its self-employed workers made up a disadvantaged class.

The Free City was of course conceived to accommodate a privileged class of those who wielded this power, namely, the entrepreneurs. Each was awarded a contract of commercial accommodation on the basis of a proposed capital venture. By Brasília's inauguration, these contracts amounted to an investment in the Free City of about U.S.$5 million (*Brasília* 1960 [40]: 28). Within this privileged class, there was considerable variation in individual worth. Enough pioneers came to Brasília with very little and made (and lost) fortunes that today their rags-to-riches stories form a sizable part of the city's lore. Most of them began either by selling construction materials (especially sand and gravel which they mined themselves) or by providing transport services. Through legendary hard work, they amassed enough savings to gain a foothold in the Free City—that is, a commercial contract from Novacap. These contracts could be had for quite modest investments. For example, one of the largest Volkswagen dealerships in the entire central west, Disbrave S/A, began in 1959 in the Free City with joint stock worth only U.S.$27. Others, like one of Brasília's most successful general retail stores, the Pioneira da Borracha LTDA, was founded in 1959 as a rubber supply outlet with a capital investment of over U.S.$2,000. But regardless of the size of the initial investment, as long as the enterprise did not fold, its proprietor held a contract that gave him long-term access to property, and thus to work and residential rights in the Federal District.

These rights enabled employers to exercise a set of class privileges and powers focused, as Novacap intended, on their monopoly of the entrepreneurial management of commerce. However, unlike the construction firm employers who held a similar monopoly in their sector of the economy, the Free City entrepreneurs found it essential to form a commercial association in early 1958 to protect their interests. The first important test of the Commercial Association of Brasília came soon after its foundation in a protracted struggle with the government of the state of Goiás over the payment of taxes on the commercial transactions of Free City enterprises. Although the federal government had exempted these enterprises from taxation as a means of attracting investors, the state of Goiás attempted to collect. It argued that until the inauguration of the capital, the Free City was still under its jurisdiction as were the other settlements in the designated Federal District. The government of Goiás found support for this argument in the very juridical ambiguity of the construction territory that Novacap used to its advantage in other circumstances. This ambiguity became especially apparent with the local and state elections of 1958 in which the federal government decided that the residents of the Free City and the construction camps could vote, in polling stations established there, as electors registered in the Goianian municipalities of Planaltina and Luziânia. In all, about 4,100 pioneers voted to elect both state officials (governor, senators, and deputies) and local officials in the two municipalities (mayors and councilmen). At that point, Goiás' statehouse countered that if it had the obligation to represent the pioneers (which it never did, in fact), then it had the right to tax them. Accordingly, at stations along the Anapolis-Brasília highway, it began to inspect trucks carrying merchandise to the Free City and to impound those that refused to pay a value-added tax.

In response, the Commercial Association threatened to close down the city with a general strike of employers. After four months of acrimonious debate between association members and state representatives, the butchers finally struck. At the same time, the association brought suit against the state of Goiás to secure a tax exempt status for the Free City. With Novacap clearly on its side, the association won the court case. This victory for the entrepreneurs consolidated the prestige and power of the Commercial Association as a class organization capable of decisively influencing both economic policy and juro-political organization in the Federal District. Paradoxically, although Novacap's support greatly enhanced this influence, the interests of the entrepreneurs soon conflicted with those of the federal government, prompting the Commercial Association to take class actions against Novacap itself.

Interestingly, the consolidation of entrepreneurial advantages did not generate a corresponding set of status issues to differentiate the living conditions of employers and workers in the Free City as it did in the construction camps. Entrepreneurs were not accorded (and to my knowledge did not attempt to usurp) any special social esteem upon which to base status monopolies. Nor, in relation to the entrepreneurs, were the workers disprivileged by virtue of negative esteem. Rather, the differences between the two tended not to be represented in special styles of life. In the rustic conditions of the Free City, both entrepreneurs and workers tended instead to adopt similar life-styles and to be considered, together, as *candangos*. As such, the Free City workers should be distinguished from the construction camp workers because the former were not eligible for the housing and food subsidies available to the latter by virtue of their employment. However, the entrepreneurs, as *candangos*, present an ambiguous case. Their designation was obviously based not on the criterion of manual labor but on a combination of two circumstances. First, while some entrepreneurs (such as the 60 liberal professionals) came from privileged backgrounds and thus were obviously "doctors," more were of humble origins from the interior of Brazil. Although these entrepreneurs belonged to the same class as the construction camp managers, their status positions were not in most cases similar because of their different upbringing and education. In other words, while their "money capital" may have been similar, their "cultural capital" was not. Rather, the entrepreneurs present another instance of the successful businessman who has little social status.

Second, unlike their construction camp counterparts, the Free City employers did not differentiate themselves from their employees by a symbolic code of special privileges, involving segregated social clubs, dining facilities, and houses. This is not to say that real differences did not exist between the living conditions of employers and employees in the Free City. It is rather to say that these differences were based on money rather than on status. Whereas construction camp workers could not have purchased the camp privileges of "doctors," Free City amenities were available to all for the price. Thus, the relative absence of status stratification in the Free City may very well have been due to its uncompromisingly capitalist market in which "money bought everything." For as Weber (1978: 936–37) observes, in such circumstances the "sheer market principle" effectively undermines the irrationalities of status esteem and therefore hinders the development of status privileges.

By the same token, however, the operation of this market rather ruthlessly consolidated the class differences upon which access to housing in the limited area of the Free City depended. Whereas housing in the construction camps was distributed on the basis of status, all housing in the Free City was based on market value rents. Those who could afford it got it according to their individual means. The demand for this housing was always high. In Novacap's original plan, the Free City was the only temporary settlement authorized to provide residence for those not lodged in the construction camps. Therefore, entrepreneurs enjoyed something of a captured market for their hotels, boarding houses, and rentable back rooms. Because there were no status restrictions on these accommodations, male migrants could either reside with their families or lodge them there if they went to work in the camps. This possibility placed a premium on Free City housing. In fact, in spite of its wild west ways, over 89% of its population lived in family households (IBGE 1959: 103).[27] To meet this increasing demand, entrepreneurs built more authorized rental units. In addition, as Novacap was desperate for workers during the first year of construction, it apparently ignored the construction of unauthorized shacks which migrants built within city limits to avoid paying the escalating rents. However, the tenuous balance between housing supply and demand was irretrievably disrupted during 1958, when the massive immigration of northeastern drought victims overwhelmed the city's limited supply of accommodations. Rents soared; serious overcrowding ensued. Both migrants and speculators responded by building huge numbers of unauthorized shacks. Rather than allow this uncontrolled growth, Novacap reacted by prohibiting any additional expansion of the Free City after December 31 that year. It even attempted to slow migration by putting up what turned out to be an ineffective police cordon around the Free City.

These events precipitated a housing crisis. Poor migrant families had little choice but to appropriate land for their houses in illegal settlements, which they founded either individually or in groups. If individually, the squatter settled at a remote site to avoid detection by Novacap's police, which adopted a policy of summarily dismantling all such dwellings. However, as there was greater safety in numbers, most land seizures were multi-family settlements. They bore such names as Sacolândia or 'Sack-land', after the discarded sacks of concrete and other construction materials that squatters used to build their shacks.

With time, these mini-occupations amalgamated into larger *vilas*, as they were called (table 6.1). The importance of these land seizures as the only viable places of residence near the construction sites for poor families is indicated in the demographic profile of the one *vila* surveyed in the 1959 census: over 99% of the population of Vila Amaury lived in family households, the highest incidence of such residence in any of the new settlements in the construction territory, and comparable only to that of the preexisting cities of Planaltina (97%) and Brazlândia (100%) (IBGE 1959: 103).

Most of the squatters clustered around the Free City in order to have access to its goods and services in a symbiosis that entrepreneurs found entirely to their liking. For in the squatter settlements, entrepreneurs had a wealth of clients constituting a profitable and expanding market, the development of which they encouraged by extending credit and such services as electricity. From their point of view, these settlements constituted a vital aspect of the Federal District's open market, the existence of which their Commercial Association had already begun to defend against Novacap's plan to demolish the Free City and to relocate its commerce to the isolated commercial areas of the Plano Piloto. For their part, the squatters saw the entrepreneurs as sources of goods, services, employment, and, not least, protection against removal. Thus, squatters and merchants became allies in a coalition of mutual interest to prevent the state from eradicating not only the land seizures but ultimately the Free City itself.

To complete the analysis of the generation of collective interests among the different subsets of pioneers, we have finally to consider the government construction camps of Novacap and the Social Security Institutes. Before doing so, the role of the latter in building Brasília requires a word of explanation.[28] When Kubitshek took office in 1955, the Brazilian system of *previdência social* (state-enforced obligatory insurance) consisted of six major welfare institutes that provided separate social insurance protection to actively employed workers in banking, transport, commerce, industry, railroad and public services, and maritime activities (see table 6.2 for a list of these institutes).[29] A seventh institute, IPASE, provided a variety of benefits to civil servants, though the vast majority of civil servants received retirement pensions from their own agencies which were generally superior to those of the *previdência* system. These welfare institutes were managed under the auspices of the Ministry of Labor, which during the 1950s was controlled by the Brazilian Labor Party (PTB). Through this ministry, the PTB was able to use the social insurance system and its approximately 62,000 jobs as a fief of political patronage (Graham 1968: 138). As a result, the mass of civil servants holding jobs in the institutes were political appointees, rather than career service bureaucrats, who had not been admitted to office on the basis of the merit system that required public examinations administered by the Administrative Department of Public Services (DASP).[30] The significant point about this situation for our analysis is that since these appointees had bypassed the merit system, they were not entitled to most of the rights and benefits of DASP classified career bureaucrats—a disadvantage important in understanding the reaction of Brasília's pioneering public sector employees to the distribution of government residences by the DASP-affiliated GTB.

Shortly after Kubitschek assumed the presidency, he confronted an urgent need to reform the entire social insurance system. Perhaps the most pressing issue was that the institutes were on the brink of financial disaster. Since 1934, they had been financed on the principle of tripartite contributions in which the government and the employer contributed an amount equal to that of the insured employee. The government's contribution was supposed to come from a variety of user taxes on services, with the remainder drawn from the general budget. In practice, however, the government seldom if ever paid its full share. As a result, the state owed the social insurance system as a whole the gargantuan sum of about Cr$2.5 billion, and its debt to the Institute for Industrial Workers (IAPI) alone amounted to Cr$1.5 billion (Malloy 1979: 182).

Confronted with this indebtedness to the financially insolvent institutes on the one hand and with the need to finance the construction of Brasília on the other, Kubitschek offered the institutes a deal: he agreed to pay the institutes what the state owed them on the condition that they build the residential units in Brasília necessary for the transfer of government. Brasília's planners considered it a masterfully executed arrangement. As one GTB official told me, "Kubitschek won in two ways with this deal: if the government had built the buildings directly, it would have continued to owe the institutes. This way, he settled the account and with the same money got the institutes to build them" (interview, Brasília, 24 October 1980). I should add that Kubitschek won in yet another way. As each of the institutes already had a real estate division for the purposes of investing in and constructing residences for its insured members, Kubitschek further requried that the institutes manage the *superquadras* and row houses they were building in Brasília. Thus, he was able to utilize the extensive resources of the Social Security Institutes to finance, construct, and manage the residences of the new capital. For their part, the institutes found themselves in a peculiar situation. They owned and managed residential units reserved for the functionaries of the federal government as determined by the GTB, in which their own members had no rights and in the distribution of which they had no say.

While those political appointees who worked for the institutes in Brasília were by and large civil servants but not career service bureaucrats, those who worked for Novacap are better considered—in those specific jobs—as public sector employees rather than as civil servants at all.[31] Such employees are found mainly in the indirect administration of the government and especially in the state enterprises (like Novacap) which have their own hiring policies, salary scales, and perquisite entitlements. In this capacity, they may be officials (like department heads), administrative staff (like secretaries), or skilled and unskilled manual laborers. Admittedly, the state enterprises are difficult entities to classify in relation to the market economy. However, I suggest that the employees of Novacap constituted a special status group in the construction territory. My argument is that their employment benefits and their privileged life-style in the camps were (*a*) available to managers (i.e., officials and staff) and to workers alike, and (*b*) not primarily determined by their fate in the market but more by their status as employees of a government corporation. The evidence for this claim is that they accepted lower wages at Novacap than they could have gotten at the private construction camps in exchange for a number of advantages that could not have been had for money. That they settled for lower wages after having signed on with Novacap is clear in table 6.5. The median income of *both* managers and workers in Novacap is less than that of the private company construction workers alone. While the data do not differentiate the wages of Novacap managers and workers, it is reasonable to conclude that they both must have been significantly lower than those of their counterparts in the private firms.

Novacap employees at all levels exchanged income for what they perceived to be both short-term and long-term job security, with the latter dominating their choice to seek employment with the state enterprise (interviews, Brasília, 1980–81; see also Lins Ribeiro 1980: 47). In the private construction camps, workers experienced especially rapid job turnovers both because the wage wars motivated them to leave one firm for another and because firms laid off workers between contracts. As long as the demand for workers remained high, such layoffs posed little threat to steady employment. But everyone realized that as Brasília approached inauguration, this demand would decrease significantly. Therefore, pioneers reasoned that while the private firms would soon have a greatly reduced presence in the Federal District, Novacap was not likely to disappear.

In addition to prospects for long-term employment, working for Novacap offered most of the *candangos* their first opportunity to become employees in the public sector and thus, potentially, to become eligible for its many prized benefits. As public sector employment is highly valued among all classes in Brazil, it is not surprising to find that the poor have least access to it. For example, in his profile of Brazilian poverty in 1960, Fishlow (1972: 393, table 2) relates that while 51% of the heads of household of poor families were self-employed and 37% were employees in the private sector, only 3% were employees in the public sector.[32] Therefore, a job in Novacap presented the *candangos* with a rare opportunity to enter public employment. Even more alluring, it offered them the possibility of modest but real structural mobility in addition to occupational advances. For not only could unskilled workers in Novacap hope to be promoted to qualified jobs as in the private camps, but they also had the expectation that they would move from being unclassified public sector employees to classified civil servants of the government of the Federal District after Brasília's inauguration. As it turned out, all of them were indeed given this offer, which was only available to Novacap members and available to all of them equally. Thus, for many it involved a significant change in status which secured eligibility for the benefits of civil service.

While such job security and status mobility were benefits for the future, Novacap employees enjoyed a daily privilege that was the most contested in the construction territory: that of family life. Novacap provided family housing for all employees and even primary schooling for their children. This provision privileged Novacap workers in a most meaningful way over workers in both the private camps and the Free City. However, although the privileges of family life were available to all Novacap employees, their distribution differentiated managers and workers; that is, although Novacap made "doctor" privileges available to *candangos*, it nevertheless separated the two with unforeseen and profound consequences for the future of Brasília.

Whereas the private firms lodged managers and workers in the same camp—though here too they were spatially segregated, often by the camp soccer field—Novacap created a separate camp, appropriately named Candangolândia, for its *candangos*. The most important privilege of this camp was that married workers were given accommodations to live with their families if they wanted to bring them to Brasília. As a result, 82% of them did so, as compared with 25% of *all* married employees (mostly managers) in the private camps. The consequence of this status privilege was that life in Candangolândia approached the demographics of a working-class neighborhood: 82% of its population lived in family households, 40% were female, and of the 414 families all but 37 had individual houses (IBGE 1959: 80, 103). According to interviews with former Candangolândia residents, it was their membership in this status group that gave them a clear sense of a future in Brasília, one that they thought would continue to be relatively privileged in comparison with that of other workers who might decide to make the new city their home. Thus, their expectations about job security, social mobility, and family life decisively influenced their decision to remain after the inauguration. Of all the workers in the construction territory, therefore, only their long-term interests were generated by a set of status privileges rather than disprivileges. Consequently, whereas other workers found their interests in direct conflict with Novacap policy, these government workers found theirs entirely served by it.

Initially, Novacap lodged both its officials and its administrative staff at its central encampment, Velhacap. Conditions at the camp for these 1,400 employees were similar to those of Candangolândia. The officials among them were the supreme bosses in Brasília, responsible for every aspect of the massive project and given commensurate authority and adequate powers to rule the territory. Moreover, with the GTB headquartered in Rio to attend to the details of the transfer, this bureaucratic elite ruled with considerable autonomy. Furthermore, as they were officials of an autarkic state corporation, they also enjoyed a real measure of independence—enhanced by their geographic remoteness—not from Kubitschek himself but more from the Congress and especially from the GTB and other authorities of the direct administration. Powerful and relatively autonomous, Novacap officialdom thus operated with few legal or political constraints, exactly as Kubitschek (1975: 41) intended: "The work of Santiago Dantas [who authored the law creating Novacap] was perfect. The board of directors of Novacap, to be nominated by me, was endowed with ample powers, giving it the right to take all measures necessary to construct the new capital, without any new hearing in Congress whatsoever." According to interviews with several of these officials, it is also clear that Novacap's elite formed a cadre dedicated to "the spirit of Brasília." Whereas most pioneers ventured to the construction territory for economic motives, they were committed to it as a mission of national development.

Nevertheless, although they combined power with considerable prestige and pioneering zeal, they lacked an essential component: according to GTB guidelines, they had no predetermined rights to reside in the city they were building. As they had been recruited for the preinaugural construction and not for the postinaugural bureaucracy, they were not part of the GTB's original distribution plan for awarding government residences to functionaries of the federal bureaucracy being transferred from Rio. The GTB's principal responsibility was to ensure that by inauguration day enough of these functionaries had been transferred, and therefore housed, to constitute the government legally in the new capital. Each completed residence in Brasília was therefore at an absolute premium for distribution to the enormous bureaucracy in Rio. As Novacap's people were already in Brasília, they simply fell outside of the GTB's priority consideration and jurisdiction. Moreover, while many of them may have been classified bureaucrats on loan to Novacap from other federal organs, as Novacap employees per se they were not civil servants in the strict sense of the term (much less ones installed through DASP's merit system). Thus, in relation to Brasília, they had few entitlements to DASP-GTB–regulated privileges. In short, as the GTB was solely in charge of Brasília's inaugural residences, Novacap administrators found themselves without inaugural rights to the city they built and ruled and to which 89% had already brought families.

In August 1958, however, a "corrective measure" presented itself. The Popular Housing Foundation was the first autarky to initiate and to complete a housing project in Brasília. This project consisted of 500 row houses (constituting the Sector of Individual Paired Dwellings) located between W-3 and W-4 in the South Wing. The prototype was a Neimeyer design featuring a living room, three bedrooms, kitchen, bathroom, veranda, garden, and a service area annexed to the kitchen. In the GTB's original distribution plan, these houses were designated for lower-echelon functionaries (drivers, guards, janitors, maids, and the like) transferred with large families. Although their design expresses a middle-class social organization, these row houses were thus intended as *casas populares*, 'popular [class] houses' for the lower-income residents of Brasília. Indeed, at their inaugural ceremonies in August 1958, Kubitschek affirmed that "what we call popular houses in other places, housing for people of few resources, in Brasília constitute palaces contested for by all the residents and workers as a prize for their efforts, for their work" (quoted from *Arquitetura & Engenharia*, July–August 1960, p. 148). In fact, so esteemed were these completed houses that 500 of Novacap's elite families immediately and illegitimately occupied all of them, usurping transferee rights. Ultimately, no one disputed Novacap's usurpation. There was, in any case, no one to evict them.

While this "official seizure" gave Novacap's elite the secure foundation in the city they thought they deserved, it also had the most important consequences on the preinaugural social planning and the postinaugural social structure of Brasília. It forced the GTB to scuttle its planned social stratification of the residential areas of the city in which the *superquadras* in the 100–300 bands were reserved for middle- and upper-echelon officials, and the W-3 houses and 400 band *superquadras* for those in the lower ranks. As the W-3 houses were now occupied, the GTB had to change completely its housing assignments and distributional criteria in order to lodge the requisite number of transferred functionaries. Instead of a socially stratified distribution of apartments, it had to adopt an explicitly egalitarian one based on objective criteria of need. Moreover, it had to distribute them to a pool of recipients now including all levels of functionaries. Ironically, out of this distribution emerged *superquadras* whose social structure bore a strong resemblence, in an unintended concordance of intentions, to those originally proposed by the utopian architects.

Having less authority than the Novacap elite, the officials of the Social Security Institutes were in an even weaker position to negotiate access to residences in the city. Moreover, having significantly less power (no security force of their own, for example), they were less capable of organizing to usurp what they thought they deserved before the inauguration of the capital. After that, they continued to live in the wooden houses of the construction camps and to be displaced from apartments by those who had transferee rights to the city, the sum total of which they considered an indelicate confirmation of their unjust status as *piotários*. While they had to pay all expenses out of pocket to bring their families and belongings to Brasília, the transferees received moving expenses, double salaries, furnished apartments, and more. Finally, however, with their faith in a just reward expiring, they seized the last apartment blocks that the institutes would build in Brasília. As these seizures constitute an unusual case of such collective action by elites, it is worth citing the description of one IPASE official who took part:

> The apartments that we built were given to the "pioneers" who came after April 1960. And these "pioneers," who found apartments with light, water, telephone, and even furniture, began to look upon us, in those shacks of wood, as a kind of squatter. Only in 1965, in a skillful and courageous maneuver by a few of IPASE's officials . . . did we succeed in obtaining apartments, exactly in the last blocks built by IPASE. . . . All this occurred because it was discovered that a certain ministry was waiting until the

end of the construction work on those blocks to requisition them for their functionaries. Receiving the request from that ministry, IPASE, through its engineering service, responded that the blocks were not yet ready to be inhabited. After that, there ensued a series of maneuvers, trying to save those blocks, to distribute the apartments among the functionaries of IPASE who were occupying wooden houses, many living in Brasília since 1957 and always passed over in the distribution of apartments. . . . We lived through tense days when we learned that some of the functionaries of that ministry, having found out about our maneuvers, were themselves planning to invade the apartments. We ourselves, in shifts, began to guard the blocks. Finally, with pressure rising and rumors multiplying and the comings and goings of the GTB . . . we decided to invade the apartments, with the prior knowledge of the administration of IPASE. The operation, as in a suspense film, was carried out in code, until the last moment when we began the move, or better, the invasion, in minutes, carrying bundles of clothes up the stairs because the buildings didn't have elevators that worked because the electricity hadn't yet been connected. That was the way we succeeded in getting apartments, eight years after being in Brasília, living in a small house of wood and after having helped to construct hundreds of them for more fortunate colleagues. (Mendes 1979: 158)

6.4 From Interests to Actions

Our aim in studying the emergence of collective interests among the pioneers has been to uncover the structure of events during the construction epoch in which the organization of Brasiliense society developed. In this investigation, we found two generative principles—or perhaps I should say one applied twice. By way of conclusion, let us review them and the social processes they generated.

The first principle was embodied in the government's plan to build an exclusively bureaucratic city and to incorporate only its own corps of employees into its public domain. This initial decision about societal incorporation logically entailed the formation of two types of populations which would be present at the capital's inauguration: one which would build the city and yet be deprived of rights to it and another which would arrive with full rights to a city already built. This entailment established the need to distinguish these populations in ways specifically related to the construction and settlement of the city. These distinctions constituted their fundamental economic, juridical, and political features, which we described in terms of recruitment to bureaucracy or to construction, eligibility for rights to the city's public residences, and capacity for collective action and political organization. On the basis of these features, we concluded that even before its inauguration Brasília was a stratified city, in which social development followed the entailments of its differential incorporation. The second principle of this development was the reiteration of the first in the planning of the construction project itself. Thus, planners established different subpopulations and types of settlements on the basis of recruitment to one market sphere or another; distributed various rights, privileges, and powers on the basis of class and status positions inherent in this recruitment; and subjugated all such differentiated categories of pioneers to the authority and power of one group of government officials.

However, these differentiations established the terms of their own transformation: the distribution of disadvantage inherent in the plan's organization of work and residence motivated the pioneers to define collective interests which in turn led them into actions against the planning authorities. On the one hand, this organization gave the pioneers of all classes numerous incentives to want to remain in the Federal District after inauguration: the workers found employment, good wages, and job mobility; the private sector managers and professionals enjoyed high income and many status privileges; the entrepreneurs built a lucrative market on tax exemptions, land grants, market monopolies, and rapidly expanding consumer demands; and, the public sector employees had job security and a set of coveted status privileges which they expected would multiply with continued government service. On the other hand, this same organization deprived all of them of postinaugural rights to remain either in the residences they were occupying or in those they were building. Only Novacap's managers had the initial political capacity to redress this dilemma: even though they lacked the authority, they had the power to do so.

Over the course of the construction period, however, all but two of the other categories of pioneers transformed their political capacities through collective actions to advance the interests that had thus emerged. The two exceptions were the construction firm managers and the government workers who found their interests adequately empowered by Novacap's. For the others, their political transformations occurred through the formation of representative associations organized around two types of interests: those concerned with conflicts of class and those concerned with status struggles.

The former resulted in the formation of two class associations: a commercial association and a labor union. The Commercial Association of the Free City arose to protect the class advantages that entrepreneurs had been accorded by government contract. When these were threatened, it consolidated its political power on the basis of its members' economic power and their solidarity in its use. By comparison, the private sector managers and professionals never had their advantages threatened and, perhaps for this reason, did not form class associations. While the Commercial Association arose to protect what it already enjoyed, the union arose among construction workers to protest the deprivation of labor rights. However, despite the legitimacy of its demands and the potential clout of an enormous membership, the labor movement remained unable to build a broad base of support during the construction era. On the one hand, the state systematically deprived the workers of their basic labor rights and suppressed union activities. On the other, however, there can be no doubt that workers remained apathetic toward unionization. Under the prevailing conditions of high labor demand, they saw little conflict between their interests concerning work and company interests concerning the pace and profit of production—a rhythm, we should not forget, effectively legitimated by the various discourses of participation.

If, with the exception of the entrepreneurs, pioneers failed to form effective solidarity associations around class interests, they mobilized decisively to contest the stratified distribution of status privileges. Only the private camp managers and the government camp workers failed to do so. The others organized into associations around the one issue that both differentiated them as a whole from the GTB civil servants (by terminating their future in the Federal District) and differentiated them internally (by establishing different conditions and qualities of daily life): access to housing. The fact that they lacked long-term residential rights meant that none of them could adequately or legally resolve their needs for housing and family accommodations within the constraints of the government plan—with the exception of the private camp managers and public camp workers which is why they did not mobilize. The very split between work and residence that the state drove to keep pioneers from establishing their own communities where they worked, prompted them to act against the state to create illegal ones. This mobilization transformed the structure of power in preinaugural Brasília and with it the destiny of the city.

TABLE 6.1
Population by Type of Settlement,
Federal District, 1959

Locality	Population	Percentage
I. Preexisting Settlements	(6,600)	(10.3)
1. Planaltina	2,245	3.5
2. Brazlândia	355	0.6
3. Rural zone	4,000	6.2
II. Planned Permanent Settlements	(2,270)	(3.5)
1. Plano Piloto		
FCP row houses[a]	2,270	3.5
III. Planned Temporary Settlements	(37,315)	(58.0)
1. Construction camps	(25,750)	(40.0)
a. Novacap	(4,186)	(6.5)
Velhacap	1,318	2.1
Candangolândia	2,868	4.5
b. Social Security Institutes[b]		
Plano Piloto—South Wing	8,737	13.6
c. Private construction firms	(12,827)	(19.9)
Plaza of the Three Powers camps	7,064	11.0
Other camps	5,763	9.0
2. Free City (Núcleo Bandeirante, 1961)	11,565	18.0
IV. Illegal Squatter Settlements	(18,129)	(28.2)
1. Urban zone[c]	(9,873)	(15.4)
a. Vila Sara Kubitschek (Taguatinga, 1958)	3,677	5.7
b. Vila Amaury (Sobradinho, 1960)	6,196	9.6
c. Vila Planalto[d] (Gama, 1960)	[6,500]	
d. Vila do IAPI[d] (Ceilândia, 1971)	[8,084]	
2. Rural zone	8,256	12.8
TOTAL	64,314	100.0

Sources: Derived from IBGE 1959: 3–4, 79, 107–8; Silva 1971: 231; Epstein 1973: 65, 69.

[a]The 500 row houses built along W-3 by the Popular Housing Foundation (FCP) were immediately occupied by upper-echelon members of the technical and administrative staff of Novacap and their families. In the IBGE census of 1959, this population is not disaggregated from the population of the construction camps in the Plano Piloto. To distinguish the former from the latter, I have used differences in their housing conditions as registered in the census, making a proportional estimate (based on 500 houses) of all those listed as "durable," "individual dwellings," with "internal water supply" and "septic tank hook-up" (as compared with those listed in contrasting categories).

[b]See table 6.2 for the itemized contribution of each Social Security Institute in the construction of the *superquadra* apartment blocks. Although the institutes themselves employed some construction workers, most of those employed among the 8,737 listed here (it is impossible to tell exactly how many) worked for private construction companies that the institutes contracted to build the *superquadras*. For example, IAPC's camp in SQS 106 was occupied by the firm Kosmos Engenharia.

[c]The government's attempt to remove and resettle the inhabitants of the illegal squatter settlements gave rise to the authorized satellite cities, listed in

parentheses with their dates of foundation. The population given for Vila Sara Kubitschek is that of the satellite city Taguatinga, which had received almost all of its residents by the date of the census.

[d]The population of Vila Planalto and Vila do IAPI, both listed in square brackets, are for the year 1964. The latter was an amalgamation of several smaller invasions, including Vila Tenório, Vila Esperança, Vila Bernardo Sayão, Morro do Querosene, and Morro do Urubu.

TABLE 6.2
Plano Piloto Residences Constructed by Federal Autarkies
for the Inauguration of Brasília, April 1960

Autarkies	Location	Apartments				Houses	Total
		1 bed	2 bed	3 bed	4 bed	3 bed	
IPASE[a]	SQS 208		48	108	96		252
IAPB[b]	SQS 108		240	216			456
IAPETC	SQS 107		144	252	24		420
IAPC	SQS 106		144	288			432
IAPI[c]	SQS 105			180			180
CAPFESP	SQS 104		144				
	SQS 304			288			432
FCP[d]	SQS 411/412	840					
	SHIGS (W-3)					500	1340
CEFRJ & SP[e]	SHIGS (W-3)					222	222
Total		840	720	1332	120	722	3734

Sources: GTB 1960: 2; Arquitetura & Engenharia, July-August 1960, pp. 148–49; Vaitsman 1968: 30–84.

[a]Social Welfare Institute for Public Servants.

[b]Institute of Retirement and Pensions for: Bank Employees (IAPB), Transport Employees (IAPETC), Commercial Employees (IAPC), Industrial Employees (IAPI), Railroad and Public Services Employees (CAPFESP).

[c]Four months after the inauguration, IAPI completed an additional 1,188 one bedroom apartments in SQS 409/410. This construction permitted the state to complete the second phase of the transfer of functionaries in the executive branch of government.

[d]The Popular Housing Foundation (FCP) constructed both the modest "JK apartments" of SQS 411/412 and the row houses along W-3 occupied by Novacap staff.

[e]Federal Savings Banks of Rio de Janeiro and São Paulo.

TABLE 6.3
Structure of the Employed Labor Force by Subsectors,
Federal District, 1959

Subsectors	Employed Population	
Construction	22,116	62.8%
Services	3,579	10.2
Agriculture	2,291	6.5
Mining[a]	1,605	4.6
Commerce	1,634	4.6
Industry[b]	1,170	3.3
Transport, communications, storage	785	2.2
Public administration	540	1.5
Social activities[c]	482	1.4
Liberal professions[d]	96	0.3
Other activities[e]	903	2.6
TOTAL	35,201	100.0%

Source: Derived from IBGE 1959: 57–60, 88–89.

[a]Primarily gravel and sand for construction purposes.

[b]Primarily construction materials and food products and processing.

[c]Activities relating to education, medical assistance, and urban services.

[d]Includes professions other than those concerned with construction.

[e]Includes real estate, credit, and insurance activities.

TABLE 6.4
Migration to the Federal District by Birthplace,
Directness of Migration, and Region of Last Residence, 1959

Region of birth or Last Residence	Birthplace of Migrants		Directness of Migration		Region of Last Residence	
	People	Percentage of total	Direct	Indirect	People	Percentage of total
North	358	0.6	49.4	50.6	297	0.5
Northeast[a]	24,511	43.0	59.2	40.8	15,489	27.2
Western northeast	3,364	5.9	62.9	37.1	2,485	4.4
Eastern northeast	13,175	23.1	65.8	34.2	8,874	15.6
Southern northeast	7,972	14.0	46.8	53.2	4,130	7.3
Southeast	16,386	28.8	66.5	33.5	17,844	31.3
South	883	1.6	51.9	48.1	987	1.7
Central west	13,459	23.6	95.5	4.5	21,979	38.6
Foreign country	1,216	2.1	6.4	93.6	78	0.1
TOTAL[b]	56,953	100.0	70.7	29.3	56,953	100.0
urban					44,753	78.6
rural					11,189	19.6

Source: Derived from IBGE 1959: 45–50, 86, 96–97.

[a]The western northeast comprises the states of Maranhão and Piauí; the eastern comprises Ceará, Rio Grande do Norte, Paraíba, Pernambuco, and Alagoas; the southern comprises Sergipe and Bahia.

[b]Total includes 140 migrants without specification of place of birth or last residence. However, the urban and rural figures do not include the 1,011 migrants who did not specify either as a condition of last residence.

TABLE 6.5
Recruitment Category of Pioneers:
Economically Active Members by Class, Occupational Field, and Income

Members by Class and Occupational Field	Total	Percentage	Median Monthly[a] Income (Cr$) ("average" Income)
TOTAL[b]	33,413	100.0	6.2
Employees	29,177	87.3	6.1
Self-employed	3,516	10.5	5.9
Employers	720	2.2	19.7
I. EMPLOYERS	933	2.8	(18.4)[c]
Commerce	151		15.5
Services	175		18.1
Transport, communication, storage	38		29.5
Construction[d]	47		25.8
Industry	98		23.0
Agriculture	130		9.2
Mining	75		22.5
Real estate, credit, insurance	4		—
Liberal professions[e]	215		18.9
II. EMPLOYEES	32,480	97.2	
A. Managerial employees	2,410	7.2	
1. Private sector executives and administrators[f]	580	1.7	
2. Public sector employees	1,830	5.5	(6.4)
Novacap officials and staff	1,378		6.4
Staff of Social Security Institutes	96		—
Other civil servants[g]	356		—
B. Manual workers	30,070	90.0	(6.0)
Construction	20,283		
Private sector employees	18,838		6.6
Public sector employees (Novacap)	1,198		
Self-employed	247		5.6
Industry	1,044		
Employees	925		5.2
Self-employed	119		5.1
Transport, communication, storage	731		
Employees	469		6.8
Self-employed	262		11.0
Agriculture	1,760		
Employees	904		3.1
Self-employed	856		3.4
Mining	1,515		
Employees	1,421		5.0
Self-employed	94		5.6
Services	3,339		
Employees[h]	2,210		2.7
Self-employed[i]	1,129		4.4
Retail and wholesale merchandise	1,398		
Employees	657		5.1
Self-employed[j]	741		10.2

Source: Derived from IBGE 1959: 60–66, 93–95, 100.

^aAt the 1959 exchange rate, U.S.$1.00 = Cr$0.184. The median income of the total is U.S.$33.70. The "average" income in parentheses is the weighted average of the median incomes for each class by occupational field.

^bTotal excludes 1,788 people listed in the 1959 census that I could not classify with confidence.

^cThe median incomes of employers are recalculations from aggregate census data, except for those of employers in commerce and services which are listed as such in the 1959 census. Separate income data for the other categories in this class are not given. See note 16 of chap. 6 for a discussion of the method used in estimating these incomes. The estimate of "average" income for the class as a whole excludes the executives and administrators, and the employers in real estate, credit, and insurance, for whom income data are lacking. As this estimate is a weighted average of medians, which is not the same as the actual median, we expect it to be lower than the actual median of Cr$19.7. The difference, however, is relatively small, only 7%.

^dThese building entrepreneurs do not represent the private construction firms contracted by government agencies to build Brasília. Rather, they are typically independent subcontractors who, in a field dominated by the firms, were notorious in their exploitation of naïve migrants "just off the bus." They were also active in the building and repairing of the shacks of the Free City.

^eThis category comprises only the private sector professionals. It includes 105 engineers in the construction firms; 68 self-employed professionals (not further discriminated in the census data) of whom 60 resided in the Free City and 8 in the illegal settlements; and 2 employers. The latter should properly be classified with the entrepreneurs, but I have found no way to disaggregate them.

^fThe construction firms listed 106 executives (directors, managers, and supervisors) and 357 administrators (office staff, inspectors, and bookkeepers). The remaining 117 are administrators in other private enterprises.

^gConsists of 198 federal, state, and municipal civil servants and 158 teachers.

^hIncludes 659 waiters, 577 cooks, 108 sales clerks, 95 guards, and 70 janitors.

ⁱIncludes 465 laundresses.

^jIncludes 148 itinerant peddlers.

SEVEN

Cities of Rebellion

The rebellion of the pioneers forced the state to recognize their rights to the city. However, it was not to the Plano Piloto itself, but rather to cities on the periphery of the capital. This development constituted a double departure from initial intentions. Neither Costa's Master Plan nor Novacap's early directives anticipated the creation of satellite cities in the Federal District. Instead, they called for the construction of one capital city to accommodate half a million people by the year 2000. These specifications were established in Law 1803 of January 1953. In addition, the Master Plan stressed that "the growth of squatter settlements [*favelas*], whether on the city outskirts or in the surrounding countryside, should at all costs be prevented" (art. 17). Thus, Brasília's planners established at the outset one of the capital's radical intentions: it should develop neither the legal nor the illegal periphery of working-class poverty that typically occurs around Brazilian metropolises. Rather, Novacap planned to develop the hinterland into agricultural cooperatives. These cooperatives constituted one option out of three planned for the labor force building the city: one-third would settle on these farms, one-third would be absorbed into local commercial services, and one-third would return home. However, in 1958, Novacap decided instead to construct satellite cities to accommodate the pioneers of Brasília. The government inaugurated the first satellite almost two years before the capital itself and founded another three by the end of 1961. To date, a total of six satellite cities have been built (map 7.1).

What motivated this radical transformation of plans? I shall argue that it both followed from and compounded Brasília's developmental structure of premise and paradox. To make this point, I shall focus on the formation of the unwanted periphery between 1958 and 1965, after which the terms of its development changed. My primary concern is with its transformation from a condition of illegality to one of legal incorporation into the administrative structure of the Federal District. I shall first describe its defiant phase when voluntary associations emerged among pioneers to create an illegal periphery of squatter settle-

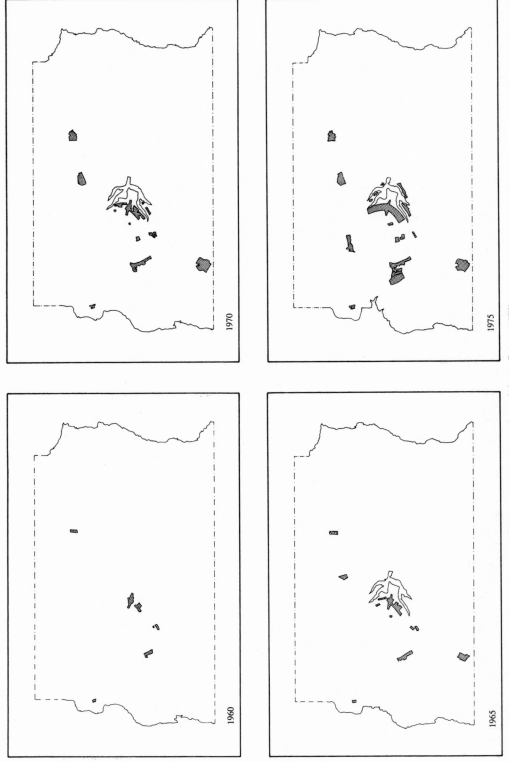

1970

1975

1960

1965

Map 7.1 Growth of urban areas in the Federal District, 1960–75. (Adapted from Geipot 1979)

ments. I shall then analyze the government's response: the organization of this illegal periphery into authorized satellite cities. My point is also to demonstrate two paradoxical consequences. On the one hand, once the rebellious associations attained their objective of legal residence, they dissolved, forfeiting the political organization they had achieved. On the other, in organizing the satellite cities, the government applied principles of stratification that set off new cycles of rebellion and legitimation that continue to this day.

7.1 The Illegal Periphery

I use the word rebellion to describe this process not only because it resulted from an organized defiance of authority, the objective of which was to transform government policy, but also because it constituted a radically new pattern of political organization and action in the Federal District. This pattern emerged as squatters formed into voluntary associations that had the primary function of representing their members in disputes with the government. These disputes focused on (a) demands for the legalization of land seizures, usually put forth as claims both for the rights of permanent settlement and for the "regularization" of titles to lots; (b) demands for urban services such as potable water, sewers, paving, and electricity; and (c) the defense of illegal settlements against eradication by government security forces. In these disputes, the associations functioned as representative groups engaged in political action. They were representative in the sense of being organized around collective interests and political in the sense of acting to influence government policy and to redirect the distribution of its powers and resources. As such, they gave their members new political identities in the Federal District. Whereas the government had denied the pioneers not only the rights of settlement but also those of local political organization, these rebellious associations provided organized representation—of a limited sort but with a considerable degree of autonomy. Therefore, they transformed their members' actions from mere individual violations of law (land seizure, clandestine house construction, refusals to vacate property, and the like) into a collective challenge to the government's organization of Brasília.

It is possible to identify three patterns in the development of these residential associations. I shall use these patterns to differentiate (a) associations that never developed formal administrative structure or corporate features; (b) associations that developed administrative structure and some corporate features but lacked the presumption of perpetuity; and (c) associations that developed as offshoots of fully corporate groups but were similar in other ways to the second type. The following discussion presents a salient example of each. I shall summarize its emergence and mobilization and focus on the conflict in which it precipitated the authorization of a satellite city. In each example, I shall also highlight one feature that while common to all the associations in their disputes with the government is best represented in the particular case I have chosen. The first example emphasizes the subversive use of state symbols against state authorities. The second highlights the importance of the patronage system linking squatter settlements and political parties. The third pays particular attention to the use of both place of birth and place of residence among migrants to form a web of patron-client relations with government officials.

These examples are given in chronological order, beginning with the foundation of the first satellite city and ending with the last one authorized before the coup of 1964. However, this chronological presentation does not mean that the periphery as a whole developed progressively from a condition of illegality to one of legality. On the contrary, as the government was reluctant to have any periphery, its development was characterized by a series of separate solutions to conflicts over settlement. Thus, while the administration acceded to the demands of one association, it rejected those of another. Therefore, at any one moment, the periphery featured multiple cycles of rebellion and legitimation in various stages of development.

Vila Sara Kubitschek (1958)/Taguatinga (1958)

The first case is of an association that never developed formal administrative or corporate features. Rather, it was a loosely defined association of squatters led by a so-called command group that negotiated the issue of settlement with the authorities. It appears that this command group neither preceded nor survived these negotiations. Nevertheless, it made an important contribution to the development of Brasília's periphery. Not only did it force the creation of the first satellite city, Taguatinga. It also established a certain style of strategic action in its dispute with the government which set a much-followed precedent.

Brasília's first satellite began with an appropriation of land near the entrance to the Free City (map 7.2). I have already described the causes of such seizures. These came to a head in the first weeks of June 1958, when, in the space of a few days, between four and five thousand Northeastern drought victims descended on the Free City in search of work. Novacap ordered its security forces (the GEB) to put up barricades on the highway

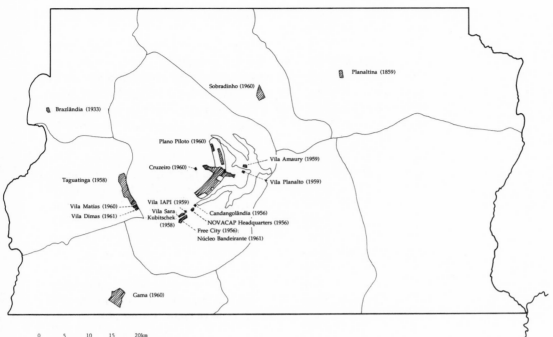

Map 7.2 Urban settlements and administrative regions of the Federal District, 1956–65

to turn them back. But rather than return—as if they had anywhere to go—these desperate migrants launched a land seizure, setting up an encampment of improvised lodgings on the other side of the barricade.

Within a few days, the highway frontage of the occupation was bannered with signs announcing, "Hail Vila Sara Kubitschek," "The residents of Vila Sara thank you," "Long live dona Sara," and the like. With these banners, the command group of the land seizure initiated an ingenious strategy to counter an expected assault by the GEB. This strategy had two elements. First, the squatters named their settlement after the wife of President Kubitschek, hoping that Novacap would hesitate to attack a *vila* dedicated to Brazil's First Lady. Second, they launched the rumor that "by order of dona Sara" anyone who staked out a plot of land in the Vila would be accorded legal rights to its occupancy; hence, the meaning of the sign, "The residents thank you, dona Sara" for supposedly authorizing the settlement and the distribution of lots. This strategem checkmated Novacap: almost immediately the site was flooded with such a mass of pioneers from the Free City, the construction camps, and the other land seizures—all after their plot in the promised land—that the security forces were outmaneuvered. Moreover, after this initial success, the lack of police action made it appear even more that the settlement had some kind of official authorization.[1]

This effective strategy was one that would be repeated many times in the various struggles for residential rights. With few resources, the association based its strategy on what was free to manipulate—the symbols of the state—for it correctly supposed that the authorities would find it more difficult to march against their own emblems. The association was especially effective in using names, exactly as the government itself does, to proclaim the existence of patronage from a purported benefactor. Even more, it understood the power of naming to invent such relations. Thus, it placed the land seizure under the protection of Brazil's First Lady with the unauthorized use of her name as its eponym. In doing so, the squatters hoped both to invest themselves with her aura of legitimacy and to force the regime to recognize the acts committed under it as legitimate.

Having defused the threat of immediate GEB retaliation, the residential association pressed its demands for legalization with the one person whose own use of charisma to legitimate the construction of Brasília made him especially vulnerable to this strategy: Juscelino Kubitschek. When the association learned that Kubitschek was to dine in the Free City at the Barbecue JK (another example of such naming practices), it planned a massive demonstration for the occasion. At the rally, it again presented the squatters' demands in the banner language of Brasília's officially legitimating discourses: "We founded the Vila Sara Kubitschek," "Long live President Juscelino," "We want to stay where we are," and the like.

Kubitschek sent one of Novacap's directors with the government's response: the administration had decided to create a satellite city, 25 kilometers from the Plano Piloto, in which migrants of very modest means would have the right to acquire a lot and to which Novacap would remove all squatters already residing in the construction territory. Thus, Brasília's first satellite city was designated as the place, at a considerable remove from the Plano Piloto, in which to accommodate Brasília's squatters.[2] Initially, the command group refused Novacap's offer, arguing that the isolation of the satellite beyond the immediate environs of the Free City and the Plano Piloto would be economically disastrous. Novacap in turn stressed the advantages of legitimate property ownership. In addition, it offered to transfer everyone to the satellite city at no expense, reconstruct their shacks there, initiate the construction of basic urban services, and provide medical assistance and transportation to work (Ernesto Silva, interview, Brasília, 1980). Finally, after a number of violent clashes, resistance to removal collapsed.

Within ten days, Novacap transferred four thousand squatters and their carefully dismantled shacks to Taguatinga, Brasília's first satellite city.

By the time the city was inaugurated on 5 July 1958, Novacap had established and staffed a local administration to supervise the distribution of lots and the provision of urban services. Although several social clubs, church-related groups, and a commercial association affiliated with that of the Free City emerged in the satellite, none was specifically organized around urban services and none engaged in political action. The political mobilization achieved by the residents' association of Vila Sara Kubitschek did not survive the transfer of its members to Taguatinga.

Vila Amaury (1959)/Sobradinho (1960)

Approximately six months after Taguatinga was founded, a new movement for residential rights began that eventuated in Brasília's second satellite city, Sobradinho. As in the first example, it was initially organized as an association lacking formal administrative or corporate features. However, under a different type of leadership and with the backing of party patronage, it developed into a corporate group with a formal hierarchy of offices.

It was initiated and led by a politically ambitious staff member of Novacap itself, Amaury de Almeida. He was known to have strong political connections within the Brazilian Labor Party (PTB) and ambitions of becoming a state deputy. In the first months of 1959, he organized a successful campaign to petition Novacap to create a new settlement near the construction sites. He proposed the settlement as a means to gather into an authorized encampment the thousands of squatters who worked for the construction companies but who for one reason or another had established illegal residences in and around the Plano Piloto. For the aspiring politician, such a gathering was a way to establish an electoral base. For Novacap, it appeared rather as a peaceful way to gather dispersed squatters into one, more easily supervised locale. To ensure that the new settlement would be temporary, like the others it had authorized for pioneers, Novacap located it on low ground destined to be flooded by the rising waters of the artificial Lake Paranoá (map 7.2). By inauguration day, the government intended its bulldozed remains to be under water. Furthermore, Novacap refused to issue any permits or to offer any assistance or resources to its inhabitants.[3] As a result, the Provisional Nucleus of Bananal, as it was officially named after a local watercourse, or the Vila Amaury, as it was popularly named after its leader, emerged as something of a contradiction: although it was temporarily authorized, it had many of the characteristics of a squatter settlement.[4]

Confronted with the rising waters of the lake, Amaury de Almeida proposed to transform both the objectives and the organization of the loosely defined association he led. He convened an assembly of about 200 residents to create the Beneficent Association of Vila Amaury. The assembly established bylaws and a hierarchy of administrative offices, elected leaders (Amaury de Almeida, president), and ratified a new set of demands. The association organized around one goal to which all of these demands referred: the right of permanent settlement in the Federal District. To achieve this objective, it followed a twofold strategy. First, it did not fight for the permanence of the Vila on its lowland site. Rather, considering the negotiated outcome of the Vila Sara Kubitschek conflict, the association demanded that Novacap authorize and sponsor the transfer of Vila Amaury residents to a satellite city. However, by the time that it had organized to fight for permanent residential rights, the planned subdivisions of Taguatinga had been almost completely filled. Therefore, the association's objective became the creation of a new satellite city, in which it demanded legal residence for its members.[5]

Second, whereas the association of Vila Sara Kubitschek succeeded with a combined strategy of militancy and propaganda, the Beneficent Association relied on the patron-client ties ties that its president cultivated within the PTB. In developing this strategy, Almeida played what is a standard role in Brazilian urban politics: that of party patron to organizations of the popular classes.[6] He used the patronage system within the PTB to wrest concessions from Novacap. In this strategy, he was effective both because the PTB had its own power base within the federal bureaucracy and because Kubitschek's own electoral and congressional victories depended on the alliance of his party (the PSD) with the PTB. Almeida's most dramatic tactic was to organize, on two occasions, a caravan of association members to travel to Rio to meet with Kubitschek's vice-president, João Goulart, the PTB leader. These meetings were arranged through the mediations of a PTB federal deputy from Goiás. Thus, a link of patronage was established that filtered down from the vice-president's office to benefit what had become, in the months just before the inauguration of the capital, a community of about 20,000 "ex"-squatters struggling in the mud of Vila Amaury.

By the time the capital was inaugurated, Novacap had established a second satellite city, Sobradinho, 22 kilometers northeast of the Plano Piloto, to accommodate these *candangos*. The Beneficent Association of Vila Amaury had thus achieved a remarkable change in status for its members. Yet, as in the first case, it dissolved upon transfer as Novacap quickly established its bureaucratic control in the new satellite city.[7]

Free City (1956)/Núcleo Bandeirante (1961)

The final case is that of a fully corporate class association of entrepreneurs which broadened its base of organization to sponsor a citywide, interclass residents' association. With considerable resources at its disposal, this association in turn sponsored a network of subsidiary associations. These were based on the crosscutting affiliations of its constituency of migrants, organized by place of residence and by place of birth. In the peculiar situation of a migrant community, the first rallied local support while the second proved an effective lobby with federal officials and especially with congressmen.[8]

On the day after Brasília's inauguration, the newspaper *Correio Braziliense* ran the headline, "Núcleo Bandeirante is illegal since yesterday." That it still stood, fully populated, violated Novacap's plan to transfer its merchants, enterprises, and employees to the Plano Piloto, and to raze the city. Before April 21, there were three types of residents in the Free City with respect to the legal rights of temporary settlement: those entrepreneurs who had contracts entitling them to establish commercial enterprises but obliging them to return their lots to Novacap by the inauguration; those who rented from the entrepreneurs; and those who squatted. After April 21, as far as Novacap was concerned, they had all become squatters.

The merchants resisted the destruction of the city because they considered a move to the Plano Piloto economically disastrous. At the time, its commercial prospects were indeed bleak. It was barely inhabited; its commercial areas, especially in the North Wing, were dispersed and isolated, and everywhere its buildings were subject to strict planning controls which prohibited exterior alteration or expansion; and most significant, its market was highly regulated. By contrast, the Free City offered unregulated commercial activity and a wealth of consumers both in its own population and in that of the squatter settlements surrounding it. Correspondingly, the squatters found in the entrepreneurial city their major source of goods, services, credit, and often employment. Such mutual interests motivated merchants and squatters to join forces in the campaign for the "fixation" of the Free City. This struggle pitted the pro-fixation forces led by the Commercial Association of Brasília (the ACB) against the forces of the state led by Novacap and the prefecture of the Federal District. The latter, Novacap's administrative superior, had been created on the inauguration of the capital and had as its first prefect Novacap's former president.

The ACB presented Novacap with a list of demands that neatly conveys the important issues. "In the name of the people," it demanded:

(1) The integration of Núcleo Bandeirante in the urbanization plan of Brasília as a district [bairro] of the future capital of the Republic, with the name District Bernardo Sayão.[9]

(2) That Novacap develop a plan with the cooperation of the association to assure, among other things, the following:

(a) the sale to the proprietor of improvements . . . of the respective lot [terreno] he occupies;[10]

(b) that this sale be concluded at a reasonable price, without down payment, to be paid over a long period of time;

(c) that the product of the sale of these lots be used in the urbanization of the future District Bernardo Sayão;

(d) that only one lot be made available to each proprietor for improvements that have actually been made;

(e) [that] it remains reserved to Novacap the right to sell or not a lot with rented real estate insofar as its legitimate owner has never resided in it and has never resided in Brasília;

(f) [that] Novacap . . . will guarantee to each pioneer inhabitant of Núcleo Bandeirante, provided he really is one, the choice of acquiring either surplus lots or lots that will be delimited in the future bairro.[11]

Provisions e and f especially were designed to protect the on-the-spot pioneer against the interests of absentee speculators, particularly those who had been awarded commercial contracts in the Free City but who had financed others to run the enterprise. These provisions were intended to assure the local ACB members an advantage over these more powerful speculators.

The government's response was contradictory. Although Novacap turned a deaf ear to these demands, Kubitschek was ambiguous. On the one hand, in the months after the inauguration, he made statements in the local press that he fully supported the fixation of the city. He assured the pioneers that he "would never permit the husk to be tossed out after squeezing and savoring the fruit" (*Cidade Livre*, 7 July 1960,

p. 4). On the other hand, he did not act on either of two bills submitted to Congress that proposed legalizing the Free City, and he left office without resolving the matter. Whereas the executive thus sent ambiguous signals to the ACB, some members of the newly installed Congress took up the issue enthusiastically. Two congressmen in particular made the cause their own: Breno da Silveira, a federal deputy from the state of Guanabara (formerly the Federal District) and a member of the Brazilian Socialist Party (PSB); and Paulo de Tarso, a federal deputy with close ties to president-elect Jânio Quadros, who expected to become the next prefect of the Federal District. These congressmen were the authors of the two bills that Kubitschek had neglected. Both espoused the ACB's demands. Furthermore, as a presidential candidate, Jânio Quadros had himself indicated that once in office he would support them. Thus, the pioneers had every expectation of realizing their demands for a change of legal status with the incoming Quadros administration.[12]

However, once in office its actions proved a consummate surprise. Prefect Tarso's first pronouncement on the fate of the city declared that it had to undergo a process of "decompression." He maintained that in order to save the city, about two-thirds of its population would have to be removed; specifically, all those who had either lived or worked illegally in the city before Brasília's inauguration. Backed by the district police and the army, he began to transfer squatters to the various satellite cities and even to other illegal settlements just to get them out of the Free City. Moreover, with the threat of forced removal, Tarso also began to pressure the entrepreneurs to fulfill their contractual obligations to move to the Plano Piloto. Considering these actions, the ACB interpreted decompression as but a prelude to eradication.

To counter these measures, the Commercial Association broadened its organizational base. It founded a citywide residents' association called the Pro-Fixation and Urbanization Movement of Núcleo Bandeirante (the MPF).[13] The ACB launched the movement as an umbrella organization. Its purpose was to coordinate the actions of the various associations that in addition to the ACB had organized to fight for the city's survival. Its own president served as MPF director and presided over a considerable array of resources. The MPF's bureaucratic structure consisted of a president, three vice-presidents, a secretary, and a treasurer as well as a set of departments including among others those of publicity, public relations, and culture. With these organizational resources, the MPF initiated a two-pronged strategy of mobilization. The objective of the first was to mobilize the local population. The objective of the second was to lobby Congress. To achieve the first, it developed an intensive media campaign utilizing its own newspaper and, most effectively, films that rebroadcast the major events of the conflict. In this effort, the MPF was quite successful. It generated widespread support from all sectors of pioneer society, counting on interclass and interstatus group affiliations (from entrepreneurs, workers, liberal professionals, and squatters and on overwhelming support among the pioneer organizations (the various residential, commercial, and labor associations in the Federal District).

Its fundamental objective was to mobilize enough support to pressure Congress into legalizing the city. To this end, the MPF implemented an additional strategy. It placed each resident of the Free City at the intersection of two sets of affiliations: it organized the population by place of residence into neighborhood associations, and by place of birth into state lobbies. The former mode of organization was important for local action, such as vigilance against removals. But as the Federal District had no form of congressional representation and no local elite in high political positions, organization by local residence was not the most effective way to reach the Congress or the executive institutions of the federal government. Rather, home state affiliations provided the only source of recognized political representation available to settlers and, among an entire adult population of migrants, it gave them a strong basis for social solidarity. Accordingly, the MPF organized the population of the Free City into state lobbies. Each lobby elected leaders to pursue the deputies, senators, ministers, and other important officials from its state who resided in the capital. Thus, the MPF's organizational strategy was based on utilizing both the ascribed (birth) and the achieved (residence) characteristics of the population. This associational web proved effective in the showdown between the prefecture and the MPF, a conflict that was finally resolved in Congress just as the MPF had planned.

Before this resolution, however, the struggle entered its most violent phase. Backed by police forces and armed with lawsuits to regain possession of the lots, the Tarso administration moved in earnest against the city. Buildings were demolished, people evicted, and businesses closed in record numbers. Pitched street battles erupted between local residents and the federal police. Rumors multiplied concerning the imminent demise of the city.[14] This climate of violence, fear, and rumor resulted in a depopulation of the city.[15] Moreover, as the violence escalated, a fissure developed in the MPF armature. Its president resigned and some of its most prominent leaders were accused by seemingly more militant members of having "sold out" to the prefecture. A new ACB president attempted to regroup the pro-fixation forces. To retake the initiative, he formed a new steering committee called the Central Commission of Núcleo Bandeirante, or simply the "grand commission." Declaring the prefect persona non grata, the commission brought the city into open rebellion by officially severing political relations with the prefecture.

At the height of this confrontation, the unexpected occurred: on 25 August, Jânio Quadros resigned the presidency. The succession crisis that followed had decisive repercussions for the local conflict. Its immediate effect was to neutralize the forces of the prefecture: shortly after Vice-President Goulart was sworn into office on 7 September, he replaced, among others, Tarso and the president of Novacap with his own appointees.

With this change of guard, the arena of conflict moved out of the streets and into the offices of the president and the Congress. Goulart had already shown himself to be sympathetic to the *candangos'* struggle for residential rights when he interceded on behalf of those in Vila Amaury. Moreover, Goulart had built his career on the federally created labor movement. Therefore, along with the labor unions and tribunals, his established political base lay with the social security institutes, which were of such importance in pioneer Brasília. In addition, as the political heir of Getúlio Vargas, he perhaps felt the need to find a popular base of support in the new capital. For these reasons, Goulart proved an ally to the Central Commission's lobby in Congress. Given his precarious political position, Goulart needed to secure an effective base within the newly created parliamentary system that could count on sustained support from the left.[16] In such circumstances, the socialist deputy Breno da Silveira was able to press his case successfully for the Free City's legalization. Thus, the outcome of the case was due not merely to Goulart's sympathies, but to effective lobbying by the state committees of the Pro-Fixation Movement. With the president's backing, they were able to enlist enough support among congressmen to secure the passage of a bill ratifying the legal status of the Free City, in situ, as a satellite of Brasília (Law 4020, 20 December 1961). Thereby, it became the first and thus far the only satellite city created by legislative act rather than executive order.

However, despite their impressive victory, the MPF, the Central Commission, and their network of neighborhood associations and state lobbies dissolved after the change in status. The Commercial Association continued to lobby the government on various issues, often claiming to represent the entire city in the absence of elected leaders. However, as in the first phase of the fixation struggle, the ACB tended to speak "in the name of the people" while in fact presenting demands that focused almost exclusively on the needs of its members, the entrepreneurs. In this respect, the list of demands reproduced above was typical of its approach. It was only under the emergency conditions of eradication that citywide, interclass mobilization occurred. Ironically, however, the new political identities created in this struggle were not sustained in victory.

Having now described the foundation of the satellite cities, we may distinguish two types of formations in the development of Brasília's periphery: the usurpative and the derivative. The satellites represent a derivative formation (like Brasília itself) in the sense that the government created them either by executive order or by legislative act. However, in authorizing their creation, the government was in each case giving legal foundation to what had in fact already been usurped: the initially denied residential rights that pioneers appropriated by forming squatter settlements. This formation usurped government authority in the sense that it encroached upon its sole right in the Federal District to found settlements, distribute residential rights, regulate property relations, authorize constructions, and the like. Thus, Brasília's legal periphery has a subversive origin in land seizures. These rebellions culminated in a recurrent pattern of urban development: those who lacked the rights to settle organized to usurp them, mobilizing around demands for legal residence in urban not rural communities. These actions created an illegal periphery of squatter settlements. Confronted with this unplanned and uncontrolled development, the government responded by founding legally constituted satellite cities of its own design to which it removed the squatters.

For *candangos,* the significance of this usurpation is that it constituted a process of status change. For in the creation of the illegal periphery, they organized to change their status from temporary migrants, denied long-term residential rights, into legal residents of the Federal District. Moreover, in mobilizing to represent their demands collectively and to defend their settlements against eradication, *candangos* created a new pattern of political organization in the district: they achieved representative associations and participatory experience in political action—both of which they had also been denied.

However, the political identities thus won evaporated in triumph. In no case did they survive the creation of the legal periphery that was the objective of the *candangos'* mobilization.[17] I suggest that their disappearance was due to their paradoxical formation: while crucial to the success of mobilization, while achieved with great effort and considerable violence, these identities were only incidental to the objective of gaining access to the entitlements of legal residence. It is important to understand that the pioneer associations only mobilized around this goal and that none presumed to continue beyond achieving it. None was organized around the denial of political rights, and none had the goal of autonomous political organization or even incorporation into the Plano Piloto's public domain. However defiant of the law, however rebellious of government policy, their political actions were thus instrumental to their residential objectives. These objectives could only be met from within the system of local-level public assistance. Therefore, if in order to gain access to public resources, the *candangos* had to rebel, then admission to the system entailed foregoing any organized opposition to it.

Hence, the abandonment of hard-won political statuses was encouraged by a combination of two circumstances: first, the associations were not organized to win political rights but to procure legal access to property and urban services. Thus, they were vulnerable to having their autonomy preempted by government initiative because state assistance was more important than autonomous political organization. Second, once they were deemed eligible to receive assistance, the logic of further demands inhibited political actions to contest the power relations upon which assistance was based. Therefore, the logics that motivated the formation of associations—namely, those of power, demand, and representation—lost significance once their members were incorporated into a system in which politically mediated access to public resources was of little value. Thus, when the authorities granted the services demanded, they dissolved.

The pattern of urban development I have described in which squatters organize to gain residential rights is common in Brazilian cities. Indeed, the literature suggests that since the 1930s squatting and other forms of illegal residence are not only one of the most traditional but also one of the most reliable ways for the urban poor to get such rights.[18] The poor seem to understand clearly the central paradox in this development: that the very illegality of their lots not only makes them accessible but moreover eventually prompts a confrontation with legitimate authority in which legal residential rights can be negotiated—in part because the authorities are more or less bound by their own rules to find a bureaucratic solution, even if one preceded by violence. Thus, squatters launch organized land seizures to precipitate such negotiations; or, if already occupying illegal sites, they organize into associations when confronted with eradication. The best outcome for squatters is fixation, as in the classic case of Brás de Pina in Rio de Janeiro (Santos 1981: 31–94); the worst is forced removal to authorized residences, as in the case of the government housing complex of Cidade de Deus, also in Rio, which received people from 63 distinct squatter settlements (Valladares 1978). In either case, the result legitimates, ex post facto, the usurpation of property rights and provides legal access to urban services—although the new contractual obligations and/or the new locations of legal residence often have contrary consequences as I shall discuss later.

Moreover, it is a general pattern throughout Brazil that residential associations of all varieties demobilize and often dissolve after achieving their objectives. As in Brasília, the very technical groups the government sends to resolve their demands tend to preempt their autonomy, authority, and function.[19] This is a telling point for the analysis of political change because urban social movements in Brazil have been almost uniformly organized to obtain property or services of one sort or another from the government. Nevertheless, to suggest the limitations inherent in such movements is not to ask that they achieve what they do not intend nor to detract from their accomplishments; it is rather to warn against overstating them.

If the development of Brasília's periphery thus reproduces a common pattern in Brazil, its lack of alternatives was nevertheless singular. Elsewhere, the poor can illegally seize, buy, or rent private lands, in which cases their disputes are with private parties and not the state. In this context, as Caldeira (1984: 23) observes for São Paulo, the many ways in which the government may actually benefit private real estate speculation, and thus aggrevate the housing crisis and its underlying systems of inequality, are not directly confronted.[20] In contrast, during the formative period of Brasília's periphery, the state owned all the land and administered all the urban services. Therefore, those who usurped residential rights opposed the state at every stage in their disputes, confronting directly its productive powers—its instruments, techniques, and tactics—to structure, stratify, and disorder Brasiliense society.

7.2 The Legal Periphery

The rebellion of the pioneers did effect a transformation in the structure of Brasília's public domain, for it ensured the inclusion of social strata previously excluded. Nevertheless, once the government organized the periphery under its administration, the substantive nature of this participation bore almost no resemblance to the political association that had generated it. The significance of the government's initiative is revealed in the alternatives it denied. On the one hand, it did not seriously attempt a military solution. Occasional skirmishes aside, it did not mobilize the armed forces to clear the Federal District of squatters or to preserve the hinterland for agricultural cooperatives as originally planned. Even if such a solution had been militarily feasible, it was politically and ideologically untenable, for it would have compromised too blatantly the planners' utopian aspirations. On the other hand, the government did not incorporate the squatters into the then nearly empty Plano Piloto. For reasons that we shall now consider, this solution was similarly perceived as untenable. Rather, the government founded the satellite cities to sustain the intentions that were threatened by the formation of the illegal periphery: it attempted to counter the Brazilianization of Brasília by developing satellites in the image of an uncompromised Plano Piloto. By projecting the order of this center to the periphery, the planners thus remained faithful to their model of the exemplary capital.

This simulacrum of intentions is evident in the ways in which the government organized the periphery, especially in its urban planning, political-administrative structure, and recruitment of settlers. With respect to the first, the government planned the periphery in terms of dormitory settlements. In so doing, it followed the principle of zoned functions underlying Costa's Master Plan. The creation of dormitory cities in the periphery reiterated the separation of work and residence in the Plano Piloto on a larger scale by extending the lines of commuter travel to the central workplace. Moreover, the planners used the Plano Piloto's fourfold typology of function to organize each satellite into exclusive and homogeneous sectors of activity. In a more modest manner, each of these sectors embodied the principle of its exemplar. Thus, with the exception of the unplanned center of Taguatinga, the satellite cities feature the modernist circulation system of the Plano Piloto. Similarly, the Master Plan's principle of collective dwelling is incorporated into the planning of the residential sectors of the satellite cities, even though these sectors are designed primarily for freestanding houses rather than for *superquadras*. Thus, the houses front onto a green area of public property that each resident is supposed to share and tend collectively with his neighbor. With their backs on the roadside, these houses therefore reproduce the front-back reversal distinctive of Brasília's urbanism.

However, in projecting the orders of the center to the periphery, the planners also reiterated the unavoidable contradiction of the utopian project: given their objectives, they had little choice but to use the mechanisms of social stratification and repression that are constituitive of the very phenomena they sought to exorcise. Two dimensions of this contradiction seems particularly significant. First, as the government planned to settle the peripheral cities while the Plano Piloto was itself only partially built and barely inhabited (map 7.1), its planners had to devise a means of preselecting who would go to each. Moreover, given their objective of maintaining the capital as a predominantly bureaucratic center, they required a recruitment policy based on some principle of nonrandom selection, that is, one that would give the bureaucrats preferential access to the Plano Piloto. Second, in organizing the administrative relations between center and periphery, they intended to maintain "the climate of tranquillity" they thought essential for the conduct of high office in the capital. Hence, they denied the satellite cities political representation in order to eliminate the turbulence of political organization. This combination of political subordination and preferential recruitment defined the satellite cities as a differentially incorporated category of settlements within the administrative structure of the Federal District. As such, the planners succeeded in reiterating, in an exemplary and even exaggerated fashion, the disfranchisement and disprivilege characteristic of the realm they thought they were negating.

7.2.1 Political-Administrative Organization: The Climate of Tranquillity

I am thus suggesting that the periphery's differential incorporation derives from Brasília's utopian premise. To understand this apparently paradoxical development, we shall consider the political subordination of the satellite cities as revealed both in the intentions and in the structure of Brasília's system of government. Both aspects of this system were established in the Organic Laws, prepared under the auspices of the GTB. This set of proposals corresponds in stature to Costa's Master Plan as the most comprehensive statement of the planners' conception of the political and administrative organization of the new Federal District.

Like the Master Plan, the Organic Laws propose a dramatic break with Brazil's past. They prescribe a system of government for Brasília that differs fundamentally from that of Brazil's previous federal capital, and indeed from that of any of its cities. Here, we need only consider its most radical proposal, the one that denies the new capital representative government. Its provisions prohibit the election of either local or national officials, and abolish the office of prefect and the institution of city council. In short, the Organic Laws deny Brasília's inhabitants the right to representation in any electoral form in the institutions of public authority governing their affairs. Rather, they argue that these institutions should be ruled by a governor in conjunction with a commission of federal senators. To this end, they give the president of Brazil the right to appoint, and dismiss at will, a governor to administer the Federal District in accordance with laws promulgated by a special commission of the Senate responsible for its legislative affairs. In addition, they vest judicial authority in a system of district courts, the judges of which would also be appointed by the president, and they place police powers under the auspices of a Federal Department of Public Security.

These proposals negate the principles of city government in force in the rest of Brazil. The report accompanying the Organic Laws justifies this negation by arguing for the need to create a "climate of tranquillity" (Ministry of Justice 1959: 9) in the nation's new capital. Moreover, it presents its case for historical rupture as a consequence of history itself: it maintains that although the governance it proposes for Brasília is similar to that of Washington, D.C. (before 1962), it should not be interpreted as a copy but rather as "the consequence of the experience of our republican practice." "Detailed studies" of this experience reveal to the authors "the great inconvenience of the coexistence of federal and local authorities, in the Federal Capital, an inconvenience that translates into a permanent conflict between the two opposite tendencies of these interests, that is, between federal centralism and municipal autonomy" (ibid.).

The report argues its case of "inconvenience" in several ways. It claims that if Brasília were allowed congressional representation, the federal government might find itself, in its own home, in conflict with local interests—especially if these interests were represented by an opposition party. The report concludes that such conflict would hinder the operation of national government. Furthermore, it suggests that such conflict would provoke the federal authorities, as the single most important source of funds and employment in the Federal District, to retaliate unfairly against the local population. In addition, it speculates that if Brasilienses were permitted to vote in elections (for president, governor, prefect, or councilmen) the same situation would inevitably arise, that is, one of predictable conflict and revenge. The report also argues that Brasília's character as an administrative city "with an absolute predominance of the interests of public servants and their families—not counterbalanced by industrial, commercial, and other interests in the Federal District—would turn its electorate into either a dangerous and active force in the sense of obtaining special favors or an easy prey for demagogic campaigns, with promises of satisfaction for its immediate demands." Thus, the authors of the Organic Laws show little confidence in the capabilities either of the people or of the federal authorities to manage their affairs within the system of electoral politics. Rather, they conclude that "in whatever form, the participation of the inhabitants of the Federal District in direct political campaigns would rob the Federal Capital of the climate of tranquillity necessary for the Federal Government to devote itself entirely to the study and solution of high national problems" (ibid.).[21]

Although the Organic Laws were submitted to Congress with Kubitschek's full support, the legislature modified their most radical intention: the version that passed gave the Federal District a restricted form of representative government.[22] Although it disallowed congressional representation, it permitted local government by a prefect and a district council with legislative authority. While agreeing to let the president of the nation nominate and dismiss the prefect, it specified that the council would be composed of twenty members "elected by the people" on the occasion of congressional elections (art. 6). However, several provisions of the law severely compromised, and in effect nullified, the apparent scope of this representation. First, the veto powers of the appointed prefect significantly reduced the autonomy and power of the council.[23] Second, although the bill went into effect upon enactment in April 1960, it stated that the council would not be elected until October 1962 (presumably to coincide with congressional elections). In the interim, the affairs of the Federal District would be administered under the executive authority of the prefecture and the legislative authority of a special senate commission.[24]

In spite of Congress's attempt to provide a form of representative government for Brasília, it was ultimately the more radical version of the Organic Laws that triumphed: for reasons that remain unclear, the council elections of October 1962 were never held. As a result, the interim suspension of political rights turned out to be perduring, and the interim administration became the de facto basis of the Federal District's system of government. As this basis was precisely the one proposed in the unadulterated version of the Organic Laws, its prescriptions for government without representation were thus realized.

This brief review of the legislation is sufficient to enable us to draw some conclusions about the relation between Brasília's political-administrative structure and the planners' "climatic concerns." First, it is evident that both the power and the authority of government were almost entirely concentrated in the executive offices of the prefecture. Second, it is evident that this concentration realized the planners' intentions. This concordance was achieved somewhat circuitously. On the one hand, the distribution of power and authority was partly established by law—only partly because it seems that the government acted illegally in not holding the prescribed elections. On the other hand, the special commission of the Senate concerned with Brasília's legislative affairs lacked sufficient power to render its modest authorities effective, and, in any case, in practice, it took a retiring view of its responsibilities. This combination of legal, illegal, and even extralegal circumstances let Brasília's planners realize—and the executives of the prefecture (and the presidential palace behind it) maintain—a "climate of tranquillity" without the turbulence of representative politics to contend with.

What were the consequences of this concentration of power for the residents of the periphery and for their political incorporation? To govern the periphery, the prefecture created and staffed subprefectures in each of the satellite cities. Based on the principle of statecraft in which the capital exemplifies the plan and the realm the capital, these subprefectures were modeled on the central bureaucracy. Thus, each had an appointed subprefect and a similar hierarchy of offices. However, perhaps because the central bureaucracy explicitly generated the foundations of its own legitimacy (the Master Plan and the Organic Laws)—in contrast, for example, to ancient exemplary courts in which legitimacy was divinely ordained—an inherent but typically submerged contradiction in this principle of statecraft surfaced: the reflection in the periphery was obviously not an "original copy" but a shadowy likeness, a simulacrum, lacking the power and autonomy of its source. Moreover, it was precisely this contradiction of the mirror that permitted the center's rule over the local administrations of the satellites. For it was the mirroring both of the center's administrative structure and of its denial of political rights that ensured that the subprefectures would function obediently.

Thus, there is an inherent deprivation of power, authority, and autonomy in the simulacrum by which the exemplar rules it. This structure of rule is evident in the contrast between the governance of the satellite cities and that of the Plano Piloto. While the prefecture ruled the periphery by creating local administrations in its image, it administered the affairs of the Plano Piloto without constituting a separate subprefecture. Rather, it functioned both as the central authority of the entire system and as the local administration of the Plano Piloto. The degree to which this merging is crucial to the power of the exemplar is suggested by the following. Two and one-half years after the creation of the first subprefecture in Taguatinga, the central office formalized its coordination of the local administrations by instituting the Department of Subprefectures (Decree 43, March 1961). At this time, it also created a subprefecture for the Plano Piloto. However, this office remained unstaffed and unweaned. Rather, the prefecture continued in its dual capacity by placing the administration of the Plano Piloto under one of its first-secretaries. Thus, by being part of the central authority, the administrators of the Plano Piloto both ruled the satellite cities and continued to exercise the power and authority in local affairs that their counterparts in the peripheral administrations lacked.[25]

This distribution of the powers of government not only deprived the subprefectures of autonomy; it also deprived the residents of the satellite cities of the capacity for collective action, representation, or organization in regulating the rule of these administrations over their affairs. Thus, the contrast could hardly have been greater between the government of the legal periphery and the governing associations of the illegal settlements that had generated it. Whereas the latter had been autonomous, the subprefectures were imposed by an outside agency. Whereas the association leaders and staff had been selected according to the orders of their own organizations, the subprefects and their staff were appointed by the central bureaucracy. Most important, whereas the associations had functioned as representative groups in trying to influence the distribution of public resources, the subprefectures, in distributing these resources, were not accountable to the residents of their cities.

In sum, for these residents, the *candangos* of Brasília, the organization of the legal periphery was a paradoxical development: although it gave them property rights, it denied them the political participation they had achieved in its creation. This denial returned them to the politically unorganized status out of which they had struggled. Moreover, it again subordinated them to the rule of others who were politically organized; that is, to the rule of those who by virtue of occupying offices in the central bureaucracy had the right to make enforceable decisions on many issues of utmost importance to them. Thus, it was in the name of "tranquillity," in the name of constructing an exemplary capital, that the state's planners differentially incorporated the residents of the satellite cities. Ironically, it was this repression and not the illegal actions of the squatters that more profoundly Brazilianized Brasília.

7.2.2 *Space and Society: An Absolute Predominance of Public Servants*

The planners had invoked the idea of a capital city to justify not only the political subordination of the *candangos* in the satellites but also their exclusion from the Plano Piloto. To have included them would have violated "the essential purpose of Brasília [as an] administrative city with an absolute predominance of the interests of public servants and their families" (Ministry of Justice 1959: 9). Hence, the *candangos* were excluded because they were not part of the established civil service for which the capital had been built. By contrast, the government gave workers at the lowest-echelons of the bureaucracy apartments within the Plano Piloto. Therefore, it did not base its rejection of the *candangos* on either practical or class considerations, such as shortage of accommodations or attempts to remove the underclasses. Rather, the decisive issue was status: they were denied a physical place within the Plano Piloto because they lacked the requisite social place within the exemplar.

Given the objective of preserving this exemplar as a predominantly bureaucratic center, the government required a policy to differentiate the settlement of the Plano Piloto from that of the satellite cities. Its solution was to maintain the spatial dichotomy between center and periphery by a principle of status differentiation: those who occupied either an established position within the civil service or an elected position within the federal government and who were recruited to work in the new capital were entitled to reside in the state-owned dwellings of the Plano Piloto; those who did not occupy such a position and who wanted to live in the Federal District had to seek residence in the satellite cities.

The government's solution was thus to make access to property in the Federal District dependent on status criteria that it established. This regulation of the real estate market was the essential means by which it sought to control settlement. Its strategy had two basic components. First, the administration maintained the dichotomy between center and satellite by restricting access to public residences in the Plano Piloto to members of the eligible status group. Second, in keeping with its exemplary projections to the periphery, it regulated the distribution of lots in the satellite cities as well. However, just as this strategy derived from Brasília's utopian premises, it also suffered its utopian paradoxes. On the one hand, the use of a status hierarchy to determine access to property established a radically unequal distribution of advantage in many ways benefiting the life chances of those in the capital. On the other, the regulations applied to the distribution of lots in the satellite cities often prevented migrants from obtaining them legally and thus established the conditions for new squatter settlements.

Three categories of people and their families were entitled to reside in the Plano Piloto: elected officials of the federal government; those who held positions in its hierarchy of bureaucratic offices, from minister to clerk to janitor, and whom the GTB had recruited for the transfer of governmental institutions from Rio; and a small number of pioneer elites. The bureaucratic functionaries constituted the overwhelming majority of those recruited to the inaugurated capital, making up almost 70% of the total. The elected officials accounted for about 10% of this group while the remaining 20% comprised the pioneer elites.[26] Among the latter were the public sector managers of Novacap and the Social Security Institutes (9%); some of the managers of the private sector construction companies who had taken jobs in the administration (2%); and a number of entrepreneurs and their employees from Núcleo Bandeirante whom Novacap had previously contracted for the capital's local commerce (9%).[27]

To these people, the government distributed similar accommodations in the Plano Piloto (either in the *superquadra* apartments or the row houses) regardless of disparities in their individual incomes. Thus, status rather than wealth was decisive in this distribution. Moreover, although two workers may have had identical class positions before migrating to Brasília, the one employed in a federal institution in the new capital with standing in the civil service had rights to a *superquadra* apartment, whereas the other employed in the same institution without such status only had access to a lot in the satellite cities. Thus, if they had different status positions with respect to the bureaucratic hierarchy in Brasília, migrants of previously identical class positions had different rights to the city.

By contrast, those who were not admitted to the Plano Piloto and who wanted to live in the Federal District had to seek residence in the satellite cities. Thus, they constituted a residual category of migrants, including (1) the construction and service workers; (2) those who worked for governmental institutions without civil service standing (typically manual laborers and clerks); (3) merchants of modest means; and (4) the unemployed.[28] These migrants had lived in the construction camps, the Free City, and the settlements of the illegal periphery.

In sum, of the preinaugural migrants, the power, status, and class elites went to the Plano Piloto while the lower strata went to the satellite cities. At the very least, these lower strata comprised about 90% of the pioneers. Of the postinaugural migrants, transferred civil servants and elected officials went to the center while industrial and service workers and small-scale merchants went to the periphery. What was the significance of this distribution?

In maintaining the spatial dichotomy between center and periphery by a principle of status differentiation, the government created two broad status groups among Brasilienses: one group comprised those people living in the Plano Piloto, and the other those living in the satellite cities. These two status groups were, with few exceptions, mutually exclusive during the formative period of these settlements, 1958–65. What preserved this exclusivity was the virtual monopoly that the one had over access to residence in the Plano Piloto. I am here speaking of the norm, for to any rule there are exceptions. For example, the subprefects of satellite cities were members of the federal civil service, and yet they lived in the periphery. Some of Novacap's workers also constituted partial exceptions as previously mentioned. A few upper-echelon bureaucrats lived outside of the modernist city but within the administrative region of the Plano Piloto. They had constructed private houses on the far side of the lake, thereby contradicting the intentions of the Master Plan (art. 20) to leave this area unbuilt. However, in this case, they were entitled to choose not to exercise their right to public accommodations within the Plano Piloto.[29] While data are lacking for me to state categorically that no other people with rights to the center lived in the periphery, I am reasonably certain that if any others did so, it was in temporary or irregular circumstances if not by personal choice.

Furthermore, those without requisite status in the bureaucracy, or without official permission as in the case of the entrepreneurs, had no legal means of obtaining a public dwelling in the Plano Piloto—no matter how much money they were willing to spend for one. For example, a professional could not have moved to the capital to open a private practice without prior institutional affiliation or permission because he would not have found a place to live.[30] Of course, there were exceptions to the general rule. Most often, these were service workers who found lodging in apartments above the shops of the commercial sectors that had been illicitly converted into boardinghouses. There were also cases of tenants who surreptitiously sublet their *superquadra* apartments to those without dwelling rights. Although the data do not permit an estimate of such exceptions, it is reasonable to suppose that they were few during this period: as government lodgings in the capital were at a premium for bureaucrats transferred from Rio, they were carefully supervised by the Department of Public Services (DASP). As these were the only residences existing at that time in the Plano Piloto, we may conclude that restricted access to them tended to create two mutually exclusive status groups in the Federal District, and, therefore, that the principle of using status discrimination to regulate access to property provided the government with an effective means of regulating the occupation of the capital and satellite cities. This distribution of statuses recapitulated an ancient theme in this most modern of exemplary capitals: it determined a dichotomous distribution of people in space with respect to the rankings of the court.

The significance of this dichotomy was that to belong to one of the status groups entailed having a set of rights, privileges, powers, and evaluations with respect to the other that significantly affected the life chances of its members. It is for this reason that we may describe this distribution of advantage as an example of social stratification. The advantages that derived from residence in a *superquadra* were many, and they were available to occupants and occupants only by virtue of their status as residents and regardless of individual disparities in income, education, social background, and the like. Thus, in theory if not always in practice, members of the privileged status group had equal rights to the *superquadras'* collective facilities, the most important being those of education, child care, medical services, organized recreation, and commerce. In addition, the government provided and maintained a full set of urban services in the Plano Piloto. Even if these were not always as complete as residents would have liked, they were incomparably better than those in the satellite cities. Moreover, in an economy dominated by the bureaucratic institutions of the Plano Piloto, simply living in the center saved residents great amounts of time, energy, and money that those in the satellites had to expend in their daily commute to work.

To belong to a status group is also to share a set of subjective evaluations about such conditions of life. These evaluations constitute the values of social esteem, style of life, symbolic interaction, behavioral codes, and patterns of consuming and acquiring goods and services. It is not difficult to imagine in these terms the ways in which, beyond the civic pride of founding settlers, evaluations about the impoverished, undeveloped, and remote satellite cities compared negatively with those about the Plano Piloto. What is significant about this comparison is the way its differences reinforced the values associated with each status group and, moreover, replicated them through its individual members. In the last chapter, I gave an example of such reinforcement in the way in which, shortly after the capital's inauguration, Plano Piloto residents began to refer to themselves as *brasilienses* while restricting the term *candango* to those of the periphery. This evaluation effectively undermined the frontier solidarity that the term *candango* had previously entailed, substituting for it a set of derogatory individual characteristics and giving this sense a specific spatial referent. Among the young elite in the Plano Piloto today, the social history of these characteristics is now completely obscured by such subjective evaluations.

In sum, the organization of an authorized periphery around the capital created a kind of dual social order which was both legally and spatially segregated. In this mapping of society, Brasília followed a familiar pattern of urban development in Brazil in which elites inhabit the center of a city and dominate disfranchised lower strata in the periphery. At that time, however, Brasília diverged from this pattern in two ways that significantly exaggerated its inequalities. The first remains as evident today as in the early 1960s, and the second has become attentuated as we shall see in the next chapter. While the central districts of other metropolitan regions featured a mixture of elite residential quarters and slums, there was an absolute spatial segregation of the two in Brasília. In fact, the Plano Piloto was and is surrounded by a moat, a so-called green belt or recreational zone, 14 kilometers wide, which separates it from the nearest satellite city (maps 7.1 and 7.2). Second, as I have suggested, Brasília's social stratification was at that time primarily based on a de jure differential incorporation of the residents of the periphery according to status criteria. Wealth was not a factor. However, in other cities, it was one of the determinants of the stratified social order. I would suggest that a social order dominated by a legally defined status hierarchy offers fewer opportunities for mobility than one dominated by wealth. If this is the case, then the status differentiation—as well as the political repression and spatial segregation—that Brasília's planners employed in organizing the periphery exaggerated the stratification characteristic of other Brazilian cities.

Having regulated access to property in the Plano Piloto, the planners could not permit the operation of an unregulated land market in the satellite cities; that is, they could not allow private real estate agents to develop the periphery as in other Brazilian cities. That would have violated their model of exemplary development. So, having already expropriated all the land in the Federal District, the government became its sole developer. Under the general supervision of Novacap, it created departments of real estate in each of the subprefectures to regulate the subdivision of the land and the distribution of lots. Its announced objective was to permit "each worker [to have] his own lot and [to acquire] it for an accessible price at favorable terms"

(Silva 1971: 231). At least this is what its spokesman told the demonstrators from Vila Sara Kubitschek when he announced the creation of Taguatinga. Although the regulation of real estate did deter speculation, which undoubtedly would have driven prices beyond the means of many of the squatter-migrants, paradoxically, it had a similar consequence. To understand this turn of events, I shall set out the more important factors regulating the distribution of lots in the satellites. These factors apply generally for the years 1958–65 and particularly to the cities of Taguatinga and Sobradinho. However, they are also relevant to the other satellites in essence and in most if not in every detail.[31]

1. Several regulations determined eligibility for lots. Only those with jobs in the Federal District qualified for residential lots, and only those among the self-employed who had sufficient start-up capital qualified for commercial ones. Moreover, subdivisions in the various cities were generally designated for specific subsets of settlers. For example, the government opened some house lots in Sobradinho only to Novacap workers, and others only to squatters removed from Vila Amaury. Therefore, the distribution of these lots was determined by status, and migrants without the requisite qualifications were ineligible.[32]

2. The determination of an applicant's eligibility for a plot involved lengthy bureaucratic procedures. Applications were made at the subprefecture, and approval required the subprefect's authorization. That was given only after the Social Service Department of Novacap had conducted a "rigorous research" of the qualifications of each applicant. Regularization (i.e., the legalities of lot measurements, house construction, transactions, paperwork, and other assorted details) was carried out by the department of real estate of each subprefecture.

3. Once approved, an applicant had to confront the most highly regulated feature of the process of acquiring a lot: the contract. The document that Novacap issued to the *compromissário*, 'prospective purchaser', was a kind of leasehold, called a "precarious title" because it was not one of outright purchase. Although it permitted the leaseholder to put up a wooden shack for immediate occupation, it attached numerous conditions to the final transfer of title.[33] To receive the title of ownership from Novacap, the applicant had (*a*) to maintain the terms of his contract continuously for three years, having done so without abandoning the lot or letting the contract lapse; (*b*) to settle his account by completing the payments due at the end of that period; and, most important, (*c*) to construct a masonry house to replace his original shack according to plans approved by the subprefecture. That construction had to be completed within

three years and certified by a title of occupancy from the local authorities.[34] If the prospective buyer moved elsewhere or otherwise failed to meet all of the terms of the contract, he automatically "lost in favor of Novacap" all of the payments and improvements to the lot he had already made.

4. Finally, I should emphasize that authorized access to a lot did not and does not now necessarily or even usually entail fully legal title to it. Such title may eventually result, but in most cases authorized access is only the first step to full possession. In between the two is the often lengthy process of regularizing the lot and its constructions, as the previous discussion concerning the distribution of lots illustrates. This process may involve substantial fees, taxes, fines, and even frauds of various sorts, any of which may eventually prove an insurmountable obstacle to full compliance with the law concerning residential status.

The sum of these distributional and contractual regulations had a predictable effect: for many migrants, it precluded the possibility of legally obtaining a lot. Although thousands of squatters had agreed to removal to satellite cities in anticipation of receiving land from the government, many ultimately found themselves ineligible for it. For a poor person, the most difficult criterion to meet was that of steady employment during the three years of monthly payments and house construction. As graph 5.2 indicates, the construction industry—the major source of employment for *candangos*—went into precipitous decline immediately after the capital's inauguration. As the boom economy ended, migrants had far fewer opportunities to find steady work and consequently less chance to qualify for house sites. Moreover, many settlers who had acquired plots on the basis of preinaugural employment lost their jobs during this period and were forced to abandon their lots for failure to meet the terms of Novacap's contract.

An additional problem confronted eligible applicants who felt that they could live with the "anxiety," as they described it, of the contract: the lack of an adequate number of regularized lots. Theoretically, all of the satellite cities had equal status as areas of resettlement. However, Novacap reserved large parts of Sobradinho as something of a showcase for its own workers, and Gama proved too distant from employment sources to be a viable option for all but a few settlers. As a result, Taguatinga was from the beginning the satellite to which Novacap sent most squatters and other migrants. Yet, only seven months after its foundation, the area designated for settlement was completely occupied. Many pioneers attributed the shortage of lots to the red tape of Novacap's procedures as well as to the corruption, illicit speculation, and fraud that had developed to circumvent its procedures (Bahouth 1978: 95–99; interviews, Brasília, 1981). As a result of these factors, it appears that the government did not subdivide enough new lots to keep up with the demand that its own settlement policies created.

For many migrants, the cumulative effects of this paradoxical situation, of the bureaucratic impediments to authorization and regularization, of the growing unemployment, and of their financial liabilities under Novacap's contracts, made the transportable assets of a wooden shack, set on illegally occupied land, seem a far more secure and accessible solution to their housing needs than the immovable investments the bureaucracy required for legal acquisition of house sites. As a result, many migrants who lacked housing rights in the Plano Piloto confronted a stark alternative: exodus or land seizure. As in the preinaugural period, most chose to squat rather than to leave the Federal District. Moreover, as in the earlier period, the problem of housing and the illegal actions taken to solve it led to the formation of new squatter associations and new illegal peripheries—peripheries in the plural because now each satellite city spawned its own fringe of illegal settlements.

Thus, by the paradoxes of utopian planning, we are led back to the beginning of the story. However, there should be no surprise in this turn of the tale since I suggested at the outset that it would not have a linear chronology. Rather, it consists of multiple, repetitive plots of similar structure—ones of rebellion and legitimation—which, for any community and at any moment, are in different stages of development. Thus, government authorization of one land seizure did not necessarily affect the others. Rather, the various satellite cities soon developed their own illegal peripheries even as the presence of squatter settlements in the Plano Piloto—what we could call first generation land seizures—remained unresolved. Hence, successive generations of illegal settlements multiplied regardless of earlier or later resolutions in specific cases.

The first land seizure on the periphery of the periphery occurred in January 1960 on the outskirts of Taguatinga. It was especially significant because it initiated the repetition of cycles of rebellion and legitimation which characterizes the development of the periphery as a whole. The land seizure was led by one Raimundo Matias, a *candango* whose passage from construction worker to squatter epitomized that of many migrants. Initially employed by one of the construction firms, he was eventually forced out of the work camps by job loss, out of the illegal settlements of the Plano Piloto, where he had lodged his family, and into Taguatinga, where he moved in the hope of gaining legal residence. However, after months of living in miserable conditions and after finding himself ineligible for a house site for lack of employment, he rebelled: he organized masses of people in similar situations to seize an area of land located just beyond the official allotments of the satellite city. According to eyewitnesses (Bahouth 1978: 105), his rebellious claim was simply that "there was plenty of land for everyone who wanted to live there."

In defending Vila Matias (map 7.2), as it came to be called after its founder, against eradication, the movement's leaders revived the strategy so effectively used during the preinaugural period: they wrapped the community in the flag, in the basic symbols and values of legal authority and Brazilian society, so that to remove them the regime would literally have to attack that which it was supposed to defend. For example, they subdivided the seized land into standard lots and distributed them in the regularized manner of legal allotments in Tagua-tinga, thus demonstrating that they were responsible but needy citizens and disarming accusations of promiscuity and criminal-ity that officialdom typically directed against squatters. Simi-larly, in response to police assaults, they deployed a concentric defense around their endangered houses which displayed the structure of an ideal family unit and evoked a patriotic trilogy of family, order, and freedom. The men stood on the perimeter (because brave men should bravely die first in this patriotic tableau), then the women, and finally the children clustered around an enormous mast on which was flown the national flag (albeit upside down).

It is not possible to say whether this strategy of pitting the nation against the regime was the decisive factor in their success. However, it did give the squatters the advantage of favorable public opinion, an advantage that attracted more squatters and handicapped the security forces in their assaults. Finally, after a year of confrontation, the administration ordered its planning department to draw up a plan to regularize the lots of Vila Matias. Officially recognizing what had already been usurped, the authorities ceremoniously presented this plan of authorization to the squatters in the central square of their settlement, appropriately baptized the Twenty-first of April Square. Thus, the government legally incorporated the illegal Vila Matias into Taguatinga, albeit under the less heroic name of Quadra South D.

The success of Vila Matias initiated a period of numerous land seizures around the satellite cities. Most of them followed the precedent that it, and Vila Sara Kubitschek before it, had established in achieving property rights for squatters. In some cases, as in Vila Matias, legal access to house sites occurred in situ (e.g., Vila Dimas, see map 7.2). In others, as in Vila Sara Kubitschek, it occurred by removal to a new subdivision in an existing satellite. However, in all cases, Brasília's periphery developed through a similar set of paradoxical circumstances. It was only through the illegal actions of land seizure that many migrants had access to lots—access that in most cases was eventually authorized. Moreover, it was only through rebellious associations that they could undertake organized political action. Thus, paradoxically, it was the illegality of their land seizures that permitted access both to property rights and to new political identities. However, all of the cases I am familiar with were true to historical type: after achieving their objectives, the residential associations dissolved, and their members accepted—or at least did not protest—the anonymity of differential incorporation into the legal but politically subordinated satellite cities.

These cycles of rebellion and legitimation, of mobilization and dissolution, were each discrete in time and space. Yet, as map 7.1 suggests, the social processes and structures they represent in the formation of the capital's periphery have been continuous over decades. During the first ten years following the foundation of the satellite cities, nearly 100,000 new migrants became squatters in the Federal District. In 1971, the government launched what was considered its final solution to this illegal periphery: it dismantled over 15,000 shacks and transferred 80,000 squatters to a new satellite city, Ceilândia, created to receive them. However, in the decade that followed that massive cleanup, the government estimates that 18 new illegal settlements have arisen around Brasília and its satellites, with a combined population of over 40,000 squatters (*Jornal de Brasília*, 2 October 1981). No doubt, as historical precedent strongly suggests, the illegal periphery of today will become the legal periphery of tomorrow. Yet, if history is a guide, one must also consider that its incorporation may only expand the periphery's political subordination, spatial segregation, and stratified inequalities, and so continue to reiterate the paradoxes of Brasília's utopian premises.

EIGHT

The Brazilianization of Brasília

Throughout this study, we have analyzed the premises and paradoxes of the two sets of intentions that constituted the planned city of Brasília, namely, those embodied in the architects' designs for a capital city and those motivating the government's plans for its construction and settlement. We found that in somewhat different but fundamentally consonant ways both sets proposed a radical break with Brazilian history. Both denied in the new city what planners considered unacceptable about prevailing conditions in Brazil: the structure of its society and the conventions of its metropolitan life. In attempting to transform these conditions, however, they stumbled repeatedly against the inherent paradox of the project itself: the necessity of having to use what existed to achieve what was imagined destroyed the utopian difference between the two that was the project's premise.

The preceding chapters focused on this subversion of first principles. They did so by juxtaposing the ways in which the planners' intentions structured the built city with the ways in which the people of Brasília, including the planners themselves, reasserted social processes and cultural values that these intentions sought to deny. This juxtaposition demonstrated that the conflict between intention and interpretation was manifested in several types of phenomena, each affording a different but related view of the subversive development of Brasiliense society. In the first two parts of the study, we concentrated on the manifestation of this conflict in Brasília's architecture and urban planning. The third part examined the embodiment and contravention of government plans. Together, the three parts illustrate the manifold ways in which Brasília recovered the history denied in both sets of intentions. However, they also demonstrate that this recovery was not a simple inversion of the initial negation. Rather, they show that this double negative had its own paradoxical development in which the interaction of intention and interpretation produced an exaggeration of some of the very conditions planners wanted to avoid.

In this concluding chapter, I shall suggest some of the ways in which the processes of reinterpretation engendered in this dialectic of premise and paradox continue to structure contemporary Brasiliense society. To make this point, I shall focus on the central processes of Brasília's recovery of history: the formation of its periphery of satellite cities, and the familiarization of its modernist center. Both resulted from the way in which the realization of plans concretized different bases for their subversion: on the one hand, it concretized an awareness of the systematic inequality of government intentions, creating a basis for challenge and resistance among the subordinate; on the other, it led to an awareness of the Master Plan's negations of Brazilian city life, creating a different basis for their contravention among the dominant. There is nothing inherently special about the ethnographic examples I use to illustrate this Brazilianization of Brasília: a squatter settlement on the outskirts of Taguatinga and one block of a street in Sobradinho. I could have chosen others because the processes of urban development they embody are everywhere expressed in the smallest details of daily life.

8.1 The Periphery in Time and Space

Since Brasília's foundation, its population has increasingly and overwhelmingly concentrated in the periphery around the Plano Piloto. Graph 8.1 illustrates this concentration. In 1980, the Plano Piloto contained less than half of its planned population of 557,000. Thus, the graph shows that it stood half empty while containing only one quarter of the Federal District's population. This distribution is a striking illustration of the thesis presented earlier that social and spatial development in Brasília follows the entailments of its differential incorporation, for it suggests that the relation between center and periphery perpetuates the policy of exclusion upon which it was founded. The initial objective of this policy was to maintain the capital as a bureaucratic center free from the social disorders that plague other Brazilian cities. Yet, this policy required planning instruments which were constitutive of these disorders and which therefore reproduced them in the capital. Thus, to preserve an uncompromised Plano Piloto, the government created a dual social order among migrants by regulating access to residence. As a result, an impoverished periphery of satellite cities filled up with those excluded from the center while the privileged center remained only partially built and occupied.[1] Graph 8.1 suggests that the government continues to expand the legal periphery

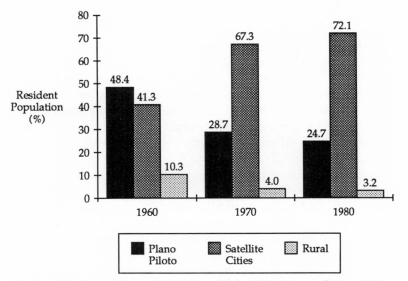

Graph 8.1 Center-periphery distribution of Federal District population, 1960, 1970, and 1980 (Source: table 5.8)

rather than incorporate migrants into the half empty Plano Piloto. To what extent, and at what cost, does this development sustain intentions threatened by such an alternative?

Approximately seven years after the foundation of the periphery its terms of incorporation were modified. In 1965, the government sold most of its residences in the Plano Piloto, giving their occupants first option to buy at extraordinarily favorable rates. With the creation of an open housing market in the Plano Piloto, the distinctions between the two previously constituted social orders changed. Yet, they did not dissolve; instead, they were maintained by a combination of new and old factors. Bureaucratic rank continued to determine who could occupy the residences that the government retained. In addition, however, wealth became a crucial factor in restricting access to the Plano Piloto and therefore in maintaining Brasília's social and spatial stratifications. This addition had several important consequences. The virtual monopoly that those recruited to government held over access to residence in the Plano Piloto ended. This change meant not only that those who previously had no rights to the residential privileges of this group were able to buy in. It also meant that lower-echelon and therefore lower-income government employees were ultimately denied the possibility of living in the Plano Piloto. Such functionaries had initially held rights to live in the city's public residences. When these residences became private, however, market forces and real estate speculation drove them beyond

their means. This marginalization occurred in two circumstances. On the one hand, those who had been assigned
apartments in the center were gradually forced out to the
satellite cities. We shall discuss the impact of this exodus on the
settlement of the periphery in a moment. On the other, those
recruited to lower-echelon positions after 1965 had no choice but
to live in the periphery. In both ways, this marginalization
consolidated the center for the upper strata—for those in the
upper echelons of the bureaucracy and/or the upper-income
brackets.

Thus, the two social orders continued after the sale of
government residences in the Plano Piloto although not as
exclusively and along somewhat different lines. To accommodate the displaced lower-echelon functionaries, the military
regimes that took command in Brasília after 1964 built tens of
thousands of subsidized housing units in the satellite cities. This
policy had a paradoxical effect on social stratification in Brasília.
In providing these units for its clerical and manual workers, the
government restricted access to the Plano Piloto according to an
inversion of earlier criteria: whereas initially those who held
government employment were entitled to reside in the center
regardless of individual disparities in wealth, after 1965 those
with bureaucratic status but low income were still given access
to government housing but only in the periphery. The result of
this policy was to segregate the lower-level functionaries in the
satellite cities far from the center where they work, contradicting
the initial objectives of Brasília's residential organization.

Moreover, planners continue to reiterate this contradiction in
new decisions to expand the periphery before completing Plano
Piloto. The most comprehensive planning study conducted to
date in the Federal District, *PEOT*, has called for the creation of
new satellite cities. In assessing the "saturation" limits of the
existing settlements, it bases its recommendation on the assumption that the stratified dichotomy between center and
periphery is inviolable.[2] Following this assessment, the Secretary of Roads and Works, the de facto regional administrator of
the Plano Piloto, has announced plans for not less than six new
satellite cities. Projected on a site between Taguatinga and
Gama, the first unveiled is intended as a dormitory city for
"public functionaries of low income."[3] Thus, once again, residential rights to public housing will segregate lower-level functionaries in the periphery; and, although its terms have partially
changed since 1965, public planning will once again promote
social stratification.

In these developments, Brasília sustains a pattern of urbanization that derives from and contradicts its first principles, a

pattern typical of Brazil's big cities in which elites inhabit the urban center and dominate disfranchised lower strata in the periphery. However, it must also be observed that Brasília exaggerates the inequalities of the typical metropolitan pattern in a number of significant ways. First, the capital has proportionately more people in its periphery and proportionately less in its center than any other major Brazilian city. In the Federal District, 75% of the population lives in the periphery. By contrast, São Paulo's periphery, numerically the most populous in Brazil, contains "only" 40% of the municipality's total population. Second, whereas the people of Brazil's urban peripheries are increasingly involved in the electoral processes of government at local, state, and national levels, the inhabitants of Brasília's satellites remain completely disfranchised.* Third, whereas other cities mix elite residential quarters and slums in their central districts, Brasília rigorously separates the one in the Plano Piloto from the other in the satellite cities. This is not to discount either the increasing number of middle-income people and middle-level bureaucrats living in the nearer satellites or the squatters who brave police assaults in the isolated areas of the Plano Piloto. It is merely to observe that in the urbanized areas of the capital there are no slums and, as tables 5.10 and 5.11 confirm, few poor people.

Furthermore, as these tables and table 1.1 suggest, the disparities in income between Brasília's center and its periphery are far greater than in other Brazilian cities, precisely because high income in the Federal District is overwhelmingly and almost uniformly concentrated in the Plano Piloto and its lake residences. Finally, what also exaggerates the differences between Brasília's center and its periphery is the way in which they are expressed spatially. Whereas other cities are continuously settled from center to periphery, Brasília dichotomizes the two in absolute terms: there is not one satellite within 14 kilometers of the Plano Piloto. Thus, the passage between center and periphery is uncompromisingly stark. Although the population of the periphery has increased by 1,350% since Brasília's inauguration,

---

*As this book went to press, the new Brazilian constitution of 1988 gave Brasília's residents the right to elect federal senators and representatives, to elect district governor, vice-governor and representatives (the latter to a so-called Legislative House), and to vote for national president and vice-president. These new rights do not, however, necessarily entail a shift in power relations between the Plano Piloto and the satellite cities because representation in Brazil is not tied to districts within an electoral unit. Rather, it is based on popular vote throughout the unit, which in this case is the entire Federal District. Although elections in Brasília will not, therefore, necessarily oppose center and periphery, they will most probably institute a new pattern of compromise.

the authorities have kept the elite center surrounded by its wide moat.

These relations between center and periphery illustrate that the construction of spatial relations is fundamental in creating the lived experiences of social stratification. In the Federal District, distance from the center is a measure—although since 1965 not an absolute measure—of where Brasilienses stand in the social order. Not only is it a measure of power, prestige, and wealth, but it is also a means by which Brasilienses deduce important social facts about each other. Not only does distance from the center determine basic features of daily life, such as type of residence, nature of employment, approximate standard of living, and amount of time spent commuting to work or school. In a society where social stratification is severe, such factors also indicate a great deal about a person's life chances. If we were to plot these indicators in terms of distance from the center of the Plano Piloto, each would appear similar to the one given for average income in graph 8.2. Such charts illustrate the great disparity in standards of living between the Plano Piloto and the satellite cities. They also show that these standards decline among the satellites themselves as one moves from closest to farthest from the center. These skewed distributions indicate the logic by which contemporary Brasiliense society is represented in space.

8.1.1 The Squatter Settlement of Vila Chaparral

One process basic to the formation of Brasília's periphery is the transformation of land seizures from illegal to legal settlements. Indeed, the satellite cities themselves owe their origins to cycles of rebellion and legitimation that date back to the pioneers and continue today. In the first phase of this process, people appropriate land rights by squatting. In the second phase, the government gives formal recognition to these usurped rights either by endowing the land seizures with legal status in situ or by removing their residents to newly subdivided house lots in an existing satellite city. This change in status results in the addition of new residents to those legally entitled to urban services and in the expansion of the urban periphery into new areas of the hinterland.

It is difficult to know precisely how many people or settlements are today involved in the first phase of this formation. Estimates vary wildly. In 1982, I tended to accept the findings of Terracap (successor to Novacap in these matters) that about 40,000 squatters resided in 23 settlements in the Federal District,

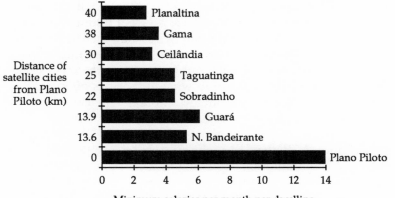

Distance of
satellite cities
from Plano
Piloto (km)

40	Planaltina
38	Gama
30	Ceilândia
25	Taguatinga
22	Sobradinho
13.9	Guará
13.6	N. Bandeirante
0	Plano Piloto

0   2   4   6   8   10   12   14

Minimum salaries per month per dwelling

Graph 8.2 Spatial distribution of average income in the Federal District, 1975
(Source: table 5.10)

5 that predate the creation in 1971 of the last satellite city,
Ceilândia.[4] What appears more certain is that in the first ten
years after the foundation of the satellite cities, approximately
100,000 migrants became squatters in the Federal District. Although the government attempted a final solution to squatting
around the capital with the creation of Ceilândia, it would seem
that in the following decade as many as 18 new land seizures
arose. However many there are today, our study of their
historical precedent in the Federal District suggests that the
illegal phase of these settlements is more or less temporary and
that they will be incorporated into the legal periphery of
tomorrow.

Following in the tradition of the pioneers, contemporary
associations of squatters in Brasília organize land takeovers to
gain legal access to urban property and services. Like squatters
elsewhere in Brazil, they achieve this objective by persuading
the authorities to change the status of their settlements. The
paradox of this situation—of which the squatters are well
aware—is that in most cases it is only through the illegal act of
squatting that they can get the services they desperately need.
Moreover, their situation is paradoxical in another sense: what
most squatters seek in addition to basic urban services is the
social respectability legitimate society denies them. Lacking
respect, they organize to achieve it by embracing one of the
most fundamental values of the social order they strive to join:
property ownership. Squatting is for them a means to acquire
the urban services and the social status of respectability that
derive from property ownership.

Knowledge of this objective helps us understand why squatters often prefigure the legal status they struggle for in the

details of their own organizations. Just as the rebellious associations of the pioneers developed a strategy of pitting the nation against the regime—of appropriating not only the land but also the symbols, values, and procedures of the state—their successors reproduce the structures and strategies of the legal settlements they border. Contrary to what authorities often charge, these land seizures are not outlaw redoubts. Their residents do not abandon accepted social bonds and morals. Much less do they attempt utopian experiments in social or economic organization.[5] Rather, Brasília's squatter settlements are "shadow communities," reiterating in perhaps surprising detail the model of the dominant social order to the limits of their resources. When resources preclude an exact reiteration, as they often do, one finds in these shadows of legitimate society an interpretation, a refashioning or resignification, of what is desired in realizable terms. This process of interpretation is fundamental to the organization of the illegal periphery. To illustrate it, I shall give an example of the ways in which the codes of Brasília's dominant institutions—such as those of bureaucracy, technology, science, law, and education—appear as organizing metaphors in these communities, focusing on one that is especially appropriate for Brasília, that of urban planning.

The invasion of QSC is one of several land takeovers recently initiated on Taguatinga's ever expanding outskirts. In official parlance, it is called "QSC" because it is located just beyond the legal residential sector Quadra Sul C in a forest reserve irrigated by the Taguatinga Stream. However, it is popularly known as the Vila Chaparral, named after a North American television show syndicated in Brazil. Times have changed. In the era of the pioneers, popular naming practices emphasized founders (Vila Matias) or purported benefactors (Vila Sara Kubitschek). In an era of mass culture, consumer items are often the focus of both popular and elite self-presentation, in what amounts to status competitions between different sectors of society played out in the knowledgeable use of fashion.

Vila Chaparral has approximately a thousand residents living in two hundred houses. Physically, it is divisible into two parts: the smaller is built on an open, flat stretch of land beyond the stream, and the greater is massed on the stream's unevenly sloping banks. The smaller part—which does not seem to have a separate name—is laid out in what can only be described as a continuation of the standardized plan of its neighboring residential sectors in legal Taguatinga. It reiterates the planning principles of the Sectors of Individual Dwellings, the subtype of residential organization designated for freestanding houses which predominates in all of the satellite cities. It is a "one street land seizure," with its houses set out in two long and straight rows on either side of a central, dirt access road—just like the residential developments in Taguatinga proper. Furthermore, just like the houses in these developments, their backs are on the road side, defined by high fences with service entrances, while their fronts face out onto an unfenced yard—exactly the front-back reversal distinctive of Brasília's urbanism.

Like the houses of the strip section, those of the riverine part are concatenations of all sizes and shapes of weather-beaten wood. But unlike the single-file orderliness of the former, the latter are assembled along serpentine paths cut into what, from afar, seems more like a continuous wooden structure than a settlement of individual buildings—like a single mass out of which the voids of passage have been carved. In these relations of solids and voids, this part of Chaparral suggests at first glance a preindustrial rather than a modernist urbanism. Formed by high batten-board fences, its paths are cavernous and tortuous like the alleys of a casbah. They are the areas of public space where neighbors converse and children play. Yet here the urban pattern stops. On closer examination, its visual unity dissolves into individual homesteads, each consisting of one or more shacks and an all-purpose yard. The shacks come in various sizes and degrees of refinement. Some are single rectangular rooms with unfinished concrete floors (dirt floors are rare) while others have several bedrooms, a living room, bathroom, and kitchen. The house lots are like farmyards. They are multifunctional areas serving as the pantry of household objects, the warehouse of construction materials, the animal yard, midden pit, vegetable and fruit garden, and playpen. When one realizes that these homesteads are almost all completely enclosed by heavily constructed fences and that the paths thus formed are the only public spaces—that there are no squares, or public or commercial buildings inside the mass of twisting paths—it becomes clearer that this part of Chaparral is more of a rural than an urban settlement. In this respect, it is unusual only in that its individual homesteads are forced into close quarters for defense against eradication.

Yet, Chaparral is not a self-contained redoubt. Despite its apparent anomalies, rural Chaparral follows one of Brasília's official residential patterns. It is the pattern designated for rural houses on the edge of an urban settlement, precisely Chaparral's situation. That the residents inhabit it as a rural settlement and that it follows this official pattern, in its own impoverished fashion, can be seen in its address system. Residents label their houses with handpainted signs according to the official address code of Brasília, exactly as if they were legally registered with the local authorities. Each house is called a *chácara*, the generic term for a small estate on the outskirts of a city. In Brasília's official residential typology, *chácaras* are only found in the elite Lake Peninsula South, where there are 290 of them. They are the largest of Brasília's house lots, measuring 10,000 m^2, and most of them are located in an area adjacent to two Internal Quadras of smaller house lots, QI-5 and QI-15. For their address, these *chácaras* take the designation of their adjacent *quadras*. For example, *chácara* number 3 in an area next to QI-15 is coded QI-15-Ch 3, that is, Internal Quadra-15-Chácara 3. In strict concordance, the houses of Chaparral follow this system: each bears the address QSC-25-Ch (*x*) because the access to Chaparral is at the end of the service road of residential unit (*conjunto*) 25 of Quadra Sul C. Thus, Vila Chaparral's address code indicates a grouping of rural houses adjacent to a *quadra*—exactly its situation in relation to the *quadras* of Taguatinga. In this way, the squatters have borrowed the logic of Brasília's official residential typology and extended it into an area of illegal settlement.

There are many other ways in which Vila Chaparral reiterates the dominant social organization around it, and I shall only suggest a few to make the point. Although it lacks running water and even the most rudimentary sanitation, there is television and electricity in all but the poorest of shacks, for television is the means in every home of keeping up with the latest of consumer culture, knowledge of which is crucial to display in the life of Chaparral.[6] As in cultural matters, so in other areas Vila Chaparral is integrated into the affairs of the Federal District. For example, its property transactions are governed by monetary and labor contracts in which houses (not, of course, land) are rented, bought, and sold in a market that is extremely competitive both with the legal and with the other illegal settlements of the Federal District.[7] These transactions are in the last instance respected by the state, as demonstrated when its officials carefully dismantle the houses of a land seizure during a removal operation so that they may be reconstructed elsewhere. But as the government rarely intervenes in the internal affairs of a squatter settlement, these contracts must be administered by the community itself. To this end, we shall not be surprised to learn that Chaparral's residential association is organized on the model of state government with multiple functions (including administration, law, police, and welfare) and officials with hierarchic titles (including president, director, and subchief) borrowed from the language of bureaucracy.[8]

These examples indicate the ways in which this squatter settlement, like others throughout Brazil, models itself on the paradigms of the legitimate social order, rehearsing its part in the wings so to speak, so that its leaders can better argue with the authorities that it deserves urban services. Indeed, Vila Chaparral passed the first step toward authorization in May 1981, when the regional administrator arranged to pipe potable water into it. Unfortunately, the governor of the Federal District ordered the water removed. When the administrator refused, he was dismissed from office. Although Chaparral thus lost a prominent ally in the regional administration, I have little doubt that eventually, either through fixation or through transfer to government-built houses in the vicinity, it will follow historical precedent and complete its transformation from an illegal to an authorized settlement of the periphery.

8.1.2 Center Street, Sobradinho

In addition to this cycle of transformation, the state's regulation of the real estate market both in the Plano Piloto and in the satellite cities has been crucial to the development of the periphery. Indeed, before their sale in 1965, it was the government's restriction of *superquadra* apartments in the Plano Piloto to federal officials that maintained the dichotomy between Brasília's center and periphery. Moreover, since the foundation of the satellite cities, the government has controlled their development through two types of real estate allotments. After describing both types, I shall focus on the effects of one over a period of 15 years on a single street in Sobradinho. This study will illustrate the ways in which real estate development initiated by the government is both displacing the poor from the nearer satellite cities and reproducing an impoverished urban periphery in new areas of the hinterland.

In the first type of allotment, the government sells house plots in subdivisions. Each sale includes a contractual obligation to build an approved masonry house within a specified period of time. The contract also gives permission to live on the land during house construction in a temporary shack built at the back of the lot. We reviewed the details of this contract in the last chapter. In addition to these contractual obligations, the distribution of lots is generally regulated by status distinctions among applicants. For example, when the government opened Ceilândia for settlement, it distributed about 15,000 lots to those it removed from squatter settlements located around Núcleo Bandeirante. Only these squatters had rights to the lots in Ceilândia, as opposed for instance to other squatters or new migrants.

Thus, in this type of real estate development, the government regulates access to land both by the status of the applicant and by contractual obligation.

In the second type of allotment, the government sells lots with houses already constructed on them. These houses are generically called *casas populares*, 'popular (class) houses', or *casas padronizadas*, 'pattern houses', because they are produced in series from a limited number of standard plans.[9] For example, of the 13,555 occupied residences registered in Sobradinho, the government has built 2,994 of them, all but 88 before 1973. In terms of the state's regulation of the housing market, it is important to understand that of these government-built houses all but 600 were reserved for lower-echelon functionaries in various bureaucratic institutions.[10] These employees were mostly manual and office workers in one of two conditions: either they were directly assigned to the periphery upon transfer to Brasília, or, having been initially given an apartment in the Plano Piloto, they were gradually forced out to the satellite cities after the creation of an open housing market in the Plano Piloto as discussed earlier. Throughout the satellites, the government has built tens of thousands of these pattern houses and has thus regulated initial access to them on the basis of status criteria of one sort or another.

In Sobradinho, the 10 x 30 m residential lots along Second Street, unofficially known as Center Street, have been developed according to the first type of real estate allotment; that is, property owners are responsible for putting an approved house on their lots within a stipulated period of time. The 33 lots on the west side of the block between Fifth and Sixth streets (officially, Quadra 6-Conjunto H) were all sold between 1966 and 1971 by Novacap on the basis of the promissory contract outlined in the last chapter. On the other side of this block (officially, Quadra Central Residencial-Conjunto A), the 18 lots were all sold between 1976 and 1977 by Terracap on the basis of a modified version of this contract. This modification has produced dramatically different blocks: in the extreme, one finds mansions facing shacks across the street (fig. 8.1; e.g., the mansion on lot 11 compared to the shack across the street on lot 41).

The west side features 12 wooden shacks, 8 pattern houses, 8 parapet or false-front houses, 2 kolonial houses, and 3 modern houses.[11] The average size of the houses is 124 m^2 and of the shacks 30 m^2. If we remove from this calculation the three largest houses (2 kolonials and one modern, all built in 1980: 250 m^2, 166 m^2, and 241 m^2, respectively), the average house is 89 m^2. Across the street, the average house measures 220 m^2, and the largest is 428 m^2 and takes up 3 lots. This side features no shacks and only 2 pattern houses. It has 2 kolonial mansions, 3 kolonial-moderns, 3 moderns, and 6 parapet houses.[12] The finishes of these houses are often luxurious; on the other side of the street, they are often economical, where finishes are an issue at all. On the east side, we find as property owners 3 entrepreneurs (an owner of a bus company, an owner of a trucking company, and an owner of several gas stations), 2 lawyers, 1 civil engineer, 1 econometrician, 1 bank employee, 1 teacher, 1 electronics technician, and 4 truck drivers who own their rigs. On the west side, we have mostly government clerks, skilled and unskilled workers (among them, 3 drivers of horse-drawn dump-carts who live in shacks), 1 teacher, and 2 bank employees (one of whom lives in the large kolonial built in 1980). In 1981, the kolonial mansion of the east side was valued at U.S.$47,000, and the average value of east-side houses was U.S.$16,500. A pattern house on the other side cost about U.S.$3,000.

That these two blocks are "neighbors" is a striking example of the effects of different policies and processes of real estate development. To find such a sharp contrast on the same street and within the same block is exceptional in the satellite cities and, as we shall see, temporary. However, precisely because it is an extreme case—one that captures two moments in antagonistic development before one subsumes the other—it neatly reveals these processes. Therefore, I shall outline the property history of each side.

The 33 west-side lots were sold under the provisions of Novacap's promissory contract, promissory because it was not a direct sale but rather a lease committing its parties to an eventual sale provided the prospective buyer fulfilled the terms of the contract. Earlier, considering the population for whom it was intended (migrants without bureaucratic status and squatters), I suggested the high potential for failure inherent in these terms and the anxiety that this potential generated among those who held them. A survey of the turnovers of property on this block confirms this rate of failure. Of the original 33 leaseholders, almost two in three failed. Of the 13 who succeeded, 10 fulfilled the terms of the contract and, as of 1981, remain on the block as owners of their lots; an additional 3 had succeeded but moved on. However, only 5 of the 13 completed their masonry houses within the stipulated three years. In a tactic frequently used to get around this stipulation, the others submitted house plans for approval at the end of the three years, requesting extensions from the authorities based on these plans. Eventually, between 1 and 5 years after their due date, 8 families in this situation completed their houses. In the interim, in some cases

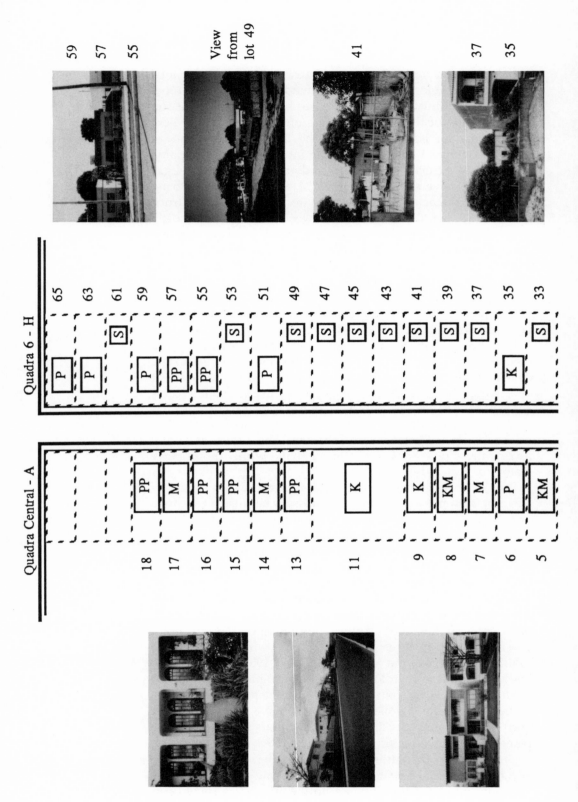

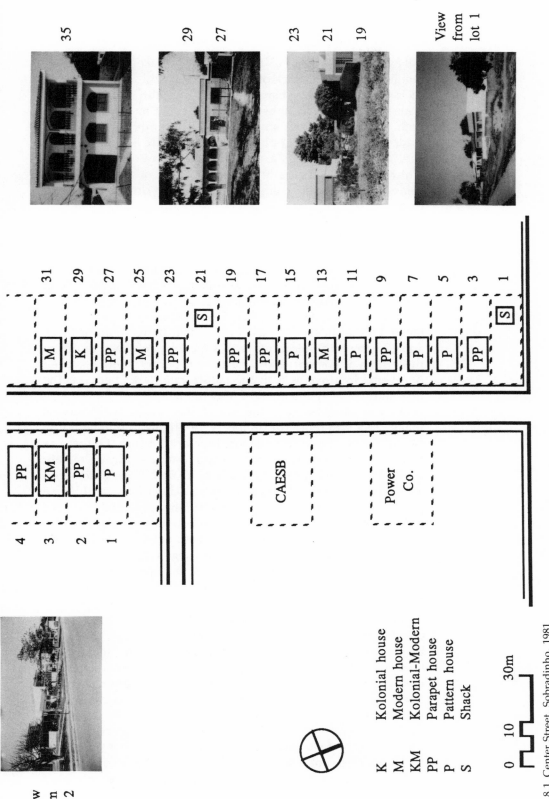

35

29
27

23
21
19

View from lot 1

View from lot 2

31
29
27
25
23
21
19
17
15
13
11
9
7
5
3
1

M
K
PP
M
PP
S
PP
PP
P
M
P
PP
P
P
PP
S

4
3
2
1

PP
KM
PP
P

CAESB

Power Co.

K   Kolonial house
M   Modern house
KM   Kolonial-Modern
PP   Parapet house
P   Pattern house
S   Shack

0   10   30m

Fig. 8.1 Center Street, Sobradinho, 1981

for as long as 8 years (5 beyond the contract's stipulated 3), families lived at the back of "their" lots, all the while investing their off-work time, energy, and savings into building their houses in the front—houses that had come to represent both their dreams and their anxieties about the future. Thus, as is evident in the plan and photographs of figure 8.1, the promissory contract generates a pattern of property development in which one finds shacks at the back of the lot and, in a state somewhere between completion and ruin, dream houses in front.

A survey of these 33 lots reveals the following history of property on the block: between 1966 and 1981, these lots have been held by 54 occupants, constituting three generations of residents. Among them, there are 51 leaseholders and 3 individuals who had purchased ownership rights directly from previously successful leaseholders. Of the 51, 21 have succeeded in their contracts to become full owners, while 30 have failed. Of the almost 60% who have failed, 18 have left the block and 12 remain in precarious legal situations. We shall return to these 12 in a moment. Over the 15-year period, there has been no overall improvement in the failure rate (60%) between the first and the last generation of leaseholders.[13]

On the other side of the street, the property history is remarkably different. The 18 lots were originally purchased by 14 individuals, three buying more than one lot each. Of these 14 people, 13 fulfilled the terms of their contracts. Eleven remain on the block and 2 have sold to others. Only 2 of the 13 required a contract extension, through the submission of a second house project, to complete their houses within the stipulated period of time. Only one of the original purchasers did not complete the terms of the contract. However, this was not a case of failure but rather a decision by the original owner, a civil engineer, to abandon a speculative venture. Even so, by holding the land for only a year and a half, he made a 53% profit on the sale. The individual to whom he sold built a house within one year.

How do we account for the radical differences in the property development of these two blocks? In an obvious way, they have to do with the different financial assets of the individuals involved. However, the distribution of this difference has everything to do with the new type of contract governing the allotments on the east and wealthier block. This contract is known as a transfer of ownership with a *pacto de retrovenda* ('sell-back agreement'). It differs from the Novacap promissory contract in the following significant ways. First, it is a contract for direct sale, not a leasehold agreement. This sale occurs at public auction, no longer by application and no longer restricted to certain status groups. Second, its terms are quite different: 30% down, and the rest in 30 payments with 6% interest per year plus inflationary correction (as opposed to 5% down, 34 payments, and in many cases no interest or monetary correction). Third, although Novacap's promissory contract obliges the leaseholder to build a house, the sell-back clause of the new contract specifies that within 4 months of the date of purchase, the owner has to provide Terracap with (a) plans for a "definitive house project" and (b) a "physical-financial chronogram" showing the schedule of construction and proof of assets to pay for each stage. Both plans and schedules are subject to approval. Moreover, within 36 months, the owner has to demonstrate that the construction is complete by obtaining an occupancy permit. Failure to comply with these three obligations gives Terracap the right at the end of 3 years to redeem the lot; that is, the owner is obliged to sell it back to Terracap, hence the name of the contract. However, the owner may sell at anytime within 3 years to anyone for any price without prior approval—all of which the earlier promissory contract forbade. In the event of repossession, Terracap will buy back the lot at the original sale price and in addition pay the owner's expenses for all existing improvements. In the earlier version, the leaseholder lost all investments upon foreclosure.

Clearly, the sell-back contract is more favorable to the buyer than the promissory one. In general, however, this advantage is only available to upper-income buyers. Working-class Brasilienses find its provisions prohibitive, especially its required down payment, submission of house plans and finance schedules after 4 months, and conditions of sell-back. As a result, they are denied access to lots sold under its provisions, an exclusion evident in the development of Center Street, Sobradinho. As Terracap creates and regulates the housing market through its allotments, one must assume that this exclusion is deliberate. If land values were kept low, perhaps it would not result. However, the average auction price of U.S.$5,100 that Terracap set in December 1976 for lots on the east side of Center Street was beyond the reach of even skilled workers. Since then, the auction prices for similar lots have spiraled ever higher. In June 1981, one went for U.S.$12,000, an appreciation of 140% in four and a half years. As Terracap has the power to set these prices, it directly influences the ebb and flow of property values and therefore of real estate speculation. We may therefore conclude that the sell-back contract awarded at public auction is a mechanism deliberately calculated to bring about the results evident in the contrast of property development between the blocks of Center Street.

From Terracap's perspective, these results are improvements that affect the entire neighborhood by raising its prestige and property value. However, such improvements also initiate a process of displacing the urban poor, a process that one might term gentrification. By this I mean government-led real estate development in which people with privileged access to government incentives—access based on wealth and/or status—displace residents without such access. The sell-back contract and its public auction may be viewed as mechanisms of such displacement because they not only attract people who can afford to build significantly more expensive houses than previously found in the periphery of Brasília; more important, they tend to restrict access to subdivisions of land sold in this way to just these people.

The processes of exclusion that these mechanisms set in motion have only just become visible in the development of the satellite cities, as the history of Center Street suggests. However, their potential long-term effects may be appreciated if we consider their impact on two groups of urban poor, those I shall call the old working poor and the new working poor. By old poor, I refer to those already residing in the satellites, especially the ones closest to the Plano Piloto; by new poor, those who will in the future migrate to the Federal District. The combined effect of these processes is to make the nearer neighborhoods in the periphery too expensive for both groups so that while the former may very likely be pushed out to farther satellites, the latter will have no choice but to go ever farther out from the center to find a place to live.

Let us first consider the effects of "improving" Center Street on its poor residents. Gentrification affects areas where the sell-back contract did not originally apply. This ripple effect can be seen on the poorer west side of Center Street when we consider both the newer residents and the fate of the remaining 12 shacks. A study of the most recent houses built by those who took over failed contracts shows that wealthier residents are replacing the lower-income ones. The three largest houses on the block (lots 35, 13, and 29) were built in 1979–80 by new leaseholders. The one on lot 35 is certainly on a par with the mansions across the street. Moreover, in the latest property turnover, the promissory title for lot 31 was taken over for U.S.$3,900 and an undisclosed amount "under the table." Immediately, the new leaseholder submitted a project to replace the lot's shack with a two storey, 352 m^2 modern house that will be the largest on the block, and second only to the kolonial mansion across the street. These new residents constitute quite a different social group from the original one. As symbolized by the houses they build, they are either comembers or aspiring comembers of the social group of mansion dwellers across the street. Needless to say, there are strained relations between the nouveaux with two cars in the garage and the "slum dwellers" with chickens and vegetables in the yard. With the passage of time, however, the latter (and their fowl) are no doubt a doomed species on the block. Not only are their shacks being replaced with opulent houses, but *they* are being displaced from Center Street altogether.

If the fate of lot 31 is any indication, the remaining 12 shack-holders should soon be bought out. Indeed, the occupant of the shack in lot 1 was recently approached with an offer of U.S.$10,000. He is "thinking about it." Certainly, these poor residents consider the precipitous increase in property values to be most fortunate for them. But if they sell out, where will they go and how will the move affect their prospects for improving *their* standard of living? Among the few families I could trace who had sold their shacks, all moved to a poorer and more distant part of Sobradinho—areas that lacked some of the basic urban services such as street paving and drainage. Moreover, all moved into another shack. If they are skillful in managing the sum of money they received from the sale of their properties on Center Street, they may improve their standard of living in another neighborhood. However, because inflation quickly erodes the purchasing power of monies received from such sales and increased distance from transportation lines affects employment negatively, there are strong indications that such sales generally lead to a reproduction of an already low standard of living. For the moment, in satellites like Sobradinho, this reproduction of poverty is occurring on the edges of the city. Yet, we can imagine that as the processes of real estate development at work on Center Street are themselves eventually reproduced in other neighborhoods, Sobradinho's working poor may very likely be displaced altogether to another satellite, inevitably one farther out into the periphery.

Moreover, as these processes raise property values dramatically, new migrants to the Federal District who are poor will soon be unable to afford to live in the satellite cities closer to the Plano Piloto. In a few years, the new poor of Brasília will have no choice but to go to the outer satellites and beyond to find affordable accommodations in legal settlements. Although the processes underlying such prospects have only become visible in the last ten years in places like Center Street, we may suggest how they will affect the overall development of Brasília's satellite cities: such processes will expand the urban periphery into new areas of the hinterland, recreating its worst conditions fartherest away from the urban center. Thus, in our analysis of events on Center Street, we have demonstrated the same processes of stratification, and the same correlations of society and space, that are illustrated in more general terms and for other variables in graph 8.2. Moreover, we have added to the list of Brasília's paradoxes: we have shown that the prime mover of both the improvement and the impoverishment of the periphery is the government itself, whose ingrained policies of stratified development reproduce the worst conditions of the periphery in new places.

8.2 The City Familiarized

Just as the reproduction of the periphery reiterates Brasília's utopian paradoxes, the familiarization of its modernist center constitutes a recovery of history that its founding premises denied. In Parts 1 and 2, we concentrated on the embodiment and contradiction of intention in Brasília's architecture and urban planning. We saw that the conventions of the city's architecture—such as the transparent glass façade, the building raised on columns, and the *superquadra* residence—were designed to create new forms of perception, experience, and interaction; and, similarly, that the principles of its modernist planning were applied not only to provide functional order for city life but also to transform personal habit and collective association. In the most important example of this application, we observed that the elimination of the street to institute a new system of traffic circulation transformed both the physical structure of the familiar Brazilian city and the nature of its public life. We therefore concluded that Brasília's architecture and planning embodied a set of intentions for creating a new social order in which urban form and organization were instruments of radical change.

However, Part 2 demonstrated that the first generations of Brasilienses, the ones that shaped the city's development, not only rejected these intentions but moreover countered them with opposing interpretations. What they rejected in the city's design was its negation of familiar patterns of urban life. What they reinterpreted was the social program the architects thought they were making manifest. Thus, they considered that the standardization of residential architecture produced anonymity among residents, not equality as intended. Similarly, they interpreted the transparent apartment façade not only as a reduction of privacy, but also as indicative of the general reduction of the influence of private interests in the spheres of social life that is essential to the modernist program of change. On both accounts, they objected to the façade. In addition, they considered the model apartment plan inconvenient but not insurmountable in its sabotage of customary stratifications of domestic space. This plan did not prevent them from hiring maids, nor did it discourage discriminatory practices in the use of residential space. Rather, it had the perverse effect of making work conditions for maids even worse. Moreover, Brasilienses tended not to use the green areas of the *superquadras* as the architects had hoped. Rather, they tended to find both the apartments and the green areas cold and even antagonistic to the traditional social relations of the Brazilian household. For these inhabitants, Brasília's residential design seems to have produced a sense both of isolation inside the apartments and yet of disinterest in the collective areas of the *superquadras*.

Brasilienses manifest their rejections of Brasília's utopian design by reasserting familiar values, conceptions, and conventions of urban life. These reassertions surface in many ways. The one we gave particular attention to was the repudiation of the antistreet design of the local commercial sector. By putting shop entrances on the curb rather than on the proposed garden side of buildings, Brasilienses attempted to reconstitute the life of the market street where it had been architecturally denied. Similarly, they rejected the transparent façade of the apartment blocks not merely by putting up curtains and blinds but by demanding a return to an opaque wall architecture in later constructions.

Many among Brasília's uppermost elite rejected the residential concept of the *superquadra* altogether: they moved out of their apartments and created their own neighborhoods of individual houses outside of the Plano Piloto. Furthermore, they constructed private clubs along the lake shore, abandoning the idea of egalitarian clubs in the *superquadras*. The very existence of these neighborhoods and clubs repudiates the aims of the Master Plan to achieve social change by instituting a new type of residential organization. Whereas the *superquadra* concretizes a set of egalitarian prescriptions in standard façades, materials, finishes, and floor plans, the houses of these neighborhoods compete with each other to display their residents' super-elite statuses with a sense of ostentation and in a *bricolage* of historical styles that fractures every tenet of the modernist aesthetic and social program.[14] By leaving the Plano Piloto, by appropriating lake frontage for private use, by creating exclusive neighborhoods and private clubs, these elites contravened the intentions of Brasília's residential organization. Without their support, important aspects of its proposed collective structure collapsed.

In sum, both those who remained in the Plano Piloto and those who moved to its lake residences rejected the city's utopian design. In so doing, they reasserted social processes and cultural values that subverted its founding premises. What resulted was not, however, a familiar Brazilian city because the architects' intentions had indeed structured the built Brasília; but neither was it the Brasília the architects imagined.

To understand what kind of city emerged out of this interaction of intention and interpretation, we earlier analyzed the consequences of eliminating the type of space and the type of social life characteristic of the street as a public room. Using examples from eighteenth-century Ouro Preto and nineteenth-century Rio de Janeiro, we identified a set of architectural conventions that define this room in terms of a contrast between public street and private building. This analysis suggested that such conventions create a setting—rather like a stage—in the outdoor spaces of the city, and also provide a set of cues for certain kinds of behavior. Thus, they physically define an outdoor public domain of social life. Chapters 4 and 5 demonstrated that modernist cities like Brasília radically transform these conventions to produce a different type of city, outdoor space, and social life. The study of these transformations showed that they were motivated by the intention of creating an egalitarian system of property relations and distribution of services and facilities in the city. However, our analysis also revealed fundamental contradictions between the architectural forms of the modernist city and its egalitarian intentions. Let us examine how the transformation of outdoor space in Brasília reveals the nature of these contradictions.

Although the new architecture was designed to stimulate new forms of public gathering in order to reinvigorate the collective realm of society, such forms have not emerged in Brasília's outdoor spaces. Rather, these spaces remain little used for other than commuter shuttles or shopping for two reasons. First, many of them are not merely overscaled and therefore cold in the proxemic sense of not inviting congregation. They are also inaccessible and thus no-man's land. It is simply an illusion of the city's plan to consider, as planners often do, the vast open spaces "freed" by antistreet planning as a setting for social activities. Rather, much of the plan's open space consists of highways and parking lots—vast areas of the city given over either to the car at rest or to the car at high speeds and therefore of limited access, utility, and interest. Furthermore, the open areas between the major highways, the parkland around the lake (what little of it has not been appropriated by private clubs and houses), the Esplanade of the Ministries, and the Plaza of the Three Powers are practically inaccessible on foot. In part because they are inaccessible and in part because they are exposed continuous spaces and not enclosed figural ones, these outdoor spaces are generally devoid of human life. Examples to the contrary, such as the blocks of inverted store fronts in a few commercial sectors of the South Wing, are precisely those that have contravened the planners' intentions.

Second, and more important, Brasília's accessible open spaces—such as the green areas of the *superquadras*—are not used because Brasilienses of the Plano Piloto no longer see themselves as participating in an outdoor public domain of social life: for them, this domain has been eliminated along with the street system of public spaces that supports it in other Brazilian cities. What is left is not just private space—which has always existed in cities—but a new and generalized urban feature that we might call elite space: space restricted by design and organization to privileged sectors of society, that is, to whichever sectors have the privileges required *by its design* to use it. As a result, social life in the Plano Piloto transpires almost entirely in these two types of spaces—the private and the elite. Moreover, in both cases, these tend to be interior spaces. Throughout this study, I have argued that these redefinitions of social space derive to a considerable degree from the way modernist architecture eliminates the public room of streets and squares by severing its unit of permeable building wall and mixed-use space into discrete parts. This operation divides a public whole into elite halves, stratifying space by making its use dependent on a prior set of privileges—car, money, *superquadra* residence, and occupational status. Moreover, the division internalizes activity into each new part: in Brasília, the pedestrian is engulfed by the car, the sidewalk transformed into an internal corridor, and commerce itself redirected toward the interior of the *superquadras* or internalized into shopping malls.

It is in such interior spaces—those of the shopping mall, the private club, and the home—that most social activity in Brasília occurs. The point that I wish to stress is that this interiorization does not constitute a simple displacement of social life from the outdoor rooms of streets to the indoor rooms of malls, clubs, and homes. Rather, this displacement stratifies space and changes the nature of the crowd that uses it. In our discussion of the street system of public spaces in Rio, we observed that it is a domain of essentially unrestricted access for all people. The most distinctive social activity of this free space is that of noncommercial exchange, such as discussion, protest, and celebration. Brasília's interior social spaces do not reproduce this outdoor city public in a new setting. The transportation center

Figs. 8.2 Popular demonstration for direct presidential elections held in the Praça da Sé, São Paulo, 25 January 1984. The headline from the news weekly *Veja* reads, "The square demands the vote." Photo: Abril Imagens/Rogério Reis

and the shopping mall, which we considered in chapter 5 as characteristic of these spaces, have not the sociality of the square. Their conversations take place between buses and between purchases. This is not to denigrate them but rather to observe that their sociality is incidental to their primary functions, their instrumental values, as centers of transport, work, and commerce. The problem is that such instrumentality characterizes all of Brasília's central sectors: whenever their respective functions are not being utilized, they are empty.

Thus, in Brasília, the outdoor city public of other Brazilian cities has all but disappeared, its room dismantled, its public transformed. Just as its space has been severed into elite halves, its public has been stratified into an indoor public of those who frequent Brasília's restricted indoor spaces and an outdoor public of those who must walk to where they have to go, braving the traffic of its speedways on foot. The former are the elites of the Plano Piloto who when outside the home and not at

Fig. 8.3 View of the Praça da Sé, São Paulo, 25 January 1984. Photo: Abril Imagens/Carlos Fenerich

work are habitually found in places such as clubs and malls that require prior privileges and assets. The latter are the working poor from the satellite cities, who beyond work have no place in the city. Throughout metropolitan Brazil, such dichotomies are not unusual. The upper and the lower classes do not generally frequent the same places; and when they do, then conventions of using space—as in the apartment building—usually ensure that they do not intersect informally. What is exceptional in Brasília is that without public spaces and urban crowds to suggest even the possibility of mediating the two, to suggest free places and situations in which interclass dialogue is of primary importance, such dichotomies are starkly apparent and apparently nonnegotiable. How different in this respect is Brasília from São Paulo, at least the São Paulo of figures 8.2 and 8.3.

Although there seems to be no simple correlation between politics and form, the creation of an elite enclave such as the Plano Piloto is not without attraction to certain types of political regimes and social orders. The elimination of streets and squares discourages the disorder of public gatherings. The compartmentalization of the city into discrete units segregates the population: those who make up its outdoor public are conspicuously out of place when not at work. This is an urban order that removes the popular classes from the city. As a means of total order, Brasília provided the military regimes that ruled Brazil for twenty years with an ideal capital. This is not to say that authoritarian and repressive regimes are not found in other types of cities. It is only to say that the modernist city is well designed to accommodate them. Where outdoor space is dominated by machines, buildings occupied by the powerful, and the populace removed beyond city limits, architecture itself becomes a great source of security: the city preserves its stratified social order in stone to such an extent that defiance, short of destruction, is difficult.

8.3 Concluding Remarks

In the way I have written this study, I have trespassed in various disciplines. I have written an ethnography, but not about tribal society. I have studied a modern city, its architecture, and its planning, and yet I have not restricted myself to formal analysis or to a history of form. I have given a historical account, but the questions that I asked of the past were meant to illuminate the present. I have focused on social change, but I have not isolated one neighborhood, community, or group within the city to bring out its particular development. I have taken an entire city as a unit of study, relating it to other cities and to global transformations in urban life, and yet I have found the whole reiterated in its smallest parts—in a block of houses, in a façade, in an address. My transgressions were not premeditated. I took what I needed to understand what I found: a society in the making, constructing itself in the experience of constructing its city, interpreting and reinterpreting its founding premises. Whether I have succeeded in describing this process is for the reader to judge, but lest it be said that I did not subordinate this process wholly to the analytical constructs of one discipline or another, I reply that this was not so much my intention as it was a necessity.

When I began my ethnographic research, I asked the reciprocal questions of how an anthropologist should study Brasília's modernism and what this study would suggest about ethnography. I have tried to let these questions provoke each other throughout the course of this book. I proposed that a critical ethnography of modernism focus on how the latter's claims are linked to social practices and thus become social forces. I argued that what defines the social effects of architecture and planning is not the consciousness their creators may have of their production but rather the status of their products in the world. To rely on the former is to confuse criticism with native interpretation, and at worst with propaganda. To avoid this conflation, and to link claim and practice, I pursued five interactive perspectives of analysis, focusing on context, intention, instrument, history, and the structures of premise and paradox which a critical study of them reveals. This critique led me to combine a formal analysis of architectural and planning conventions with a social history of their use, a study of the values and discourses they embody, and an assessment of the contributions they make in defining the city as a domain of social and political life—in short, an anthropology and not only a semiotics or a history of modernism in Brasília.

My focus on the utopian paradoxes of the planning process itself raised a complex problem: the need for utopia in imagining a better world. Modernist planning arose in the context of the European avant-gardes as an attempt to develop alternatives to bourgeois capitalist society and consciousness. Its aim was subversive: to disrupt the imagery of what bourgeois society understood as the real and the natural, to defamiliarize the normative, moral, aesthetic, and familiar categories of social life. I have argued that its failures derive from the utopian nature of its counter-formulations, especially from its dehistoricizing and decontextualizing premises. Modernist projects such as Brasília tend to get caught in the contradictions of such formulations when they engage existing conditions for their realization, often exacerbating the very social and cultural discontents that motivate them.

We have seen that modernist intentions end up dialectically reversed with enough regularity that we are justified in repudiating their utopian project and demanding an alternative. Yet, the most interesting alternatives to appear recently seem similarly trapped in an unsatisfactory relation with history. The architectural historian Tafuri (1976, 1980) advances the most rigorously pessimistic of them. He maintains that under current global conditions of capitalism the architect cannot be a builder of revolutionary architecture, of exemplars of a future society. Denouncing the modernist conflation of the political and the aesthetic, he (1980: iii) writes that "one cannot 'anticipate' a class architecture (an architecture 'for a liberated society'); what is possible is the introduction of class criticism into architecture." Commenting on this text, Jameson (1985: 55) establishes the importance of Tafuri's position: "It follows, then, that . . . an architecture of the future will be concretely and practically possible only when the future has arrived, that is to say, after a total social revolution, a systematic transformation of this mode of production into something else." What Tafuri would eliminate from current architectural practice (and criticism) is the possibility of projecting alternative futures. Yet, without a utopian factor, are not plans likely to reproduce the oppressive status quo? Is not the elimination of desire for the future equally oppressive? Is not the notion of total revolution an indefinite postponement, as totalizing and self-perpetuating as the capitalist system it attacks?

Jameson's response to Tafuri is to call for a "Gramscian architecture" based on "an *enclave* theory of social transition" (1985: 70). He argues that the postmodern aesthetic of this architecture will generate a "new kind of perception" focused on contradiction and fragmentation which will (somehow) not slide over into the "stylistic fiat" of modernism (p. 86). This position seems difficult to maintain because, as Jameson himself admits, the notion that an architectural project could serve as an enclave of subversion to transform the social order around it is precisely one of modernism's fundamental premises. As the anthropological study of Brasília has shown, either such a project remains totally decontextualized, disconnected, and ahistorical; or, if it has history, its defamiliarizations are very likely to end in perversion. Moreover, whereas modernism had a vision of a desired alternative to embody architecturally, the fragmentations of postmodernism tend complacently to reflect the social fractures around it. While this lack of transcendence may paradoxically be one of its redeeming features, it would seem that in rejecting modernism, postmodernism also needs to reject its enclave theory of social transformation which is based on the transcendence of context.

A different and more common sort of postmodern critique has emerged in recent years, one that uses an image of the preindustrial city as its inspiration. It draws precisely on those features that modernism overturned: the discourse of reversals of the solid-void/figure-ground relations; the distinction of public monuments and civic institutions as exceptional, figural solids; the treatment of streets and squares as figural, roomlike spaces; the celebration of the outdoor public nature of these spaces at a pedestrian and not an automotive scale, the heroes of which are the consumer and the *flâneur* engaged in an unprogrammed enjoyment of the city (the image of Debret's "little capitalists" comes to mind; cf. fig. 4.15); nontotalizing, heterogeneous typologies of form and function; and the use of historical quotation in ornament to suggest a layering of historical context. Our discussion in previous chapters of all of these features has suggested their importance. However, the problem with their application in today's city is paradoxically a question of context: they are out of context in their nostalgic reference to (an imagined) social and economic order of the past. Colquhoun (1985: 116) captures this predicament in his comparison of modernist and postmodernist space: "Against this [the postmodern city] we must set not only the urban [modernist] utopias of 1920 to 1970, but also the actual modern city, where the image is one of chance, competition, profit, and corporate power"—not to mention class and race warfare. In its rejection of this actual city, the foundations of this nostalgic postmodernism are utopian; in its assumptions about the past in favor of the present, its utopias are a regressive response to the progressive utopias of modernism.

Both varieties of utopia run a similar risk: on the one hand, to remain disconnected from the conditions that generate a desire for them; on the other, to exacerbate the very issues they intend to negate. The study of Brasília demonstrates that these utopian paradoxes are coextensive and mutually reinforcing. Yet, it also suggests that without a utopian factor, plans remain locked in the prison-house of existing conditions. These conclusions leave me with an unsettling question at the end of this study: what possibilities are left for intellectual and artistic production that wants to retain an image of a better or different world with which to point to an emergent future?

For me, the reciprocal provocations of anthropology and modernism suggest that we need not attempt to resolve the paradoxes of planning and development, or devise schemes that supposedly do not have any. Rather, we might accept them and the tensions they create as constitutive elements in a critical perspective of the modern world. Nor, however, need we advocate what might be called the easy postmodernist way out which abandons the attempt to articulate alternative social-cultural visions. Instead, as social critics, we need to retain the kind of commitment to planning, to alternative futures, which acknowledges and even emphasizes the necessary dilemma of being caught between the utopian contradictions of imagining a better world and the unacceptability of reproducing the status quo. This is not a plea for a modernist type of rational domination of the future. It is rather the more modest suggestion that architects and planners learn to work with social analysis and to appropriate the social effects of their projects in the processes of planning, without imposing a teleology that disembodies history or abandoning the goal of new social and aesthetic possibilities. It is thus to conceive of planning as a dialectic of provocations between alternative futures and existing conditions which must hold fast to its inherent tensions; a project, moreover, which might be well informed by, and even a counterpart to, the kind of critical ethnography I have attempted here.

To that end, I have focused the study of Brasília's development from founding premises on the tensions between premise and paradox, between intention and interpretation. To grasp the significance of these tensions for contemporary society required that I analyze them from both historical and cross-class perspectives. For on the one hand, I found it impossible to understand the organization of either the elites in the Plano Piloto or the lower strata in the periphery without analyzing the history of their interactions; in fact, without seeing the organization of the one as in large measure a response to the organization of the other. On the other, I found that architecture is of special importance to Brasilienses largely because it expresses their differences and aspirations in a way legible to all groups in Brasília. The ethnography of the preceding chapters focused on the structures of premise and paradox to show how their insoluble problems are the conditions of their own subversion and transformation. In these processes, one may find clues to the alternatives of Brasília's future as a living city—alternatives that planners and architects may work with rather than attempt to impose.

At the conclusion of this study, I am aware that the complexity of these processes has also in some measure subverted my intentions to describe them—for my intentions as ethnographer also had a utopian factor, and I too constructed an imaginary city to explore. This was the city I made during fieldwork out of the social, historical, spatial, and architectural relations I found. For each of these relations, I erected a set of posts and strung a cord of different color until the cords became numerous enough to detect patterns. As I look back on the structure I made in this way, I know that it is stretched too tautly in some parts and too loosely in others; that it is only one version of what another would have done differently; and that, in a certain sense, it is already in ruins as the city it embodied at one moment has changed.

Notes

Chapter 1

1. Recently, a powerful and remarkable exception has appeared in Taussig's study of terror and healing. It explicitly sets out "to disrupt the imagery of natural order through which, in the name of the real, power exercises its domain . . . to work with a different conflation of modernism and the primitivism it conjures into life—namely, the carrying over into history of the principle of montage" (1987: xiv).

2. I have in mind, for example, an ethnography of American adolescence to interact with, and perhaps disrupt, Margaret Mead's study of Samoan youth; or of modern English concepts and uses of time to make sense of, or to debunk, Evans-Pritchard's (1940: 103) ungrounded, but potentially subversive claim that "Nuer are fortunate" because their lives are not ordered by an abstract and autonomous system of time. One notable exception is J. Favret-Saada's (1980) ethnography of witchcraft in contemporary rural France which explicitly engages Evans-Pritchard's study of witchcraft among the Azande, and which both enriches the Zande material and benefits from an interactive reading of it.

3. A growing number of ethnographies written in the context of first-world academic institutions address these concerns. Among the most stimulating for me have been Comaroff (1985), Nash (1979), Taussig (1980 and 1987), and Willis (1981). Produced in the same institutional milieu are the complementary theoretical discussions found in Clifford (1983), Clifford and Marcus (1986), and Rabinow (1985), in addition to works already mentioned. In this context, I should note Bourdieu's (1984) monograph on discrimination and taste in modern France. This work is pioneering in many ways among those studies of the developed West which do not treat culture as epiphenomenal superstructure. Nevertheless, its almost exclusive reliance on survey data would make most ethnographers uncomfortable.

4. I am not, however, counterposing against the hubris of master planning either an alternative notion of organic or natural growth in which cities somehow take care of themselves (a notion I criticize in a later chapter), or a celebration of commercialized urban sprawl (as Venturi suggests in his powerful endorsement of a vernacular, if complacent, free play of symbols in *Learning from Las Vegas*). In this sense, I do not doubt the importance of planning. Rather, I want to cut through such unsatisfying juxtapositions by historicizing and contex-

tualizing intention and plan, by taking the imposition of the Master Plan of Brasília as a planned event in 1957 from which developed both the orders and the disorders of the built city.

5. Two contextualizing issues I have not addressed are nineteenth-century Brazilian positivism and 1920s Brazilian modernism. The former contributed philosophically to notions of space, power, and national territorial sovereignty, notions that were important in legitimating the project of Brasília. A general text on this New World positivism is by Cruz Costa (1956). The latter is a fascinating subject about which a number of good studies have been written, including those by Martins (1969) and Lafetá (1974). One of its main concerns was to find new forms of Brazilian nationalism by combining European literary modernism with an appropriation of images from Brazilian and Amerindian folklore. Some of the foundational works in this project are Mário de Andrade's *Macunaíma* (1928) and Oswald de Andrade's *Manifesto da Poesia Pau-Brasil* (1924) and *Manifesto Antropófago* (1928). While of great interest to the history of ethnographic surrealism, Brasília's modernists, as architects and planners, had other concerns.

6. I should point out that intentions are not the same as beliefs and that a description of them is much less likely than one of beliefs to promote the author-anthropologist as the voice of culture (as in "The Nuer think . . . ").

7. For a discussion of their conceptions of this method see Held 1980: 183–87 and passim.

8. The average population density varies within this region: for Goiás, it is 6; for Mato Grosso do Sul, 4; for Mato Grosso, 1. As map 1.1 indicates, the anomaly is the Federal District with 218 persons per square kilometer. Since the map compares population density by state, however, it does not show that the district's density remains lower than that of all but one of Brazil's nine largest metropolitan regions. For example, the population density per square kilometer of São Paulo is 1,583; of Recife, 1,067; of Belo Horizonte, 693; and of Porto Alegre, 384 (Codeplan 1976: 17 and IBGE 1981b: 4–9, 14–16).

9. Unless otherwise noted, all translations are by the author. They are set into the text with the following conventions. Glosses of a given foreign word or phrase are enclosed in single quotation marks. Translated words are enclosed in double quotation marks when a bibliographic source is cited or, occasionally, to indicate that they are translations of Portuguese terms recorded in my fieldnotes.

10. I might note here that this rhetoric has been remarkably well internalized by all classes of people in Brasília: both of these phrases were given in interviews with, among others, an impoverished squatter living on the periphery of the city and a Bank of Brazil executive living in one of its elite neighborhoods.

11. It is beyond the scope of this study to evaluate the effects that the construction of Brasília may have had on the accelerating rate of inflation of the late fifties and early sixties. However, I should note that estimates of the costs involved vary considerably. Perhaps the most reliable one is given in ECLA's 1964 study of the Target Program: "It is difficult to calculate the amount invested in the construction of Brasília

for want of official figures. Those available, at current prices, were estimated by the Getúlio Vargas Foundation for the period between 1957 and mid-1962, as follows: [in millions of cruzeiros] public sector, 139,000; private sector—10,000; total, 149,000. At 1961 prices, this expenditure was calculated to be between 250,000 and 300,000 million cruzeiros [between U.S.\$926 million and 1 billion], which means that Brasília mobilized 2–3% of the gross domestic product for that period" (ECLA 1964: 171). However, using congressional reports, the journalist Vaitsman (1968: 87) claims that until the end of 1961 total expenditures amounted to much less: Cr\$81,805 million (U.S.\$303 million).

12. The portrayal of Brasília as a fantasy in the popular imagination comes across in a samba by Billy Blanco that became a hit in 1958: "I'm not going to Brasília, neither me nor my family, I'm not an Indian or anything; I don't have a pierced ear . . . Even to get rich with pockets full of money, I prefer to die poor without leaving Copacabana," i.e., Rio de Janeiro; cited in Mendes 1979: 121.

13. In the Federal District, 54.4% of the population 10 years of age and older is economically active as compared with 54.2% in the state of São Paulo and 49.7% nationally (IBGE 1981a: 21,437,619).

14. The 1980 census shows that among women 10 years of age and older 37.2% are economically active in the Federal District, 32.8% in São Paulo, and 26.9% in Brazil. Corresponding to the high percentage of working women in Brasília is the low proportion of those in the labor force between 10 and 14 years of age: 5.9% in Brasília as compared with 12.8% in São Paulo and 14.2% in Brazil (IBGE 1981a: 21,437,619).

15. The comparison with Sobradinho is even more revealing: 99% of its residences had sanitary sewage, 58% telephones, and 100% trash removal. Moreover, by 1983, 88% of its streets were paved and 75% had public lighting. Although Sobradinho is not Brasília's poorest satellite, its conditions are more typical of the capital's periphery than Ceilândia's.

16. The data for urban services in São Paulo are from IBGE 1984; in São Miguel Paulista, from Caldeira 1984; and in Ceilândia and Sobradinho, from Codeplan 1984. The division of São Paulo into eight areas of homogeneous socioeconomic characteristics derives from Seplan 1977.

17. I found out who held the highest positions in 1977 and then inquired as to where they lived and what jobs they held both before the change of government in 1974 and after the change in 1979. The Ministry of the Interior presents a typical example in the survey. Of those in the top 22 positions, 18 (82%) resided in Brasília before President Geisel took office in 1974 and 19 (86%) of them remained after President Figueiredo assumed power in 1979. In the latter transition, only four retained the same job. Of the 18 who changed jobs, 16 (89%) remained in Brasília and 15 (83%) remained in the highest echelons of government at other institutions. Furthermore, interviews with some of these superbureaucrats revealed that their decision to stay in the capital even when offered a similar job elsewhere was based on a strong preference for the conveniences of life in Brasília.

18. In fact, this distribution is even sharper than table 1.1 suggests: as studies presented in chap. 5 demonstrate, the average income per

residence in the Plano Piloto is three and one-half times, and in the lake suburbs five times, that of residences in the satellite cities.

19. Perquisites are normally awarded in varying measures to all officials holding a position of established rank in the federal bureaucracy. What makes Brasília's case scandalous is the quantity of butlerisms top-level bureaucrats receive. These officials are found principally in the executive institutions of government. They occupy what are officially called positions of Superior Supervision and Counsel (DAS), and constitute what is unofficially called "a caste of superfunctionaries." Little is publicly known about the organization of this "caste." The information that follows derives from my own investigations into the congressional record (published in the *Diário Oficial*); from the files of Congressman Maurício Fruet, who led a congressional campaign denouncing excessive *mordomias* in Brasília; and from the archives of the newspaper *O Estado de São Paulo*. There are six levels of DAS bureaucrats. The lowest level receives 13 minimum salaries per month—the same as the top salary for career bureaucrats under the merit system of the Department of Public Administration (DASP). The highest DAS level officially receives 30 minimum salaries. However, it is reported that DAS officials frequently hold multiple positions so that they commonly "earn" as much as 70 salaries. In addition, they receive considerable perquisites; in fact, most of Brasília's *mordomia* budget goes to them. In a series of reports, Congressman Fruet revealed that for 1981 the proposed budget of *mordomias* in Brasília just for the 15 ministries of state and for the presidency amounted to approximately U.S.$20,400,000. The significance of this figure becomes apparent in comparison to other aspects of the federal budget. In 1981, the proposed expenditures for the Ministry of Health for all federal health programs amounted to U.S.$3 per Brazilian. If we accept the estimate that there are about 5000 DAS bureaucrats in Brasília (the exact number is "unavailable"), then the city's 1981 *mordomia* budget for executive institutions provided U.S.$4,100 per DAS official!

Chapter 2

1. For a history of modern architecture and urban planning in Brazil, see Bruand 1981.

2. See chap. 3 for a discussion of the competition; see also Evenson 1973: 117–44 for a summary of the top five entries, all of which are of the CIAM type. These projects are published in *Módulo* 8 (1957) and *Habitat* 40–41, 42, and 45 (1957). Costa's Master Plan is published in *Módulo* 8 in Portuguese, Spanish, French, and English. These four versions were reissued as an offprint in *Módulo* 18 (1960) and have become the standard texts in their respective languages, reprinted in special editions by the Brazilian government and in professional journals. The English translation may be found, for example, in *Architectural Review* 122 (1957): 399–402. I use it for all of my citations of the Master Plan.

3. Readers unfamiliar with the history of modern architecture and city planning may find the following introductory references helpful:

for general studies, Banham 1960, Benevolo 1977, Frampton 1980, Hitchcock and Johnson 1966, and Jencks 1973; for manifestos and other primary documents, Conrads 1970; for urban planning, Benevolo 1967 and Fishman 1982; for studies of individual architects, Pevsner 1960. However, as I suggested in the previous chapter, readers should be aware that this literature is for the most part internal to the claims of modernist architecture. Readers should also note that as my focus is architecture and planning, I shall not as a rule cite works on other areas of modernism, about which there is an enormous scholarly, and often more critical, production.

4. For a general study of the Soviet case, see Kopp 1970. Also see Kreis 1980 on the "communal house" and its restructuring of domestic organization; Cohen 1981 and Starr 1981 on the relation between Le Corbusier and Soviet constructivism; and Lodder 1983 on the relation of the several art forms of constructivism (but with less focus on architecture) to modernism in Western Europe. For pre-Stalin primary sources, see Ginzburg 1982 [1928] (OSA Constructivism) and Lissitzky 1970 [1929] (ASNOVA Constructivism). For post-Stalin "modern functionalism," see Gutnov, et al. 1968.

5. The history of avant-garde contributions to CIAM may be found in the general studies of modern architecture and planning cited in this chapter. Girouard (1985: 233–54) provides an introduction to the importance of colonialism in the development of master planning. Rabinow (1986: 258–61) briefly discusses the significance of French urban planning in colonial North Africa, both in terms of the use of space for political control and in terms of new areas of anthropological research. For French urbanists at home, see Sutcliffe (1970), who provides a great deal of material on the planning of central Paris from 1850 to 1970. He sets the concept of Grand Design within the tensions of city government, reform movements, modernization, and conservation, evaluating its premises and consequences from its beginnings during the reign of Louis XVI, to its peak under Napoleon III and Haussmann, and its decline after 1914. Though he does not link this study with modernist planning, his documentation lets us understand the degree to which the modernists appropriated its planning instruments and strategies, as I shall discuss later.

6. Rabinow (1983: 277–78) suggests that the origins of the need for such articulation may be located toward the end of the previous century: "Partially under the spur of the defeat of 1870 and the Commune, Frenchmen concerned with such issues began to look abroad, and they found in Germany and England the beginnings of a new discipline, urbanism, which sought to combine the planning of space with political control based on a scientific understanding of society. It was to be a long time indeed before any comprehensive urban planning was done in France—really not until after the Second World War. But in the interim a good deal of discourse about the need for it was generated." See Vidler (1972) for a discussion of the urban utopias of late nineteenth-century France, around which a significant part of this discourse revolved.

7. See Jencks (1973: 37) for a revealing example of compromise in the 1928 resolution on the "redistribution of private property in land."

8. Brazil has been an important member of CIAM since 1930. During his 1929 lecture tour in São Paulo, Le Corbusier invited the "first" Brazilian modern architect, Ukrainian-Italian immigrant Gregori Warchavchik, to become CIAM's South American delegate (cf. Bruand 1981: 68). However, Brazil does not appear to have sent a representative to the 1933 Congress.

9. In her essay on Le Corbusier's Algiers project (1931–42), McLeod (1980) suggests what such political differences could mean in the conception of modernist city planning. She compares his first scheme (1932), proposed when he was immersed in the regional syndicalist movement, with his last scheme (1942), formulated under the auspices of the Vichy government. However, McLeod often accepts Le Corbusier's own terms for her analytic categories, and thus at times writes largely from within his dogma. This is especially the case in her use of the same biological analogies (e.g., organic, dynamic, cellular, and so forth) that Le Corbusier developed to describe the chaos of unplanned cities and the salvation of his plans (see Sutcliffe 1977: 227–31 on these medical metaphors and their application as well by French geographers and sociologists). Nevertheless, hers is one of the few detailed studies of a single project to examine seriously the modernist link between architecture and politics. From the perspective of Le Corbusier's overall career, Fishman (1977) covers the same years in discussing the relation between his political affiliations and his planning concepts.

10. An introductory account is given in Benevolo 1977, chap. 16. There are, however, several case studies that describe the political affiliations of various national groups. For German modernist architecture and planning, Lane 1968 and Taylor 1974; for Soviet, Kopp 1970, Miliutin 1974, and Gutnov, et al. 1968; for Dutch, Jaffé 1986; for Le Corbusier, Fishman 1977 and 1982: 182–257, and McLeod 1980.

11. The following discussion of the origins of city planning legislation draws on Benevolo 1967: 85–104 for a European overview, Sutcliffe 1970 for France, and essays in Sutcliffe 1980 for Britain.

12. Yet, even in this prescription, CIAM was developing rather than breaking with the various discourses of salvation that the Industrial Revolution had spawned. As E. P. Thompson (1967: 87, n. 102) notes with a citation from 1673, the mechanical had from early modern times been promoted as a model for the moral organization of life: "A wise and well skilled Christian should bring his matters into such order, that every ordinary duty should know his [sic] place, and all should be . . . as the parts of a Clock or other Engine, which must be all conjunct, and each right placed."

13. I should note that although the Radiant City is indeterminate and open in *form* like a modular system, each of its units is complete in terms of its four functions. In this sense, the machine rationality of CIAM overcomes the old oppositions between whole and part, city and individual building, and urbanism and architecture. Tafuri (1976: 105) suggests that in this "rigid process of planned production . . . the architectural object is completely dissolved." Discussing Hilberseimer's theories of the relation between the "urban organism as a whole" and the "elementary cell," Tafuri writes: "The single building is no longer

an 'object.' It is only the place in which the elementary assemblage of single cells assumes physical form. Since these cells are elements reproducible *ad infinitum*, they conceptually embody the prime structures of a production line that excludes the old concepts of 'place' or 'space' " (1976: 105).

14. For a sample of the Soviet modernists' attack on the family, one typical of their position from 1905 to 1930, see the statement by N. A. Miliutin accompanying figs. 3.1–3.4.

15. Of course, the modernists were neither the first nor the only ones to conceive of architecture as a means of social change. Architecture and utopia have been related in an instrumental manner in Western culture generally and Mediterranean culture specifically at least since the notion of the Garden (with its plan and structures) was associated with paradise both in Christian and in Islamic traditions.

16. For a discussion of Brecht's theory of *Verfremdung*, see Jameson 1972: 58–59. In this passage, Jameson contrasts Brecht's emphasis on historical and political change with Shklovsky's attention to literary change in the latter's comparable theory of *ostranenie*.

17. On the distinction between the private (or domestic-kinship) and the public (or juro-political) domains of social organization, see Kuper and Smith 1969: 38–39, 42–49, and 93–97. I do not use the terms public or public sphere to refer to the state. Although such identification is common, especially in political science, it seems to me that it may obfuscate the social and political processes by which a particular state may have subsumed the institutions that regulate the collective relations of a given society.

Chapter 3

1. For a classic study of the genealogy as a means of validating present circumstance, see Laura Bohannan, "A Genealogical Charter," *Africa* 22 (1952): 301–15.

2. The competition program stated that entries would be evaluated in relation to four "functional elements": (1) consideration of topographical data; (2) the size of the city, projected to accommodate a population of 500,000, in relation to population density; (3) integration of urban elements within the city; and (4) the relation of the city to the surrounding region. The complete program may be found in Portuguese in *Brasília* 3 (1957): 19–20.

3. The role in foundation mythology of a special place of origin is always crucial. For example, according to Malinowski (1954: 112–15), each Trobrian Island village (and especially its headman's house) is located near its spot of mythical origin. A heap of stones or a coral outcrop mark these spots out of which, as the myths relate, the first human couples emerged "and took possession of the lands, and gave the totemic, industrial, magical, and sociological character to the communities thus begun." In the case of the founding of Brasília in Costa's plan, the crossing of two axes at the center of Brazil marks a spot accorded an analogous status (see below, chap. 3).

4. For the distinctions between sign, icon, and index, see below and Lyons 1977: 99–109.

5. For a discussion of the Egyptian glyph and the Roman *templum*, see Rykwert 1976: 44–71 and 192–93.

6. Law 3273 of 1 October 1957 set the date of Brasília's inauguration. The date appears to have been chosen for its symbolic efficacy: 21 April is the Day of Tiradentes, commemorating the failed independence movement of 1789, known as the Inconfidência Mineira; 22 April is the Day of the Discovery of Brazil, commemorating Pedro Álvares Cabral's landfall in 1500 and his dedication of the "land of the Holy Cross" to the king of Portugal. Moreover, 21 April is one of the traditional dates of the founding of Rome. To commemorate this event and the analogy between Brasília and Rome, the Italian government presented the Brazilian government at the inaugural ceremonies with a freestanding column carrying the figures of the she-wolf suckling Romulus and Remus. The column was erected in front of the Municipal Administration Building. Thus, the selection of 21 April appropriates the significance of all of these legendary events for the inauguration of Brasília.

7. The typological inversion "palaces for the people" is commonplace in the architecture of social reform and utopian socialism. By the early nineteenth century, the royal palace provided the type form for numerous proposals of collective dwellings for the working classes, including Fourier's phalanstery and the workers barracks conceived by the architects of Napoleon III. In the early twentieth century, Soviet modernists adopted the palatial inversion, but not its form, for their workers clubs and cultural centers, calling them "palaces of labor"—an expression that Lissitzky (1970) suggested should more properly be applied to the new factories of socialist society.

8. Trotsky (1959: 3–4) was even more explicit in arguing for the necessity of a leap in the development process of "backward" countries: "The privilege of historic backwardness—and such a privilege exists—permits, or rather compels, the adoption of whatever is ready in advance of any specified date, skipping a whole series of intermediate stages. . . . Unevenness, the most general law of the historic process, reveals itself most sharply and complexly in the destiny of backward countries. Under the whip of external necessity their backward culture is compelled to make leaps. From the universal law of unevenness thus derives another law which . . . we may call the law of *combined development*—by which we mean a drawing together of the different stages of the journey, a combining of separate steps, an amalgam of archaic with more contemporary forms."

9. See the appendixes in Lissitzky 1970 for extensive documentation on the theories of development and the actual work of these architects in Russia. See also Benevolo 1977: 560.

10. For an analysis of these proposals, see McLeod 1980 and Tafuri 1976: 125–49.

11. The discussion that follows in the rest of this chapter illustrates an important but neglected aspect of development ideology in Brazil and the third world generally: that of the affinity between modernism and modernization. Although I am limited in this discussion to the

example of Brasília, it nevertheless suggests basic themes for a more comprehensive study of the topic.

12. For a concise description of the Target Program, see Jaguaribe 1968: 151–62; for a comprehensive account including compiled economic data, see ECLA 1964: 153–214. An in-depth exposition and analysis of the program is found in Lafer 1970, and a brief discussion of its reception by Brazil's political parties, especially the PSD and the PTB, in Benevides 1976: 213–20. The reader is also referred to M. L. Cardoso 1978 for a thematic analysis of Kubitschek's ideology of development.

13. Wheatley 1969; 1971: 411–76; and Geertz 1977; 1980: 13–19 and passim.

14. See Geertz 1977: 150–53 for a discussion of Shil's concept of charisma and its application to the theory of the exemplary center.

15. In terms of urban planning, this model derives from Le Corbusier's (1971b: 83–100) scheme to reorganize regional and national space in terms of a new paradigm of settlements. There are three types of settlements in this classification: agricultural farm units, linear settlements of industrial production that are stretched along major transportation lines, and radiocentric cities that function as administrative and distributive centers. In this paradigm, all cities are capitals; that is, they are solely administrative in function. They consist of the institutions of government, management, finance, education and art, and the services that they require. They are regional capitals, from which radiate lines of industrial and agricultural development. Thus, in terms of this modernist typology of settlements, Brasília is a typical city in that it has only one function, that of administration. Yet, as a capital of capitals, it is a model of the way all cities in the new paradigm of dispersed and concentrated populations should be organized.

16. Interview with Jayme de Assis Almeida, September 1982. The Working Group of Brasília, its proposals, and those of other commissions are discussed in chaps. 6 and 7.

17. Niemeyer, interview, August 1981; see Bruand 1981: 93 and 28, n. 43.

18. Epstein 1973 and Evenson 1973: 164–82 offer this type of explanation. Indeed, both Costa (1962: 339–40) and Niemeyer (1974: lxxxiii; 1980a: 46–47; 1983: 4) use such an argument when they maintain that their egalitarian intentions were perverted by "the capitalist society" that invaded Brasília and specifically by the bureaucratic-authoritarian regime that began its rule of the city and the nation in 1964.

Chapter 4

1. Le Corbusier proclaimed the death of the street in an article first published in the French syndicalist newspaper *L'Intransigeant* in 1929. A slightly different and expanded version was republished in the syndicalist review *Plans* 5 (May 1931). This version is reprinted in Le Corbusier's *Radiant City*.

2. The Crown's instructions of 1548 to Tomé de Sousa, first governor general of Brazil, contain stipulations with respect to the site selection and planning of urban settlements that recall earlier and later Spanish master plans. However, it was not until the period under consideration that a pattern emerged throughout Brazil of orthogonal planning with baroque embellishments, regularizing the architectural and planning conventions that concern us in this chapter. For an overview of Brazil's urban development as colony and empire, see Morse 1974. A study of city plans and planning in eighteenth-century Brazil may be found in Delson 1979.

3. See Schmitter 1971: 35–36 for a discussion of this point.

4. For a historical and morphological study of the square from antiquity to the nineteenth century, principally concerned with Europe but with some attention to the New World, see Zucker 1959.

5. Published in France between 1834 and 1839 as *Voyage Pittoresque et Historique au Brésil*, Debret's illustrations were the product of fifteen years of continuous research and documentation in Brazil. As a member of the French Artistic Mission invited by the Crown to found the Academy of Fine Arts, Debret arrived in 1816, eight years after the flight of the Portuguese court from Lisbon to Rio and one year after the elevation of Brazil to the status of a kingdom. When his work appeared, the official Brazilian Institute of History and Geography condemned it as "shocking that it should depict customs of slaves and scenes of popular life with such realism" (Debret 1978: 13). It is of course precisely this condemnation which confirms our interest in Debret's ethnography today.

6. Walsh wrote in 1830 that "old and respectable creole families . . . repaired to the capital, where frequent galas, levees, and birth-day ceremonies at court, attracted crowds together. Here, from mixing with strangers, both Portuguese and English, they soon rubbed off the rust of retirement, and returned home with new ideas and modes of life, which were again adopted by their neighbours" (cited in Morse 1974: 65).

7. In contemporary Brazilian cities that still feature the preindustrial pattern of solids and voids, the immediacy of contact between house and street distinguishes the *casa colonial*, 'colonial house' (a type referring to new as well as old houses), from the *casa moderna*, 'modern house'. It is perhaps an even more significant distinction than the one between pitched (colonial) and flat (modern) roofs. Thus, in these cities, Brazilians classify houses that have any space between their façades and the sidewalk as *tipo moderno*, 'the modern kind'. My study of this distinction confirms similar observations by Wagley (1963: 152) and Harris (1971: 30, 34).

8. People quite consciously experience the street and square as a room. For example, to indicate the place where people socialize in Rio, its inhabitants have the popular expression "the living room is in the street" (*a sala está na rua*). Or again, in his study of Rio's civic square (fig. 4.13), Ferrez (1978: 9) calls the Largo do Carmo (Praça XV) "for three centuries the parlor of our city" (*a sala de visitas*). Thus, the house and the city stand in a reiterative relation to each other, in which the rooms and corridors of the one are conceived of as a reiteration (in plan,

section, and elevation) of the squares and streets of the other. One of the earliest theoretical statements on this relation of house and city is found in Alberti's *Ten Books on Architecture*, a work which decisively influenced the design and conceptualization of Western cities after its publication in Italy in 1485. For a complementary analysis of the "house and the street" as domains of Brazilian society, see Da Matta's (1978: 70–95) insightful discussion.

9. The notion of convention in semiotic theory is discussed in Eco 1976 and Lyons 1977 (vol. 1): 99–109.

10. For an extremely useful analysis of the visual world in terms of these perceptual relations and others, see Arnheim 1974.

11. A classic discussion of the figure-ground relationship and its complexities is Ruben 1958.

12. With important exceptions that we shall consider in a moment, the blackened solids of the figure-ground plans of the preindustrial cities in figs. 4.21, 4.23, 4.24, and 4.25 do not represent *single* buildings. Rather, they represent entire blocks of many, *contiguous* buildings, none of which has an individuating shape in plan (with the exceptions noted). This representation should be compared to the modernist plan in which the blackened solids normally represent single buildings, each a freestanding object in space. This contrast is clearly shown in Le Corbusier's Plan Voisin (fig. 4.27). It presents both orders of solids and voids in the same drawing. Le Corbusier uses the figure-ground plan to emphasize the inversion of object-space relations in his plan for a new Paris as compared with that in the plan of old Paris. Note that each Cartesian cross in his new Paris represents a single building.

13. However, with some notable exceptions, it is not an essential feature of North American cities, where buildings tend to be freestanding in their lots and separated from the street by a front yard.

14. Population and gold statistics from Vasconcellos 1977: 35–36, 50.

15. The possibility of effacing the "old order" and inscribing a new one complements, at an architectural level, the possibility of a development leap proposed in the theory of the modernist city (discussed in sec. 3.3). It is this aesthetic of erasure and reinscription that makes modernist architecture especially appealing both to radical Right and to radical Left political ideologies.

16. Private buildings, especially bourgeois urban villas, become such monuments by using the figural conventions of public architecture for private aggrandizement. For the architectural basis of this appropriation, see the discussion above on the reversal of figure and ground as a means of transforming wealth into public display.

17. This relation between lexical proscription and physical elimination was made explicit in Le Corbusier's 1946 proposal: "The word *street* nowadays means chaotic circulation. Let us replace the word (and the thing itself) by the terms *footpath* and *automobile road* or *highway*" (Le Corbusier 1971b: 59).

18. The organization of the city into a Monumental Axis and a Residential Axis does not represent a public-private division. In Brasília, the Monumental and the Residential are different types of public spaces both sponsored by the state.

19. At the heart of the city, the axial crossing itself consists of a series of under- and overpasses creating a multilevel highway platform (fig. 2.7). Here, the high-speed center lanes of the Residential Axis pass under the Monumental Axis while the side lanes designated for local residential traffic pass over it. The two axes communicate through a series of ramps and cloverleaf interchanges. This assemblage of interconnecting speedways defines the area of the platform and constitutes its ceilings, floors, and walls. The platform is thus neither all building nor all roadway, but a carefully orchestrated fusion of the two. Its upper level contains parking lots and the Touring Club and features an unobstructed view of the eastern axis. On the west, it is contiguous with the Entertainment sectors, and on the east it provides stair access to the National Theater. Its lower level contains its prime function, that of the Interurban Bus Terminal, the hub of Brasília's commuter bus service between the Plano Piloto and the satellite cities.

20. Moreover, contrary to popular belief, most of the preinaugural settlers (construction workers, merchants, engineers, and administrative staff) were also from cities. See table 6.4, which shows that about 79% were urban migrants.

Chapter 5

1. Without doubt, the Monumental Axis, especially the eastern, federal half, is for Brasilienses the most memorable part of the city. In their reading of the city's form as an airplane, the plane's body is taken as a metaphor for the body politic of the city: its cockpit, the center of command, corresponds to the Plaza of the Three Powers; its fuselage, to the ministerial and service sectors; its tail section to the municipal administration ("at the back of the plane" politically); and, in the wings, with no voice along the axis of command, the residents in their *superquadras*.

2. In the Commercial Sector South, the rational address system has been altogether abandoned and replaced by a landmark-type system: buildings are named after companies and capitalists, states and statesmen, and the like. Thus, one finds the Antonio Venâncio Building, the Gilberto Salamão Building (named after local entrepreneurs), the President Dutra Building, the JK Building (for President Juscelino Kubitschek), the City Bank Building, the São Paulo Building, and so on. In other words, there has been a return to the use of buildings as monuments of individual privilege and of collective memory. Nevertheless, the result is a kind of oversubscribed "valley of the kings" in which so many monuments shoulder each other that it becomes very difficult to remember, identify, or even find one of them.

3. These functions are divided into approximately 80 sectors according to the most comprehensive survey of the city (Geipot 1975: 57). A full listing may be found in Holston 1986: table 5.2.

4. An example of this illusion of the plan is the way in which maps of the Plano Piloto (e.g., the one in Brasília's telephone directory) label the two strips of grass on either side of the Bus Terminal Platform as *praças*, 'squares'. These strips border the upper-level parking lots and

are visible in fig. 2.7. To my knowledge they are not used by human beings for any sort of activity. Nor are they identified in peoples' minds as particular places, certainly not as squares. The same deception occurs with the Square (*read* parking lot) of the Superior Tribunals. If such areas can be called squares, then one wonders about the impoverishment of architectural concepts—not to mention the quality of city life—in modernist planning.

5. For the purpose of understanding the organization of work in terms of the organization of space, the distribution of jobs available by locality is more revealing than that of employed population. While the latter distribution is the one usually given in statistical surveys, it is based on where people live and not where they work. It reveals that so many people living in a designated area are either employed or unemployed. It does not reveal where the jobs are located and thus the relative concentrations of activities in different areas.

6. For the study of the Federal District and especially of the Plano Piloto, we are fortunate in having a number of surveys conducted under the auspices of the Ministry of Transportation (Geipot) that are based on a division of the district into relatively small traffic zones (map 5.3, accompanying table 5.10). Within the Plano Piloto, these zones generally correspond exactly to the sectoral divisions of the city. They are therefore an ideal unit of survey for our purposes. Moreover, Geipot compiled two types of data based on these zones: a "diagnostic" set of conditions in the years 1973 and 1975, and a "prognostic" set for the year 2000. These sets thus compare actual conditions with planner's intentions and also give us a view of Brasília when it is fully built. In part, the prognostic set is based less on projections from the 1975 data than on an ideal model of the way Brasília ought to be organized. The ideality of this set of data is indicated by the fact that the composite projections for the year 2000 depend on the existence of six new satellite cities. These are to offer nothing less than 28% of the tertiary-sector jobs in the entire Federal District and are to be built in a mere twenty years. However, the projections for sectors within the Plano Piloto are more realistic, for they are based on the completion of construction already underway. In the relevant tables, I have correlated Geipot's traffic zones with Brasília's sectoral plan.

7. The variation between 1973 and 1975 of the proportion of Plano Piloto and Federal District jobs available in the Monumental sectors (table 5.4) may be explained by several factors. The 1973 figures reflect the transfer from Rio de Janeiro to Brasília between 1971 and 1973 of several enormous government agencies, including the Bank of Brazil and the Ministry of Foreign Relations, both of which are located in the Monumental sectors. At the same time, the early years of the decade brought significant development in the satellite cities. The 1975 figures show that the Residential sectors had expanded their local commercial services significantly during the two years to accommodate those just transferred, thus the percentage of Monumental-Sector jobs decreased from 71% to 58%. As the government was spending considerable sums building up the Residential sectors of the Plano Piloto, work in the satellite cities slowed. This slowdown accounts for the marked increases from 1973 to 1975 of both the Monumental and the Residential

sectors' portion of the total number of jobs in the Federal District (33% to 43% and 9% to 21%, respectively).

8. In the designated Commercial sectors one does not find retail establishments as one might expect, but the professional service sector of the city: the offices of architects, lawyers, accountants, and the like (what Brazilians call the "liberal professionals") and of local entrepreneurs, lobbyists, commercial and professional associations, real estate agencies, clinics, foreign banks, international organizations, and state enterprises. It is difficult to call this the private sector of the city because almost all of its jobs depend either indirectly or directly on state patronage. Rather, they are sectors in which anyone can rent an office and in which renters are generally those ineligible for offices in other Monumental sectors. With over 20% of the jobs, they are second in importance only to the sectors of the Esplanade of the Ministries as a place of work. Because they are populous and because the buildings of the Esplanade and Public Service sectors are not freely accessible to the public, the Commercial sectors also contain the city's informal market of goods and services, including those of fruit sellers, shoe shiners, and an assortment of pavement jewelers and craftsmen. However, this informal market functions precariously because the police never issue licenses for this type of activity and regularly chase out the unlicensed.

9. Cruzeiro Novo and Cruzeiro Velho (zones 57 and 56 on map 5.3) are primarily the places of residence for rank-and-file military personnel. Middle- and upper-echelon officers live elsewhere, mostly in *superquadras* affiliated with the Ministries of the Armed Forces.

10. In *The Radiant City*, Le Corbusier (1967 [1933]: 7) emphasizes this displacement of social institutions centered in the private sphere of social relations to a new state-sponsored sphere of collective services: "The dwelling unit must be considered as part of public services."

11. I am here referring to Lévi-Strauss's (1966) argument that certain peoples have used the natural differences between plant and animal species to differentiate human groups which are naturally similar. The use of plants and animals as "logical operators" to differentiate human kind is for Lévi-Strauss exemplary of the passage from nature to culture that such systems of classification achieve.

12. Table 5.14 in Holston 1986 presents an inventory of shops and services offered in the local commercial sectors at the time of the author's fieldwork to suggest the range of commerce associated with the *superquadras*.

13. We may note here that Brasília's interblock and neighborhood club are closely related in design and program to the workers' clubs associated with the new Soviet residential units and factories. See chap. 3, n. 7.

14. See Gardel 1967: 15–18, 62–88 for an account of the organization of *carnaval* and its relation to the city block and neighborhood.

15. Indeed, it is often reported that when these children move from Brasília, they have great difficulty adapting to the urban life of other Brazilian cities.

16. I should stress that initially income was not an issue of tenancy in either *superquadra* as all occupants, regardless of bureaucratic status,

paid a nominal "occupation tax" as rent. This tax was one of the means by which Brasília's planners hoped to prohibit the spatial stratification of different income groups, one of their radical intentions for the capital's residential organization. Although most of the apartments in SQS 108 were sold after 1965, and most in SQS 308 after 1971, table 5.11 suggests that they continue to house similar income groups.

17. I should note that all of the architects I interviewed, and all of the middle-class family apartments I studied in several Brazilian cities, confirmed this conventional organization of residential space.

18. I should add that I know of several cases of new house (but not apartment) construction which represent the beginnings of a change in the relation between the kitchen and the social areas. Usually called an "Americanization," this change involves eroding the separations between the two, as well as providing the kitchen with better ventilation, natural light, and views to the outside. It is an expression of the changing roles of middle-class women both within the house and without, which at least in this case owes much to the influence of North American family life-styles and feminist values. However, it is a change that does not include a rethinking of the servant quarters and work areas. Nor, in one case I investigated, was it carried out with the approval of the head of the construction crew who could not understand why anyone would want to devalue a house that way.

19. "The problem was no longer that of the family cell itself, but that of the group; it was no longer that of the individual lot but that of development" (Le Corbusier 1957 [1941]: 16).

20. Article 19 of the Master Plan reads: "The city's cemeteries . . . will be planted with grass lawns and suitably wooded. The gravestones will be simple, flat slabs as used in England, the idea being to avoid any sign of ostentation."

21. This figure-ground relation presents the same visual paradox that we found in the relation between the entire façade and the figural space of the street it frames: although the wall surface is physically terminated at each opening, the edges thus created belong visually to the apertures (the figures) and not to the wall (the ground). The reader is referred to the last chapter for a discussion of this paradox and its traditional solution of banding each aperture with a raised surface (i.e., door and window frames) behind which the wall can comfortably end. Such ornaments therefore have the important visual function of confirming both the figural character of the openings and the ground character of the wall surface.

22. As passage and barrier are fundamentally paired experiences, it may be the case that a particular opening makes us aware of the barrier of a wall. However, this association does not deny that walls primarily communicate barrier and openings the possibility of passage.

Chapter 6

1. The sources for this investigation reflect its combined character as anthropology and history. They include interviews with pioneers and

civil servants who were among the first recruited; published memoirs by pioneers of the construction epoch (Bahouth 1978, Kubitschek 1975, Mendes 1979, and Silva 1971); materials from the personal archives of key officials in the construction of the capital and the transfer of the government; documents from the archives of relevant government agencies; period newspaper and magazine articles; secondary studies (Bicalho 1978, Lins Ribeiro 1980, and etc.); and IBGE's 1959 population census of Brasília which like so much else planned for the new capital was experimental and innovative and designed to establish national guidelines.

2. The indirect administration consists of a miscellany of autonomous autarkies (foundations, agencies, institutions, departments, and services); state corporations; and mixed enterprises. The direct administration consists of the ministries, agencies, and commissions directly responsible to the president of the republic.

3. An executive agency, almost a superministry, the Administrative Department of Public Service (DASP) was created in 1938 to oversee the federal administrative system.

4. In this analysis, I shall draw on M. G. Smith's (1974: 182–92, 333–37 and passim) theoretical and comparative study of societal incorporation.

5. The concept of differential incorporation is useful in this case because it focuses our attention on the constitution of Brasília's public domain, the conditions under which people participate in it, and the criteria of legitimate social action. Smith (1974: 334) defines differential incorporation, distinguishing it from universalistic and consociational modes, as based on an individual's identification with "one or other of a series of closed collectivities which are ordered unequally as superior and inferior by their differential access to the public domain of the inclusive unit. Normally, one of these collectivities dominates the others and thus the society, by denying them access to the public domain and thus prescribing their political and legal subordination." Therefore, differential incorporation creates highly stratified polities, such as South Africa, of mutually exclusive and closed sections, ranked in terms of a differential distribution of juro-political status and social advantage. I should add that while differential incorporation has its own purely logical entailments and ideal conditions, none predetermines the actual distribution of political rights, the type of governing regime and its relation to society, or the specific principles of recruitment to social groups. These must all be determined by historical and ethnographic study.

6. It has been a source of much ambiguity in the debate surrounding Brasília whether the architects originally intended the city to include the construction workers. Niemeyer (1960: 22) resolutely maintains that the urban plan did in such statements as "It only saddened us to find out that it would be unfeasible to ensure the workers the standard of living assigned to them by the Master Plan, which situated them, as would have been only just, within the collective housing areas so as to allow their children to grow up in brotherhood with the other children of Brasília, without frustrations, fit for the new station that would be

theirs when in time the just claims of humanity were fully granted." However, I can find not a shred of evidence to support this claim about the Master Plan's intentions. As I have discussed in chap. 3, the plan does specify that all government functionaries—including those at the lowest echelons—should reside in the *superquadras*. Yet, however radical by Brazilian standards, this intention to create an equality of living conditions among public functionaries is a decidedly different matter than extending them to the citizenry at large and the industrial working classes in particular.

7. These and subsequent media citations from the construction period are from newspapers and magazines in the archives of the author.

8. The term *bandeirante* derives from military classification in medieval Portugal, in which a group of soldiers equal to the size of a company was called a *bandeira*, 'flag', after its distinctive banner.

9. See Esterci 1977; she analyzes the colonization and migration policies of the Estado Novo in terms of its legitimating ideologies. She gives a rather structuralist account of the significance of the *bandeirante* as a symbol of frontier democracy.

10. Thus, *candangos* delight in describing the way Kubitschek walked around the sites without police protection, gave an enormous barbecue for *candangos* at his improvised residence during which he embraced them and ate with them, and sent each worker employed at Novacap a "personal letter" on leaving the presidency to express his gratitude for their efforts. Actually, the letter I saw was mimeographed, but nevertheless the several *candangos* who showed me their copies considered each personal and had kept it for more than twenty years among their most intimate papers.

One of the *candangos* well-known among pioneers as "the man who received Juscelino" (at the airport) told me that when his twins were born in Brasília he let it be known that he wanted Kubitschek and an important engineer to be their godfathers. Both showed up at the baptism, but "when it was time to pay the priest for the service, Juscelino didn't have the money. He had to borrow it. Just like me, right? A man of the people!"

11. One of the most accessible studies of the Eastern European monumentalization of the construction worker may be seen in the recent Polish film *Man of Marble*, directed by Andrzej Wajda, about the fate of one such working-class hero. I appreciated the ironic lessons of this film even more because I saw it in Brasília. The twin statues in the Plaza of the Three Powers seen in fig. 4.4 are sometimes intentionally misnamed *The Candangos*. Officially, however, they are titled *The Warriors*. The only official commemoration to the *candangos*, let alone to the pioneers as a whole, is found in an auditorium at the University of Brasília that was named *Two Candangos* after two laborers who were killed during its construction by being, as the story goes, accidentally embalmed in its concrete foundations.

12. When we look at the migration profile in terms of the place of last residence, it is interesting to note that the majority of those who migrated indirectly to Brasília did so from the central west—a pattern

which may be explained by the fact that this region had become increasingly important since the 1940s as an area of internal colonization.

13. The migrants who reached Brasília under these conditions became known as the city's *pau-de-araras*, 'parrot-perches', because they made the journey in open trucks that were fitted with rows of benches upon which they sat holding on to a rail overhead.

14. In newspaper clippings from 1960 cited in Lins Ribeiro (1980: 22), these recruiters are described as slave-traders; for example: "Subcontractors, ranchers and even families, when they wanted to buy Northeasterners, went to the trucks and made a deal. The prices varied between U.S.$3.00 and U.S.$10.00 in accordance with the physical condition of each. . . . In the act of the sale, the driver delivered to the buyer the documents of this strange merchandise (work card, birth certificate, etc.) and the Northeasterners became the slaves of their buyers. When they asked for wages, the owners claimed that they had paid their passage to the driver that brought them and that they would have to work until they paid off the debt—which was never."

15. This concession of lots in the Free City was one of the first acts of the Administrative Council of Novacap. It was announced in *Boletim*, no. 1, of Novacap, January 1957, under "Acts of the Council" and "authorize[d] the Directorate [of Novacap] to prepare, for the period of four years, leases for installations, in precarious title, of industries necessary to the construction of the New Capital, and of local commerce, realizing contracts of accommodation for this end" (cited in Silva 1971: 111).

16. Table 6.5 has been compiled from data collected in the *Experimental Census of Brasília, 1959*. In some instances, the categories of the census are not identical to the ones I have used in my classification of pioneers. In these cases, my figures derive from cross-tabulations based on reasonable but ultimately unverifiable assumptions. For example, although the census does not distinguish between public and private sector liberal professionals, it does distinguish the settlements in which they lived. To arrive at the number of private sector professionals, I subtracted from the totals the data pertaining to those professionals living in the camps of Novacap and the Social Security Institutes and those listed under the category of public administration living elsewhere. With regard to income, the census presents its data in terms of median income, classifying the total economically active population and the population of each category of economic activity into ten income brackets. For the total, it gives separate income data on employees, the self-employed, and employers. Unfortunately, only for services and retail trade does it list the income distributions of all three. For the remaining eight categories of activity, it lists the distribution of the total and of the employees, and in four of the cases it also lists the self-employed. Fortunately, however, the census elsewhere gives the number of employees, self-employed, and employers in each category. To estimate the income of the latter two in the categories in which they are not given, I used the following method. Based on the fact that the reported median monthly income for the total number of employers is

Cr$19.70, the highest of the three and over three times higher than that for employees, and that the income for the total number of the self-employed is Cr$5.90, the lowest of the three, I assumed that the "missing" employers were contained in the top income brackets of the unaccounted total for each category of activity and that the "missing" self-employed were in the bottom brackets. As the number of employers and self-employed is known for each, I counted half the number of the former from the top and half the number of the latter from the bottom to arrive at the median income bracket. Within this bracket, I assumed an equal distribution to estimate the median income. Thus, the income estimates especially cannot be viewed as "hard" data. Nevertheless, their distribution appears consistent with expectations based on other criteria (i.e., an analysis of rights and privileges), and therefore to lend support to the proposed classification. At the very least, it indicates the range of income differences between the three subdivisions of pioneers.

17. Through the hospital of the Institute of Retirement and Pensions for Industrial Employees (IAPI), the government provided health services for all of the pioneers who were registered, depending on their sector of employment, with any of the various Social Security Institutes. Therefore, the provision of health services should not be seen as a benefit offered by the construction firms to which workers had a right by virtue of their employment. However, free transportation to the work site may be viewed as such a benefit, albeit a relatively inconsequential one as the work camps were almost always located in the immediate vicinity of the work sites. Nevertheless, rather than worker benefits, it may be better in this situation to understand the provision of both medical and transportation services as means developed by the private firms and the state to ensure the productivity of their labor force, by securing its fitness for work, punctuality, attendance on the job, and the like. In this sense, these services are cost reduction mechanisms benefiting employers. I have little doubt that without them Novacap and the firms would still have been able to recruit an equal number of workers, but that they would have had much greater difficulties meeting their project deadlines.

18. It is indeed difficult to establish more exactly the comparative worth of this income in national or even regional terms, both for lack of data and for the problems inherent in determining the comparability of those data available. For example, if we try to compare it with the monthly income estimates calculated by Fishlow (1973: table 3.3) for urban employees in several regions of Brazil in August 1960, we must make two difficult assumptions. As my estimates refer to median income and Fishlow's to mean income, we must first assume that the two are comparable. Due to the nature of the sample populations involved, such a comparison is probably unreasonable. Second, to make the comparison, I must inflate my May 1959 figures to August 1960 values (or vice versa) by an appropriate index (such as the consumer price or the wholesale price index), which assumes an equivalence of the baskets of goods and services the two sets of income cover that we know to be false in the case of the camp construction

workers. It may be possible to correct for this difference by increasing the consumer price index by 80% in that specific case. If we make these assumptions, we arrive at the following comparisons between the income of Brasília's construction and agricultural employees and that of urban and rural employees elsewhere. I give these comparisons, for their suggestive value, as the percent by which the income of Brasília's workers is above (+) or below (−) that of others in each of the following regions. For Brazil as a whole: (1) Brasília's construction employees = +114%, (2) its agricultural employees = +77%. For the northeast region: (1) Brasília's construction employees = +256%, (2) its agricultural employees = +130%. For Guanabara state and Rio de Janeiro: (1) Brasília's construction employees = +56%, (2) its agricultural employees = +53%. For São Paulo state: (1) Brasília's construction employees = +84%, (2) its agricultural employees = +35%. Regrettably, I cannot give comparative data for the employers and the self-employed using Fishlow's study because it conflates the two categories.

19. Moreover, a 1958 national labor ordinance required industrial firms employing more than 100 workers to establish internal committees for accident protection, known as CIPAs. It appears that none was established in preinaugural Brasília.

20. In his history of Brasília, Silva (1971: 259) notes: "During the construction of Brasília, Novacap did not have a Justice Department. To speak frankly, the Department was organized at the end of 1959, but only really functioned after the move [inauguration]. Novacap had in its services only one lawyer . . . and one Counselor. One day, [the lawyer] brought to the attention of Israel [Pinheiro, the president of Novacap] a certain clause in a particular contract. Dr. Israel replied: 'Look here, I want a lawyer to help me and not to complicate things. To comply with what is in the Law, I don't need a lawyer; I am going to carry on without your opinions. What I need a lawyer for is to justify what is not clear in the Law.' "

21. Racial type—or "color" as it is measured in the census survey (IBGE 1959: 19–21)—must be considered a weak class indicator in Brasília during the construction period because those classified as white (55% of the total) constituted at least an absolute majority of the population in all but three localities in the territory: in Planaltina (50%), in the rural zone (48%), and in the largest squatter settlement, Vila Amaury (41%). Thus, even though census color classifications are notoriously unreliable in Brazil, it seems evident that the majority of *candangos* were classified white. Nevertheless, there existed a secondary correlation between color and status as the highest concentration of whites occurred at Novacap headquarters (76%), while the highest concentration of both blacks and browns occurred in Vila Amaury. Moreover, there was a significantly higher proportion of whites among the female population than among the males in all localities except the Free City, while the opposite was the case among blacks. For example, in the south zone of the Plano Piloto, 70% of the women and 54% of the men were white. Such proportions suggest that whites were more

likely than others to have the privilege of residing with their families, a distribution of privilege that may correlate with the fact that "doctors" were far more likely to be white. Thus, a much more explicit correlation between color and status probably existed for women and children than for men.

22. Mendes (1979: 87) gives an example of a "doctors' " cook who was beaten up by fellow *candangos* for "putting on airs."

23. The worst food riot occurred on the Sunday night of *carnaval* in 1959. It became known as the Massacre of Pacheco Fernandes after the construction company in whose canteen it occurred. The security forces responded by machine-gunning an unknown number of men (perhaps one, perhaps forty) who were hastily buried in an unmarked grave somewhere in the *cerrado* around Planaltina according to unofficial reports (*Jornal do Brasil*, 18 February 1968: 26). Many workers felt aggrieved enough to attend meetings of the association of construction workers to condemn the action. Even though the association's call for justice did not produce an official inquest, it was able to use the event to legitimate its mission and strengthen its membership.

24. As we might expect, there was some ambiguity in the distribution: occasionally, the firms also provided houses for some of their job foremen, master tradesmen, and even a few of their senior skilled workers.

25. I should note here that the importance of the union increased dramatically among construction workers as working conditions (especially employment, wages, and overtime) deteriorated after Brasília's inauguration. These conditions hit rock-bottom in the period 1961–64 (see graph 5.2), initiating a period of increasingly turbulent relations between government and labor until the military coup of 1964 stifled dissent.

26. In this case, we may consider economic power to be reflected essentially in income although it may be the consequence of power existing on other than economic grounds.

27. The census classified coresidents as members of family households if they were related by kinship ties, either as consanguineals or affines.

28. The role of these institutes in the construction of Brasília constitutes an interesting development in the history of the Brazilian social insurance system, which to my knowledge is not discussed in the major sources on the subject. I am referring to the full-length study by Malloy (1979) and to the discussions of the social insurance administration in Graham (1968) and Lafer (1970), all in English. Brazilian sources I have consulted on these topics include Celso Barroso Leite and Luiz Paranhos Velloso, *Previdência Social* (Rio de Janeiro: Zahar, 1963), and several other works by the first author.

29. See Malloy 1979: passim, for a comprehensive view of this insurance system in its political context, and especially pp. 83–115 for the period 1945–64.

30. The ratio of political appointees to career service bureaucrats in the institutes appears unavailable. However, Graham (1968: 129) cites a report prepared by DASP in July 1961 which estimates that of the total

of 300,000 federal civil servants, only 15% had been admitted through public examinations.

31. By public sector employee, I mean a person who works for a federal, state, or municipal organization but whose position in that specific employment is not that of a civil servant (although he or she may hold that status in another situation). I use the term 'civil servant' (*servidor civil*) to refer to those who occupy a legally defined position in the government as specified in the bureaucracy's classification plan. In the case of preinaugural Brasília, this plan was the Law of Readjustment (Law 284) of 1936, in effect until 1960, when Congress passed a new classification plan. The term civil servant covers several categories of officials distinguished by the manner in which they occupy their positions. Thus, a public sector employee is someone who works for a government organization in a job that has no classificatory status in the federal, state, or local bureaucracy.

32. In this profile, poverty is defined in terms of the real minimum wage for 1960 in the northeast, the poorest region of Brazil, which is taken as the lower limit of acceptable income for a family of 4.3 persons (Fishlow 1972: 393).

Chapter 7

1. According to several reports, this second subterfuge may have been concocted by Free City entrepreneurs in league with association leaders (interviews, Brasília, 1981; also suggested in Silva [1971: 231–33] and reported in the *Correio do Povo* [Porto Alegre, 17 August 1958, cited in Lins Ribeiro 1980: 180]). The merchants stood to gain substantially in the sale to squatters not only of building materials and subsistence items but even more of "property rights." In what seems like transparent fraud, they reportedly marked off the best sites along the highway and sold their "stakes" to latecomers for considerable sums of cash. This type of thievery has become increasingly common in Brazil's major cities. Such illegal residential allotments are called *loteamentos grilados*, and their illicit realtors, *grileiros*. See Caldeira (1984: 13–29) for a concise discussion of the development of São Paulo's periphery and especially of its various conditions of illegality.

2. Officials frequently assert that the placement of the satellite cities at considerable distances from the Plano Piloto was based on purely ecological considerations (interviews, Brasília, 1980–82). They maintain that the cities were located in areas outside of the watershed of Lake Paranoá so that their sewage would not pollute the Plano Piloto's recreational waterway and limnological environment. However, as of 1982, the lake remains in a highly polluted and mephitic condition not because of the excesses of the satellite cities but because of the dumping of raw waste principally from residential areas surrounding the lake: the North Wing of the Plano Piloto itself, the elite North Lake, the near suburb Guará, and Núcleo Bandeirante. Moreover, as of 1977, neither of the two existing sewage treatment plants in the Plano Piloto (one in the South and one in the North Wing) had been completed. As a result,

they continued to dump only partially treated waste from the rest of the Plano Piloto into the lake (*PEOT* 1977: vol. 1, 87).

3. Novacap's intentions in creating the settlement are documented in congressional testimony, November 1959 (*Diário de Brasília* 1959: 282).

4. By May 1959, the Vila Amaury had 6,200 residents (IBGE 1959: 79). As it was the only squatter-type settlement surveyed in preinaugural Brasília, its demographic characteristics suggest what conditions may have been like in the others. In almost all aspects, it was unlike the settlements of officially recruited migrants (i.e., the construction camps and the Free City). At 35%, its economically active population was the lowest of any surveyed in the Plano Piloto, but similar to that of the distant Planaltina (31%), Brazlândia (33%), and the new satellite Taguatinga (31%). Of its employed residents, 62% were in construction, 18% in services, and 7% in commerce (ibid., 54). At most, 7% were employees of Novacap (ibid., 58). Unlike the neighboring construction camps, Vila Amaury approached a balanced ratio of men to women, comparable to that of the preexisting and other authorized settlements. Moreover, 99% of its residents lived in family households, similar in this respect to the outlying cities of Taguatinga, Planaltina, and Brazlândia (ibid., 68). Of the dwellings, 82% were shacks made of nonmasonry materials or unfinished wood. In terms of infrastructural facilities, 72% of its residences had no local water supply (compared to 34% in the Free City, the next "driest"); almost 70% had no sewage installations of any kind beyond rudimentary ditches (compared to 35% in the next least sanitary); and 95% did not have electricity (compared to 54% in the Free City, the next least illuminated)(ibid., 73). Finally, 88% of the dwellings in Vila Amaury were owned by someone living in them. This figure should be compared with that of 81% for Brazlândia, indicating the absence of real estate speculation in rentals in both cases (one for reason of impermanence, the other for reason of remoteness); and at the other extreme with that of 36% in the Free City, indicating here the effects of such speculation (ibid., 107).

5. In addition, the association argued that since the inhabitants of Vila Amaury could not afford to move, Novacap had to assist them with the following: trucks to carry their shacks and possessions; carpenters to dismantle and reassemble their houses; temporary lodging in the new satellite; unemployment compensation for the time required to move and set up new residences; medical assistance; and last, dependable transportation to and from the satellite so that people could continue to work in the Plano Piloto.

6. For examples of this type of political patronage in other cities, see Diniz 1982: 64–72; Santos 1981: 89, n. 12; and Perlman 1976: 50. In the case of squatter settlements, it should be noted that this type of patronage tends to be personalistic, depending on informal networks of specific individuals, and not patronage based on formal party sponsorship.

7. Law 3751 of 13 April 1960 gave the administration sweeping powers to implant and administer the satellite cities of the Federal District. By May, it had used these powers to inaugurate Sobradinho and to initiate plans for a third satellite city, Gama, 38 kilometers south of the Plano Piloto.

8. In the following discussion, the names Free City and Núcleo Bandeirante refer to the same settlement. The former was its unofficial designation, the latter its official. Following the *unofficial* custom of the times, I use Free City to refer to this settlement before it achieved legal status as a satellite city, and Núcleo Bandeirante to refer to it after this change.

9. Bernardo Sayão was one of the three founding directors of Novacap. Even before Brasília, during Vargas's agricultural colonization of the central west, he had become legendary as an indefatigable pioneer, an "opener of the wilderness." In 1958, President Kubitschek placed him in charge of one of his major development projects: cutting the Belém-Brasília highway through the Amazon forest. In January 1959, only 31 kilometers from his destination, Sayão was struck dead by a gigantic tree. Many *candangos* believed that his death occurred in mysterious circumstances, and to this day tell bizarre stories about the "revenge of the forest" that killed him. His death shocked Brasília. It is reported that the day of his funeral was the only day that the construction of the city ever stopped. The *candangos* revered him as a true pioneer and thus as the appropriate eponym of the Free City.

10. The "proprietor of improvements" is thus called because one could not own the land, only the improvements on it (such as buildings).

11. From *A Tribuna,* 20 September 1959. I thank Gustavo Lins Ribeiro for providing me with this list of demands.

12. As I have emphasized the importance of names and naming in these urban movements, it is interesting to note that as the Quadros government became the anticipated hero of the fixation struggle, residents of the city circulated a proposal to change the name of its main street from Central Avenue to Broom Avenue, the broom being the symbol of Quadros's presidential campaign (to "sweep out corruption").

13. Throughout Brazil, the terms "urbanization" and "to urbanize" commonly denote the provision of services such as potable water, sewage, trash removal, paving, and electricity.

14. For example, it was rumored that the administration had gone to Sumoc (the Superintendency for Monetary Coordination) to request the closing of the city's banks; that it planned to cut bus service with the Plano Piloto; that it intended to transfer the city's auto repair sector, one of its most important, to the western end of the Plano Piloto; and that it had designated the market, the bus station, and the movie theaters for demolition. In Congress, these events and rumored events were intensely debated, if one may judge from speeches reported in the congressional record of the period. The profixation forces continued to be led by PSB deputy Breno da Silveira, who in the heat of the debate actually came to blows with another congressman over the issue.

15. In September 1960, the Free City registered 21,033 inhabitants, an increase of 82% over the previous census of May 1959. However, by September 1961, the concerted destabilization efforts of the administration had reduced the population to 15,000.

16. See Skidmore 1967: 200–302, and especially 200–215, for an account of Goulart's situation during the period under discussion.

17. We should note that in the case of the mobilizations of elite Novacap and Social Security Institute officials, the specific organizations required to carry them out also dissolved as soon as the government formally accepted their usurpations.

18. The following are among the better case studies of such residential conditions: for Rio de Janeiro, Chinelli 1980, Perlman 1976, Santos 1981, Valladares 1978, and Zaluar 1985; for São Paulo, Bonduki 1983 and Caldeira 1984; and for Salvador, Brandão 1979. A useful review of the literature is found in Valladares 1982. It is important to note that in other Brazilian cities squatting is only one of several types of illegal land occupation found among the poor. If squatting is defined by the occupation of land to which the resident has no legal claim whatsoever either as owner or tenant, the others include fraudulent sales (*loteamento grilado*), illegal subdivisions (*loteamento clandestino*), and unapproved constructions (*construção clandestina*). In her study of São Paulo's periphery, Caldeira (1984: 23) notes that these forms of illegality characterize approximately half the allotments of the greater metropolitan region. Therefore, she concludes that "as paradoxical as it may seem, it is exactly this condition of 'illegality' that ends up making lots accessible to the lower-income groups of the population." Moreover, as she and others show, all of these forms motivate residents to organize for legal rights.

19. See Santos (1981: 75–83) for a detailed description of the demise of the Residents' Association of Brás de Pina in such circumstances.

20. Nevertheless, I should note that according to data summarized in Valladares (1982: 29) 50% of Rio's squatter settlements in 1964 and 44% of São Paulo's in 1974 were located on public lands.

21. The argument for political tranquillity was waged on several fronts. In discourses of the day among legislators, politicians, and planners, it was also advanced to exclude industry from the city and thus not only the labor conflicts but the very presence of an industrialized proletariat. Moreover, it appears that initially some government planners, though not Lúcio Costa, were against the idea of creating a university in Brasília for fear of disruptive student demonstrations.

22. Law 3751 of 13 April 1960, known as the Santiago Dantas Law after its principal author.

23. The law gave the prefect the power of veto over all council legislation while denying the council the requisite authority to overturn it. Instead, it determined that a vetoed bill would be submitted to a special senate commission for final ratification or rejection.

24. To augment the prefecture's executive capacities, Law 3751 gave it control of 51% of the shares of the state enterprise Novacap. Moreover, it gave the prefect the authority to fill all of its executive offices and the power to dismiss its president. This transfer brought the prefecture considerable resources, for at the time Novacap had 20 departments and a staff of almost 1,400.

25. The central administration has maintained this double identity under both democratic and military regimes. Under military dictatorship, Law 4545 (December 1964) was enacted to restructure the administrative organization of the Federal District. The law created eight administrative regions, each under a regional administrator appointed

directly by the governor of the district (map 1.3): AR I, Brasília (including the Plano Piloto, its elite suburbs South Lake, North Lake, and Parkway Mansions, Núcleo Bandeirante, Cruzeiro, and Guará I and II); AR II, Gama; AR III, Taguatinga (including Ceilândia); AR IV, Brazlândia; AR V, Sobradinho; AR VI, Planaltina; AR VII, Paranoá; and AR VIII, Jardim. Of the eight regional administrations, three have never been implemented: the two rural regions, AR VII (subordinated under Gama) and AR VIII (subordinated under Brazlândia); and, most important, AR I, Brasília itself, which is administered by the governor's Secretary of Roads and Works. On the essential issues of autonomy, autocephaly, and representation in local government, the new law changed some of the labels (prefect = governor, subprefecture = regional administration, and so forth) but therefore kept the existing arrangements in place.

26. These figures are estimates based on various surveys I conducted in 1980–82.

27. When Novacap was incorporated into the prefecture, all of the employees of this statutory body were given the opportunity to join the federal civil service. As Novacap's managers had already appropriated accommodations in the Plano Piloto, this transformation of status legitimated their residence in the government houses.

28. Among those in the periphery, Novacap's 1,200 workers constituted a partial exception to the eligibility rules concerning residence. Along with their managers, they had had the opportunity to join the prefecture and gain civil service rank, but they were nonetheless excluded from the Plano Piloto. Their case represents only a partial exception because in distributing residences in the Plano Piloto the GTB gave priority to those it transferred from Rio whereas Novacap's workers had migrated on their own account.

29. On the issue of choice and rights, Lúcio Costa had been adamant. In a letter to the president of Novacap in 1961, he protested the decision to construct low-income houses for lower-echelon civil servants at the western end of the Monumental Axis in what is today Cruzeiro: "No [civil] servant should live outside of the residential area concentrated along the Residential Axis [i.e., in the *superquadras*]; if he does so, it should be out of his own wish or initiative, not compelled by circumstances" (Costa 1962: 340).

30. This restriction does not mean that there were no professionals in private practice in the Plano Piloto; only that their primary work affiliation was with a public institution.

31. This information derives from interviews with the head of the real estate department of Sobradinho's regional administration (June 1981), from archival research in his office, and from copies of original lot contracts obtained there.

32. Purchase of either residential or commercial property was limited to one lot per person. This restriction applied not only within each satellite city but moreover within the entire Federal District. Thus, those who had lots in one satellite could not acquire them in another. Significantly, however, those who had renters' rights to government dwellings in the Plano Piloto (which could not be bought) were *not* prohibited from purchasing lots in the satellite cities.

33. Lots sold for approximately U.S.$50, with a downpayment of about U.S.$2.50. The rest had to be paid in 34 monthly installments of about U.S.$1.30 (without interest or correction for inflation, an important advantage for those who purchased before rates were added in 1967). In effect, the prospective purchaser opened an account with Novacap, the legal proprietor. The prospective owner then had to pay to Novacap all taxes, service charges, and fines resulting from mandatory upkeep and improvements, even though the property remained in Novacap's name for the duration of the contract. If the prospective purchaser fell behind in any of the payments, Novacap would pay the account and charge a penalty.

34. To avoid real estate speculation Novacap initially prohibited the transfer of contractual rights to another party. However, this rule was changed, apparently in 1966, to permit transfers to third parties, but only at the original contract price and with Novacap's written consent. Moreover, to deter transfers and to insure that unstable marital bonds would not result in family members' being put out of their house if the head of household abandoned them, both the contract and the final title were made out in the name of the family.

Chapter 8

1. The one exception to this pattern was the depopulation of Núcleo Bandeirante after it won legal status as a satellite city. Its depopulation was the result of a master plan approved for its urbanization in 1965. According to sources cited in Epstein (1973: 79–80), officials estimated that this plan provided residential lots for only 37% of the city's residents. The rest were to make their homes elsewhere, i.e., in the other satellite cities. In keeping with the "spirit of Brasília," the plan accomplished this depopulation by combining status criteria for lot acquisition with a strict enforcement of the promissory contract for masonry construction on the lots. Between 1960 and 1970, the city's population declined by almost 50% while the other satellites were more than tripling theirs.

2. "In this way, the Plano Piloto and the existing peripheral nuclei [i.e., the satellite cities], maintained with their current characteristics of occupation (residential typology and net density), will have the capacity to absorb, at saturation levels, approximately 55% of the 2,400,000 inhabitants anticipated, so that the remaining 45% . . . constitutes a population to be placed in new nuclei" (PEOT 1977: vol. 1, 121–22).

3. Interview, Brasília, August 1982. It is worth mentioning that according to the secretary, the project incorporates a number of suggestions from Lúcio Costa, who reviewed it without major objection in his capacity as consultant to the GDF on matters of urban planning.

4. Jornal de Brasília, 2 October 1981. However, the 1980 national census reports that there are only 12,384 people residing in six land seizures (IBGE 1981c: 11). Surpassing this estimate, the Office of Social Services (GDF 1982: 8) states that in an undisclosed number of settlements the total population of squatters in the Federal District reached 27,015 in 1977 and 93,000 in 1982!

5. In fact, there are several utopian communities in the rural zone of the Federal District and in nearby Goiás to which the squatter settlements should be contrasted. The former are mostly millenarian and curing cults of varying fanaticism such as the Cidade Eclética and the Vale do Amanhecer. The social, religious, and economic orders that they construct are proposed as alternatives to the very society that the squatters want to join. However, even in these ostensibly alternative social orders, the symbolic codes of society's dominant institutions often appear as organizing metaphors (Holston 1982, field data).

6. Because they live in an illegal settlement, the residents of Chaparral cannot open accounts directly with the electric company. Instead, they must pay higher rates than normal for the service. They buy electricity from an entrepreneur in Taguatinga who charges by the number of outlets in a shack, regardless of how much wattage is used. As is common in such situations, the entrepreneur had a meter legally installed on a spot of urbanized land not far from the main entrance to Chaparral, from which he sells the electricity to the squatters.

7. For example, a small wooden shack measuring 10×20 feet sold in 1981 for about U.S.$765 whereas a similar shack in a squatter settlement near Núcleo Bandeirante went for three times that amount. The higher price of the latter was due to its proximity to the employment sources of the Plano Piloto. Similarly, there is a correlation in the rental market of illegal settlements between rent and distance from the Plano Piloto, exactly as in the official market: on average, during the time I did fieldwork, a one-room shack in a land seizure in Núcleo Bandeirante rented for U.S.$40 a month, in Sobradinho for U.S.$30, and in Gama for U.S.$20.

8. Everywhere in Brazil, it is common practice for squatter settlements to model their organizations on those of society's dominant institutions. Gardel (1967) gives a detailed description of how the famous *samba* schools and clubs of Rio de Janeiro's *favelas* are organized on the model of legal corporations. Zaluar (1985: 173–217) analyzes the relation between residential associations and *samba* clubs among the former squatters of Cidade de Deus in Rio, the relation between the cultural and political activities of these organizations, and their articulation with the bureaucratic institutions of city government. In her survey of 103 squatter associations in Rio, Diniz (1982: 44) notes that she found a "certain degree of standardization" in their organizational structure, "since the statutes [registered documents for the most part] of the squatter associations follow criteria defined by legislation that regulated the conditions of their recognition by the State." In São Paulo, the statutes of the Neighborhood Friends' Associations are based on a single model written by the Department of Social Promotion of the City of São Paulo, and only those associations that adopt this model can be officially recognized.

9. These inexpensive, government-issue houses are by statute 68 m^2 or less (recently raised from 60 m^2) although in the mid-sixties Novacap built a larger version (80 m^2) in Sobradinho for its manual workers and office clerks.

10. For instance, in 1969 and 1970, in Quadra 2, the Corporation of Housing of Social Interest constructed 122 houses earmarked for the

functionaries of the Supreme Military Tribunal, 158 for those of the Bank of Brazil, and 384 for those of the Ministry of Agriculture and the Ministry of Labor. This information is from the archives of the Regional Administration, Sobradinho.

11. According to local classifications, these house types may be defined in terms of the following architectural criteria. They are given in order of decreasing prestige. A kolonial house (*casa colonial*) is a thoroughly modern house in structure and plan (hence I distinguish it by the "k" in kolonial), which features a pyramidal clay tile roof and other quotations from colonial architecture (principally arches, rosette windows, shutters, stucco surfaces, and white and blue trim). A modern house (*casa moderna*) is typified by its exposed flat roof, often of serrated fiber-cement (called a *canalete* roof). A parapet or false-front house (*casa platibanda*) hides either a pitched or a flat roof behind a parapet along the front façade. Usually, this façade extends well beyond the body of the house at the top and often at the sides as well. The part that extends beyond the roof line is often used for decoration. This type of house is also called a *casa quadrada*, 'square', *caixote*, 'box', or *moderna*, 'modern'. The government-issue pattern houses come in several varieties. The more prestigious feature parapets; the less show a pitched crenulated fiber or metal roof (called *ondulada*). The government gives plans for these pattern houses free of charge to prospective home builders.

12. In local usage, a kolonial-modern (*casa colonial-moderna*) is a hybrid category (as if the others were not!). It almost always results from the renovation of a modern or parapet house in which a colonial tile roof is added. Sometimes a second storey bearing the new roof is also constructed, in which case the added storey will usually feature colonial quotations, especially arches. The house on lot 8 in Quadra Central (fig. 8.1) is an example of a two-storey modern—originally similar to its neighbor in lot 7—retopped with a colonial-style roof. The kolonial-modern on lot 3 on the same side of the street is an example of a renovated parapet house to which was added a second storey and a tile roof.

13. A profile of property transactions by generation reveals the following. Twenty of the original 33 leaseholders failed to carry out their contractual obligations. Of these, 13 have moved out while 7 remain in "irregular situations," all of them living in shacks. Nine of the 13 had left before 1971 without attempting to extend their contracts, three shortly thereafter, and one in 1981 after many extensions. Therefore, there were 13 second-generation leaseholders who took over failed contracts and the shacks left behind, which according to the terms of the contract became the property of Novacap. Of the 13 second-generation residents, more than half failed. Only 6 built masonry houses, and all of them remain on the block. Of the 7 who failed, 5 exited leaving their shacks behind, 3 at or before the end of term and 2 after several extensions. Two remain in "irregular situations." Of the 5 third-generation leaseholders who took over from those who had left, 2 succeeded in building houses and remain on the block; 3 failed but remain despite contract violations. Why the families in contract violation have not been evicted is a complex matter. In small part, it has to

do with the fact that most of them worked for Novacap as pioneers and as a result benefit from the nostalgia of contemporary officials who were themselves pioneers. In larger part, it depends on the delay tactic of periodically submitting house plans for approval.

14. This display of "personality" in architecture, as Brasilienses call it, is also the rage of house renovations in the satellite cities where demonstrations of personality, taste, respectability, and place in the social structure are equally important. House transformations among both rich and poor provide people with a model for thinking about themselves, their place in society, and other social groups, and, moreover, with a means for displaying these thoughts. A future study will focus on this public discourse about social linkages and cultural attitudes, one which evokes the values of social classification by means of a system of aesthetic judgments.

Bibliography

Arnheim, Rudolph. 1974. *Art and Visual Perception*. Berkeley: University of California Press.

Arquitetura e Engenharia. 1960. *Brasília*. Special edition, July–August.

Bahouth, Jr., Alberto. 1978. *Taguatinga: Pioneiros e Precursores*. Brasília: H. P. Mendes.

Banham, Reyner. 1960. *Theory and Design in the First Machine Age*. London: Architectural Press.

Barboza, Inez C., and Aldo Paviani. 1972. Commuting in the Federal District. *Revista Geográfica 77*.

Barthes, Roland. 1972. *Mythologies*. New York: Hill & Wang.

Benevides, Maria Victória de Mesquita. 1976. *O Governo Kubitschek: Desenvolvimento Econômico e Estabilidade Política*. Rio de Janeiro: Paz e Terra.

Benevolo, Leonardo. 1967. *The Origins of Modern Town Planning*. Cambridge: MIT Press.

———. 1977. *History of Modern Architecture*. Cambridge: MIT Press.

Benjamin, Walter. 1973. Paris—the capital of the nineteenth century. *Charles Baudelaire: A Lyric Poet in the Era of High Capitalism*. Trans. H. Zohn. London: New Left Books.

Bicalho, Nair H. 1978. Operários e Política: Estudo sobre os Trabalhadores da Construção Civil em Brasília. M.A. thesis, University of Brasília.

Bonduki, Nabil Georges. 1983. Habitação popular: contribuição para o estudo da evolução urbana de São Paulo. In Lícia do Prado Valladares, ed., *Repensando a Habitação no Brasil*, pp. 135–68. Rio de Janeiro: Zahar Editores.

Bourdieu, Pierre. 1984. *Distinction: A Social Critique of the Judgement of Taste*. Cambridge: Harvard University Press.

Brandão, Maria de Azevedo. 1980. O último dia da criação: mercado, propriedade e uso do solo em Salvador. In Lícia do Prado Valladares, ed., *Habitação em Questão*, pp. 125–42. Rio de Janeiro: Zahar Editores.

Brasília (Journal of Companhia Urbanizadora da Nova Capital do Brasil—Novacap)

Bruand, Yves. 1981. *Arquitetura Contemporânea no Brasil*. São Paulo: Editora Perspectiva.

Bürger, Peter. 1984. *Theory of the Avant-Garde*. Minneapolis: University of Minnesota Press.

Caldeira, Teresa Pires do Rio. 1984. *A Política dos Outros: O Cotidiano dos Moradores da Periferia e o que Pensam do Poder e dos Poderosos*. São Paulo: Editora Brasiliense.

Cardoso, Miriam Limoeiro. 1978. *Ideologia do Desenvolvimento—Brasil: JK–JQ.* Rio de Janeiro: Paz e Terra.

Chinelli, Filippina. 1980. Os loteamentos de periferia. In Lícia do Prado Valladares, ed., *Habitação em Questão*, pp. 49–68. Rio de Janeiro: Zahar Editores.

Clifford, James. 1981. On ethnographic surrealism. *Comparative Studies in Society and History* 23(4): 539–64.

———. 1983. On ethnographic authority. *Representations* 1(2): 118–46.

Clifford, James, and George E. Marcus, eds. 1986. *Writing Culture: The Poetics and Politics of Ethnography.* Berkeley: University of California Press.

Codeplan (Companhia de Desenvolvimento do Planalto Central). 1974. *Cadastro Industrial do Distrito Federal.* Brasília: Codeplan.

———. 1976. *Diagnóstico do Espaço Natural do Distrito Federal.* Brasília: Codeplan.

———. 1980. *Anuário Estatístico do Distrito Federal.* Brasília: Codeplan.

———. 1984. *Caracterização do Território e da População do Distrito Federal.*, vols. 1–10. Brasília: Codeplan.

Cohen, Jean-Louis. 1981. Le Corbusier and the mystique of the U.S.S.R. *Oppositions* 23: 84–121.

Colquhoun, Alan. 1985. On modern and postmodern space. In Joan Ockman, ed., *Architecture, Criticism, Ideology*, pp. 103–17. Princeton: Princeton Architectural Press.

Comaroff, Jean. 1985. *Body of Power, Spirit of Resistance: The Culture and History of a South African People.* Chicago: University of Chicago Press.

Conrads, Ulrich. 1970. *Programs and Manifestoes on Twentieth-Century Architecture.* Cambridge: MIT Press.

Costa, Lúcio. 1952. O arquiteto e a sociedade contemporânea. In Costa 1962: 230–51.

———. 1957. O relatório do Plano Piloto de Brasília [multilingual edition]. *Módulo* 8.

———. 1960. [Offprint of Costa 1957]. *Módulo* 18.

———. 1962. *Sôbre Arquitetura.* Porto Alegre: Centro dos Estudantes de Arquitetura.

———. 1980. Razões da nova arquitetura [1930]. *Arte em Revista* 4: 15–23.

Cruz Costa, João. 1956. *O Positivismo na República.* São Paulo: Cia. Editora Nacional.

Da Matta, Roberto. 1978. *Carnavais, Malandros e Heróis: Para uma Sociologia do Dilema Brasileiro.* Rio de Janeiro: Zahar Editores.

Debret, Jean Baptiste. 1978. *Viagem Pitoresca e Histórica ao Brasil* [1834–39]. São Paulo: Editora da Universidade de São Paulo.

Delson, Roberta Marx. 1979. *New Towns for Colonial Brazil: Spatial and Social Planning of the Eighteenth Century.* Ann Arbor: University Microfilms International.

Diário de Brasília. 1957–60. Rio de Janeiro: Serviço de Documentação da Presidência da República.

DIEESE (Inter-Trade Union Department of Statistics and Socio-Economic Studies). 1974. Família assalariada: padrão e custo de vida. *Estudos Sócio-Econômicos* 2.

Diniz, Eli. 1982. Favela: associativismo e participação social. In Renato Boschi, ed., *Movimentos Coletivos no Brasil Urbano*, pp. 27–74. Rio de Janeiro: Zahar Editores.

ECLA (Economic Commission for Latin America). 1964. Fifteen years of economic policy in Brazil. *Economic Bulletin for Latin America* 9(2): 153–214.

Eco, Umberto. 1976. *A Theory of Semiotics*. Bloomington: Indiana University Press.

Emplasa (Empresa Metropolitana de Planejamento da Grande São Paulo S.A.). 1978. *Pesquisa Origem-Destino/77—Resultados Básicos—Documento Bilingue*. São Paulo: Emplasa.

Engels, Friedrich. 1872. *The Housing Question*. New York: International Publishers.

Epstein, David G. 1973. *Brasília: Plan and Reality*. Berkeley: University of California Press.

Esterci, Neide. 1977. *O Mito da Democracia no País das Bandeiras*. Brasília: Department of Anthropology, University of Brasília (Pesquisa Antropológica 18).

Evans-Pritchard, E. E. 1940. *The Nuer: A Description of the Modes of Livelihood and Political Institutions of a Nilotic People*. Oxford: Oxford University Press.

Evenson, Norma. 1973. *Two Brazilian Capitals: Architecture and Urbanism in Rio de Janeiro and Brasília*. New Haven: Yale University Press.

Fabian, Johannes. 1983. *Time and the Other: How Anthropology Makes Its Object*. New York: Columbia University Press.

Faria, Vilmar. 1983. Desenvolvimento, urbanização e mudanças na estrutura do emprego: a experiência brasileira dos últimos trinta anos. In Bernardo Sorj and Maria Hermínia Tavares de Almeida, eds., *Sociedade e Política no Brasil Pós-64*, pp. 118–63. São Paulo: Brasiliense.

Favret-Saada, Jeanne. 1980. *Deadly Words: Witchcraft in the Bocage*. [1977.] Cambridge: Cambridge University Press.

Ferrez, Gilberto. 1978. *A Praça 15 de Novembro, Antigo Largo do Carmo*. Rio de Janeiro: Riotur.

Fishlow, Albert. 1972. Brazilian size distribution of income. *American Economic Review* 62: 391–402.

———. 1973. Some reflections on post-1964 Brazilian economic policy. In Alfred Stepan, ed., *Authoritarian Brazil: Origins, Policies, and Future*, pp. 69–118. New Haven: Yale University Press.

Fishman, Robert. 1977. From the Radiant City to Vichy: Le Corbusier's plans and politics, 1928–1942. In Russell Walden, ed., *The Open Hand: Essays on Le Corbusier*, pp. 243–83. Cambridge: MIT Press.

———. 1982. *Urban Utopias in the Twentieth Century: Ebenezer Howard, Frank Lloyd Wright, and Le Corbusier*. Cambridge: MIT Press.

Foucault, Michel. 1973. *Madness and Civilization: A History of Insanity in the Age of Reason*. New York: Vintage Press.

Frampton, Kenneth. 1968. Notes on Soviet urbanism, 1917–32. In David Lewis, ed., *Urban Structure*, pp. 238–52. New York: John Wiley & Sons.

———. 1980. *Modern Architecture: A Critical History*. New York: Oxford University Press.

Furtado, Celso. 1971. *The Economic Growth of Brazil*. [1959.] Berkeley: University of California Press.

Gardel, Luis D. 1967. *Escolas de Samba*. Rio de Janeiro: Livraria Kosmos Editora.

GDF (Governo do Distrito Federal). 1980. *Indicadores Conjunturais* 8(3). Brasília: Codeplan.

_____. 1981. *O Fenômeno Migratório em Brasília (Relatório—Ano Base 1980)*. Brasília: Siamig.

_____. 1982. *Sistema Secretaria de Serviços Sociais*. Brasília. Internal report.

Geertz, Clifford. 1977. Centers, kings, and charisma: Reflections on the symbolics of power. In J. Ben-David and T. N. Clark, eds., *Culture and Its Creators: Essays in Honor of Edward Shils*, pp. 150–71. Chicago: University of Chicago Press.

_____. 1980. *Negara: The Theatre State in Nineteenth-Century Bali*. Princeton: Princeton University Press.

Geipot (Ministério dos Transportes). 1975. *Plano Diretor de Transportes Urbanos do Distrito Federal: Levantamentos, Pesquisas e Estudos Básicos*. Brasília: Geipot.

_____. 1979. *Plano Diretor de Transportes Urbanos do Distrito Federal: Relatório Final*. Brasília: Geipot.

Ginzburg, Moisei, 1982. *Style and Epoch*. [1928.] Cambridge: MIT Press.

Girouard, Mark. 1985. *Cities and People: A Social and Architectural History*. New Haven: Yale University Press.

Graham, Lawrence S. 1968. *Civil Service Reform in Brazil: Principles versus Practice*. Austin: University of Texas Press.

GTB (Grupo de Trabalho de Brasília). 1960. *Boletim Informativo* 6.

Gutnov, Alexei, et al. 1968. *The Ideal Communist City*. New York: George Braziller.

Harris, Marvin. 1971. *Town and Country in Brazil*. [1956.] New York: W. W. Norton & Co.

Held, David. 1980. *Introduction to Critical Theory: Horkheimer to Habermas*. Berkeley: University of California Press.

Hitchcock, Henry-Russell, and Philip Johnson. 1966. *International Style*. New York: W. W. Norton & Co.

Holford, William. 1957. Brasília: A new capital city for Brazil. *Architectural Review* 122: 394–402.

Holston, James. 1986. The Modernist City: Architecture, Politics, and Society in Brasília. Ph.D. diss., Department of Anthropology, Yale University.

IBGE (Instituto Brasileiro de Geografia e Estatística). 1959. *Censo Experimental de Brasília*. Rio de Janeiro: IBGE.

_____. 1960. *Censo Demográfico de 1960*. Rio de Janeiro: IBGE.

_____. 1973. *Censo Demográfico de 1970*. Rio de Janeiro: IBGE.

_____. 1975–80. *Anuários Estatísticos do Brasil*. Rio de Janeiro: IBGE.

_____. 1981a. *Tabulações Avançadas do Censo Demográfico de 1980: Resultados Preliminares*. Rio de Janeiro: IBGE.

_____. 1981b. *Sinopse Preliminar do Censo Demográfico de 1980*, vol. 1.1.1 (Brasil). Rio de Janeiro: IBGE.

_____. 1981c. *Sinopse Preliminar do Censo Demográfico de 1980*, vol. 1.1.25 (Distrito Federal). Rio de Janeiro: IBGE.

_____. 1984. *Recenseamento Geral do Brasil—1980: Censo Demográfico*, vol. 1.1.18 (São Paulo). Rio de Janeiro: IBGE.

Jaffé, H. L. C. 1986. *De Stijl, 1917–1931: The Dutch Contribution to Modern Art*. Cambridge: Harvard University Press.

Jaguaribe, Hélio. 1968. *Economic and Political Development: A Theoretical Approach and a Brazilian Case Study*. Cambridge: Harvard University Press.

Jameson, Fredric. 1972. *The Prison-House of Language: A Critical Account of Structuralism and Russian Formalism*. Princeton: Princeton University Press.

_____. 1981. *The Political Unconscious: Narrative as a Socially Symbolic Act*. Ithaca: Cornell University Press.

_____. 1985. Architecture and the critique of ideology. In Joan Ockman, ed., *Architecture, Criticism, Ideology*, pp. 51–87. Princeton: Princeton Architectural Press.

Jencks, Charles. 1973. *Modern Movements in Architecture*. Garden City: Anchor Books.

Kopp, Anatole. 1970. *Town and Revolution: Soviet Architecture and City Planning, 1917–1935*. New York: George Braziller.

Kreis, Barbara. 1980. The idea of the dom-kommuna and the dilemma of the Soviet avant-garde. *Oppositions* 21: 52–77.

Kuper, Leo, and M. G. Smith, eds. 1969. *Pluralism in Africa*. Berkeley: University of California Press.

Kubitschek, Juscelino. 1975. *Por Que Construí Brasília*. Rio de Janeiro: Bloch Editores.

Lafer, Celso. 1970. The Planning Process and the Political System in Brazil: A Study of Kubitschek's Target Plan. Ph.D. diss., Cornell University Dissertation series, no. 16.

Lafetá, João Luiz. 1974. *1930: A Crítica e o Modernismo*. São Paulo: Duas Cidades.

Lane, Barbara M. 1968. *Architecture and Politics in Germany, 1918–1945*. Cambridge: Harvard University Press.

Le Corbusier (Charles Edouard Jeanneret). 1937. *Oeuvre complète, 1910–1929*. With Pierre Jeanneret. Zurich: Editions Girsberger.

_____. 1939. *Oeuvre complète, 1934–1938*. With Pierre Jeanneret. Zurich: Editions Girsberger.

_____. 1957. *La Charte d'Athenes*. [1941.] Paris: Editions de Minuit.

_____. 1967. *The Radiant City: Elements of a Doctrine of Urbanism to Be Used as the Basis of Our Machine-Age Civilization*.[1933.] New York: Orion Press.

_____. 1971a. *The City of Tomorrow*. [1924.] Cambridge: MIT Press.

_____. 1971b. *Looking at City Planning*. [1946.] New York: Grossman Publishers.

_____. 1974. *Towards a New Architecture*. [1923.] New York: Praeger.

Lemos, Carlos A. C. 1978. *Cozinhas, Etc. (Um Estudo Sobre as Zonas de Serviço da Casa Paulista)*. 2d ed. São Paulo: Editora Perspectiva.

Lévi-Strauss, Claude. 1966. *The Savage Mind*. Chicago: University of Chicago Press.

Lins Ribeiro, Gustavo S. 1980. O Capital da Esperança. Brasília: Estudo sobre uma Grande Obra da Construção Civil. M.A. thesis, Graduate Program in Anthropology, University of Brasília.

Lissitzky, El. 1970. *Russia: An Architecture for World Revolution*. [1930.] Cambridge: MIT Press.

Lodder, Christina. 1983. *Russian Constructivism*. New Haven: Yale University Press.

Lyons, John. 1977. *Semantics*, vol. 1. Cambridge: Cambridge University Press.

Malinowski, Bronislaw. 1954. *Magic, Science, and Religion*. Garden City: Doubleday.

Malloy, James M. 1979. *The Politics of Social Security in Brazil*. Pittsburgh: University of Pittsburgh Press.

Marcus, George E., and Michael M. J. Fischer. 1986. *Anthropology as Cultural Critique: An Experimental Moment in the Human Sciences*. Chicago: University of Chicago Press.

Martins, Wilson. 1969. *O Modernismo, 1916–1945*. São Paulo: Editora Cultrix.

McLeod, Mary. 1980. Le Corbusier and Algiers. *Oppositions* 19–20: 55–85.

Mendes, Manuel. 1979. *Meu Testemunho de Brasília*. Brasília: Horizonte Editora.

Miliutin, N. A. 1974. *Sotsgorod: The Problem of Building Socialist Cities*. [1930.] Cambridge: MIT Press.

Ministry of Justice (Minister Carlos Cyrillo, Jr., et al.). 1959. *Brasília: Medidas Legislativas Sugeridas à Comissão Mista pelo Ministro da Justiça e Negócios Interiores*. Rio de Janeiro: Departamento de Imprensa Nacional.

Morse, Richard M. 1974. Brazil's urban development: Colony and empire. *Journal of Urban History* 1(1): 39–72.

Nash, June. 1979. *We Eat the Mines and the Mines Eat Us: Dependency and Exploitation in Bolivian Tin Mines*. New York: Columbia University Press.

Niemeyer, Oscar. 1974. Excerpt from Oscar Niemeyer's speech of acceptance of the Lenin Prize awarded at Brasília. [1962.] *L'Architecture d'aujourd'hui* 171 (special edition on Niemeyer): lxxxiii.

––––––. 1960. Minha experiência em Brasília. *Arquitetura e Engenharia*, July–August: 22–24.

––––––. 1961. *Minha Experiência em Brasília*. Rio de Janeiro: Editora Vitória.

––––––. 1980a. *A Forma na Arquitetura*. Rio de Janeiro: Avenir Editora.

––––––. 1980b. O problema social na arquitetura. [1955.] *Arte em Revista* 4: 53–55.

––––––. 1980c. Forma e função na arquitetura. [1959.] *Arte em Revista* 4: 57–60.

––––––. 1980d. Oscar Niemeyer: Entrevista. *Status* (April): 21–23, 138–43.

––––––. 1983. Brasília, hoje: uma cidade como outra qualquer. *Jornal do Brasil*, 31 August.

Novo Michaelis Dicionário Ilustrado. 1979. São Paulo: Melhoramentos.

Papadaki, Stamo. 1960. *Oscar Niemeyer.* New York: George Braziller.

Pastore, José. 1969. *Brasília: A Cidade e o Homem.* São Paulo: Editora da Universidade de São Paulo.

Peirce, Charles S. 1931–58. *Collected Papers,* vols. 1–8. Edited by C. Hartshorne and P. Weiss. Cambridge: Harvard University Press.

PEOT. 1977. *Plano Estrutural de Organização Territorial do Distrito Federal,* vols. 1 and 2. Brasília: Codeplan.

Perlman, Janice. 1976. *The Myth of Marginality.* Berkeley: University of California Press.

Perugine, Erdna, and Maria Luísa C. Aroeira, Maria José Caldeira. 1980. *Gente, Terra Verde, Céu Azul: Estudos Sociais.* São Paulo: Editora Ática.

Pevsner, Nikolaus. 1960. *Pioneers of Modern Design.* Harmondsworth: Penguin Books.

Rabinow, Paul. 1983. Ordonnance, discipline, regulation: Some reflections on urbanism. *Humanities in Society* 6: 267–78.

_____. 1985. Discourse and power: On the limits of ethnographic texts. *Dialectical Anthropology* 10: 1–13.

_____. 1986. Representations are social facts: Modernity and post-modernity in anthropology. In James Clifford and George E. Marcus, eds., *Writing Culture: The Poetics and Politics of Ethnography,* pp. 234–61. Berkeley: University of California Press.

Rowe, Colin, and Fred Koetter. 1978. *Collage City.* Cambridge: MIT Press.

Ruben, Edgar. 1958. Figure and ground. In D. C. Beardslee and M. Wertheimer, eds., *Readings in Perception,* pp. 194–203. Princeton: D. Van Nostrand.

Rykwert, Joseph. 1976. *The Idea of a Town: The Anthropology of Urban Form in Rome, Italy, and the Ancient World.* Princeton: Princeton University Press.

Salvador, Frei Vicente do. 1931. *História do Brasil, 1500–1627.* São Paulo: Cia. Melhoramentos.

Santos, Carlos Nelson Ferreira dos. 1981. *Movimentos Urbanos no Rio de Janeiro.* Rio de Janeiro: Zahar Editores.

Schmitter, Philippe C. 1971. *Interest, Conflict, and Political Change in Brazil.* Stanford: Stanford University Press.

Seplan (Secretaria de Economia e Planejamento do Estado de São Paulo). 1977. *Subdivisão do Município de São Paulo em Áreas Homogêneas.* São Paulo: Seplan.

Serenyi, Peter. 1967. Le Corbusier, Fourier, and the Monastery at Ema. *Art Bulletin* 49: 277–86.

Shils, Edward. 1965. Charisma, order, and status. *American Sociological Review* 30(2): 199–213.

Shklovsky, Victor. 1965. Art as technique. [1916.] In *Russian Formalist Criticism: Four Essays,* trans. Lee J. Lemon and Marion J. Reis. Lincoln: University of Nebraska Press.

Silva, Ernesto. 1971. *História de Brasília: Um Sonho, Uma Esperança, Uma Realidade.* Brasília: Coordenada-Editora de Brasília.

Skidmore, Thomas E. 1967. *Politics in Brazil, 1930–1964: An Experiment in Democracy.* London: Oxford University Press.

Smith, M. G. 1974. *Corporations and Society: The Social Anthropology of Collective Action.* Chicago: Aldine Publishing Co.

Starr, S. Frederick. 1981. Le Corbusier and the U.S.S.R.: New documentation. *Oppositions* 23: 123–37.

Sutcliffe, Anthony. 1970. *The Autumn of Central Paris: The Defeat of Town Planning, 1850–1970.* London: Edward Arnold.

———. 1977. A vision of utopia: optimistic foundations of Le Corbusier's *doctrine d'urbanisme.* In Russell Walden, ed., *The Open Hand: Essays on Le Corbusier,* pp. 217–43. Cambridge: MIT Press.

Sutcliffe, Anthony, ed. 1980. *The Rise of Modern Urban Planning, 1800–1914.* New York: St. Martin's Press.

Tafuri, Manfredo. 1976. *Architecture and Utopia: Design and Capitalist Development.* Cambridge: MIT Press.

———. 1980. *Theories and History of Architecture.* New York: Harper & Row.

Taussig, Michael. 1980. *The Devil and Commodity Fetishism in South America.* Chapel Hill: University of North Carolina Press.

———. 1987. *Shamanism, Colonialism, and the Wild Man: A Study in Terror and Healing.* Chicago: University of Chicago Press.

Taylor, Robert R. 1974. *The World in Stone: The Role of Architecture in the National Socialist Ideology.* Berkeley: University of California Press.

Thompson, E. P. 1967. Time, work-discipline, and industrial capitalism. *Past and Present* 38: 56–97.

Trotsky, Leon. 1959. *The Russian Revolution.* Garden City: Doubleday.

Vaitsman, Maurício. 1968. *Quanto Costou Brasília.* Rio de Janeiro: Editora Posto de Serviço.

Valladares, Lícia do Prado. 1978. *Passa-se uma Casa: Análise do Programa de Remoção de Favelas do Rio de Janeiro.* Rio de Janeiro: Zahar Editores.

———. 1982. Estudos recentes sobre a habitação no Brasil: resenha da literatura. In Lícia do Prado Valladares, ed., *Repensando a Habitação no Brasil,* pp. 21–77. Rio de Janeiro: Zahar Editores.

Vasconcellos, Sylvio de. 1977. *Vila Rica.* São Paulo: Editora Perspectiva.

Venturi, Robert, Denise Scott Brown, and Steven Izenour. 1977. *Learning from Las Vegas: The Forgotten Symbolism of Architectural Form.* Rev. ed. Cambridge: MIT Press.

Vidler, Anthony. 1972. The new world: The reconstruction of urban utopia in late nineteenth century France. *Perspecta* 13: 243–56.

———. 1978. The scenes of the street: Transformations in ideal and reality, 1750–1871. In Sanford Anderson, ed., *On Streets,* pp. 29–111. Cambridge: MIT Press.

Wagley, Charles. 1963. *An Introduction to Brazil.* New York: Columbia University Press.

Weber, Adna F. 1963. *The Growth of Cities in the Nineteenth Century: A Study in Statistics.* Ithaca: Cornell University Press.

Weber, Max. 1978. *Economy and Society.* Edited by Guenther Roth and Claus Wittich. Berkeley: University of California Press.

Wheatley, Paul. 1969. *The City as Symbol*. An inaugural lecture delivered at University College, London, 20 November 1967. London: H. K. Lewis & Co.

_____. 1971. *The Pivot of the Four Quarters: A Preliminary Enquiry into the Origins and Character of the Ancient Chinese City*. Chicago: Aldine Publishing Co.

Willis, Paul. 1981. *Learning to Labor: How Working Class Kids Get Working Class Jobs* [1977.] New York: Columbia University Press.

Zaluar, Alba. 1985. *A Máquina e a Revolta: As Organizações Populares e o Significado da Pobreza*. São Paulo: Editora Brasiliense.

Zucker, Paul. 1959. *Town and Square: From the Agora to the Village Green*. New York: Columbia University Press.

INDEX

ACB. *See* Commercial Association of
Brasília
Address systems: Plano Piloto,
143–44, 149–51, 166, 298,
330 n. 2; Vila Chaparral, 297–98
Agency: historical, 10; in modernism,
9
Agricultural cooperatives, 257
Alberti, Leone Battista, 328 n. 8
Almeida, Guilherme de, 72
Anápolis, 221
Anthropology: as critique, 6–10,
12–14, 315, 317–18; and history,
9–10, 200; and modernism, 5–14,
319 n. 1; of modern society, 7,
314–15, 319 n. 3; postmodernist
critique, 13–14; and the study of
power, 8. *See also* Counter-
discourse; Ethnography
Apartment building: class
conventions, 178–81;
middle-class organization of
space, 171, 174–79
Aragão, João Guilherme de, 202
Architecture: antimodernist
reactions, 24, 139–40, 182–84,
186–87, 308–9; and conflicting
interpretations, 96–97; as
embodiment of intention, 11–12,
72–73; house types, 303, 328 n. 7,
347 nn. 11, 12, 348 n. 14; and
innovation, 52, 56, 88–90, 92,
183–84; as instrument of social
change, 3–4, 20–23, 31, 52–58,
60, 75–82, 92–93, 153, 172–73,
184, 308, 315–17, 325 n. 15,
326 n. 7; internal reading vs.
critique, 8, 315; modernist,
denotations, 36; organization of
public and private, 91, 103, 111,
117–19, 128–36, 165, 172–73,
181, 184–87, 329 n. 16;
postmodernist, 316–17, 319 n. 4;

semiotic structures, 56, 119–27,
129–36, 150, 185–86, 329 n. 12; as
social management, 12; in
squatter settlements, 296–97;
and standardization, 21, 24, 78,
167, 172–73, 182–84, 300; and
status, 78, 173, 179, 183–84, 309,
333 n. 20, 348 n. 14; street system
of public space, 105, 109–19,
118–27, 129–30, 310–12; as
subversive fragment, 52–53, 56,
57, 92, 316; as symbol of Brazil's
modernity, 95–97, 101–2; urban
and rural patterns, 107–9, 297;
and utopia, 56–57, 85, 315–18.
See also Façades; Figure-ground;
Monumentality; Ornament;
Streets
Associations: corporate features,
259–60, 263–65; demobilization,
263, 265, 269–72, 288; of
employers, 230–32, 238–39,
249–50, 265; and government
cooptation, 271; mobilization,
236, 249–50, 261–62, 264, 265,
267–68, 271, 341 n. 5; as
representative political groups,
259, 268, 270–72, 278;
residential, 170, 257–72, 298,
346 n. 8; residential vs. labor, 236;
types of disputes, 259; of
workers, 231, 250, 339 nn. 23, 25.
See also Squatter settlements

Bahouth, Jr., Alberto, 286, 287
Bairro, 169–72
Bandeirantes, 209–10
Barthes, Roland, 66
Beneficent Association of Vila
Amaury, 264–65, 341 n. 5
Benevolo, Leonardo, 42, 48
Benjamin, Walter, 182
Bicalho, Nair H., 226, 229, 231

359

201–2, 326 n. 8; rhetoric, 18, 96, 320 n. 10

Developmentalism, 18, 94. *See also* Kubitschek, Juscelino

Differential incorporation of Brasília, 203–6, 248–49, 274, 277–78, 283, 288, 290–92, 334 n. 5

Diniz, Eli, 346 n. 8

Direct administration, 202, 334 n. 2

Dogmatism: in critique, 12–13; in modernism, 13

Dom-kommuna, 60–61, 76, 165

Doutor: as status term, 232–33

ECLA (Economic Commission for Latin America): and developmentalism, 18; evaluation of Target Program, 320 n. 11

Economic conditions: and bureaucratic state, 157–59, 219; comparative, 25–29; labor market, construction epoch, 219, 253; labor market, Federal District, 156–59, 188–90. *See also* Labor; Property; Work

Education, 168, 169

Egalitarianism: in CIAM doctrine, 46, 50; intended in Brasília, 20–23, 78–80, 136–37, 153–54, 167, 206, 247, 280, 282, 334 n. 6. *See also* Modernist city: contradiction of intentions

Elections, disfranchisement in Brasília, 275–77, 293

Elite clubs, 309, 311

Elite space, 311–12

Engels, Friedrich, 49

Entertainment sectors, 161

Entrepreneurs: class organization, 238, 250; contractual rights in Brasília, 224, 238; economic conditions, 236–37; fight for Free City permanence, 265–70; relations with squatters, 241, 265, 340 n. 1, 346 n. 6. *See also* Free City; Recruitment

Epstein, David G., 327 n. 18

Esso Oil Corporation of Brazil, 211

Ethnography: and analysis of context, 11; and analysis of intentions, 11–12, 23, 320 n. 6; and analysis of opinion, 24, 27–28; critical potential, 7, 318, 319 n. 2; and immanent critique,

13–14; of modernism, 6–9, 315; research framework, 8, 10–14, 314–15; units of analysis, 10, 290. *See also* Anthropology; Counter-discourse

Evans-Pritchard, E. E., 319 n. 2

Evenson, Norma, 327 n. 18

Exemplary center, 85–87, 273, 277, 282

Fabian, Johannes, 7

Façades; load-bearing wall, 118–22,129, 183, 185–86, 333 n. 21; and personality, 24, 173, 183–84; transparent glass, 56, 173, 183–87. *See also* Figure-ground; Houses; Ornament; Streets

Familiarization, 6, 290, 308–10

Family: household life, 118, 177–82, 333 n. 18; in *superquadras,* 171–73, 180–82

Favela, 257

Favret-Saada, Jeanne, 319 n. 2

Federal autarkies, 252

Federal District: area, 14; center-periphery relations, 160–63, 273–74, 277–83, 290–95; denial of political representation, 274–78, 293, 343 n. 21; income, 28–29, 193, 293, 295; labor conditions, 189–90; population, 192–93, 290–91, 293–95, 345 n. 4; religious cults, 346 n. 5. *See also* Construction of Brasília; Periphery; Political-administrative organization; Satellite cities

Figure-ground: plans, 124, 126, 134; and solid-void relations, 91, 120–27, 129–36, 138, 144, 150, 185–86, 329 n. 12, 333 n. 21

First Mass, 201

Fischer, Michael M. J., 6, 7

Fishlow, Albert, 244, 337 n. 18

Fishman, Robert, 42, 49

Fixation, 265

Flagelados, 220, 240, 260

Food riots, 234–35, 339 n. 23

Foucault, Michel, 7

Frampton, Kenneth, 81

Frankfurt school, 13

Free City (Núcleo Bandeirante, satellite city): authorized organization, 218, 223–25; class